W9-DHU-851

Religious Commitment and Salvation

Readings in Secular and
Theistic Religion

1|10|75

Religious Commitment and Salvation

Readings in Secular and Theistic Religion

Edited by

Claudia F. Card
University of Wisconsin

Robert R. Ammerman
University of Wisconsin

CHARLES E. MERRILL PUBLISHING COMPANY
A Bell & Howell Company
Columbus, Ohio

Published by
Charles E. Merrill Publishing Company
A Bell & Howell Company
Columbus, Ohio 43216

ISBN: 0-675-08871-2

Library of Congress Catalog Card Number: 73-87527

1 2 3 4 5 6 7 8—81 80 79 78 77 76 75 74

Printed in the United States of America

To Bob, Bruce, and John

Preface

Part I

This book is intended to fill a need felt by many teachers of philosophy of religion courses. The vast majority of anthologies currently available for use in such courses restrict themselves to selections from the Judaic-Christian religious tradition. The problems they emphasize are, almost exclusively, God-centered—the nature of God, proofs of the existence of God, our knowledge of God, theodicy, theistic language, and supernaturalist eschatology. Atheism and theistic agnosticism are typically represented only as nonreligious alternative life-orientations. Up until relatively recent times, many people have identified the problems of religion with the problems of the Judaic-Christian religion, especially as those problems have been defined by theologians and philosophers through the centuries. This identification has been increasingly corroded during the past two hundred years, as can be seen by the selections chronologically arranged in this book.

We believe that the scope of religious commitment is much broader than that of the issues encompassed by the varieties of Judaic-Christianity; or, for that matter, the varieties of Eastern mysticism or any other body of tradition. Contemporary radical theology, to cite but one source, has shown that the important questions concerning religious commitment and its relationship to individual and social life can be raised and discussed fruitfully with little or no reference to God conceived as a personal Being, or to any form of supernaturalism. The idea of "secular religion" no longer strikes one as a contradiction in terms.

Instead of taking the concept of God as central to religion, it is much more illuminating to use the concept of Salvation as the organizing theme. Salvation need not be conceived in supernaturalist terms at all. Most of the traditional problems of religion can be viewed in a fresh and more interesting light, if they are stated in a more general fashion and not restricted to the limited terminology and concerns of the Judaic-Christian tradition. When salvation is taken as the central concept, the problems of religion become more closely allied with problems of ethics and social philosophy, as well as philosophical psychology. In more traditional approaches, the alliance has been almost exclusively with cosmology and epistemology. This point of contrast marks a significant difference between this book and most others designed for use in teaching the philosophy of religion.

The philosophers and theologians whose writings are represented in this book reflect a variety of different interests in religion. Some, for example Marx, Nietzsche, and Freud, were avowed atheists and highly critical of the dogmas of traditional religion. Others, e.g. Robinson, Bultmann, and Tillich, were or are affiliated with one or another Christian sect. Yet, all the authors who are included in this book share at least one common trait: they refuse to allow that anything about religion is so sacred that it cannot be questioned. They are all, in other words, at least in their writings included here, philosophers *of* religion and not apologists *for* religion. It is our belief that exposure to this kind of honest confrontation between philosophers and theologians from many different traditions can best help the concerned student today to arrive at his or her own beliefs on these most important of matters.

The selections in this book have been ordered chronologically. No attempt has been made to separate them into problem areas. There are many reasons why we have felt this procedure to be best. The most compelling rationale is that a large number of the selections are classics of, or taken from classics of, western philosophy and literature. Most of them are so rich in content that it would be artificial and restrictive to try to present them in any neat, topical ordering. Another reason why we have refrained from dividing them into sections is that the chronological ordering serves to underline a function of this book by emphasizing the historical secularization of religion and showing its salient developments. The book is intended to serve both courses which are historically-oriented and courses which are topic-oriented. In the case of the latter, we leave it for the most part to the imagination and skill of the teachers of philosophy of religion to organize and utilize the selections contained herein in the way that will be most meaningful for their students and fits best with other materials used in the course. Since, however, there are many connections between the selections, not all of them equally obvious, we have provided in the second part of this Preface a brief discussion of some of the interrelationships between selections.

Many of the selections are complete, but some have been excerpted from longer works. Some have been internally edited, and we have indicated this fact by the use of ellipses and editorial comment in the footnotes. Complete biographical references are to be found in the footnotes and additional bibliography is given at the end of the book.

The editors would like the thank Robert T. Ammerman for his assistance in compiling the manuscript.

C.F.C.
R.R.A.

Part II

There are many different ways in which the selections in this book might be grouped under various topics. The editors themselves have made use of many of these selections in rather different ways for different courses in the philosophy of religion. We think the following connections between selections are worth noting and may prove helpful to the instructor who wishes to organize his course around topics, rather than to present the material chronologically.

The questions *What is religion? What is it to be religious?* and *What is religious experience?* are dealt with in a general way by James (10). On what is distinctive about theistic religion, there are the highly polemical and provocative discussions by Feuerbach (2) and Freud (12). The selections by Bultmann (15), Tillich (18), and Robinson (20) could be read as responses to Feuerbach and Freud and as attempts to define what is essential for modern Christianity.

Closely related to the question "What is religion?" are the questions *Are religious claims intelligible?* and *What is the meaning of religious commitment?* The latter problem has been explored primarily by the existentialists, while the former problem has been the focus of much discussion in analytic philosophy. The Robinson selection (20) discusses these issues on a popular level and from a contemporary Christian viewpoint as a peculiarly modern need to show the relevance of religion to aspects of our lives which seem incompatible with it but which we cannot abandon either. For deeper consideration on the existentialist side, the selections by Bultmann (15) and Tillich (18)—upon which Robinson draws heavily—and the selection of Kierkegaard (3) might be contrasted with those by Sartre (16) and Camus (17). From an analytic viewpoint, the now-classic logical positivist statement by Ayer (13) sets the challenge to which the pieces from Wisdom (14) and Van Buren (21) respond. Nagel's paper (22) might be treated as bringing out connections between the existentialist and analytic problems and attempting a unified response to them. It also provides an interesting contrast to Camus' treatment of the absurd.

Discussions of the intelligibility and meaningfulness of religious claims and commitments inevitably lead to questions as to *the validity or soundness of religious views.* The topic of miracles has acquired an important place in this issue, since miracles have been traditionally invoked as demonstrations of God's concern for man, if not as demonstrations of His very existence. Miracles are dealt with by Hume (1), by Bultmann (15), in his project for "demythologizing" the Gospels, and, to a limited extent, by Dostoyevsky (6), in his "Legend of the Grand Inquisitor."

Miracles also may be treated as part of the topic of *religious experience,* which has generally played an important role in the assessment of religious claims and commitments. Religious experience is often associated with revelation and cited as the foundation of religious faith. Bultmann (15) and Wisdom (14) offer very different and suggestive contemporary re-examinations of the idea of revelation. James' discussion (11) and citation of cases of the "sense of presence" is a classic. The significance of apparent encounter with the Unseen presented by Kierkegaard (3) or Bultmann (15) should be contrasted with Freud's account (12) of what religious experiences really consists in. In Tolstoy (9), Tillich (18), and Camus (17), the focus of attention is shifted from experience of unseen beings or powers to experience of oneself in the world and to the practical questions whether faith in or hope for the eventual achievement of certain ideals is humanly possible, necessary, courageous, or even sane.

The above questions— *What is religion? How can we evaluate religious claims? What is the significance of religious experience?*—lead again and again to confrontation with *the idea of salvation.* Many of the selections in this book can be read in terms of the fundamental question whether individual or social salvation on earth is possible for modern man. The problem of evil, for such writers as Dostoyevsky (6), Nietzsche (7, 8), Marx (4), Engels (5), Freud (12), and Brown (19), is no longer the problem of attempting to reconcile the existence of an omnipotent perfectly good Creator with the existence of evil in His creation, but rather, the problem of *how to face* or *what to do about* the evils we find—or produce—in our world, evil in ourselves and in our social institutions. The selections by Marx (4) and Engels (5) point toward faith in a socialistic utopia, as an alternative to theism. Dostoyevsky (6), on the other hand, can be read as providing a remarkable critique of both the Church and Socialism. Nietzsche and Brown (who can profitably be read in connection with the selection from Freud) develop the idea that there is no possibility of salvation for man until he overcomes his neurotic inability to accept his body and its inevitable death.

Contents

1. Of Miracles

Part I

There is in Dr. Tillotson's writings an argument against the *real presence,* which is as concise and elegant and strong as any argument can possibly be supposed against a doctrine so little worthy of a serious refutation. It is acknowledged on all hands, says that learned prelate, that the authority, either of the scripture or of tradition, is founded merely in the testimony of the apostles, who were eyewitnesses to those miracles of our Saviour, by which he proved his divine mission. Our evidence, then, for the truth of the *Christian* religion is less than the evidence for the truth of our senses, because, even in the first authors of our religion, it was no greater; and it is evident it must diminish in passing from them to their disciples; nor can anyone rest such confidence in their testimony as in the immediate object of his senses. But a weaker evidence can never destroy a stronger; and therefore, were the doctrine of the real presence ever so clearly revealed in scripture, it were directly contrary to the rules of just reasoning to give

Reprinted from David Hume, *An Enquiry Concerning Human Understanding,* ed. L. A. Selby-Bigge (Oxford-Clarendon Press, 1902), sec. x.

our assent to it. It contradicts sense, though both the scripture and tradition, on which it is supposed to be built, carry not such evidence with them as sense, when they are considered merely as external evidences, and are not brought home to everyone's breast by the immediate operation of the Holy Spirit.

Nothing is so convenient as a decisive argument of this kind, which must at least *silence* the most arrogant bigotry and superstition, and free us from their impertinent solicitations. I flatter myself that I have discovered an argument of a like nature, which, if just, will, with the wise and learned, be an everlasting check to all kinds of superstitious delusion, and consequently will be useful as long as the world endures. For so long, I presume, will the accounts of miracles and prodigies be found in all history, sacred and profane.

Though experience be our only guide in reasoning concerning matters of fact, it must be acknowledged that this guide is not altogether infallible, but in some cases is apt to lead us into errors. One who in our climate should expect better weather in any week of June than in one of December, would reason justly, and conformably to experience; but it is certain that he may happen, in the event, to find himself mistaken. However, we may observe that, in such a case, he would have no cause to complain of experience, because it commonly informs us beforehand of the uncertainty, by that contrariety of events which we may learn from a diligent observation. All effects follow not with like certainty from their supposed causes. Some events are found, in all countries and all ages, to have been constantly conjoined together: others are found to have been more variable, and sometimes to disappoint our expectations; so that, in our reasonings concerning matter of fact, there are all imaginable degrees of assurance, from the highest certainty to the lowest species of moral evidence.

A wise man, therefore, proportions his belief to the evidence. In such conclusions as are founded on an infallible experience, he expects the event with the last degree of assurance, and regards his past experience as a full *proof* of the future existence of that event. In other cases he proceeds with more caution: he weighs the opposite experiments: he considers which side is supported by the greater number of experiments: to that side he inclines, with doubt and hesitation; and when at last he fixes his judgment, the evidence exceeds not what we properly call *probability*. All probability, then, supposes an opposition of experiments and observations, where the one side is found to overbalance the other, and to produce a degree of evidence proportioned to the superiority. A hundred instances or experiments on one side, and fifty on another, afford a doubtful expectation of any event; though a hundred uniform experiments, with only one that is contradictory, reasonably beget a pretty strong degree of assurance. In all cases we must balance the opposite experiments, where they are opposite, and deduct the smaller number from the greater, in order to know the exact force of the superior evidence.

To apply these principles to a particular instance; we may observe that there is no species of reasoning more common, more useful, and even necessary to human life, than that which is derived from the testimony of men, and the reports of eyewitnesses and spectators. This species of reasoning, perhaps, one may deny to be founded on the relation of cause and effect. I shall not dispute about a word. It will be sufficient to observe that our assurance in any argument of this kind is derived from no other principle than our observation of the veracity of human testimony, and of the usual conformity of facts to the reports of witnesses. It being a general maxim that no objects have any discoverable connexion together, and that all the inferences which we can draw from one to another are founded merely on our experience of their constant and regular conjunction; it is evident that we ought not to make an exception to this maxim in favour of human testimony, whose connexion with any event seems, in itself, as little necessary as any other. Were not the memory tenacious to a certain degree; had not men commonly an inclination to truth and a principle of probity; were they not sensible to shame, when detected in a falsehood; were not these, I say, discovered by *experience* to be qualities inherent in human nature, we should never repose the least confidence in human testimony. A man delirious, or noted for falsehood and villainy, has no manner of authority with us.

And as the evidence derived from witnesses and human testimony is founded on past experience, so it varies with the experience, and is regarded either as a *proof* or a *probability,* according as the conjunction between any particular kind of report and any kind of object has been found to be constant or variable. There are a number of circumstances to be taken into consideration in all judgments of this kind; and the ultimate standard, by which we determine all disputes that may arise concerning them, is always derived from experience and observation. Where this experience is not entirely uniform on any side, it is attended with an unavoidable contrariety in our judgments, and with the same opposition and mutual destruction of argument as in every other kind of evidence. We frequently hesitate concerning the reports of others. We balance the opposite circumstances which cause any doubt or uncertainty; and when we discover a superiority on any side, we incline to it; but still with a diminution of assurance in proportion to the force of its antagonist.

This contrariety of evidence, in the present case, may be derived from several different causes; from the opposition of contrary testimony; from the character or number of the witnesses; from the manner of their delivering their testimony; or from the union of all these circumstances. We entertain a suspicion concerning any matter of fact when the witnesses contradict each other; when they are but few, or of a doubtful character; when they have an interest in what they affirm; when they deliver their testimony with hesitation or, on the contrary, with too violent asseverations. There are many other particulars of the same kind which may diminish or destroy the force of any argument derived from human testimony.

Suppose, for instance, that the fact which the testimony endeavours to establish partakes of the extraordinary and the marvellous; in that case the evidence resulting from the testimony admits of a diminution, greater or less, in proportion as the fact is more or less unusual. The reason why we place any credit in witnesses and historians is not derived from any *connexion* which we perceive *a priori,* between testimony and reality, but because we are accustomed to find a conformity between them. But when the fact attested is such a one as has seldom fallen under our observation, here is a contest of two opposite experiences; of which the one destroys the other, as far as its force goes, and the superior can only operate on the mind by the force which remains. The very same principle of experience, which gives us a certain degree of assurance in the testimony of witnesses, gives us also, in this case, another degree of assurance against the fact which they endeavour to establish; from which contradiction there necessarily arises a counterpoise, and mutual destruction of belief and authority.

I should not believe such a story were it told me by Cato, was a proverbial saying in Rome, even during the lifetime of that philosophical patriot.[1] The incredibility of a fact, it was allowed, might invalidate so great an authority.

The Indian prince who refused to believe the first relations concerning the effects of frost reasoned justly; and it naturally required very strong testimony to engage his assent to facts that arose from a state

---

1. Plutarch, *in Vita Catonis*

of nature with which he was unacquainted, and which bore so little analogy to those events of which he had had constant and uniform experience. Though they were not contrary to his experience, they were not conformable to it.[2]

But in order to increase the probability against the testimony of witnesses, let us suppose that the fact which they affirm, instead of being only marvellous, is really miraculous; and suppose also, that the testimony considered apart and in itself amounts to an entire proof; in that case, there is proof against proof, of which the strongest must prevail, but still with a diminution of its force in proportion to that of its antagonist.

A miracle is a violation of the laws of nature; and as a firm and unalterable experience has established these laws, the proof against a miracle, from the very nature of the fact, is as entire as any argument from experience can possibly be imagined. Why is it more than probable that all men must die; that lead cannot, of itself, remain suspended in the air; that fire consumes wood, and is extinguished by water; unless it be that these events are found agreeable to the laws of nature, and there is required a violation of these laws or, in other words, a miracle, to prevent them? Nothing is esteemed a miracle if it ever happen in the common course of nature. It is no miracle that a man, seemingly in good health, should die on a sudden, because such a kind of death, though more unusual than any other, has yet been frequently observed to happen. But it is a miracle that a dead man should come to life, because that has never been observed in any age or country. There must, therefore, be a uniform experience against every miraculous event, otherwise the event would not merit that appellation. And as a uniform experience amounts to a proof, there is here a direct and full *proof,* from the nature of the fact, against the existence of any

---

2. No Indian, it is evident, could have experience that water did not freeze in cold climates. This is placing nature in a situation quite unknown to him; and it is impossible for him to tell *a priori* what will result from it. It is making a new experiment, the consequence of which is always uncertain. One may sometimes conjecture from analogy what will follow; but still this is but conjecture. And it must be confessed that, in the present case of freezing, the event follows contrary to the rules of analogy, and is such as a rational Indian would not look for. The operations of cold upon water are not gradual according to the degrees of cold; but whenever it comes to the freezing point, the water passes in a moment from the utmost liquidity to perfect hardness. Such an event, therefore, may be denominated *extraordinary,* and requires a pretty strong testimony to render it credible to people in a warm climate; but still it is not *miraculous,* nor contrary to uniform experience of the course of nature in cases where all the circumstances are the same. The inhabitants of Sumatra have always seen water fluid in their own climate, and the freezing of their rivers ought to be deemed a prodigy: but they never saw water in Muscovy during the winter; and therefore they cannot reasonably be positive what would there be the consequence.

miracle; nor can such a proof be destroyed, or the miracle rendered credible, but by an opposite proof which is superior.[3]

The plain consequence is (and it is a general maxim worthy of our attention), "that no testimony is sufficient to establish a miracle, unless the testimony be of such a kind that its falsehood would be more miraculous than the fact which it endeavours to establish; and even in that case there is a mutual destruction of arguments, and the superior only gives us an assurance suitable to that degree of force which remains after deducting the inferior." When anyone tells me that he saw a dead man restored to life, I immediately consider with myself whether it be more probable that this person should either deceive or be deceived, or that the fact which he relates should really have happened. I weigh the one miracle against the other; and according to the superiority which I discover, I pronounce my decision, and always reject the greater miracle. If the falsehood of his testimony would be more miraculous than the event which he relates, then, and not till then, can he pretend to command my belief or opinion.

Part II

In the foregoing reasoning we have supposed that the testimony upon which a miracle is founded may possibly amount to an entire proof, and that the falsehood of that testimony would be a real prodigy, but it is easy to show that we have been a great deal too liberal in our concession, and that there never was a miraculous event established on so full an evidence.

For, *first,* there is not to be found in all history any miracle attested by a sufficient number of men of such unquestioned good sense, edu-

---

3. Sometimes an event may not, *in itself, seem* to be contrary to the laws of nature, and yet, if it were real, it might, by reason of some circumstances, be denominated a miracle; because, in *fact,* it is contrary to these laws. Thus if a person, claiming a divine authority, should command a sick person to be well, a healthful man to fall down dead, the clouds to pour rain, the winds to blow, in short, should order many natural events which immediately follow upon his command; these might justly be esteemed miracles, because they are really, in this case, contrary to the laws of nature. For if any suspicion remain that the event and command concurred by accident, there is no miracle and no transgression of the laws of nature. If this suspicion be removed, there is evidently a miracle, and a transgression of these laws; because nothing can be more contrary to nature than that the voice or command of a man should have such an influence. A miracle may be accurately defined—*a transgression of a law of nature by a particular volition of the Deity, or by the interposition of some invisible agent.* A miracle may either be discoverable by men or not. This alters not its nature and essence. The raising of a house or ship into the air is a visible miracle. The raising of a feather, when the wind wants ever so little of a force requisite for that purpose, is as real a miracle, though not so sensible with regard to us.

cation, and learning, as to secure us against all delusion in themselves; of such undoubted integrity as to place them beyond all suspicion of any design to deceive others; of such credit and reputation in the eyes of mankind as to have a great deal to lose in case of their being detected in any falsehood; and at the same time, attesting facts performed in such a public manner and in so celebrated a part of the world, as to render the detection unavoidable: all which circumstances are requisite to give us a full assurance in the testimony of men.

Secondly, we may observe in human nature a principle which, if strictly examined, will be found to diminish extremely the assurance which we might, from human testimony, have in any kind of prodigy. The maxim by which we commonly conduct ourselves in our reasonings is that the objects of which we have no experience resemble those of which we have; that what we have found to be most usual is always most probable; and that where there is an opposition of arguments, we ought to give the preference to such as are founded on the greatest number of past observations. But though, in proceeding by this rule, we readily reject any fact which is unusual and incredible in an ordinary degree; yet in advancing farther, the mind observes not always the same rule; but when anything is affirmed utterly absurd and miraculous, it rather the more readily admits of such a fact, upon account of that very circumstance which ought to destroy all its authority. The passion of *surprise* and *wonder,* arising from miracles being an agreeable emotion, gives a sensible tendency towards the belief of those events from which it is derived. And this goes so far that even those who cannot enjoy this pleasure immediately, nor can believe those miraculous events of which they are informed, yet love to partake of the satisfaction at second-hand or by rebound, and place a pride and delight in exciting the admiration of others.

With what greediness are the miraculous accounts of travellers received, their descriptions of sea and land monsters, their relations of wonderful adventures, strange men, and uncouth manners? But if the spirit of religion join itself to the love of wonder, there is an end of common sense; and human testimony, in these circumstances, loses all pretensions to authority. A religionist may be an enthusiast, and imagine he sees what has no reality: he may know his narrative to be false, and yet persevere in it with the best intentions in the world, for the sake of promoting so holy a cause: or even where this delusion has not place, vanity, excited by so strong a temptation, operates on him more powerfully than on the rest of mankind in any other circumstances; and self-interest with equal force. His auditors may not have, and commonly have not, sufficient judgment to canvass his evidence: what judgment they have, they renounce by the principle in these sublime and mysterious subjects: or if they were ever so willing to employ it, passion and a heated imagination disturb the regularity of its operations. Their credulity increases his impudence: and his impudence overpowers their credulity.

Eloquence, when at its highest pitch, leaves little room for reason or reflection; but addressing itself entirely to the fancy or the affections, captivates the willing hearers, and subdues their understanding. Happily, this pitch it seldom attains. But what a Tully or a Demosthenes could scarcely effect over a Roman or Athenian audience, every *Capuchin,* every itinerant or stationary teacher can perform over the generality of mankind, and in a higher degree, by touching such gross and vulgar passions.

The many instances of forged miracles, and prophecies, and supernatural events, which, in all ages, have either been detected by contrary evidence, or which detect themselves by their absurdity, prove sufficiently the strong propensity of mankind to the extraordinary and the marvellous, and ought reasonably to beget a suspicion against all relations of this kind. This is our natural way of thinking, even with regard to the most common and most credible events. For instance, there is no kind of report which rises so easily, and spreads so quickly, especially in country places and provincial towns, as those concerning marriages; insomuch that two young persons of equal condition never see each other twice, but the whole neighbourhood immediately join them together. The pleasure of telling a piece of news so interesting, of propagating it, and of being the first reporters of it, spreads the intelligence. And this is so well known that no man of sense gives attention to these reports, till he find them confirmed by some greater evidence. Do not the same passions, and others still stronger, incline the generality of mankind to believe and report, with the greatest vehemence and assurance, all religious miracles?

Thirdly, it forms a strong presumption against all supernatural and miraculous relations that they are observed chiefly to abound among ignorant and barbarous nations; or if a civilized people has ever given admission to any of them, that people will be found to have received them from ignorant and barbarous ancestors, who transmitted them with that inviolable sanction and authority which always attends received opinions. When we peruse the first histories of all nations, we are apt to imagine ourselves transported into some new world, where the whole frame of nature is disjointed, and every element performs its operations in a different manner from what it does at present. Battles, revolutions, pestilence, famine and death, are never the effect of those natural causes which we experience. Prodigies, omens, oracles, judgments, quite obscure the few natural events that are intermingled with them. But as the former grow thinner every page, in proportion as we advance nearer the enlightened ages, we soon learn that there is nothing mysterious or supernatural in the case, but that all proceeds from the usual propensity of mankind towards the marvellous, and that, though this inclination may at intervals receive a check from sense and learning, it can never be thoroughly extirpated from human nature.

It is strange, a judicious reader is apt to say, upon the perusal of these wonderful historians, *that such prodigious events never happen in our days.* But it is nothing strange, I hope, that men should lie in all ages. You must surely have seen instances enough of that frailty. You have yourself heard many such marvellous relations started, which, being treated with scorn by all the wise and judicious, have at last been abandoned even by the vulgar. Be assured that those renowned lies, which have spread and flourished to such a monstrous height, arose from like beginnings; but being sown in a more proper soil, shot up at last into prodigies almost equal to those which they relate.

It was a wise policy in that false prophet, Alexander, who, though now forgotten, was once so famous, to lay the first scene of his impostures in Paphlagonia, where, as Lucian tells us, the people were extremely ignorant and stupid, and ready to swallow even the grossest delusion. People at a distance, who are weak enough to think the matter at all worth enquiry, have no opportunity of receiving better information. The stories come magnified to them by a hundred circumstances. Fools are industrious in propagating the imposture; while the wise and learned are contented, in general, to deride its absurdity, without informing themselves of the particular facts by which it may be distinctly refuted. And thus the impostor above mentioned was enabled to proceed from his ignorant Paphlagonians to the enlisting of votaries, even among the Grecian philosophers, and men of the most eminent rank and distinction in Rome: nay, could engage the attention of that sage emperor Marcus Aurelius; so far as to make him trust the success of a military expedition to his delusive prophecies.

The advantages are so great, of starting an imposture among an ignorant people, that, even though the delusion should be too gross to impose on the generality of them *(which, though seldom, is sometimes the case)* it has a much better chance for succeeding in remote countries, than if the first scene had been laid in a city renowned for arts and knowledge. The most ignorant and barbarous of these bar-

barians carry the report abroad. None of their countrymen have a large correspondence, or sufficient credit and authority to contradict and beat down the delusion. Men's inclination to the marvellous has full opportunity to display itself. And thus a story which is universally exploded in the place where it was first started, shall pass for certain at a thousand miles distance. But had Alexander fixed his residence at Athens, the philosophers of that renowned mart of learning had immediately spread, throughout the whole Roman empire, their sense of the matter; which, being supported by so great authority, and displayed by all the force of reason and eloquence, had entirely opened the eyes of mankind. It is true, Lucian, passing by chance through Paphlagonia, had an opportunity of performing this good office. But, though much to be wished, it does not always happen that every Alexander meets with a Lucian, ready to expose and detect his impostures.

I may add as a *fourth* reason, which diminishes the authority of prodigies, that there is no testimony for any, even those which have not been expressly detected, that is not opposed by an infinite number of witnesses; so that not only the miracle destroys the credit of testimony, but the testimony destroys itself. To make this the better understood, let us consider that, in matters of religion, whatever is different is contrary; and that it is impossible the religions of ancient Rome, of Turkey, of Siam and of China should, all of them, be established on any solid foundation. Every miracle, therefore, pretended to have been wrought in any of these religions (and all of them abound in miracles), as its direct scope is to establish the particular system to which it is attributed, so has it the same force, though more indirectly, to overthrow every other system. In destroying a rival system, it likewise destroys the credit of those miracles on which that system was established; so that all the prodigies of different religions are to be regarded as contrary facts, and the evidences of these prodigies, whether weak or strong, as opposite to each other. According to this method of reasoning, when we believe any miracle of Mohammed or his successors, we have for our warrant the testimony of a few barbarous Arabians: and on the other hand, we are to regard the authority of Titus Livius, Plutarch, Tacitus and, in short, of all the authors and witnesses, Grecian, Chinese, and Roman Catholic, who have related any miracle in their particular religion; I say, we are to regard their testimony in the same light as if they had mentioned that Mohammedan miracle, and had in express terms contradicted it, with the same certainty as they have for the miracle they relate. This argument may appear over subtle and refined, but is not in reality different from the reasoning of a judge, who supposes that the credit of two witnesses, maintaining a crime against anyone, is destroyed by the testimony of two others, who affirm him to have been two hundred leagues distant at the same instant when the crime is said to have been committed.

One of the best attested miracles in all profane history is that which Tacitus reports of Vespasian, who cured a blind man in Alexandria by means of his spittle, and a lame man by the mere touch of his foot, in obedience to a vision of the god Serapis, who had enjoined them to have recourse to the Emperor for these miraculous cures. The story may be seen in that fine historian;[4] where every circumstance seems to add weight to the testimony, and might be displayed at large with all the force of argument and eloquence, if anyone were now concerned to enforce the evidence of that exploded and idolatrous superstition. The gravity, solidity, age, and probity of so great an emperor, who, through the whole course of his life, conversed in a familiar manner with his friends and courtiers, and never affected those extraordinary airs of divinity assumed by Alexander and Demetrius: the historian, a contemporary writer, noted for candour and veracity, and, withal, the greatest and most penetrating genius, perhaps, of all antiquity; and so free from any tendency to credulity that he even lies under the contrary imputation of atheism and profaneness: the persons, from whose authority he related the miracle, of established character for judgment and veracity, as we may well presume; eyewitnesses of the fact, and confirming their testimony after the Flavian family was despoiled of the empire, and could no longer give any reward as the price of a lie. *Utrumque, qui interfuere, nunc quoque memorant, postquam nullum mendacio pretium.* To which if we add the public nature of the facts as related, it will appear that no evidence can well be supposed stronger for so gross and so palpable a falsehood.

There is also a memorable story related by Cardinal de Retz, which may well deserve our consideration. When that intriguing politician fled into Spain to avoid the persecution of his enemies, he passed through Saragossa, the capital of Aragon, where he was shown, in the cathedral, a man who had served seven years as a doorkeeper, and was well known to everybody in town that had ever paid his devotions at that church. He had been seen, for so long a time, wanting a leg, but recovered that limb by the rubbing of holy oil upon the stump; and the cardinal assures us that he saw him with two legs. This miracle was vouched by all the canons of the church; and the whole company in town were appealed to for a confirmation of the fact; whom the cardinal found, by their zealous devotion, to be thorough believers of the

---

4. *Hist.,* Lib. v, cap. 8. Suetonius gives nearly the same account in *Vita Vespasiani.*

miracle. Here the relater was also contemporary to the supposed prodigy, of an incredulous and libertine character, as well as of great genius; the miracle of *so singular* a nature as could scarcely admit of a counterfeit, and the witnesses very numerous, and all of them, in a manner, spectators of the fact to which they gave their testimony. And what adds mightily to the force of the evidence, and may double our surprise on this occasion, is that the cardinal himself, who relates the story, seems not to give any credit to it, and consequently cannot be suspected of any concurrence in the holy fraud. He considered justly that it was not requisite, in order to reject a fact of this nature, to be able accurately to disprove the testimony and to trace its falsehood through all the circumstances of knavery and credulity which produced it. He knew that as this was commonly altogether impossible at any small distance of time and place, so was it extremely difficult, even where one was immediately present, by reason of the bigotry, ignorance, cunning, and roguery of a great part of mankind. He therefore concluded, like a just reasoner, that such an evidence carried falsehood upon the very face of it, and that a miracle, supported by any human testimony, was more properly a subject of derision than of argument.

There surely never was a greater number of miracles ascribed to one person than those which were lately said to have been wrought in France upon the tomb of Abbé Pâris, the famous Jansenist, with whose sanctity the people were so long deluded. The curing of the sick, giving hearing to the deaf, and sight to the blind, were everywhere talked of as the usual effects of that holy sepulchre. But what is more extraordinary, many of the miracles were immediately proved upon the spot, before judges of unquestioned integrity, attested by witnesses of credit and distinction, in a learned age, and on the most eminent theatre that is now in the world. Nor is this all: a relation of them was published and dispersed everywhere; nor were the Jesuits, though a learned body supported by the civil magistrate, and determined enemies to those opinions in whose favour the miracles were said to have been wrought, ever able distinctly to refute or detect them. Where shall we find such a number of circumstances, agreeing to the corroboration of one fact? And what have we to oppose to such a cloud of witnesses, but the absolute impossibility or miraculous nature of the events which they relate? And this, surely, in the eyes of all reasonable people, will alone be regarded as a sufficient refutation.

Is the consequence just, because some human testimony has the utmost force and authority in some cases—when it relates the battle of Philippi or Pharsalia for instance—that therefore all kinds of testimony must, in all cases, have equal force and authority? Suppose that the Caesarean and Pompeian factions had, each of them, claimed the victory in these battles, and that the historians of each party had uni-formly ascribed the advantage to their own side; how could mankind, at this distance, have been able to determine between them? The contrariety is equally strong between the miracles related by Herodo-tus or Plutarch, and those delivered by Mariana, Bede, or any monkish historian.

The wise lend a very academic faith to every report which favours the passion of the reporter; whether it magnifies his country, his fam-ily, or himself, or in any other way strikes in with his natural inclina-tions and propensities. But what greater temptation than to appear a missionary, a prophet, an ambassador from heaven? Who would not encounter many dangers and difficulties, in order to attain so sublime a character? Or if, by the help of vanity and a heated imagination, a man has first made a convert of himself, and entered seriously into the delusion; who ever scruples to make use of pious frauds, in support of so holy and meritorious a cause?

The smallest spark may here kindle into the greatest flame, because the materials are always prepared for it. The *avidum genus auricu-larum,*[5] the gazing populace, receive greedily, without examination, whatever soothes superstition and promotes wonder.

How many stories of this nature have, in all ages, been detected and exploded in their infancy? How many more have been celebrated for a time, and have afterwards sunk into neglect and oblivion? Where such reports, therefore, fly about, the solution of the phenomenon is obvious; and we judge in conformity to regular experience and obser-vation, when we account for it by the known and natural principles of credulity and delusion. And shall we, rather than have a recourse to so natural a solution, allow of a miraculous violation of the most established laws of nature?

I need not mention the difficulty of detecting a falsehood in any private or even public history, at the place where it is said to happen; much more when the scene is removed to ever so small a distance. Even a court of judicature, with all the authority, accuracy, and judg-ment which they can employ, find themselves often at a loss to distin-guish between truth and falsehood in the most recent actions. But the matter never comes to any issue, if trusted to the common method of altercation and debate and flying rumours; especially when men's pas-sions have taken part on either side.

In the infancy of new religions, the wise and learned commonly esteem the matter too inconsiderable to deserve their attention or regard. And when afterwards they would willingly detect the cheat, in

---

5. Lucretius.

order to undeceive the deluded multitude, the season is now past, and the records and witnesses, which might clear up the matter, have perished beyond recovery.

No means of detection remain, but those which must be drawn from the very testimony itself of the reporters: and these, though always sufficient with the judicious and knowing, are commonly too fine to fall under the comprehension of the vulgar.

Upon the whole, then, it appears that no testimony for any kind of miracle has ever amounted to a probability, much less to a proof; and that, even supposing it amounted to a proof, it would be opposed by another proof, derived from the very nature of the fact which it would endeavour to establish. It is experience only which gives authority to human testimony, and it is the same experience which assures us of the laws of nature. When, therefore, these two kinds of experience are contrary, we have nothing to do but subtract the one from the other, and embrace an opinion, either on one side or the other, with that assurance which arises from the remainder. But according to the principle here explained, this subtraction with regard to all popular religions, amounts to an entire annihilation; and, therefore, we may establish it as a maxim that no human testimony can have such force as to prove a miracle, and make it a just foundation for any such system of religion.

I beg the limitations here made may be remarked, when I say that a miracle can never be proved, so as to be the foundation of a system of religion. For I own that otherwise there may possibly be miracles, or violations of the usual course of nature, of such a kind as to admit of proof from human testimony; though, perhaps, it will be impossible to find any such in all the records of history. Thus, suppose all authors, in all languages, agree that, from the first of January 1600, there was a total darkness over the whole earth for eight days: suppose that the tradition of this extraordinary event is still strong and lively among the people: that all travellers who return from foreign countries bring us accounts of the same tradition, without the least variation or contradiction: it is evident that our present philosophers, instead of doubting the fact, ought to receive it as certain, and ought to search for the causes whence it might be derived. The decay, corruption, and dissolution of nature is an event rendered probable by so many analogies, that any phenomenon which seems to have a tendency towards that catastrophe comes within the reach of human testimony, if that testimony be very extensive and uniform.

But suppose that all the historians who treat of England should agree that on the first of January 1600, Queen Elizabeth died; that both before and after her death she was seen by her physicians and the whole court, as is usual with persons of her rank; that her successor was acknowledged and proclaimed by the parliament; and that, after being interred a month, she again appeared, resumed the throne, and governed England for three years: I must confess that I should be surprised at the concurrence of so many odd circumstances, but should not have the least inclination to believe so miraculous an event. I should not doubt of her pretended death, and of those other public circumstances that followed it: I should only assert it to have been pretended, and that it neither was, nor possibly could be, real. You would in vain object to me the difficulty, and almost impossibility, of deceiving the world in an affair of such consequence; the wisdom and solid judgment of that renowned queen, with the little or no advantage which she could reap from so poor an artifice: all this might astonish me; but I would still reply that the knavery and folly of men are such common phenomena, that I should rather believe the most extraordinary events to arise from their concurrence, than admit of so signal a violation of the laws of nature.

But should this miracle be ascribed to any new system of religion; men, in all ages, have been so much imposed on by ridiculous stories of that kind, that this very circumstance would be a full proof of a cheat, and sufficient, with all men of sense, not only to make them reject the fact, but even reject it without farther examination. Though the Being to whom the miracle is ascribed be, in this case, Almighty, it does not, upon that account, become a whit more probable; since it is impossible for us to know the attributes or actions of such a Being, otherwise than from the experience which we have of his productions in the usual course of nature. This still reduces us to past observation, and obliges us to compare the instances of the violation of truth in the testimony of men with those of the violation of the laws of nature by miracles, in order to judge which of them is most likely and probable. As the violations of truth are more common in the testimony concerning religious miracles than in that concerning any other matter of fact, this must diminish very much the authority of the former testimony, and make us form a general resolution never to lend any attention to it, with whatever specious pretence it may be covered.

Lord Bacon seems to have embraced the same principles of reasoning. "We ought," says he, "to make a collection or particular history of all monsters and prodigious births or productions, and in a word of everything new, rare, and extraordinary in nature. But this must be done with the most severe scrutiny, lest we depart from truth. Above all, every relation must be considered as suspicious which depends in any degree upon religion, as the prodigies of Livy: and no less so, everything that is to be found in the writers of natural magic or alchemy, or such authors who seem, all of them, to have an unconquerable appetite for falsehood and fable."[6]

I am the better pleased with the method of reasoning here delivered, as I think it may serve to confound those dangerous friends or disguised enemies to the *Christian Religion,* who have undertaken to defend it by the principles of human reason. Our most holy religion is founded on *faith,* not on reason; and it is a sure method of exposing it to put it to such a trial as it is by no means fitted to endure. To make this more evident let us examine those miracles related in scripture; and not to lose ourselves in too wide a field, let us confine ourselves to such as we find in the Pentateuch, which we shall examine according to the principles of these pretended Christians, not as the word or testimony of God himself, but as the production of a mere human writer and historian. Here, then, we are first to consider a book presented to us by a barbarous and ignorant people, written in an age when they were still more barbarous, and in all probability long after the facts which it relates, corroborated by no concurring testimony, and resembling those fabulous accounts which every nation gives of its origin. Upon reading this book, we find it full of prodigies and miracles. It gives an account of a state of the world and of human nature entirely different from the present; of our fall from that state; of the age of man extended to near a thousand years; of the destruction of the world by a deluge; of the arbitrary choice of one people as the favourites of heaven, and that people the countrymen of the author; of their deliverance from bondage by prodigies the most astonishing imaginable: I desire anyone to lay his hand upon his heart, and after a serious consideration declare whether he thinks that the falsehood of such a book, supported by such a testimony, would be more extraordinary and miraculous than all the miracles it relates; which is, however, necessary to make it be received, according to the measures of probability above established.

What we have said of miracles may be applied, without any variation, to prophecies; and, indeed, all prophecies are real miracles, and as such only can be admitted as proofs of any revelation. If it did not exceed the capacity of human nature to foretell future events, it would be absurd to employ any prophecy as an argument for a divine mission or authority from heaven. So that, upon the whole, we may conclude that the *Christian Religion* not only was at first attended with miracles,

---

6. *Nov. Organ.* Lib. ii, aph. 29.

but even at this day cannot be believed by any reasonable person without one. Mere reason is insufficient to convince us of its veracity: and whoever is moved by *faith* to assent to it, is conscious of a continued miracle in his own person, which subverts all the principles of his understanding, and gives him a determination to believe what is most contrary to custom and experience.

2. The Essence of Christianity

What we have hitherto been maintaining generally, even with regard to sensational impressions, of the relation between subject and object, applies especially to the relation between the subject and the religious object.

In the perceptions of the senses consciousness of the object is distinguishable from consciousness of self; but in religion, consciousness of the object and self-consciousness coincide. The object of the senses is out of man, the religious object is within him, and therefore as little forsakes him as his self-consciousness or his conscience; it is the intimate, the closest object. "God," says Augustine, for example, "is nearer, more related to us, and therefore more easily known by us, than sensible, corporeal things." The object of the senses is in itself indifferent—independent of the disposition or of the judgment; but the object of religion is a selected object; the most excellent, the first, the supreme being; it essentially presupposes a critical judgment, a discrimination between the divine and the nondivine, between that which is worthy of adoration and that which is not worthy. And here may be applied, without any limitation, the proposition: the object of any subject is nothing else than the subject's own nature taken objec-

Reprinted from Ludwig Feuerbach, *The Essence of Christianity,* trans. Marian Evans (George Eliot), (Boston: Houghton Mifflin, 1854), chap. i, sec. 2.

tively. Such as are a man's thoughts and dispositions, such is his God; so much worth as a man has, so much and no more has his God. Consciousness of God is self-consciousness, knowledge of God is self-knowledge. By his God thou knowest the man, and by the man his God; the two are identical. Whatever is God to a man, that is his heart and soul; and conversely, God is the manifested inward nature, the expressed self of a man,—religion the solemn unveiling of a man's hidden treasures, the revelation of his intimate thoughts, the open confession of his love-secrets.

But when religion—consciousness of God—is designated as the self-consciousness of man, this is not to be understood as affirming that the religious man is directly aware of this identity; for, on the contrary, ignorance of it is fundamental to the peculiar nature of religion. To preclude this misconception, it is better to say, religion is man's earliest and also indirect form of self-knowledge. Hence, religion everywhere precedes philosophy, as in the history of the race, so also in that of the individual. Man first of all sees his nature as if *out of* himself, before he finds it in himself. His own nature is in the first instance contemplated by him as that of another being. Religion is the childlike condition of humanity; but the child sees his nature—man—out of himself; in childhood a man is an object to himself, under the form of another man. Hence the historical progress of religion consists in this: that what by an earlier religion was regarded as objective, is now recognised as subjective; that is, what was formerly contemplated and worshipped as God is now perceived to be something *human.* What was at first religion becomes at a later period idolatry; man is seen to have adored his own nature. Man has given objectivity to himself, but has not recognised the object as his own nature: a later religion takes this forward step; every advance in religion is therefore a deeper self-knowledge. But every particular religion, while it pronounces its predecessors idolatrous, excepts itself—and necessarily so, otherwise it would no longer be religion—from the fate, the common nature of all religions: it imputes only to other religions what is the fault, if fault it be, of religion in general. Because it has a different object, a different tenor, because it has transcended the ideas of preceding religions, it erroneously supposes itself exalted above the necessary eternal laws which constitute the essence of religion—it fancies its object, its ideas, to be superhuman. But the essence of religion, thus hidden from the religious, is evident to the thinker, by whom religion is viewed objectively, which it cannot be by its votaries. And it is our task to show that the antithesis of divine and human is altogether illusory, that it is nothing else than the antithesis between the human nature in general

and the human individual; that, consequently, the object and contents
of the Christian religion are altogether human.

Religion, at least the Christian, is the relation of man to himself, or
more correctly to his own nature (i.e., his subjective nature); but a
relation to it, viewed as a nature apart from his own. The divine being
is nothing else than the human being, or, rather, the human nature
purified, freed from the limits of the individual man, made objective
—i.e., contemplated and revered as another, a distinct being. All the
attributes of the divine nature are, therefore, attributes of the human
nature.

In relation to the attributes, the predicates, of the Divine Being, this
is admitted without hesitation, but by no means in relation to the
subject of these predicates. The negation of the subject is held to be
irreligion, nay, atheism; though not so the negation of the predicates.
But that which has no predicates or qualities, has no effect upon me;
that which has no effect upon me has no existence for me. To deny all
the qualities of a being is equivalent to denying the being himself. A
being without qualities is one which cannot become an object to the
mind, and such a being is virtually non-existent. Where man deprives
God of all qualities, God is no longer anything more to him than a
negative being. To the truly religious man, God is not a being without
qualities, because to him he is a positive, real being. The theory that
God cannot be defined, and consequently cannot be known by man,
is therefore the offspring of recent times, a product of modern unbelief.

As reason is and can be pronounced finite only where man regards
sensual enjoyment, or religious emotion, or aesthetic contemplation,
or moral sentiment, as the absolute, the true; so the proposition that
God is unknowable or undefinable, can only be enunciated and
become fixed as a dogma, where this object has no longer any interest
for the intellect; where the real, the positive, alone has any hold on
man, where the real alone has for him the significance of the essential,
of the absolute, divine object, but where at the same time, in contradiction with this purely worldly tendency, there yet exist some old remains of religiousness. On the ground that God is unknowable, man
excuses himself to what is yet remaining of his religious conscience for
his forgetfulness of God, his absorption in the world: he denies God
practically by his conduct,—the world has possession of all his
thoughts and inclinations,—but he does not deny him theoretically, he
does not attack his existence; he lets that rest. But this existence does
not affect or incommode him; it is a merely negative existence, an
existence without existence, a self-contradictory existence,—a state of

being which, as to its effects, is not distinguishable from non-being. The denial of determinate, positive predicates concerning the divine nature is nothing else than a denial of religion, with, however, an appearance of religion in its favour, so that it is not recognised as a denial; it is simply a subtle, disguised atheism. The alleged religious horror of limiting God by positive predicates is only the irreligious wish to know nothing more of God, to banish God from the mind. Dread of limitation is dread of existence. All real existence, i.e., all existence which is truly such, is qualitative, determinative existence. He who earnestly believes in the Divine existence is not shocked at the attributing even of gross sensuous qualities to God. He who dreads an existence that may give offence, who shrinks from the grossness of a positive predicate, may as well renounce existence altogether. A God who is injured by determinate qualities has not the courage and the strength to exist. Qualities are the fire, the vital breath, the oxygen, the salt of existence. An existence in general, an existence without qualities, is an insipidity, an absurdity. But there can be no more in God than is supplied by religion. Only where man loses his taste for religion, and thus religion itself becomes insipid, does the existence of God become an insipid existence—an existence without qualities.

There is, however, a still milder way of denying the divine predicates than the direct one just described. It is admitted that the predicates of the divine nature are finite, and, more particularly, human qualities, but their rejection is rejected; they are even taken under protection, because it is necessary to man to have a definite conception of God, and since he is man he can form no other than a human conception of him. In relation to God, it is said, these predicates are certainly without any objective validity; but to me, if he is to exist for me, he cannot appear otherwise than as he does appear to me, namely, as a being with attributes analogous to the human. But this distinction between what God is in himself, and what he is for me destroys the peace of religion, and is besides in itself an unfounded and untenable distinction. I cannot know whether God is something else in himself or for himself than he is for me; what he is to me is to me all that he is. For me, there lies in these predicates under which he exists for me, what he is in himself, his very nature; he is for me what he can alone ever be for me. The religious man finds perfect satisfaction in that which God is in relation to himself; of any other relation he knows nothing, for God is to him what he can alone be to man. In the distinction above stated, man takes a point of view above himself, i.e., above his nature, the absolute measure of his being; but this transcendentalism is only an illusion; for I can make the distinction between the object as it is in itself, and the object as it is for me, only where an object can really appear otherwise to me, not where it appears to me such as the absolute measure of my nature determines it to appear— such as it must appear to me. It is true that I may have a merely subjective conception, i.e., one which does not arise out of the general constitution of my species; but if my conception is determined by the constitution of my species, the distinction between what an object is in itself, and what it is for me ceases; for this conception is itself an absolute one. The measure of the species is the absolute measure, law, and criterion of man. And, indeed, religion has the conviction that its conceptions, its predicates of God, are such as every man ought to have, and must have, if he would have the true ones—that they are the conceptions necessary to human nature; nay, further, that they are objectively true, representing God as he is. To every religion the gods of *other* religions are only notions concerning God, but its own conception of God is to it God himself, the true God—God such as he is in himself. Religion is satisfied only with a complete Deity, a God without reservation; it will not have a mere phantasm of God; it demands God himself. Religion gives up its own existence when it gives up the nature of God; it is no longer a truth when it renounces the possession of the true God. Scepticism is the arch-enemy of religion; but the distinction between object and conception—between God as he is in himself, and God as he is for me—is a sceptical distinction, and therefore an irreligious one.

That which is to man the self-existent, the highest being, to which he can conceive nothing higher—that is to him the Divine Being. How then should he inquire concerning this being, what he is in himself? If God were an object to the bird, he would be a winged being: the bird knows nothing higher, nothing more blissful, than the winged condition. How ludicrous would it be if this bird pronounced: To me God appears as a bird, but what he is in himself I know not. To the bird the highest nature is the bird-nature; take from him the conception of this, and you take from him the conception of the highest being. How, then, could he ask whether God in himself were winged? To ask whether God is in himself what he is for me, is to ask whether God is God, is to lift oneself above one's God, to rise up against him.

Wherever, therefore, this idea, that the religious predicates are only anthropomorphisms, has taken possession of a man, there has doubt, has unbelief, obtained the mastery of faith. And it is only the inconsequence of faint-heartedness and intellectual imbecility which does not proceed from this idea to the formal negation of the predicates, and from thence to the negation of the subject to which they relate. If thou doubtest the objective truth of the predicates, thou must also doubt the objective truth of the subject whose predicates they are. If thy predicates are anthropomorphisms, the subject of them is an anthropomorphism too. If love, goodness, personality, &c., are human attributes, so also is the subject which thou presupposest, the existence of God, the belief that there is a God, an anthropomorphism—a presupposition purely human. Whence knowest thou that the belief in a God at all is not a limitation of man's mode of conception? Higher beings—and thou supposest such—are perhaps so blest in themselves, so at unity with themselves, that they are not hung in suspense between themselves and a yet higher being. To know God and not oneself to be God, to know blessedness and not oneself to enjoy it, is a state of disunity, of unhappiness. Higher beings know nothing of this unhappiness; they have no conception of that which they are not.

Thou believest in love as a divine attribute because thou thyself lovest; thou believest that God is a wise, benevolent being because thou knowest nothing better in thyself than benevolence and wisdom; and thou believest that God exists, that therefore he is a subject—whatever exists is a subject, whether it be defined as substance, person, essence, or otherwise—because thou thyself existest, art thyself a subject. Thou knowest no higher human good than to love, than to be good and wise; and even so thou knowest no higher happiness than to exist, to be a subject; for the consciousness of all reality, of all bliss, is for thee bound up in the consciousness of being a subject, of existing. God is an existence, a subject to thee, for the same reason that he is to thee a wise, a blessed, a personal being. The distinction between the divine predicates and the divine subject is only this, that to thee the subject, the existence, does not appear an anthropomorphism, because the conception of it is necessarily involved in thy own existence as a subject, whereas the predicates do appear anthropomorphisms, because their necessity—the necessity that God should be conscious, wise, good, &c.,—is not an immediate necessity, identical with the being of man, but is evolved by his self-consciousness, by the activity of his thought. I am a subject, I exist, whether I be wise or unwise, good or bad. To exist is to man the first datum; it constitutes the very idea of the subject; it is presupposed by the predicates. Hence man relinquishes the predicates, but the existence of God is to him a settled, irrefragable, absolutely certain, objective truth. But, nevertheless, this distinction is merely an apparent one. The necessity of the subject lies only in the necessity of the predicate. Thou art a subject only in so far as thou art a human subject; the certainty and reality of thy existence lie only in the certainty and reality of thy human attributes. What the subject is lies only in the predicate; the predicate is the *truth* of the subject—the subject only the personified, existing predicate, the predicate conceived as existing. Subject and predicate are distinguished only as existence and essence. The negation of the predicates is therefore the negation of the subject. What remains of the human subject when abstracted from the human attributes? Even in the language of common life the divine predicates—Providence, Omniscience, Omnipotence—are put for the divine subject.

The certainty of the existence of God, of which it has been said that it is as certain, nay, more certain to man than his own existence, depends only on the certainty of the qualities of God—it is in itself no immediate certainty. To the Christian the existence of the Christian God only is a certainty; to the heathen that of the heathen God only. The heathen did not doubt the existence of Jupiter, because he took no offence at the nature of Jupiter, because he could conceive of God under no other qualities, because to him these qualities were a certainty, a divine reality. The reality of the predicate is the sole guarantee of existence.

Whatever man conceives to be true, he immediately conceives to be real (that is, to have an objective existence), because, originally, only the real is true to him—true in opposition to what is merely conceived, dreamed, imagined. The idea of being, of existence, is the original idea of truth; or, originally, man makes truth dependent on existence, subsequently, existence dependent on truth. Now God is the nature of man regarded as absolute truth,—the truth of man; but God, or, what is the same thing, religion, is as various as are the conditions under which man conceives this his nature, regards it as the highest being. These conditions, then, under which man conceives God, are to him the truth, and for that reason they are also the highest existence, or rather they are existence itself; for only the emphatic, the highest existence, is existence, and deserves this name. Therefore, God is an existent, real being, on the very same ground that he is a particular, definite being; for the qualities of God are nothing else than the essential qualities of man himself, and a particular man is what he is, has his existence, his reality, only in his particular conditions. Take away from the Greek the quality of being Greek, and you take away his existence. On this ground it is true that for a definite positive religion—that is, relatively—the certainty of the existence of God is *immediate;* for just as involuntarily, as necessarily, as the Greek was a Greek, so necessarily were his gods Greek beings, so necessarily were they real, existent beings. Religion is that conception of the nature of the world and of man which is essential to, i.e., identical with, a man's nature. But man does not stand above this his necessary conception; on the contrary, it stands above him; it animates, determines, governs him. The necessity of a proof, of a middle term to unite qualities with existence, the possibility of a doubt, is abolished. Only that which is apart from my own being is capable of being doubted by me. How then can I doubt of God, who is my being? To doubt of God is to doubt of myself. Only when God is thought of abstractly, when his predicates are the result of philosophic abstraction, arises the distinction or separation between subject and predicate, existence and nature—arises the fiction that the existence or the subject is something else than the predicate, something immediate, indubitable, in distinction from the predicate, which is held to be doubtful. But this is only a fiction. A God who has abstract predicates has also an abstract existence. Existence, being, varies with varying qualities.

The identity of the subject and predicate is clearly evidenced by the progressive development of religion, which is identical with the progressive development of human culture. So long as man is in a mere state of nature, so long is his god a mere nature-god—a personification of some natural force. Where man inhabits houses, he also encloses his gods in temples. The temple is only a manifestation of the value which man attaches to beautiful buildings. Temples in honour of religion are in truth temples in honour of architecture. With the emerging of man from a state of savagery and wildness to one of culture, with the distinction between what is fitting for man and what is not fitting, arises simultaneously the distinction between that which is fitting and that which is not fitting for God. God is the idea of majesty, of the highest dignity: the religious sentiment is the sentiment of supreme fitness. The later more cultured artists of Greece were the first to embody in the statues of the gods the ideas of dignity, of spiritual grandeur, of imperturbable repose and serenity. But why were these qualities in their view attributes, predicates of God? Because they were in themselves regarded by the Greeks as divinities. Why did those artists exclude all disgusting and low passions? Because they perceived them to be unbecoming, unworthy, unhuman, and consequently ungodlike. The Homeric gods eat and drink;—that implies eating and drinking is a divine pleasure. Physical strength is an attribute of the Homeric gods: Zeus is the strongest of the gods. Why? Because physical strength, in and by itself, was regarded as something glorious, divine. To the ancient Germans the highest virtues were those of the warrior; therefore their supreme god was the god of war, Odin,—war, "the original or oldest law." Not the attribute of the divinity, but the divineness or deity of the attribute, is the first true Divine Being. Thus what theology and philosophy have held to be God, the Absolute, the Infinite, is not God; but that which they have held not to be God is God: namely, the attribute, the quality, whatever has reality. Hence he alone is the true atheist to whom the predicates of the Divine Being,—for example, love, wisdom, justice,—are nothing; not he to whom merely the subject of these predicates is nothing. And in no wise is the negation of the subject necessarily also a negation of the predicates considered in themselves. These have an intrinsic, independent reality; they force their recognition upon man by their very nature; they are self-evident truths to him; they prove, they attest themselves. It does not follow that goodness, justice, wisdom, are chimaeras because the existence of God is a chimaera, nor truths because this is a truth. The idea of God is dependent on the idea of justice, of benevolence; a God who is not benevolent, not just, not wise, is no God; but the converse does not hold. The fact is not that a quality is divine because God has it, but that God has it because it is in itself divine: because without it God would be a defective being. Justice, wisdom, in general every quality which constitutes the divinity of God, is determined and known by itself independently, but the idea of God is determined by the qualities which have thus been previously judged to be worthy of the divine nature; only in the case in which I identify God and justice, in which I think of God immediately as the reality of the idea of justice, is the idea of God self-determined. But if God as a subject is the determined, while the quality, the predicate, is the determining, then in truth the rank of the godhead is due not to the subject, but to the predicate.

Not until several, and those contradictory, attributes are united in one being, and this being is conceived as personal—the personality being thus brought into especial prominence—not until then is the origin of religion lost sight of, is it forgotten that what the activity of the reflective power has converted into a predicate distinguishable or separable from the subject, was originally the true subject. Thus the Greeks and Romans deified accidents as substances; virtues, states of mind, passions, as independent beings. Man, especially the religious man, is to himself the measure of all things, of all reality. Whatever strongly impresses a man, whatever produces an unusual effect on his mind, if it be only a peculiar, inexplicable sound or note, he personifies as a divine being. Religion embraces all the objects of the world: everything existing has been an object of religious reverence; in the nature and consciousness of religion there is nothing else than what lies in the nature of man and in his consciousness of himself and of the world. Religion has no material exclusively its own. In Rome even the passions of fear and terror had their temples. The Christians also made mental phenomena into independent beings, their own feelings into qualities of things, the passions which governed them into powers which governed the world, in short, predicates of their own nature, whether recognised as such or not, into independent subjective existences. Devils, cobolds, witches, ghosts, angels, were sacred truths as long as the religious spirit held undivided sway over mankind.

In order to banish from the mind the identity of the divine and human predicates, and the consequent identity of the divine and human nature, recourse is had to the idea that God, as the absolute, real Being, has an infinite fulness of various predicates, of which we here know only a part, and those such as are analogous to our own; while the rest, by virtue of which God must thus have quite a different nature from the human or that which is analogous to the human, we shall only know in the future—that is, after death. But an infinite plenitude or multitude of predicates which are really different, so different that the one does not immediately involve the other, is realised only in an infinite plenitude or multitude of different beings or individuals. Thus the human nature presents an infinite abundance of different predicates, and for that very reason it presents an infinite abundance of different individuals. Each new man is a new predicate, a new phasis of humanity. As many as are the men, so many are the powers, the properties of humanity. It is true that there are the same elements in every individual, but under such various conditions and modifications that they appear new and peculiar. The mystery of the inexhaustible fulness of the divine predicates is therefore nothing else than the mystery of human nature considered as an infinitely varied, infinitely modifiable, but consequently, phenomenal being. Only in the realm of the senses, only in space and time, does there exist a being of really infinite qualities or predicates. Where there are really different predicates there are different times. One man is a distinguished musician, a distinguished author, a distinguished physician; but he cannot compose music, write books, and perform cures in the same moment of time. Time, and not the Hegelian dialectic, is the medium of uniting opposites, contradictories, in one and the same subject. But distinguished and detached from the nature of man, and combined with the idea of God, the infinite fulness of various predicates is a conception without reality, a mere phantasy, a conception derived from the sensible world, but without the essential conditions, without the truth of sensible existence, a conception which stands in direct contradiction with the Divine Being considered as a spiritual, i.e., an abstract, simple, single being; for the predicates of God are precisely of this character, that one involves all the others, because there is no real difference between them. If, therefore, in the present predicates I have not the future, in the present God not the future God, then the future God is not the present, but they are two distinct beings.[1] But this distinction is in contradiction with the unity and simplicity of the theological God. Why is a given predicate a predicate of God? Because it is divine in its nature, i.e., because it expresses no limitation, no defect. Why are other predicates applied to him? Because, however various in themselves, they agree in this, that they all alike express perfection, unlimitedness. Hence I can conceive innumerable predicates of God, because they must all agree with the abstract idea of the Godhead, and must have in common that which constitutes every single predicate a divine attribute. Thus it is in the system of Spinoza. He speaks of an infinite number of attributes of the divine substance, but he specifies none except Thought and Extension. Why? Because it is a matter of indifference to know them; nay, Because they are in themselves indifferent, superfluous; for with all these innumerable predicates, I yet always mean to say the same thing as when I speak of Thought and Extension. Why is Thought an attribute of substance? Because, according to Spinoza, it is capable of being conceived by itself, because it expresses something indivisible, perfect, infinite. Why Extension or Matter? For the same reason. Thus, substance can have an indefinite number of predicates, because it is not their specific definition, their difference, but their identity, their equivalence, which makes them attributes of substance. Or rather, substance has innumerable predicates only because (how strange!) it has properly no predicate; that is, no definite, real predicate. The indefinite unity which is the product of thought, completes itself by the indefinite multiplicity which is the product of the imagination. Because the predicate is not *multum,* it is *multa.* In truth, the positive predicates are Thought and Extension. In these two infinitely more is said than in the nameless innumerable predicates; for they express something definite—in them I have something. But substance is too indifferent, too apathetic to be *something;* that is, to have qualities and passions; that it may not be something, it is rather nothing.

Now, when it is shown that what the subject is lies entirely in the attributes of the subject; that is, that the predicate is the true subject; it is also proved that if the divine predicates are attributes of the human

---

1. For religious faith there is no other distinction between the present and future God than that the former is an object of faith, of conception, of imagination, while the latter is to be an object of immediate, that is, personal, sensible perception. In this life and in the next he is the same God; but in the one he is incomprehensible, in the other comprehensible.

nature, the subject of those predicates is also of the human nature. But the divine predicates are partly general, partly personal. The general predicates are the metaphysical, but these serve only as external points of support to religion; they are not the characteristic definitions of religion. It is the personal predicates alone which constitute the essence of religion—in which the Divine Being is the object of religion. Such are, for example, that God is a Person, that he is the moral Lawgiver, the Father of mankind, the Holy One, the Just, the Good, the Merciful. It is, however, at once clear, or it will at least be clear in the sequel, with regard to these and other definitions, that, especially as applied to a personality, they are purely human definitions, and that consequently man in religion—in his relation to God—is in relation to his own nature; for to the religious sentiment these predicates are not mere conceptions, mere images, which man forms of God, to be distinguished from that which God is in himself, but truths, facts, realities. Religion knows nothing of anthropomorphisms; to it they are not anthropomorphisms. It is the very essence of religion, that to it these definitions express the nature of God. They are pronounced to be images only by the understanding, which reflects on religion, and which while defending them yet before its own tribunal denies them. But to the religious sentiment God is a real Father, real Love and Mercy; for to it he is a real, living, personal being, and therefore his attributes are also living and personal. Nay, the definitions which are the most sufficing to the religious sentiment are precisely those which give the most offence to the understanding, and which in the process of reflection on religion it denies. Religion is essentially emotion; hence, objectively also, emotion is to it necessarily of a divine nature. Even anger appears to it an emotion not unworthy of God, provided only there be a religious motive at the foundation of this anger.

But here it is also essential to observe, and this phenomenon is an extremely remarkable one, characterising the very core of religion, that in proportion as the divine subject is in reality human, the greater is the apparent difference between God and man; that is, the more, by reflection on religion, by theology, is the identity of the divine and human denied, and the human, considered as such, is depreciated. The reason of this is, that as what is positive in the conception of the divine being can only be human, the conception of man, as an object of consciousness, can only be negative. To enrich God, man must become poor; that God may be all, man must be nothing. But he desires to be nothing in himself, because what he takes from himself is not lost to him, since it is preserved in God. Man has his being in God; why then should he have it in himself? Where is the necessity of positing the same thing twice, of having it twice? What man withdraws from himself, what he renounces in himself, he only enjoys in an incomparably higher and fuller measure in God.

The monks made a vow of chastity to God; they mortified the sexual passion in themselves, but therefore they had in heaven, in the Virgin Mary, the image of woman—an image of love. They could the more easily dispense with real woman in proportion as an ideal woman was an object of love to them. The greater the importance they attached to the denial of sensuality, the greater the importance of the heavenly virgin for them: she was to them in the place of Christ, in the stead of God. The more the sensual tendencies are renounced, the more sensual is the God to whom they are sacrificed. For whatever is made an offering to God has an especial value attached to it; in it God is supposed to have especial pleasure. That which is the highest in the estimation of man is naturally the highest in the estimation of his God; what pleases man pleases God also. The Hebrews did not offer to Jehovah unclean, ill-conditioned animals; on the contrary, those which they most highly prized, which they themselves ate, were also the food of God (*Cibus Dei,* Lev. iii. 2). Wherever, therefore, the denial of the sensual delights is made a special offering, a sacrifice well-pleasing to God, there the highest value is attached to the senses, and the sensuality which has been renounced is unconsciously restored, in the fact that God takes the place of the material delights which have been renounced. The nun weds herself to God; she has a heavenly bridegroom, the monk a heavenly bride. But the heavenly virgin is only a sensible presentation of a general truth, having relation to the essence of religion. Man denies as to himself only what he attributes to God. Religion abstracts from man, from the world; but it can only abstract from the limitations, from the phenomena; in short, from the negative, not from the essence, the positive, of the world and humanity: hence, in the very abstraction and negation it must recover that from which it abstracts, or believes itself to abstract. And thus, in reality, whatever religion consciously denies—always supposing that what is denied by it is something essential, true, and consequently incapable of being ultimately denied—it unconsciously restores in God. Thus, in religion man denies his reason; of himself he knows nothing of God, his thoughts are only worldly, earthly; he can only believe what God reveals to him. But on this account the thoughts of God are human, earthly thoughts: like man, he has plans in his mind, he accommodates himself to circumstances and grades of intelligence, like a tutor with his pupils; he calculates closely the effect of his gifts and revelations; he observes man in all his doings; he knows all things, even the most earthly, the commonest, the most trivial. In brief, man in relation to God denies his own knowledge, his own thoughts, that he may place them in God. Man gives up his personality; but in return, God, the Almighty, infinite, unlimited being, is a person; he denies human dignity, the human *ego;* but in return God is to him a selfish, egoistical being, who in all things seeks only himself, his own honour, his own ends; he represents God as simply seeking the satisfaction of his own selfishness, while yet he frowns on that of every other being; his God is the very luxury of egoism. Religion further denies goodness as a quality of human nature; man is wicked, corrupt, incapable of good; but, on the other hand, God is only good—the Good Being. Man's nature demands as an object goodness, personified as God; but is it not hereby declared that goodness is an essential tendency of man? If my heart is wicked, my understanding perverted, how can I perceive and feel the holy to be holy, the good to be good? Could I perceive the beauty of a fine picture if my mind were aesthetically an absolute piece of perversion? Though I may not be a painter, though I may not have the power of producing what is beautiful myself, I must yet have aesthetic feeling, aesthetic comprehension, since I perceive the beauty that is presented to me externally. Either goodness does not exist at all for man, or, if it does exist, therein is revealed to the individual man the holiness and goodness of human nature. That which is absolutely opposed to my nature, to which I am united by no bond of sympathy, is not even conceivable or perceptible by me. The holy is in opposition to me only as regards the modifications of my personality, but as regards my fundamental nature it is in unity with me. The holy is a reproach to my sinfulness; in it I recognise myself as a sinner; but in so doing, while I blame myself, I acknowledge what I am not, but ought to be, and what, for that very reason, I, according to my destination, can be; for an "ought" which has no corresponding capability does not affect me, is a ludicrous chimaera without any true relation to my mental constitution. But when I acknowledge goodness as my destination, as my law, I acknowledge it, whether consciously or unconsciously, as my own nature. Another nature than my own, one different in quality, cannot touch me. I can perceive sin as sin, only when I perceive it to be a contradiction of myself with myself—that is, of my personality with my fundamental nature. As a contradiction of the absolute, considered as another being, the feeling of sin is inexplicable, unmeaning.

The distinction between Augustinianism and Pelagianism consists only in this, that the former expresses after the manner of religion what the latter expresses after the manner of Rationalism. Both say the same thing, both vindicate the goodness of man; but Pelagianism does it directly, in a rationalistic and moral form; Augustinianism indirectly, in a mystical, that is, a religious form.[2] For that which is given to man's God is in truth given to man himself; what a man declares concerning God, he in truth declares concerning himself. Augustinianism would be a truth, and a truth opposed to Pelagianism, only if man had the devil for his God, and, with the consciousness that he was the devil, honoured, reverenced, and worshipped him as the highest being. But so long as man adores a good being as his God, so long does he contemplate in God the goodness of his own nature.

As with the doctrine of the radical corruption of human nature, so is it with the identical doctrine, that man can do nothing good, i.e., in truth, nothing of himself—by his own strength. For the denial of human strength and spontaneous moral activity to be true, the moral activity of God must also be denied; and we must say, with the Oriental nihilist or pantheist: the Divine being is absolutely without will or action, indifferent, knowing nothing of the discrimination between evil and good. But he who defines God as an active being, and not only so, but as morally active and morally critical,—as a being who loves, works, and rewards good, punishes, rejects, and condemns evil,—he who thus defines God only in appearance denies human activity, in fact, making it the highest, the most real activity. He who makes God act humanly, declares human activity to be divine; he says: A god who is not active, and not morally or humanly active, is no god; and thus he makes the idea of the Godhead dependent on the idea of activity, that is, of human activity, for a higher he knows not.

Man—this is the mystery of religion—projects his being into objectivity,[3] and then again makes himself an object to this projected image

2. Pelagianism denies God, religion—isti tantam tribuunt potestatem voluntati, ut pietati auferant orationem. (Augustin de Nat. et Grat. cont. Pelagium, c. 58). It has only the creator, i.e., Nature, as a basis, not the Saviour, the true God of the religious sentiment—in a word, it denies God; but, as a consequence of this, it elevates man into a God, since it makes him a being not needing God, self-sufficing, independent. (See on this subject Luther against Erasmus and Augustine, l. c. c. 33.) Augustinianism denies man; but, as a consequence of this, it reduces God to the level of man, even to the ignominy of the cross, for the sake of man. The former puts man in the place of God, the latter puts God in the place of man; both lead to the same result—the distinction is only apparent, a pious illusion. Augustinianism is only an inverted Pelagianism; what to the latter is a subject, is to the former an object.

3. The religious, the original mode in which man becomes objective to himself, is (as is clearly enough explained in this work) to be distinguished from the mode in which this occurs in reflection and speculation; the latter is voluntary, the former involuntary, necessary—as necessary as art, as speech. With the progress of time, it is true, theology coincides with religion.

of himself thus converted into a subject; he thinks of himself as an object to himself, but as the object of an object, of another being than himself. Thus here. Man is an object to God. That man is good or evil is not indifferent to God; no! He has a lively, profound interest in man's being good; he wills that man should be good, happy—for without goodness there is no happiness. Thus the religious man virtually retracts the nothingness of human activity, by making his dispositions and actions an object to God, by making man the end of God—for that which is an object to the mind is an end in action; by making the divine activity a means of human salvation. God acts, that man may be good and happy. Thus man, while he is apparently humiliated to the lowest degree is in truth exalted to the highest. Thus, in and through God, man has in view himself alone. It is true that man places the aim of his action in God, but God has no other aim of action than the moral and eternal salvation of man: thus man has in fact no other aim than himself. The divine activity is not distinct from the human.

How could the divine activity work on me as its object, nay, work in me, if it were essentially different from me; how could it have a human aim, the aim of ameliorating and blessing man, if it were not itself human? Does not the purpose determine the nature of the act? When man makes his moral improvement an aim to himself, he has divine resolutions, divine projects; but also, when God seeks the salvation of man, he has human ends and a human mode of activity corresponding to these ends. Thus in God man has only his own activity as an object. But for the very reason that he regards his own activity as objective, goodness only as an object, he necessarily receives the impulse, the motive not from himself, but from this object. He contemplates his nature as external to himself, and this nature as goodness; thus it is self-evident, it is mere tautology to say that the impulse to good comes only from thence where he places the good.

God is the highest subjectivity of man abstracted from himself; hence man can do nothing of himself, all goodness comes from God. The more subjective God is, the more completely does man divest himself of his subjectivity, because God is, *per se,* his relinquished self, the possession of which he however again vindicates to himself. As the action of the arteries drives the blood into the extremities, and the action of the veins brings it back again, as life in general consists in a perpetual systole and diastole; so is it in religion. In the religious systole man propels his own nature from himself, he throws himself outward; in the religious diastole he receives the rejected nature into his heart again. God alone is the being who acts of himself,—this is the force of repulsion in religion; God is the being who acts in me, with me, through me, upon me, for me, is the principle of my salvation, of my good dispositions and actions, consequently my own good principle and nature,—this is the force of attraction in religion.

The course of religious development which has been generally indicated consists specifically in this, that man abstracts more and more from God, and attributes more and more to himself. This is especially apparent in the belief in revelation. That which to a later age or a cultured people is given by nature or reason, is to an earlier age, or to a yet uncultured people, given by God. Every tendency of man, however natural—even the impulse to cleanliness, was conceived by the Israelites as a positive divine ordinance. From this example we again see that God is lowered, is conceived more entirely on the type of ordinary humanity, in proportion as man detracts from himself. How can the self-humiliation of man go further than when he disclaims the capability of fulfilling spontaneously the requirements of common decency?[4] The Christian religion, on the other hand, distinguished the impulses and passions of man according to their quality, their character; it represented only good emotions, good dispositions, good thoughts, as revelations, operations—that is, as dispositions, feelings, thoughts,—of God; for what God reveals is a quality of God himself: that of which the heart is full overflows the lips; as is the effect such is the cause; as the revelation, such the being who reveals himself. A God who reveals himself in good dispositions is a God whose essential attribute is only moral perfection. The Christian religion distinguishes inward moral purity from external physical purity; the Israelites identified the two.[5] In relation to the Israelitish religion, the Christian religion is one of criticism and freedom. The Israelite trusted himself to do nothing except what was commanded by God; he was without will even in external things; the authority of religion extended itself even to his food. The Christian religion, on the other hand, in all these external things made man dependent on himself, i.e., placed in man what the Israelite placed out of himself in God. Israel is the most complete presentation of Positivism in religion. In relation to the Israelite, the Christian is an *esprit fort,* a free-thinker. Thus do things change. What yesterday was still religion is no longer such to-day; and what to-day is atheism, tomorrow will be religion.

---

4. Deut. xxiii. 12, 13.

5. See, for example, Gen. xxxv. 2; Levit. xi. 44; xx. 26; and the Commentary of Le Clere on these passages.

3. Fear and Trembling

Once upon a time there was a man who as a child had heard the beautiful story about how God tempted Abraham, and how he endured temptation, kept the faith, and a second time received again a son contrary to expectation. When the child became older he read the same story with even greater admiration, for life had separated what was united in the pious simplicity of the child. The older he became, the more frequently his mind reverted to that story, his enthusiasm became greater and greater, and yet he was less and less able to understand the story. At last in his interest for that he forgot everything else; his soul had only one wish, to see Abraham, one longing, to have been witness to that event. His desire was not to behold the beautiful countries of the Orient, or the earthly glory of the Promised Land, or that godfearing couple whose old age God had blessed, or the venerable figure of the aged patriarch, or the vigorous young manhood of Isaac whom God had bestowed upon Abraham—he saw no reason why the same thing might not have taken place on a barren heath in Denmark. His yearning was to accompany them on the three days' journey when Abraham rode with sorrow before him and with

---

Reprinted from Søren Kierkegaard, *Fear and Trembling and the Sickness Unto Death* transl. with an Introduction and Notes, by Walter Lowrie (Princeton Paperback, 1968), pp. 26 through 37. Reprinted by permission of Princeton University Press.

Isaac by his side. His only wish was to be present at the time when Abraham lifted up his eyes and saw Mount Moriah afar off, at the time when he left the asses behind and went alone with Isaac up unto the mountain; for what his mind was intent upon was not the ingenious web of imagination but the shudder of thought.

That man was not a thinker, he felt no need of getting beyond faith; he deemed it the most glorious thing to be remembered as the father of it, an enviable lot to possess it, even though no one else were to know it.

That man was not a learned exegete, he didn't know Hebrew, if he had known Hebrew, he perhaps would easily have understood the story and Abraham.

I

"And God tempted Abraham and said unto him, Take Isaac, thine only son, whom thou lovest, and get thee into the land of Moriah, and offer him there for a burnt offering upon the mountain which I will show thee."

It was early in the morning, Abraham arose betimes, he had the asses saddled, left his tent, and Isaac with him, but Sarah looked out of the window after them until they had passed down the valley and she could see them no more. They rode in silence for three days. On the morning of the fourth day Abraham said never a word, but he lifted up his eyes and saw Mount Moriah afar off. He left the young men behind and went on alone with Isaac beside him up to the mountain. But Abraham said to himself, "I will not conceal from Isaac whither this course leads him." He stood still, he laid his hand upon the head of Isaac in bene-diction, and Isaac bowed to receive the blessing. And Abraham's face was fatherliness, his look was mild, his speech encouraging. . But Isaac was unable to understand him, his soul could not be exalted; he embraced Abraham's knees, he fell at his feet imploringly, he begged for his young life, for the fair hope of his future, he called to mind the joy in Abraham's house, he called to mind the sorrow and loneliness. Then Abraham lifted up the boy, he walked with him by his side, and his talk was full of comfort and exhortation. But Isaac could not understand him. He climbed Mount Moriah, but Isaac understood him not. Then for an instant he turned away from him, and when Isaac again saw Abraham's face it was changed, his glance was wild, his form was horror. He seized Isaac by the throat, threw him to the ground, and said, "Stupid boy, dost thou then suppose that I am thy father?

I am an idolater. Dost thou suppose that this is God's bidding? No, it is my desire." Then Isaac trembled and cried out in his terror, "O God in heaven, have compassion upon me. God of Abraham, have compassion upon me. If I have no father upon earth, be Thou my father!" But Abraham in a low voice said to himself, "O Lord in heaven, I thank Thee. After all it is better for him to believe that I am a monster, rather than that he should lose faith in Thee."

When the child must be weaned, the mother blackens her breast, it would indeed be a shame that the breast should look delicious when the child must not have it. So the child believes that the breast has changed, but the mother is the same, her glance is as loving and tender as ever. Happy the person who had no need of more dreadful expedients for weaning the child!

II

It was early in the morning, Abraham arose betimes, he embraced Sarah, the bride of his old age, and Sarah kissed Isaac, who had taken away her reproach, who was her pride, her hope for all time. So they rode on in silence along the way, and Abraham's glance was fixed upon the ground until the fourth day when he lifted up his eyes and saw afar off Mount Moriah, but his glance turned again to the ground. Silently he laid the wood in order, he bound Isaac, in silence he drew the knife —then he saw the ram which God had prepared. Then he offered that and returned home. . . . From that time on Abraham became old, he could not forget that God had required this of him. Isaac throve as before, but Abraham's eyes were darkened, and he knew joy no more.

When the child has grown big and must be weaned, the mother virginally hides her breast, so the child has no more a mother. Happy the child which did not in another way lose its mother.

III

It was early in the morning, Abraham arose betimes, he kissed Sarah, the young mother, and Sarah kissed Isaac, her delight, her joy at all times. And Abraham rode pensively along the way, he thought of Hagar and of the son whom he drove out into the wilderness, he climbed Mount Moriah, he drew the knife.

It was a quiet evening when Abraham rode out alone, and he rode to Mount Moriah; he threw himself upon his face, he prayed God to forgive him his sin, that he had been willing to offer Isaac, that the father had forgotten his duty toward the son. Often he rode his lonely way, but he found no rest. He could not comprehend that it was a sin to be willing to offer to God the best thing he possessed, that for which he would many times have given his life; and if it was a sin, if he had not loved Isaac as he did, then he could not understand that it might be forgiven. For what sin could be more dreadful?

When the child must be weaned, the mother too is not without sorrow at the thought that she and the child are separated more and more, that the child which first lay under her heart and later reposed upon her breast will be so near to her no more. So they mourn together for the brief period of mourning. Happy the person who has kept the child as near and needed not to sorrow any more!

IV

It was early in the morning, everything was prepared for the journey in Abraham's house. He bade Sarah farewell, and Eleazar, the faithful servant, followed him along the way, until he turned back. They rode together in harmony, Abraham and Isaac, until they came to Mount Moriah. But Abraham prepared everthing for the sacrifice, calmly and quietly; but when he turned and drew the knife, Isaac saw that his left hand was clenched in despair, that a tremor passed through his body —but Abraham drew the knife.

Then they returned again home, and Sarah hastened to meet them, but Isaac had lost his faith. No word of this had ever been spoken in the world, and Isaac never talked to anyone about what he had seen, and Abraham did not suspect that anyone had seen it.

When the child must be weaned, the mother has stronger food in readiness, lest the child should perish. Happy the person who has stronger food in readiness!

Thus and in many like ways that man of whom we are speaking thought concerning this event. Every time he returned home after wandering to Mount Moriah, he sank down with weariness, he folded his hands and said, "No one is so great as Abraham! Who is capable of understanding him?"

If there were no eternal consciousness in a man, if at the foundation of all there lay only a wildly seething power which writhing with obscure passions produced everything that is great and everything that is insignificant, if a bottomless void never satiated lay hidden beneath all— what then would life be but despair? If such were the case, if there were no sacred bond which united mankind, if one generation arose after another like the leafage in the forest, if the one generation replaced the other like the song of birds in the forest, if the human race passed through the world as the ship goes through the sea, like the wind through the desert, a thoughtless and fruitless activity, if an eternal oblivion were always lurking hungrily for its prey and there was no power strong enough to wrest it from it's maw—how empty then and comfortless life would be! But therefore it is not thus, but as God created man and woman, so too He fashioned the hero and the poet or orator. The poet cannot do what the other does, he can only admire, love and rejoice in the hero. Yet he too is happy, and not less so, for the hero is as it were his better nature, with which he is in love, rejoicing in the fact that this after all is not himself, that his love can be admiration. He is the genius of recollection, can do nothing except call to mind what has been done, do nothing but admire what has been done; he contributes nothing of his own, but is jealous of the intrusted treasure. He follows the option of his heart, but when he has found what he sought, he wanders before every man's door with his song and with his oration, that all may admire the hero as he does, be proud of the hero as he is. This is his achievement, his humble work, this is his faithful service in the house of the hero. If he thus remains true to his love, he strives day and night against the cunning of oblivion which would trick him out of his hero, then he has completed his work, then he is gathered to the hero, who has loved him just as faithfully, for the poet is as it were the hero's better nature, powerless it may be as a memory is, but also transfigured as a memory is. Hence no one shall be forgotten who was great, and though time tarries long, though a cloud of misunderstanding takes the hero away, his lover comes nevertheless, and the longer the time that has passed, the more faithfully will he cling to him.

No, not one shall be forgotten who was great in the world. But each was great in his own way, and each in proportion to the greatness of that which he *loved.* For he who loved himself became great by himself, and he who loved other men became great by his selfless devotion, but he who loved God became greater than all. Everyone shall be remembered, but each became great in proportion to his *expectation.* One became great by expecting the possible, another by expecting the eternal, but he who expected the impossible became greater than all. Everyone shall be remembered, but each was great in proportion to the greatness of that with which he *strove.* For he who strove with the world became great by overcoming the world, and he who strove with himself became great by overcoming himself, but he who strove with God became greater than all. So there was strife in the world, man against man, one against a thousand, but he who strove with God was greater than all. So there was strife upon earth: there was one who

overcame all by his power, and there was one who overcame God by
his impotence. There was one who relied upon himself and gained all,
there was one who secure in his strength sacrificed all, but he who
believed God was greater than all. There was one who was great by
reason of his power, and one who was great by reason of his wisdom,
and one who was great by reason of his hope, and one who was great
by reason of his love; but Abraham was greater than all, great by reason
of his power whose strength is impotence, great by reason of his
wisdom whose secret is foolishness, great by reason of his hope whose
form is madness, great by reason of the love which is hatred of oneself.

By faith Abraham went out from the land of his fathers and became
a sojourner in the land of promise. He left one thing behind, took one
thing with him: he left his earthly understanding behind and took faith
with him—otherwise he would not have wandered forth but would
have thought this unreasonable. By faith he was a stranger in the land
of promise, and there was nothing to recall what was dear to him, but
by its novelty everything tempted his soul to melancholy yearning—
and yet he was God's elect, in whom the Lord was well pleased! Yea,
if he had been disowned, cast off from God's grace, he could have
comprehended it better; but now it was like a mockery of him and of
his faith. There was in the world one too who lived in banishment from
the fatherland he loved. He is not forgotten, nor his Lamentations
when he sorrowfully sought and found what he had lost. There is no
song of Lamentations by Abraham. It is human to lament, human to
weep with them that weep, but it is greater to believe, more blessed
to contemplate the believer.

By faith Abraham received the promise that in his seed all races of
the world would be blessed. Time passed, the possibility was there,
Abraham believed; time passed, it became unreasonable, Abraham
believed. There was in the world one who had an expectation, time
passed, the evening drew nigh, he was not paltry enough to have
forgotten his expectation, therefore he too shall not be forgotten.
Then he sorrowed, and sorrow did not deceive him as life had done,
it did for him all it could, in the sweetness of sorrow he possessed his
delusive expectation. It is human to sorrow, human to sorrow with
them that sorrow, but it is greater to believe, more blessed to contemplate the believer. There is no song of Lamentations by Abraham. He
did not mournfully count the days while time passed, he did not look
at Sarah with a suspicious glance, wondering whether she were growing old, he did not arrest the course of the sun, that Sarah might not
grow old, and his expectation with her. He did not sing lullingly before
Sarah his mournful lay. Abraham became old, Sarah became a laugh-

ingstock in the land, and yet he was God's elect and inheritor of the promise that in his seed all the races of the world would be blessed. So were it not better if he had not been God's elect? What is it to be God's elect? It is to be denied in youth the wishes of youth, so as with great pains to get them fulfilled in old age. But Abraham believed and held fast the expectation. If Abraham had wavered, he would have given it up. If he had said to God, "Then perhaps it is not after all Thy will that it should come to pass, so I will give up the wish. It was my only wish, it was my bliss. My soul is sincere, I hide no secret malice because Thou didst deny it to me"—he would not have been forgotten, he would have saved many by his example, yet he would not be the father of faith. For it is great to give up one's wish, but it is greater to hold it fast after having given it up, it is great to grasp the eternal, but it is greater to hold fast to the temporal after having given it up.

Then came the fulness of time. If Abraham had not believed, Sarah surely would have been dead of sorrow, and Abraham, dulled by grief, would not have understood the fulfilment but would have smiled at it as at a dream of youth. But Abraham believed, therefore he was young; for he who always hopes for the best becomes old, and he who is always prepared for the worst grows old early, but he who believes preserves an eternal youth. Praise therefore to that story! For Sarah, though stricken in years, was young enough to desire the pleasure of motherhood, and Abraham, though gray-haired, was young enough to wish to be a father. In an outward respect the marvel consists in the fact that it came to pass according to their expectation, in a deeper sense the miracle of faith consists in the fact that Abraham and Sarah were young enough to wish, and that faith had preserved their wish and therewith their youth. He accepted the fulfilment of the promise, he accepted it by faith, and it came to pass according to the promise and according to his faith—for Moses smote the rock with his rod, but he did not believe.

Then there was joy in Abraham's house, when Sarah became a bride on the day of their golden wedding.

But it was not to remain thus. Still once more Abraham was to be tried. He had fought with that cunning power which invents everything, with that alert enemy which never slumbers, with that old man who outlives all things—he had fought with Time and preserved his faith. Now all the terror of the strife was concentrated in one instant. "And God tempted Abraham and said unto him, Take Isaac, thine only son, whom thou lovest, and get thee into the land of Moriah, and offer him there for a burnt offering upon the mountain which I will show thee."

So all was lost—more dreadfully than if it had never come to pass! So the Lord was only making sport of Abraham! He made miraculously the preposterous actual, and now in turn He would annihilate it. It was indeed foolishness, but Abraham did not laugh at it like Sarah when the promise was announced. All was lost! Seventy years of faithful expectation, the brief joy at the fulfilment of faith. Who then is he that plucks away the old man's staff, who is it that requires that he himself shall break it? Who is he that would make a man's gray hairs comfortless, who is it that requires that he himself shall do it? Is there no compassion for the venerable oldling, none for the innocent child? And yet Abraham was God's elect, and it was the Lord who imposed the trial. All would now be lost. The glorious memory to be preserved by the human race, the promise in Abraham's seed—this was only a whim, a fleeting thought which the Lord had had, which Abraham should now obliterate. That glorious treasure which was just as old as faith in Abraham's heart, many, many years older than Isaac, the fruit of Abraham's life, sanctified by prayers, matured in conflict—the blessing upon Abraham's lips, this fruit was now to be plucked prematurely and remain without significance. For what significance had it when Isaac was to be sacrificed? That sad and yet blissful hour when Abraham was to take leave of all that was dear to him, when yet once more he was to lift up his head, when his countenance would shine like that of the Lord, when he would concentrate his whole soul in a blessing which was potent to make Isaac blessed all his days—this time would not come! For he would indeed take leave of Isaac, but in such a way that he himself would remain behind; death would separate them, but in such a way that Isaac remained its prey. The old man would not be joyful in death as he laid his hands in blessing upon Isaac, but he would be weary of life as he laid violent hands upon Isaac. And it was God who tried him. Yea, woe, woe unto the messenger who had come before Abraham with such tidings! Who would have ventured to be the emissary of this sorrow? But it was God who tried Abraham.

Yet Abraham believed, and believed for this life. Yea, if his faith had been only for a future life, he surely would have cast everything away in order to hasten out of this world to which he did not belong. But Abraham's faith was not of this sort, if there be such a faith; for really this is not faith but the furthest possibility of faith which has a presentiment of its object at the extremest limit of the horizon, yet is separated from it by a yawning abyss within which despair carries on its game. But Abraham believed precisely for this life, that he was to grow old in the land, honored by the people, blessed in his generation, remembered forever in Isaac, his dearest thing in life, whom he embraced with a love for which it would be a poor expression to say that he loyally fulfilled the father's duty of loving the son, as indeed is evinced in the words of the summons, "the son whom thou lovest." Jacob had twelve sons, and one of them he loved; Abraham had only one, the son whom he loved.

Yet Abraham believed and did not doubt, he believed the preposterous. If Abraham had doubted—then he would have done something else, something glorious; for how could Abraham do anything but what is great and glorious! He would have marched up to Mount Moriah, he would have cleft the fire-wood, lit the pyre, drawn the knife —he would have cried out to God, "Despise not this sacrifice, it is not the best thing I possess, that I know well, for what is an old man in comparison with the child of promise; but it is the best I am able to give Thee. Let Isaac never come to know this, that he may console himself with his youth." He would have plunged the knife into his own breast. He would have been admired in the world, and his name would not have been forgotten; but it is one thing to be admired, and another to be the guiding star which saves the anguished.

But Abraham believed. He did not pray for himself, with the hope of moving the Lord—it was only when the righteous punishment was decreed upon Sodom and Gomorrha that Abraham came forward with his prayers.

We read in those holy books: "And God tempted Abraham, and said unto him, Abraham, Abraham, where are thou? And he said, Here am I." Thou to whom my speech is addressed, was such the case with thee? When afar off thou didst see the heavy dispensation of providence approaching thee, didst thou not say to the mountains, Fall on me, and to the hills, Cover me? Or if thou wast stronger, did not thy foot move slowly along the way, longing as it were for the old path? When a call was issued to thee, didst thou answer, or didst thou not answer perhaps in a low voice, whisperingly? Not so Abraham: joyfully, buoyantly, confidently, with a loud voice, he answered, "Here am I." We read further: "And Abraham rose early in the morning"—as though it were to a festival, so he hastened, and early in the morning he had come to the place spoken of, to Mount Moriah. He said nothing to Sarah, nothing to Eleazar. Indeed who could understand him? Had not the temptation by its very nature exacted of him an oath of silence? He cleft the wood, he bound Isaac, he lit the pyre, he drew the knife. My hearer, there was many a father who believed that with his son he lost everything that was dearest to him in the world, that he was deprived of every hope for the future, but yet there was none that was the child of promise in the sense that Isaac was for Abraham. There was many a father who lost his child; but then it was God, it was the unalterable, the unsearchable will of the Almighty, it was His hand took the child. Not so with Abraham. For him was reserved a harder trial, and Isaac's fate was laid along with the knife in Abraham's hand. And there he stood, the old man, with his only hope! But he did not doubt, he did not look anxiously to the right or to the left, he did not challenge heaven with his prayers. He knew that it was God the Almighty who was trying him, he knew that it was the hardest sacrifice that could be required of him; but he knew also that no sacrifice was too hard when God required it—and he drew the knife.

Who gave strength to Abraham's arm? Who held his right hand up so that it did not fall limp at his side? He who gazes at this becomes paralyzed. Who gave strength to Abraham's soul, so that his eyes did not grow dim, so that he saw neither Isaac nor the ram? He who gazes at this becomes blind.—And yet rare enough perhaps is the man who becomes paralyzed and blind, still more rare one who worthily re-counts what happened. We all know it—it was only a trial.

If Abraham when he stood upon Mount Moriah had doubted, if he had gazed about him irresolutely, if before he drew the knife he had by chance discovered the ram, if God had permitted him to offer it instead of Isaac—then he would have betaken himself home, everything would have been the same, he has Sarah, he retained Isaac, and yet how changed! For his retreat would have been a flight, his salvation an accident, his reward dishonor, his future perhaps perdition. Then he would have borne witness neither to his faith nor to God's grace, but would have testified only how dreadful it is to march out to Mount Moriah. Then Abraham would not have been forgotten, nor would Mount Moriah, this mountain would then be mentioned, not like Ara-rat where the Ark landed, but would be spoken of as a consternation, because it was here that Abraham doubted.

Venerable Father Abraham! In marching home from Mount Moriah thou hadst no need of a panegyric which might console thee for thy loss; for thou didst gain all and didst retain Isaac. Was it not so? Never again did the Lord take him from thee, but thou didst sit at table joyfully with him in thy tent, as thou dost in the beyond to all eternity. Venerable Father Abraham! Thousands of years have run their course since those days, but thou hast need of no tardy lover to snatch the memorial of thee from the power of oblivion, for every language calls thee to remembrance—and yet thou dost reward thy lover more glori-ously than does any other; hereafter thou dost make him blessed in thy bosom; here thou dost enthral his eyes and his heart by the marvel of thy deed. Venerable Father Abraham! Second Father of the human race! Thou who first wast sensible of and didst first bear witness to that prodigious passion which disdains the dreadful conflict with the rage of the elements and with the powers of creation in order to strive with God; thou who first didst know that highest passion, the holy, pure and humble expression of the divine madness which the pagans admired —forgive him who would speak in praise of thee, if he does not do it fittingly. He spoke humbly, as if it were the desire of his own heart, he spoke briefly, as it becomes him to do, but he will never forget that thou hadst need of a hundred years to obtain a son of old age against expectation, that thou didst have to draw the knife before retaining Isaac; he will never forget that in a hundred and thirty years thou didst not get further than to faith.

4. Private Property, Communism and Money

I. Private Property and Communism

. . . The antithesis of *propertylessness* and *property* so long as it is not comprehended as the antithesis of *labour* and *capital,* still remains an antithesis of indifference, not grasped in its *active connection,* its *internal* relation—an antithesis not yet grasped as a *contradiction.* It can find expression in this *first* form even without the advanced development of private property (as in ancient Rome, Turkey, etc.). It does not yet *appear* as having been established by private property itself. But labour, the subjective essence of private property as exclusion of property, and capital, objective labour as exclusion of labour, constitute *private property* as its developed state of contradiction—hence a dynamic relationship moving inexorably to its resolution.

. . . The transcendence of self-estrangement follows the same course as self-estrangement. *Private property* is first considered only in its objective aspect—but nevertheless with labour as its essence. Its form of existence is therefore *capital,* which is to be annulled "as such" (Proudhon). Or a *particular form* of labour—labour levelled down, parcelled, and therefore unfree—is conceived as the source of private

---

Reprinted from Karl Marx, *Philosophic and Economic Manuscripts of 1844,* trans. and notes by Martin Milligan (Moscow: Foreign Languages Publishing House, 1961).

property's *perniciousness* and of its existence in estrangement from men; for instance, *Fourier,* who, like the physiocrats, also conceived *agricultural labour* to be at least the *exemplary* type, whilst *Saint-Simon* declares in contrast that *industrial labour* as such is the essence, and now also aspires to the *exclusive* rule of the industrialists and the improvement of the workers' condition. Finally, *communism* is the *positive* expression of annulled private property—at first as *universal* private property. By embracing this relation as a *whole,* communism is:

(1) In its first form only a *generalization* and *consummation* of this relationship. It shows itself as such in a twofold form: on the one hand, the dominion of *material* property bulks so large that it wants to destroy *everything* which is not capable of being possessed by all as *private property.* It wants to abstract *by force* from talent, etc. For it the sole purpose of life and existence is direct, physical *possession.* The category of *labourer* is not done away with, but extended to all men. The relationship of private property persists as the relationship of the community to the world of things. Finally, this movement of counterposing universal private property to private property finds expression in the bestial form of counterposing to *marriage* (certainly a *form of exclusive private property*) the *community of women,* in which a woman becomes a piece of *communal* and *common* property. It may be said that this idea of the *community of women* gives away the *secret* of this as yet completely crude and thoughtless communism. Just as the woman passes from marriage to general prostitution,[1] so the entire world of wealth (that is, of man's objective substance) passes from the relationship of exclusive marriage with the owner of private property to a state of universal prostitution with the community. In negating the *personality* of man in every sphere, this type of communism is really nothing but the logical expression of private property, which is this negation. General *envy* constituting itself as a power is the disguise in which *avarice* re-establishes itself and satisfies itself, only in *another* way. The thoughts of every piece of private property—inherent in each piece as such—are *at least* turned against all *wealthier* private property in the form of envy and the urge to reduce to a common level, so that this envy and urge even constitute the essence of competition. The crude communism is only the consummation of this envy and of this levelling-down proceeding from the *preconceived* minimum. It has a

---

1. Prostitution is only a *specific* expression of the *general* prostitution of the *labourer,* and since it is a relationship in which falls not the prostitute alone, but also the one who prostitutes—and the latter's abomination is still greater—the capitalist, etc., also comes under this head. [*Marx*]

definite, limited standard. How little this annulment of private property is really an appropriation is in fact proved by the abstract negation of the entire world of culture and civilization, the regression to the *unnatural* simplicity of the *poor and undemanding* man who has not only failed to go beyond private property, but has not yet even attained to it.

The community is only a community of *labour,* and an equality of *wages* paid out by the communal capital—the *community* as the universal capitalist. Both sides of the relationship are raised to an *imagined* universality—*labour* as a state in which every person is put, and *capital* as the acknowledged universality and power of the community.

In the approach to *woman* as the spoil and handmaid of communal lust is expressed the infinite degradation in which man exists for himself, for the secret of this approach has its *unambiguous,* decisive, *plain* and undisguised expression in the relation of *man* to *woman* and in the manner in which the *direct* and *natural* procreative relationship is conceived. The direct, natural, and necessary relation of person to person is the *relation of man to woman.* In this *natural* relationship of the sexes man's relation to nature is immediately his relation to man, just as his relation to man is immediately his relation to nature—his own *natural* function. In this relationship, therefore, is *sensuously manifested,* reduced to an observable *fact,* the extent to which the human essence has become nature to man, or to which nature has to him become the human essence of man. From this relationship one can therefore judge man's whole level of development. It follows from the character of this relationship how much *man* as a *species being,* as *man,* has come to be himself and to comprehend himself; the relation of man to woman is *the most natural* relation of human being to human being. It therefore reveals the extent to which man's *natural* behaviour has become *human,* or the extent to which the *human* essence in him has become a *natural* essence—the extent to which his *human nature* has come to be *nature to him.* In this relationship is revealed, too, the extent to which man's *need* has become a *human* need; the extent to which, therefore, the *other* person as a person has become for him a need—the extent to which he in his individual existence is at the same time a social being. The first positive annulment of private property—*crude* communism—is thus merely one *form* in which the vileness of private property, which wants to set itself up as the *positive community, comes to the surface.*

(2) Communism (a) of a political nature still—democratic or despotic; (b) with the annulment of the state, yet still incomplete, and being still affected by private property (i.e., by the estrangement of

man). In both forms communism already knows itself to be re-integration or return of man to himself, the transcendence of human self-estrangement; but since it has not yet grasped the positive essence of private property, and just as little the *human* nature of need, it remains captive to it and infected by it. It has, indeed, grasped its concept, but not its essence.

(3) *Communism* as the *positive* transcendence of *private property,* or *human self-estrangement,* and therefore as the real *appropriation of the human* essence by and for man; communism therefore as the complete return of man to himself as a *social* (i.e., human) being—a return become conscious, and accomplished within the entire wealth of previous development. This communism, as fully-developed naturalism, equals humanism, and as fully-developed humanism equals naturalism; it is the *genuine* resolution of the conflict between man and nature and between man and man—the true resolution of the strife between existence and essence, between objectification and self-confirmation, between freedom and necessity, between the individual and the species. Communism is the riddle of history solved, and it knows itself to be this solution.

The entire movement of history is, therefore, both its *actual* act of genesis (the birth act of its empirical existence) and also for its thinking consciousness the *comprehended* and *known* process of its *coming-to-be.* That other, still immature communism, meanwhile, seeks an *historical* proof for itself—a proof in the realm of the existent— amongst disconnected historical phenomena opposed to private property, tearing single phases from the historical process and focussing attention on them as proofs of its historical pedigree (a horse ridden hard especially by Cabet, Villegardelle, etc.). By so doing it simply makes clear that by far the greater part of this process contradicts its claims, and that, if it has once been, precisely its being in the *past* refutes its pretension to being *essential.*

That the entire revolutionary movement necessarily finds both its empirical and its theoretical basis in the movement of *private property* —in that of the economy, to be precise—is easy to see.

This *material,* immediately *sensuous* private property is the material sensuous expression of *estranged human* life. Its movement— production and consumption—is the *sensuous* revelation of the movement of all production hitherto—i.e., the realization or the reality of man. Religion, family, state, law, morality, science, art, etc., are only *particular* modes of production, and fall under its general law. The positive transcendence of *private property* as the appropriation of *human* life is, therefore, the positive transcendence of all estrangement—that is to say, the return of man from religion, family, state, etc., to his *human,* i.e., *social* mode of existence. Religious estrangement as such occurs only in the realm of *consciousness,* of man's inner life, but economic estrangement is that of *real life;* its transcendence therefore embraces both aspects. It is evident that the *initial* stage of the movement amongst the various peoples depends on whether the true and for them *authentic* life of the people manifests itself more in consciousness or in the external world—is more ideal or real. Communism begins from the outset (*Owen*) with atheism; but atheism is at first far from being *communism;* indeed, it is still mostly an abstraction.

The philanthropy of atheism is therefore at first only *philosophical,* abstract, philanthropy, and that of communism is at once *real* and directly bent on *action.*

We have seen how on the premise of positively annulled private property man produces man—himself and the other man; how the object, being the direct embodiment of his individuality, is simultaneously his own existence for the other man, the existence of the other man, and that existence for him. Likewise, however, both the material of labour and man as the subject, are the point of departure as well as the result of the movement (and precisely in this fact, that they must constitute the *point of departure,* lies the historical *necessity* of private property). Thus the *social* character is the general character of the whole movement: *just as* society itself produces *man as man,* so is society *produced* by him. Activity and consumption, both in their content and in their *mode of existence,* are *social: social* activity and *social* consumption; the *human* essence of nature first exists only for *social* man; for only here does nature exist for him as a *bond* with *man* —as his existence for the other and other's existence for him—as the life-element of the human world; only here does nature exist as the *foundation* of his own *human* existence. Only here has what is to him his *natural* existence become his *human* existence, and nature become man for him. Thus *society* is the consummated oneness in substance of man and nature—the true resurrection of nature—the naturalism of man and the humanism of nature both brought to fulfilment.

Social activity and social consumption exist by no means *only* in the form of some *directly* communal activity and directly *communal* consumption, although *communal* activity and *communal* consumption— i.e., activity and consumption which are manifested and directly confirmed in *real association* with other men—will occur wherever such a *direct* expression of sociality stems from the true character of the activity's content and is adequate to the nature of consumption.

But again when I am active *scientifically,* etc.,—when I am engaged in activity which I can seldom perform in direct community with others —then I am *social,* because I am active as a *man.* Not only is the material of my activity given to me as a social product (as is even the language in which the thinker is active): my *own* existence *is* social activity, and therefore that which I make of myself, I make of myself for society and with the consciousness of myself as a social being.

My *general* consciousness is only the *theoretical* shape of that of which the *living* shape is the *real* community, the social fabric, although at the present day *general* consciousness is an abstraction from real life and as such antagonistically confronts it. Consequently, too, the *activity* of my general consciousness, as an activity, is my *theoretical* existence as a social being.

What is to be avoided above all is the re-establishing of "Society" as an abstraction *vis-à-vis* the individual. The individual *is the social being.* His life, even if it may not appear in the direct form of a *communal* life carried out together with others—is therefore an expression and confirmation of *social life.* Man's individual and species life are not *different,* however much—and this is inevitable—the mode of existence of the individual is a more *particular,* or more *general* mode of the life of the species, or the life of the species is a more *particular* or more *general* individual life.

In his *consciousness of species* man confirms his real *social life* and simply repeats his real existence in thought, just as conversely the being of the species confirms itself in species-consciousness and is for *itself* in its generality as a thinking being.

Man, much as he may therefore be a *particular* individual (and it is precisely his particularity which makes him an individual, and a real *individual* social being), is just as much the *totality*—the ideal totality —the subjective existence of thought and experienced society present for itself; just as he exists also in the real world as the awareness and the real enjoyment of social existence, and as a totality of human life-activity.

Thinking and *being* are thus no doubt *distinct,* but at the same time they are in *unity* with each other.

Death seems to be a harsh victory of the species over the *definite* individual and to contradict their unity. But the determinate individual is only a *determinate species being,* and as such mortal.

(4) Just as *private property* is only the sensuous expression of the fact that man becomes *objective* for himself and at the same time becomes to himself a strange and inhuman object; just as it expresses the fact that the assertion of his life is the alienation of his life, that his

realization is his loss of reality, is an *alien* reality: conversely, the positive transcendence of private property—i.e., the *sensuous* appropriation for and by man of the human essence and of human life, of objective man, of human *achievements*—is not to be conceived merely in the sense of *direct,* one-sided *gratification*—merely in the sense of *possessing,* of *having.* Man appropriates his total essence in a total manner, that is to say, as a whole man. Each of his *human* relations to the world—seeing, hearing, smelling, tasting, feeling, thinking, being aware, sensing, wanting, acting, loving—in short, all the organs of his individual being, like those organs which are directly social in their form, are in their *objective* orientation or in their *orientation to the object,* the appropriation of that object, the appropriation of the *human* world; their orientation to the object is the *manifestation of the human world;*[2] it is human *efficaciousness* and human *suffering,* for suffering, apprehended humanly, is an enjoyment of self in man.

Private property has made us so stupid and one-sided that an object is only *ours* when we have it—when it exists for us as capital, or when it is directly possessed, eaten, drunk, worn, inhabited, etc.,—in short, when it is *used* by us. Although private property itself again conceives all these direct realizations of possession as *means of life,* and the life which they serve as means is the *life of private property*—labour and conversion into capital.

In place of *all* these physical and mental senses there has therefore come the sheer estrangement of *all* these senses—the sense of *having.* The human being had to be reduced to this absolute poverty in order that he might yield his inner wealth to the outer world. (On the category of *"having,"* see Hess in the *Twenty-One Sheets.*)

The transcendence of private property is therefore the complete *emancipation* of all human senses and attributes; but it is this emancipation precisely because these senses and attributes have become, subjectively and objectively, *human.* The eye has become a *human* eye, just as its *object* has become a social, *human* object—an object emanating from man for man. The *senses* have therefore become directly in their practice *theoreticians.* They relate themselves to the *thing* for the sake of the thing, but the thing itself is an *objective human* relation to itself and to man,[3] and vice versa. Need or enjoy-

---

2. For this reason it is just as highly priced as the *determinations* of human *essence* and *activities.* [Marx]

3. In practice I can relate myself to a thing humanly only if the thing relates itself to the human being humanly. [*Marx*]

ment have consequently lost their *egotistical* nature, and nature has lost its mere *utility* by use becoming *human* use.

In the same way, the senses and enjoyments of other men have become my *own* appropriation. Besides these direct organs, therefore, *social* organs develop in the *form* of society; thus, for instance, activity in direct association with others, etc., has become an organ for *expressing* my own *life,* and a mode of appropriating *human life.*

It is obvious that the *human* eye gratifies itself in a way different from the crude, non-human eye; the human *ear* different from the crude ear, etc.

To recapitulate; man is not lost in his object only when the object becomes for him a *human* object or objective man. This is possible only when the object becomes for him a *social* object, he himself for himself a social being, just as society becomes a being for him in this object.

On the one hand, therefore, it is only when the objective world becomes everywhere for man in society the world of man's essential powers[4] —human reality, and for that reason the reality of his *own* essential powers—that all *objects* become for him the *objectification of himself,* become objects which confirm and realize his individuality, become *his* objects: that is, *man himself* becomes the object. The manner in which they become *his* depends on the *nature of the objects* and on the nature of the *essential power* corresponding *to it;* for it is precisely the *determinateness* of this relationship which shapes the particular, *real* mode of affirmation. To the *eye* an object comes to be other than it is to the *ear,* and the object of the eye is another object than the object of the *ear.* The peculiarity of each essential power is precisely its *peculiar essence,* and therefore also the peculiar mode of its objectification, of its *objectively actual* living *being.* Thus man is affirmed in the objective world not only in the act of thinking, but with *all* his senses.

On the other hand, looking at this in its subjective aspect: just as music alone awakens in man the sense of music, and just as the most beautiful music has *no* sense for the unmusical ear—is no object for it, because my object can only be the confirmation of one of my essential powers and can therefore only be so for me as my essential power is present for itself as a subjective capacity, because the sense of an object for me goes only so far as *my* senses go (has only sense for a

---

4. "Essential powers"—*Wesenskräfte:* i.e., powers belonging to me as part of my essential nature, my very being.

sense corresponding to that object)—for this reason the *senses* of the social man are *other* senses than those of the non-social man. Only through the objectively unfolded richness of man's essential being is the richness of subjective *human* sensibility (a musical ear, an eye for beauty of form—in short, *senses* capable of human gratifications, senses confirming themselves as essential powers of *man*) either cultivated or brought into being. For not only the five senses but also the so-called mental senses—the practical senses (will, love, etc.)—in a word, *human* sense—the humanness of the senses—comes to be by virtue of its object, by virtue of *humanized* nature. The *forming* of the five senses is a labour of the entire history of the world down to the present.

The *sense* caught up in crude practical need has only a *restricted* sense. For the starving man, it is not the human form of food that exists, but only its abstract being as food; it could just as well be there in its crudest form, and it would be impossible to say wherein this feeding-activity differs from that of *animals*. The care-burdened man in need has no sense for the finest play; the dealer in minerals sees only the mercantile value but not the beauty and the unique nature of the mineral: he has no mineralogical sense. Thus, the objectification of the human essence both in its theoretical and practical aspects is required to make man's *sense human*, as well as to create the *human sense* corresponding to the entire wealth of human and natural substance.

Just as resulting from the movement of *private property*, of its wealth as well as its poverty—or of its material and spiritual wealth and poverty—the budding society finds to hand all the material for this *development:* so *established* society produces man in this entire richness of his being—produces the *rich* man *profoundly endowed with all the senses*—as its enduring reality.

It will be seen how subjectivism and objectivism, spiritualism and materialism, activity and suffering, only lose their antithetical character, and thus their existence, as such antitheses in the social condition; it will be seen how the resolution of the *theoretical* antitheses is *only* possible *in a practical* way, by virtue of the practical energy of men. Their resolution is therefore by no means merely a problem of knowledge, but a *real* problem of life, which *philosophy* could not solve precisely because it conceived this problem as *merely* a theoretical one.

It will be seen how the history of *industry* and the established *objective* existence of industry are the *open* book of *man's essential powers,* the exposure to the senses of human *psychology*. Hitherto this was not conceived in its inseparable connection with man's *essential being,* but only in an external relation of utility, because, moving in the realm of estrangement, people could only think man's general mode of being —religion or history in its abstract-general character as politics, art, literature, etc.,—to be the reality of man's essential powers and *man's species-activity*. We have before us the *objectified essential powers* of man in the form of *sensuous, alien, useful objects,* in the form of estrangement, displayed in *ordinary material industry* (which can be conceived as a part of that general movement, just as that movement can be conceived as a particular part of industry, since all human activity hitherto has been labour—that is, industry—activity estranged from itself).

A *psychology* for which this, the part of history most contemporary and accessible to sense, remains a closed book, cannot become a genuine, comprehensive and *real* science. What indeed are we to think of a science which *airily* abstracts from this large part of human labour and which fails to feel its own incompleteness, while such a wealth of human endeavour unfolded before it means nothing more to it than, perhaps, what can be expressed in one word— *"need," "vulgar need"?*

The *natural sciences* have developed an enormous activity and have accumulated a constantly growing mass of material. Philosophy, how-ever, has remained just as alien to them as they remain to philosophy. Their momentary unity was only a *chimerical illusion.* The will was there, but the means were lacking. Even historiography pays regard to natural science only occasionally, as a factor of enlightenment and utility arising from individual great discoveries. But natural science has invaded and transformed human life all the more *practically* through the medium of industry; and has prepared human emancipation, how-ever directly and much it had to consummate dehumanization. *Indus-try* is the *actual,* historical relation of nature, and therefore of natural science, to man. If, therefore, industry is conceived as the *exoteric* revelation of man's *essential powers,* we also gain an understanding of the *human* essence of nature or the *natural* essence of man. In consequence, natural science will lose its abstractly material—or rather, its idealistic—tendency, and will become the basis of *human* science, as it has already become the basis of actual human life, albeit in an estranged form. *One* basis for life and another basis for *science* is *a priori* a lie. The nature which comes to be in human history—the genesis of human society—is man's *real* nature; hence nature as it comes to be through industry, even though in an *estranged* form, is true *anthropological* nature.

Sense-perception (see Feuerbach) must be the basis of all science. Only when it proceeds from sense-perception in the twofold form both of *sensuous* consciousness and of *sensuous* need—that is, only when science proceeds from nature—is it *true* science. All history is the preparation for *"man"* to become the object of *sensuous* consciousness, and for the needs of "man as man" to become [natural, sensuous] needs. History itself is a *real* part of *natural history*—of nature's coming to be man. Natural science will in time subsume under itself the science of man, just as the science of man will subsume under itself natural science: there will be *one* science.

Man is the immediate object of natural science: for immediate, *sensuous nature* for man is, immediately, human sensuousness (the expressions are identical)—presented immediately in the form of the *other* man sensuously present for him. For his own sensuousness first exists as human sensuousness for himself through the *other* man. But *nature* is the immediate object of the *science of man:* the first object of man—man—is nature, sensuousness; and the particular human sensuous essential powers can only find their self-knowledge in the science of the natural world in general, since they can find their objective realization in *natural* objects only. The element of thought itself —the element of thought's living expression—*language*—is of a sensuous nature. The *social* reality of nature, and *human* natural science, or the *natural science about man,* are identical terms.

It will be seen how in place of the *wealth* and *poverty* of political economy come the *rich human being* and rich *human* need. The *rich* human being is simultaneously the human being *in need of* a totality of human life-activities—the man in whom his own realization exists as an inner necessity, as *need.* Not only *wealth,* but likewise the *poverty* of man—given socialism—receives in equal measure a *human* and therefore social significance. Poverty is the passive bond which causes the human being to experience the need of the greatest wealth—the *other* human being. The dominion of the objective being in me, the sensuous outburst of my essential activity, is *emotion,* which thus becomes here the *activity* of my being.

(5) *A being* only considers himself independent when he stands on his own feet; and he only stands on his own feet when he owes his *existence* to himself. A man who lives by the grace of another regards himself as a dependent being. But I live completely by the grace of another if I owe him not only the sustenance of my life, but if he has, moreover, *created* my *life*—if he is the *source* of my life; and if it is not of my own creation, my life has necessarily a source of this kind outside it. The *Creation* is therefore an idea very difficult to dislodge from popular consciousness. The self-mediated being of nature and of

man is *incomprehensible* to it, because it contradicts everything *palpable* in practical life.

The creation of the *earth* has received a mighty blow from *geogeny* —i.e., from the science which presents the formation of the earth, the coming-to-be of the earth, as a process, as self-generation. *Generatio aequivoca*[5] is the only practical refutation of the theory of creation.

Now it is certainly easy to say to the single individual what Aristotle has already said. You have been begotten by your father and your mother; therefore in you the mating of two human beings—a species-act of human beings—has produced the human being. You see, therefore, that even physically, man owes his existence to man. Therefore you must not only keep sight of the *one* aspect—the *infinite* progression which leads you further to enquire: "Who begot my father? Who his grandfather?", etc. You must also hold on to the *circular movement* sensuously perceptible in that progression, by which *man* repeats himself in procreation, thus always remaining the subject. You will reply, however: I grant you this circular movement; now grant me the progression which drives me even further until I ask: Who begot the first man, and nature as a whole? I can only answer you: Your question is itself a product of abstraction. Ask yourself how you arrived at that question. Ask yourself whether your question is not posed from a standpoint to which I cannot reply, because it is a perverse one. Ask yourself whether that progression as such exists for a reasonable mind. When you ask about the creation of nature and man, you are abstracting, in so doing, from man and nature. You postulate them as *non-existent,* and yet you want me to prove them to you as *existing.* Now I say to you: Give up your abstraction and you will also give up your question. Or if you want to hold on to your abstraction, then be consistent, and if you think of man and nature as *non-existent,* then think of yourself as non-existent, for you too are surely nature and man. Don't think, don't ask me, for as soon as you think and ask, your *abstraction* from the existence of nature and man has no meaning. Or are you such an egoist that you postulate everything as nothing, and yet want yourself to be?

You can reply: I do not want to postulate the nothingness of nature. I ask you about *its genesis,* just as I ask the anatomist about the formation of bones, etc.

But since for the socialist man the *entire so-called history of the world* is nothing but the begetting of man through human labour,

---

5. Spontaneous generation.

nothing but the coming-to-be of nature for man, he has the visible, irrefutable proof of his *birth* through himself, of his *process* of *coming-to-be*. Since the *real existence* of man and nature has become practical, sensuous and perceptible—since man has become for man as the being of nature, and nature for man as the being of man—the question about an *alien* being, about a being above nature and man —a question which implies the admission of the inessentiality of nature and of man—has become impossible in practice. *Atheism,* as the denial of this inessentiality, has no longer any meaning, for atheism is a *negation of God,* and postulates the *existence of man* through this negation; but socialism as socialism no longer stands in any need of such a mediation. It proceeds from the *practically and theoretically sensuous consciousness* of man and of nature as the *essence.* Socialism is man's *positive self-consciousness* no longer mediated through the annulment of religion, just as *real life* is man's positive reality, no longer mediated through the annulment of private property, through *communism.* Communism is the position as the negation of the negation, and is hence the *actual* phase necessary for the next stage of historical development in the process of human emancipation and recovery. *Communism* is the necessary pattern and the dynamic principle of the immediate future, but communism as such is not the goal of human development—the structure of human society.

II. The Power of Money in Bourgeois Society

If man's *feelings,* passions, etc., are not merely anthropological phenomena in the [narrower][6] sense, but truly *ontological* affirmations of essential being (of nature), and if they are only really affirmed because their *object* exists for them as an object of *sense,* then it is clear:

(1) That they have by no means merely one mode of affirmation, but rather that the distinctive character of their existence, of their life, is constituted by the distinctive mode of their affirmation. In what manner the object exists for them, is the characteristic mode of their *gratification.*

(2) Whenever the sensuous affirmation is the direct annulment of the object in its independent form (as in eating, drinking, working up of the object, etc.), this is the affirmation of the object.

(3) In so far as man, and hence also his feeling, etc., are *human,* the affirmation of the object by another is likewise his own enjoyment.

---

6. This word is illegible.

(4) Only through developed industry—i.e., through the medium of private property—does the ontological essence of human passion come to be both in its totality and in its humanity; the science of man is therefore itself a product of man's establishment of himself by practical activity.

(5) The meaning of private property—liberated from its estrangement—is the *existence of essential objects* for man, both as objects of enjoyment and as objects of activity.

By possessing the *property* of buying everything, by possessing the property of appropriating all objects, *money* is thus the *object* of eminent possession. The universality of its *property* is the omnipotence of its being. It therefore functions as the almighty being. Money is the *pimp* between man's need and the object, between his life and his means of life. But that which mediates *my* life for me, also *mediates* the existence of other people *for me*. For me it is the *other* person.

> "What, man! confound it, hands and feet
> And head and backside, all are yours!
> And what we take while life is sweet,
> Is that to be declared not ours?
>   Six stallions, say, I can afford,
>   Is not their strength my property?
>   I tear along, a sporting lord,
>   As if their legs belonged to me."
>   (Mephistopheles, in *Faust*)[7]

Shakespeare in *Timon of Athens:*

> "Gold? Yellow, glittering, precious gold? No, Gods,
> I am no idle votarist! . . . Thus much of this will
>   make black white, foul fair,
> Wrong right, base noble, old young, coward valiant.
> . . . Why, this
> Will lug your priests and servants from your sides,
> Pluck stout men's pillows from below their heads:
> This yellow *slave*
> Will knit and break religions, bless the accursed;
> Make the hoar leprosy adored, place thieves
> And give them title, knee and approbation
> With senators on the bench: This is it
> That makes the wappen'd widow wed again;

---

7. Goethe, *Faust*, (Part I—Faust's study,III), translated by Philip Wayne (Penguin, 1949), p. 91.

> She, whom the spital-house and ulcerous sores
> Would cast the gorge at, this embalms and spices
> To the April day again. . . . Damned earth,
> Thou common whore of mankind, that putt'st odds
> Among the rout of nations."[8]

And also later:

> "O thou sweet king-killer, and dear divorce
> Twixt natural son and sire! thou bright defiler
> Of Hymen's purest bed! thou valiant Mars!
> Thou ever young, fresh, loved and delicate wooer,
> Whose blush doth thaw the consecrated snow
> That lies on Dian's lap! Thou *visible God!*
> That solder'st *close impossibilities,*
> And mak'st them kiss! That speak'st with every tongue,
> To every purpose! O thou touch of hearts!
> Think thy slave man rebels, and by thy virtue
> Set them into confounding odds, that beasts
> May have the world in empire!"[9]

Shakespeare excellently depicts the real nature of *money.* To understand him, let us begin, first of all, by expounding the passage from Goethe.

That which is for me through the medium of *money*—that for which I can pay (i.e., which money can buy)—that am *I,* the possessor of the money. The extent of the power of money is the extent of my power. Money's properties are my properties and essential powers—the properties and powers of its possessor. Thus, what I *am* and *am capable* of is by no means determined by my individuality. I am ugly, but I can buy for myself the most *beautiful* of women. Therefore I am not *ugly,* for the effect of *ugliness*—its deterrent power— is nullified by money. I, in my character as an individual, am *lame,* but money furnishes me with twenty-four feet. Therefore I am not lame. I am bad, dishonest, unscrupulous, stupid; but money is honoured, and therefore so is its possessor. Money is the supreme good, therefore its possessor is good. Money, besides, saves me the trouble of being dishonest: I am therefore presumed honest. I am *stupid,* but money is the *real mind* of all things and how then should its possessor be stupid? Besides, he can buy talented people for himself, and is he who has power over the

---

8. Shakespeare, *Timon of Athens,* Act 4, Scene 3. Marx quotes the Schlegel-Tieck German translation. (Marx's emphasis.)

9. Ibid.

talented not more talented than the talented? Do not I, who thanks to money am capable of *all* that the human heart longs for, possess all human capacities? Does not my money therefore transform all my incapacities into their contrary?

If *money* is the bond binding me to *human* life, binding society to me, binding me and nature and man, is not money the bond of all *bonds?* Can it not dissolve and bind all ties? Is it not, therefore, the universal *agent of divorce?* It is the true *agent of divorce* as well as the true *binding agent*—the [universal][10] *galvano-chemical* power of Society.

Shakespeare stresses especially two properties of money:

(1) It is the visible divinity—the transformation of all human and natural properties into their contraries, the universal confounding and overturning of things: it makes brothers of impossibilities. (2) It is the common whore, the common pimp of people and nations.

The overturning and confounding of all human and natural qualities, the fraternization of impossibilities—the *divine* power of money —lies in its *character* as men's estranged, alienating and self-disposing *species-nature.* Money is the alienated *ability of mankind.*

That which I am unable to do as a *man,* and of which therefore all my individual essential powers are incapable, I am able to do by means of *money.* Money thus turns each of these powers into something which in itself it is not—turns it, that is, into its *contrary.*

If I long for a particular dish or want to take the mail-coach because I am not strong enough to go by foot, money fetches me the dish and the mail-coach: that is, it converts my wishes from something in the realm of imagination, translates them from their meditated, imagined or willed existence into their *sensuous, actual* existence—from imagination to life, from imagined being into real being. In effecting this mediation, money is the *truly creative* power.

No doubt *demand* also exists for him who has no money, but his demand is a mere thing of the imagination without effect or existence for me, for a third party, for the others, and which therefore remains for me *unreal* and *objectless.* The difference between effective demand based on money and ineffective demand based on my need, my passion, my wish, etc., is the difference between *being* and *thinking,* between the imagined which *exists* merely within me and the imagined as it is for me outside me as a *real object.*

If I have no money for travel, I have no *need*—that is, no real and self-realizing need—to travel. If I have the *vocation* for study but no

---

10. An end of the page is torn out of the manuscript.

money for it, I have *no* vocation for study—that is, no *effective,* no *true* vocation. On the other hand, if I have really *no* vocation for study but have the will *and* the money for it, I have an *effective* vocation for it. Being the external, common *medium* and *faculty* for turning an *image* into *reality* and *reality* into a mere *image* (a faculty not springing from man as man or from human society as society), *money* transforms the *real essential powers of man and nature* into what are merely abstract conceits and therefore *imperfections*—into tormenting chimeras—just as it transforms *real imperfections and chimeras*—essential powers which are really impotent, which exist only in the imagination of the individual—into *real powers* and *faculties.*

In the light of this characteristic alone, money is thus the general overturning of *individualities* which turns them into their contrary and adds contradictory attributes to their attributes.

Money, then, appears as this *overturning* power both against the individual and against the bonds of society, etc., which claim to be *essences* in themselves. It transforms fidelity into infidelity, love into hate, hate into love, virtue into vice, vice into virtue, servant into master, master into servant, idiocy into intelligence and intelligence into idiocy.

Since money, as the existing and active concept of value, confounds and exchanges all things, it is the general *confounding* and *compounding* of all things—the world upside-down—the confounding and compounding of all natural and human qualities.

He who can buy bravery is brave, though a coward. As money is not exchanged for any one specific quality, for any one specific thing, or for any particular human essential power, but for the entire objective world of man and nature, from the standpoint of its possessor it therefore serves to exchange every property for every other, even contradictory, property and object: it is the fraternization of impossibilities. It makes contradictions embrace.

Assume *man* to be *man* and his relationship to the world to be a human one: then you can exchange love only for love, trust for trust, etc. If you want to enjoy art, you must be an artistically-cultivated person; if you want to exercise influence over other people, you must be a person with a stimulating and encouraging effect on other people. Every one of your relations to man and to nature must be a *specific expression,* corresponding to the object of your will, of your *real individual* life. If you love without evoking love in return—that is, if your loving as loving does not produce reciprocal love; if through a *living expression* of yourself as a loving person you do not make yourself a *loved person,* then your love is impotent—a misfortune.

5. The Inevitability of Scientific Socialism

The materialist conception of history starts from the proposition
that the production of the means to support human life and, next to
production, the exchange of things produced, is the basis of all social
structure; that in every society that has appeared in history, the manner
in which wealth is distributed and society divided into classes or orders
is dependent upon what is produced, how it is produced, and how the
products are exchanged. From this point of view the final causes of all
social changes and political revolutions are to be sought, not in men's
brains, not in men's better insight into eternal truth and justice, but
in changes in the modes of production and exchange. They are to be
sought not in the *philosophy,* but in the *economics* of each particular
epoch. The growing perception that existing social institutions are
unreasonable and unjust, that reason has become unreason and right
wrong,[1] is only proof that in the modes of production and exchange
changes have silently taken place with which the social order, adapted
to earlier economic conditions, is no longer in keeping. From this it

---

Reprinted from Friedrich Engels, *Socialism: Utopian and Scientific,* trans. Edward
Aveling (London: Swan Sonnenschein & Co., 1892), part III. The text is that of the
authorized English edition of 1892. Title supplied by the editors.

1. Mephistopheles, in Goethe's *Faust.*

also follows that the means of getting rid of the incongruities that have been brought to light must also be present, in a more or less developed condition, within the changed modes of production themselves. These means are not to be invented by deduction from fundamental principles, but are to be discovered in the stubborn facts of the existing system of production.

What is, then, the position of modern socialism in this connection?

The present structure of society—this is now pretty generally conceded—is the creation of the ruling class of today, of the bourgeoisie. The mode of production peculiar to the bourgeoisie, known, since Marx, as the capitalist mode of production, was incompatible with the feudal system, with the privileges it conferred upon individuals, entire social ranks and local corporations, as well as with the hereditary ties of subordination which constituted the framework of its social organisation. The bourgeoisie broke up the feudal system and built upon its ruins the capitalist order of society, the kingdom of free competition, of personal liberty, of the equality, before the law, of all commodity owners, of all the rest of the capitalist blessings. Thenceforward the capitalist mode of production could develop in freedom. Since steam, machinery, and the making of machines by machinery transformed the older manufacture into modern industry, the productive forces evolved under the guidance of the bourgeoisie developed with a rapidity and in a degree unheard of before. But just as the older manufacture, in its time, and handicraft, becoming more developed under its influence, had come into collision with the feudal trammels of the guilds, so now modern industry, in its more complete development, comes into collision with the bounds within which the capitalistic mode of production holds it confined. The new productive forces have already outgrown the capitalistic mode of using them. And this conflict between productive forces and modes of production is not a conflict engendered in the mind of man, like that between original sin and divine justice. It exists, in fact, objectively, outside us, independently of the will and actions even of the men that have brought it on. Modern socialism is nothing but the reflex, in thought, of this conflict in fact; its ideal reflection in the minds, first, of the class directly suffering under it, the working class.

Now, in what does this conflict consist?

Before capitalistic production, i.e., in the Middle Ages, the system of petty industry obtained generally, based upon the private property of the labourers in their means of production; in the country, the agriculture of the small peasant, freeman or serf; in the towns, the handicrafts organised in guilds. The instruments of labour—land, agricultural implements, the workshop, the tool—were the instruments of labour of single individuals, adapted for the use of one worker, and, therefore, of necessity, small, dwarfish, circumscribed. But, for this very reason they belonged, as a rule, to the producer himself. To concentrate these scattered, limited means of production, to enlarge them, to turn them into the powerful levers of production of the present day—this was precisely the historic role of capitalist production and of its upholder, the bourgeoisie. In the fourth section of *Capital* Marx has explained in detail how since the fifteenth century this has been historically worked out through the three phases of simple co-operation, manufacture and modern industry. But the bourgeoisie, as is also shown there, could not transform these puny means of production into mighty productive forces without transforming them, at the same time, from means of production of the individual into *social* means of production only workable by a collectivity of men. The spinning-wheel, the hand-loom, the blacksmith's hammer, were replaced by the spinning-machine, the power-loom, the steam-hammer; the individual workshop, by the factory implying the co-operation of hundreds and thousands of workmen. In like manner, production itself changed from a series of individual into a series of social acts, and the products from individual to social products. The yarn, the cloth, the metal articles that now came out of the factory, were the joint product of many workers, through whose hands they had successively to pass before they were ready. No one person could say of them; "I made that; this is *my* product."

But where, in a given society, the fundamental form of production is that spontaneous division of labour which creeps in gradually and not upon any preconceived plan, there the products take on the form of *commodities,* whose mutual exchange, buying and selling, enable the individual producers to satisfy their manifold wants. And this was the case in the Middle Ages. The peasant, e.g., sold to the artisan agricultural products and bought from him the products of handicraft. Into this society of individual producers, of commodity producers, the new mode of production thrust itself. In the midst of the old division of labour, grown up spontaneously and upon *no definite plan,* which had governed the whole of society, now arose division of labour upon a *definite* plan, as organised in the factory; side by side with *individual* production appeared *social* production. The products of both were sold in the same market, and, therefore, at prices at least approximately equal. But organisation upon a definite plan was stronger than spontaneous division of labour. The factories working with the combined social forces of a collectivity of individuals produced their commodities far more cheaply than the individual small producers. Individual production succumbed in one department after another. Socialised production revolutionised all the old methods of production. But its revolutionary character was, at the same time, so little recognised that it was, on the contrary, introduced as a means of increasing and developing the production of commodities. When it arose, it found ready-made, and made liberal use of, certain machinery for the production and exchange of commodities: merchants' capital, handicraft, wage-labour. Socialised production thus introducing itself as a new form of the production of commodities, it was a matter of course that under it the old forms of appropriation remained in full swing, and were applied to its products as well.

In the mediaeval stage of evolution of the production of commodities, the question as to the owner of the product of labour could not arise. The individual producer, as a rule, had, from raw material belonging to himself, and generally his own handiwork, produced it with his own tools, by the labour of his own hands or of his family. There was no need for him to appropriate the new product. It belonged wholly to him, as a matter of course. His property in the product was, therefore, based *upon his own labour.* Even where external help was used, this was, as a rule, of little importance, and very generally was compensated by something other than wages. The apprentices and journeymen of the guilds worked less for board and wages than for education, in order that they might become master craftsmen themselves.

Then came the concentration of the means of production and of the producers in large workshops and manufactories, their transformation into actual socialised means of production and socialised producers. But the socialised producers and means of production and their products were still treated, after this change, just as they had been before, i.e., as the means of production and the products of individuals. Hitherto, the owner of the instruments of labour had himself appropriated the product, because, as a rule, it was his own product and the assistance of others was the exception. Now the owner of the instruments of labour always appropriated to himself the product, although it was no longer *his* product but exclusively the product of the *labour of others.* Thus, the products now produced socially were not appropriated by those who had actually set in motion the means of production and actually produced the commodities, but by the *capitalists.* The means of production, and production itself, had become in essence socialised. But they were subjected to a form of appropriation which presupposes the private production of individuals, under which, therefore, everyone owns his own product and brings it to market. The mode of production is subjected to this form of appropriation, although it abolishes the conditions upon which the latter rests.[2]

This contradiction, which gives to the new mode of production its capitalistic character, *contains the germ of the whole of the social antagonisms of today.* The greater the mastery obtained by the new mode of production over all important fields of production and in all manufacturing countries, the more it reduced individual production to an insignificant residuum, *the more clearly was brought out the incompatibility of socialised production with capitalistic appropriation.*

The first capitalists found, as we have said, alongside of other forms of labour, wage-labour ready-made for them on the market. But it was exceptional, complementary, accessory, transitory wage-labour. The agricultural labourer, though, upon occasion, he hired himself out by the day, had a few acres of his own land on which he could at all events live at a pinch. The guilds were so organized that the journeyman of today became the master of tomorrow. But all this changed as soon as the means of production became socialised and concentrated in the hands of capitalists. The means of production, as well as the product, of the individual producer became more and more worthless; there was nothing left for him but to turn wage-worker under the capitalist. Wage-labour, aforetime the exception and accessory, now became the rule and basis of all production; aforetime complementary, it now became the sole remaining function of the workers. The wage-worker for a time became a wage-worker for life. The number of these permanent wage-workers was further enormously increased by the breaking-up of the feudal system that occurred at the same time, by the disbanding of the retainers of the feudal lords, the eviction of the peasants from their homesteads, etc. The separation was made complete between the means of production concentrated in the hands of the capitalists, on the one side, and the producers, possessing nothing but their labour-power, on the other. *The contradiction between so-*

2. It is hardly necessary in this connection to point out that, even if the *form* of appropriation remains the same, the *character* of the appropriation is just as much revolutionised as production is by the changes described above. It is, of course, a very different matter whether I appropriate to myself my own product or that of another. Note in passing that wage-labour, which contains the whole capitalistic mode of production in embryo, is very ancient; in a sporadic, scattered form it existed for centuries alongside of slave-labour. But the embryo could duly develop into the capitalistic mode of production only when the necessary historical preconditions had been furnished. [*Engels*]

cialised production and capitalistic appropriation manifested itself as the antagonism of proletariat and bourgeoisie.

We have seen that the capitalistic mode of production thrust its way into a society of commodity-producers, of individual producers, whose social bond was the exchange of their products. But every society based upon the production of commodities has this peculiarity: that the producers have lost control over their own social interrelations. Each man produces for himself with such means of production as he may happen to have, and for such exchange as he may require to satisfy his remaining wants. No one knows how much of his particular article is coming on the market, nor how much of it will be wanted. No one knows whether his individual product will meet an actual demand, whether he will be able to make good his costs of production or even to sell his commodity at all. Anarchy reigns in socialised production.

But the production of commodities, like every other form of production, has its peculiar, inherent laws inseparable from it; and these laws work, despite anarchy, in and through anarchy. They reveal themselves in the only persistent form of social inter-relations, i.e., in exchange, and here they affect the individual producers as compulsory laws of competition. They are, at first, unknown to these producers themselves, and have to be discovered by them gradually and as the result of experience. They work themselves out, therefore, independently of the producers, and in antagonism to them, as inexorable natural laws of their particular form of production. The product governs the producers.

In mediaeval society, especially in the earlier centuries, production was essentially directed towards satisfying the wants of the individual. It satisfied, in the main, only the wants of the producer and his family. Where relations of personal dependence existed, as in the country, it also helped to satisfy the wants of the feudal lord. In all this there was, therefore, no exchange; the products, consequently, did not assume the character of commodities. The family of the peasant produced almost everything they wanted: clothes and furniture, as well as means of subsistence. Only when it began to produce more than was sufficient to supply its own wants and the payments in kind to the feudal lord, only then did it also produce commodities. This surplus, thrown into socialised exchange and offered for sale, became commodities.

The artisans of the towns, it is true, had from the first to produce for exchange. But they, also, themselves supplied the greatest part of their own individual wants. They had gardens and plots of land. They turned their cattle out into the communal forest, which, also, yielded them timber and firing. The women spun flax, wool, and so forth. Production for the purpose of exchange, production of commodities, was only in its infancy. Hence, exchange was restricted, the market narrow, the methods of production stable; there was local exclusiveness without, local unity within; the Mark in the country; in the town, the guild.

But with the extension of the production of commodities, and especially with the introduction of the capitalist mode of production, the laws of commodity production, hitherto latent, came into action more openly and with greater force. The old bonds were loosened, the old exclusive limits broken through, the producers were more and more turned into independent, isolated producers of commodities. It became apparent that the production of society at large was ruled by absence of plan, by accident, by anarchy; and this anarchy grew to greater and greater height. But the chief means by aid of which the capitalist mode of production intensified this anarchy of socialised production was the exact opposite of anarchy. It was the increasing organisation of production, upon a social basis, in every individual productive establishment. By this, the old, peaceful, stable condition of things was ended. Wherever this organisation of production was introduced into a branch of industry, it brooked no other method of production by its side. The field of labour became a battle-ground. The great geographical discoveries, and the colonisation following upon them, multiplied markets and quickened the transformation of handicraft into manufacture. The war did not simply break out between the individual producers of particular localities. The local struggles begot in their turn national conflicts, the commercial wars of the seventeenth and eighteenth centuries.

Finally, modern industry and the opening of the world market made the struggle universal, and at the same time gave it an unheard-of virulence. Advantages in natural or artificial conditions of production now decide the existence or non-existence of individual capitalists, as well as of whole industries and countries. He that falls is remorselessly cast aside. It is the Darwinian struggle of the individual for existence transferred from Nature to society with intensified violence. The conditions of existence natural to the animal appear as the final term of human development. The contradiction between socialised production and capitalistic appropriation now presents itself as *an antagonism between the organisation of production in the individual workshop and the anarchy of production in society generally.*

The capitalistic mode of production moves in these two forms of the antagonism immanent to it from its very origin. It is never able to get out of that "vicious circle" which Fourier had already discovered. What Fourier could not, indeed, see in his time is that this circle is gradually narrowing; that the movement becomes more and more a spiral, and must come to an end, like the movement of the planets, by collision with the centre. It is the compelling force of anarchy in the production of society at large that more and more completely turns the great majority of men into proletarians; and it is the masses of the proletariat again who will finally put an end to anarchy in production. It is the compelling force of anarchy in social production that turns the limitless perfectibility of machinery under modern industry into a compulsory law by which every individual industrial capitalist must perfect his machinery more and more, under penalty of ruin.

But the perfecting of machinery is making human labour superfluous. If the introduction and increase of machinery means the displacement of millions of manual by a few machine-workers, improvement in machinery means the displacement of more and more of the machine-workers themselves. It means, in the last instance, the production of a number of available wage-workers in excess of the average needs of capital, the formation of a complete industrial reserve army, as I called it in 1845, available at the times when industry is working at high pressure, to be cast out upon the street when the inevitable crash comes, a constant dead weight upon the limbs of the working class in its struggle for existence with capital, a regulator for the keeping of wages down to the low level that suits the interests of capital. Thus it comes about, to quote Marx, that machinery becomes the most powerful weapon in the war of capital against the working class; that the instruments of labour constantly tear the means of subsistence out of the hands of the labourer; that the very product of the worker is turned into an instrument for his subjugation. Thus it comes about that the economising of the instruments of labour becomes at the same time, from the outset, the most reckless waste of labour power, and robbery based upon the normal conditions under which labour functions; that machinery, "the most powerful instrument for shortening labour time, becomes the most unfailing means for placing every moment of the labourer's time and that of his family at the disposal of the capitalist for the purpose of expanding the value of his capital." (*Capital,* English edition, p. 406.) Thus it comes about that the overwork of some becomes the preliminary condition for the idleness of others, and that modern industry, which hunts after new consumers over the whole world, forces the consumption of the masses at home down to a starvation minimum, and in doing thus destroys its own home market. "The law that always equilibrates the relative surplus population, or industrial reserve army, to the extent and energy of accumulation, this law rivets the labourer to capital more firmly than the wedges of Vulcan did Prometheus to the rock. It establishes an accumulation of misery, corresponding with accumulation of capital. Accumulation of wealth at one pole is, therefore, at the same time, accumulation of misery, agony of toil, slavery, ignorance, brutality, mental degradation, at the opposite pole, i.e. on the side of the class that produces *its own product in the form of capital.*" (*Capital*, p. 661.) And to expect any other division of the products from the capitalistic mode of production is the same as expecting the electrodes of a battery not to decompose acidulated water, not to liberate oxygen at the positive, hydrogen at the negative pole, so long as they are connected with the battery.

We have seen that the ever-increasing perfectibility of modern machinery is, by the anarchy of social production, turned into a compulsory law that forces the individual industrial capitalist always to improve his machinery, always to increase its productive force. The bare possibility of extending the field of production is transformed for him into a similar compulsory law. The enormous expansive force of modern industry, compared with which that of gases is mere child's play, appears to us now as a *necessity* for expansion, both qualitative and quantitative, that laughs at all resistance. Such resistance is offered by consumption, by sales, by the markets for the products of modern industry. But the capacity for extension, extensive and intensive, of the markets is primarily governed by quite different laws that work much less energetically. The extension of the markets cannot keep pace with the extension of production. The collision becomes inevitable, and as this cannot produce any real solution so long as it does not break in pieces the capitalist mode of production, the collisions become periodic. Capitalist production has begotten another "vicious circle."

As a matter of fact, since 1825, when the first general crisis broke out, the whole industrial and commercial world, production and exchange among all civilised peoples and their more or less barbaric hangers-on, are thrown out of joint about once every ten years. Commerce is at a standstill, the markets are glutted, products accumulate, as multitudinous as they are unsaleable, hard cash disappears, credit vanishes, factories are closed, the mass of the workers are in want of the means of subsistence, because they have produced too much of the means of subsistence; bankruptcy follows upon bankruptcy, execution upon execution. The stagnation lasts for years; productive forces and products are wasted and destroyed wholesale, until the accumulated mass of commodities finally filters off, more or less depreciated in value, until production and exchange gradually begin to move again. Little by little the pace quickens. It becomes a trot. The industrial trot breaks into a canter, the canter in turn grows into the headlong gallop of a perfect steeplechase of industry, commercial credit, and speculation which finally, after breakneck leaps, ends where it began—in the ditch of a crisis. And so over and over again. We have now, since the year 1825, gone through this five times, and at the present moment (1877) we are going through it for the sixth time. And the character of these crises is so clearly defined that Fourier hit all of them off when he described the first as "*crise pléthorique,*" a crisis from plethora.

In these crises, the contradiction between socialised production and capitalist appropriation ends in a violent explosion. The circulation of commodities is, for the time being, stopped. Money, the means of circulation, becomes a hindrance to circulation. All the laws of production and circulation of commodities are turned upside down. The economic collision has reached its apogee. *The mode of production is in rebellion against the mode of exchange.*

The fact that the socialised organisation of production within the factory has developed so far that it has become incompatible with the anarchy of production in society, which exists side by side with and dominates it, is brought home to the capitalists themselves by the violent concentration of capital that occurs during crises, through the ruin of many large, and a still greater number of small, capitalists. The whole mechanism of the capitalist mode of production breaks down under the pressure of the productive forces, its own creations. It is no longer able to turn all this mass of means of production into capital. They lie fallow, and for that very reason the industrial reserve army must also lie fallow. Means of production, means of subsistence, available labourers, all the elements of production and of general wealth, are present in abundance. But "abundance becomes the source of distress and want" (Fourier), because it is the very thing that prevents the transformation of the means of production and subsistence into capital. For in capitalistic society the means of production can only function when they have undergone a preliminary transformation into capital, into the means of exploiting human labour power. The necessity of this transformation into capital of the means of production and subsistence stands like a ghost between these and the workers. It alone prevents the coming together of the material and personal levers of production; it alone forbids the means of production to function, the workers to work and live. On the one hand, therefore, the capitalistic mode of production stands convicted of its own incapacity to further direct these productive forces. On the other, these productive forces themselves, with increasing energy, press forward to the removal of the existing contradiction to the abolition of their quality as capital, to the *practical recognition of their character as social productive forces.*

This rebellion of the productive forces, as they grow more and more powerful, against their quality as capital, this stronger and stronger command that their social character shall be recognised, forces the capitalist class itself to treat them more and more as social productive forces, so far as this is possible under capitalist conditions. The period of industrial high pressure, with its unbounded inflation of credit, not less than the crash itself, by the collapse of great capitalist establishments, tends to bring about that form of the socialisation of great masses of means of production which we meet with in the different kinds of joint-stock companies. Many of these means of production and of distribution are, from the outset, so colossal that, like the railways, they exclude all other forms of capitalistic exploitation. At a further stage of evolution this form also becomes insufficient. The producers on a large scale in a particular branch of industry in a particular country unite in a trust, a union for the purpose of regulating production. They determine the total amount to be produced, parcel it out among themselves, and thus enforce the selling price fixed beforehand. But trusts of this kind, as soon as business becomes bad, are generally liable to break up, and on this very account compel a yet greater concentration of association. The whole of the particular industry is turned into one gigantic joint-stock company; internal competition gives place to the internal monopoloy of this one company. This has happened in 1890 with the English alkali production, which is now, after the fusion of 48 large works, in the hands of one company, conducted upon a single plan, and with a capital of £6,000,000.

In the trusts, freedom of competition changes into its very opposite —into monopoly; and the production without any definite plan of capitalistic society capitulates to the production upon a definite plan of the invading socialistic society. Certainly this is so far still to the benefit and advantage of the capitalists. But in this case the exploitation is so palpable that it must break down. No nation will put up with production conducted by trusts, with so barefaced an exploitation of the community by a small band of dividend-mongers.

In any case, with trusts or without, the official representative of capitalist society—the state—will ultimately have to undertake the direction of production.[3] This necessity for conversion into state property is felt first in the great institutions for intercourse and communication—the post office, the telegraphs, the railways.

If the crises demonstrate the incapacity of the bourgeoisie for managing any longer modern productive forces, the transformation of the great establishments for production and distribution into joint-stock companies, trusts and state property shows how unnecessary the bourgeoisie are for that purpose. All the social functions of the capitalist are now performed by salaried employees. The capitalist has no further social function than that of pocketing dividends, tearing off coupons, and gambling on the Stock Exchange, where the different capitalists despoil one another of their capital. At first the capitalistic mode of production forces out the workers. Now it forces out the capitalists, and reduces them, just as it reduced the workers, to the ranks of the surplus population, although not immediately into those of the industrial reserve army.

But the transformation, either into joint-stock companies and trusts, or into state ownership, does not do away with the capitalistic nature of the productive forces. In the joint-stock companies and trusts this is obvious. And the modern state, again, is only the organisation that bourgeois society takes on in order to support the external conditions of the capitalist mode of production against the encroachments as well of the workers as of individual capitalists. The modern state, no matter what its form, is essentially a capitalist machine, the state of the capitalists, the ideal personification of the total national capital. The more it proceeds to the taking over of productive forces, the more does it

---

3. I say "have to." For only when the means of production and distribution have *actually* outgrown the form of management by joint-stock companies, and when, therefore, the taking them over by the state has become *economically* inevitable, only then —even if it is the state of today that effects this—is there an economic advance, the attainment of another step preliminary to the taking over of all productive forces by society itself. But of late, since Bismarck went in for state ownership of industrial establishments, a kind of spurious socialism has arisen, degenerating, now and again, into something of flunkeyism, that without more ado declares *all* state ownership, even of the Bismarckian sort, to be socialistic. Certainly, if the taking over by the state of the tobacco industry is socialistic, then Napoleon and Metternich must be numbered among the founders of socialism. If the Belgian state, for quite ordinary political and financial reasons, itself constructed its chief railway lines; if Bismarck, not under any economic compulsion, took over for the state the chief Prussian lines, simply to be the better able to have them in hand in case of war, to bring up the railway employees as voting cattle for the government, and especially to create for himself a new source of income independent of parliamentary votes—this was, in no sense, a socialistic measure, directly or indirectly, consciously or unconsciously. Otherwise, the Royal Maritime Company, the Royal porcelain manufacture, and even the regimental tailor shops of the Army would also be socialistic institutions, or even, as was seriously proposed by a sly dog in Frederick William III's reign, the taking over by the state of the brothels. [*Engels*]

actually become the national capitalist, the more citizens does it exploit. The workers remain wage-workers—proletarians. The capitalist relation is not done away with. It is rather brought to a head. But, brought to a head, it topples over. State ownership of the productive forces is not the solution of the conflict, but concealed within it are the technical conditions that form the elements of that solution.

This solution can only consist in the practical recognition of the social nature of the modern forces of production, and therefore in the harmonising of the modes of production, appropriation, and exchange with the socialised character of the means of production. And this can only come about by society openly and directly taking possession of the productive forces which have outgrown all control except that of society as a whole. The social character of the means of production and of the products today reacts against the producers, periodically disrupts all production and exchange, acts only like a law of Nature working blindly, forcibly, destructively. But with the taking over by society of the productive forces, the social character of the means of production and of the products will be utilised by the producers with a perfect understanding of its nature, and instead of being a source of disturbance and periodical collapse, will become the most powerful lever of production itself.

Active social forces work exactly like natural forces: blindly, forcibly, destructively, so long as we do not understand, and reckon with, them. But when once we understand them, when once we grasp their action, their direction, their effects, it depends only upon ourselves to subject them more and more to our own will, and by means of them to reach our own ends. And this holds quite especially of the mighty productive forces of today. As long as we obstinately refuse to understand the nature and the character of these social means of action—and this understanding goes against the grain of the capitalist mode of production and its defenders—so long these forces are at work in spite of us, in opposition to us, so long they master us, as we have shown above in detail.

But when once their nature is understood, they can, in the hands of the producers working together, be transformed from master demons into willing servants. The difference is as that between the destructive force of electricity in the lightning of the storm, and electricity under command in the telegraph and the voltaic arc; the difference between a conflagration, and fire working in the service of man. With this recognition, at last, of the real nature of the productive forces of today, the social anarchy of production gives place to a social regulation of production upon a definite plan, according to the needs of the community and of each individual. Then the capitalist mode of appropriation, in which the product enslaves first the producer and then the appropriator, is replaced by the mode of appropriation of the products that is based upon the nature of the modern means of production; upon the one hand, direct social appropriation, as means to the maintenance and extension of production—on the other, direct individual appropriation, as means of subsistence and of enjoyment.

Whilst the capitalist mode of production more and more completely transforms the great majority of the population into proletarians, it creates the power which, under penalty of its own destruction, is forced to accomplish this revolution. Whilst it forces on more and more the transformation of the vast means of production, already socialised, into state property, it shows itself the way to accomplishing this revolution. *The proletariat seizes political power and turns the means of production into state property.*

But, in doing this, it abolishes itself as proletariat, abolishes all class distinctions and class antagonisms, abolishes also the state as state. Society thus far, based upon class antagonisms, had need of the state. That is, of an organisation of the particular class which was *pro tempore* the exploiting class, an organisation for the purpose of preventing any interference from without with the existing conditions of production, and, therefore, especially, for the purpose of forcibly keeping the exploited classes in the condition of oppression corresponding with the given mode of production (slavery, serfdom, wagelabour). The state was the official representative of society as a whole; the gathering of it together into a visible embodiment. But it was this only in so far as it was the state of that class which itself represented, for the time being, society as a whole: in ancient times, the state of slaveowning citizens; in the Middle Ages, the feudal lords; in our own time, the bourgeoisie. When at last it becomes the real representative of the whole of society, it renders itself unnecessary. As soon as there is no longer any social class to be held in subjection; as soon as class rule, and the individual struggle for existence based upon our present anarchy in production, with the collisions and excesses arising from these, are removed, nothing more remains to be repressed, and a special repressive force, a state, is no longer necessary. The first act by virtue of which the state really constitutes itself the representative of the whole of society—this is, at the same time, its last independent act as a state. State interference in social relations becomes, in one domain after another, superfluous, and then dies out of itself; the government of persons is replaced by the administration of things, and by the conduct of processes of production. The state is not "abolished." *It dies out.* This gives the measure of the value of the phrase *"a free state,"* both as to its justifiable use at times by agitators, and as to its ultimate scientific insufficiency; and also of the demands of the so-called anarchists for the abolition of the state out of hand.

Since the historical appearance of the capitalist mode of production, the appropriation by society of all the means of production has often been dreamed of, more or less vaguely, by individuals, as well as by sects, as the ideal of the future. But it could become possible, could become a historical necessity, only when the actual conditions for its realisation were there. Like every other social advance, it becomes practicable, not by men understanding that the existence of classes is in contradiction to justice, equality, etc., not by the mere willingness to abolish these classes, but by virtue of certain new economic conditions. The separation of society into an exploiting and an exploited class, a ruling and an oppressed class, was the necessary consequence of the deficient and restricted development of production in former times. So long as the total social labour only yields a product which but slightly exceeds that barely necessary for the existence of all; so long, therefore, as labour engages all or almost all the time of the great majority of the members of society—so long, of necessity, this society is divided into classes. Side by side with the great majority, exclusively bond slaves to labour, arises a class freed from directly productive labour, which looks after the general affairs of society: the direction of labour, state business, law, science, art, etc. It is, therefore, the law of division of labour that lies at the basis of the division into classes. But this does not prevent this division into classes from being carried out by means of violence and robbery, trickery and fraud. It does not prevent the ruling class, once having the upper hand, from consolidating its power at the expense of the working class, from turning its social leadership into an intensified exploitation of the masses.

But if, upon this showing, division into classes has a certain historical justification, it has this only for a given period, only under given social conditions. It was based upon the insufficiency of production. It will be swept away by the complete development of modern productive forces. And, in fact, the abolition of classes in society presupposes a degree of historical evolution at which the existence, not simply of this or that particular ruling class, but of any ruling class at all, and, therefore, the existence of class distinction itself has become an obsolete anachronism. It presupposes, therefore, the development of production carried out to a degree at which appropriation of the means of production and of the products, and, with this, of political domination, of the monopoly of culture, and of intellectual leadership by a particular class of society, has become not only superfluous but economically, politically, intellectually, a hindrance to development.

This point is now reached. Their political and intellectual bankruptcy is scarcely any longer a secret to the bourgeoisie themselves. Their economic bankruptcy recurs regularly every ten years. In every crisis, society is suffocated beneath the weight of its own productive forces and products, which it cannot use, and stands helpless, face to face with the absurd contradiction that the producers have nothing to consume, because consumers are wanting. The expansive force of the means of production bursts the bonds that the capitalist mode of production had imposed upon them. Their deliverance from these bonds is the one precondition for an unbroken, constantly accelerated development of the productive forces, and therewith for a practically unlimited increase of production itself. Nor is this all. The socialised appropriation of the means of production does away, not only with the present artificial restrictions upon production, but also with the positive waste and devastation of productive forces and products that are at the present time the inevitable concomitants of production, and that reach their height in the crises. Further, it sets free for the community at large a mass of means of production and of products, by doing away with the senseless extravagance of the ruling classes of today and their political representatives. The possibility of securing for every member of society, by means of socialised production, an existence not only fully sufficient materially, and becoming day by day more full, but an existence guaranteeing to all the free development and exercise of their physical and mental faculties—this possibility is now for the first time here, but *it is here.* [4]

With the seizing of the means of production by society, production of commodities is done away with, and, simultaneously, the mastery of the product over the producer. Anarchy in social production is replaced by systematic, definite organisation. The struggle for individual

---

4. A few figures may serve to give an approximate idea of the enormous expansive force of the modern means of production, even under capitalist pressure. According to Mr. Giffen, the total wealth of Great Britain and Ireland amounted, in round numbers in

1814 to £2,200,000,000.
1865 to £6,100,000,000.
1875 to £8,500,000,000.

As an instance of the squandering of means of production and of products during a crisis, the total loss in the German iron industry alone, in the crisis 1873–78, was given at the second German Industrial Congress (Berlin, February 21, 1878) as £22,-750,000. [*Engels*]

existence disappears. Then for the first time man, in a certain sense, is finally marked off from the rest of the animal kingdom, and emerges from mere animal conditions of existence into really human ones. The whole sphere of the conditions of life which environ man, and which have hitherto ruled man, now comes under the dominion and control of man, who for the first time becomes the real, conscious lord of Nature, because he has now become master of his own social organisation. The laws of his own social action, hitherto standing face to face with man as laws of Nature foreign to, and dominating him, will then be used with full understanding, and so mastered by him. Man's own social organisation, hitherto confronting him as a necessity imposed by Nature and history, now becomes the result of his own free action. The extraneous objective forces that have hitherto governed history pass under the control of man himself. Only from that time will man himself, more and more consciously, make his own history—only from that time will the social causes set in movement by him have, in the main and in a constantly growing measure, the results intended by him. It is the ascent of man from the kingdom of necessity to the kingdom of freedom.

Let us briefly sum up our sketch of historical evolution.

I. *Mediaeval Society.* Individual production on a small scale. Means of production adapted for individual use; hence primitive, ungainly, petty, dwarfed in action. Production for immediate consumption, either of the producer himself or of his feudal lord. Only where an excess of production over his consumption occurs is such excess offered for sale, enters into exchange. Production of commodities, therefore, only in its infancy. But already it contains within itself, in embryo, *anarchy in the production of society at large.*

II. *Capitalist Revolution.* Transformation of industry, at first by means of simple co-operation and manufacture. Concentration of the means of production, hitherto scattered, into great workshops. As a consequence, their transformation from individual to social means of production—a transformation which does not, on the whole, affect the form of exchange. The old forms of appropriation remain in force. The capitalist appears. In his capacity as owner of the means of production, he also appropriates the products and turns them into commodities. Production has become a *social* act. Exchange and appropriation continue to be *individual* acts, the acts of individuals. *The social product is appropriated by the individual capitalist.* Fundamental contradiction, whence arise all the contradictions in which our present-day society moves, and which modern industry brings to light.

A. Severance of the producer from the means of production. Condemnation of the worker to wage-labour for life. *Antagonism between the proletariat and the bourgeoisie.*

B. Growing predominance and increasing effectiveness of the laws governing the production of commodities. Unbridled competition. *Contradiction between socialised organisation in the individual factory and social anarchy in production as a whole.*

C. On the one hand, perfecting of machinery, made by competition compulsory for each individual manufacturer, and complemented by a constantly growing displacement of labourers. *Industrial reserve army.* On the other hand, unlimited extension of production, also compulsory under competition, for every manufacturer. On both sides, unheard-of development of productive forces, excess of supply over demand, over-production, glutting of the markets, crises every ten years, the vicious circle: excess here, of means of production and products—excess there, of labourers, without employment and without means of existence. But these two levers of production and of social well-being are unable to work together, because the capitalist form of production prevents the productive forces from working and the products from circulating, unless they are first turned into capital—which their very superabundance prevents. The contradiction has grown into an absurdity. *The mode of production rises in rebellion against the form of exchange.* The bourgeoisie are convicted of incapacity further to manage their own social productive forces.

D. Partial recognition of the social character of the productive forces forced upon the capitalists themselves. Taking over of the great institutions for production and communication, first by joint-stock companies, later on by trusts, then by the state. The bourgeoisie demonstrated to be a superfluous class. All its social functions are now performed by salaried employees.

III. *Proletarian Revolution.* Solution of the contradictions. The proletariat seizes the public power, and by means of this transforms the socialised means of production, slipping from the hands of the bourgeoisie, into public property. By this act, the proletariat frees the means of production from the character of capital they have thus far borne, and gives their socialised character complete freedom to work itself out. Socialised production upon a predetermined plan becomes henceforth possible. The development of production makes the existence of different classes of society thenceforth an anachronism. In proportion as anarchy in social production vanishes, the political authority of the state dies out. Man, at last the master of his own form of social organisation, becomes at the same time the lord over Nature, his own master—free.

To accomplish this act of universal emancipation is the historical mission of the modern proletariat. To thoroughly comprehend the historical conditions and thus the very nature of this act, to impart to the new oppressed proletarian class a full knowledge of the conditions and of the meaning of the momentous act it is called upon to accomplish, this is the task of the theoretical expression of the proletarian movement, scientific socialism.

6.   Rebellion and the Grand Inquisitor

I. Rebellion

"I must make you one confession," Ivan began. "I could never understand how one can love one's neighbours. It's just one's neighbours, to my mind, that one can't love, though one might love those at a distance. I once read somewhere of John the Merciful, a saint, that when a hungry, frozen beggar came to him, he took him into his bed, held him in his arms, and began breathing into his mouth, which was putrid and loathsome from some awful disease. I am convinced that he did that from 'self-laceration,' from the self-laceration of falsity, for the sake of the charity imposed by duty, as a penance laid on him. For any one to love a man, he must be hidden, for as soon as he shows his face, love is gone."

"Father Zossima has talked of that more than once," observed Alyosha, "he, too, said that the face of a man often hinders many people not practised in love, from loving him. But yet there's a great deal of love in mankind, and almost Christ-like love. I know that myself, Ivan."

"Well, I know nothing of it so far, and can't understand it, and the

---

Reprinted from Fyodor Dostoyevsky, *The Brothers Karamazov,* trans. Constance Garnett and with an introduction by Marc Slonim (New York: Random House, 1950), bk. V, chaps. iv and v.

innumerable mass of mankind are with me there. The question is, whether that's due to men's bad qualities or whether it's inherent in their nature. To my thinking, Christ-like love for men is a miracle impossible on earth. He was God. But we are not gods. Suppose I, for instance, suffer intensely. Another can never know how much I suffer, because he is another and not I. And what's more, a man is rarely ready to admit another's suffering (as though it were a distinction). Why won't he admit it, do you think? Because I smell unpleasant, because I have a stupid face, because I once trod on his foot. Besides there is suffering and suffering; degrading, humiliating suffering such as humbles me—hunger, for instance,—my benefactor will perhaps allow me; but when you come to higher suffering—for an idea, for instance—he will very rarely admit that, perhaps because my face strikes him as not at all what he fancies a man should have who suffers for an idea. And so he deprives me instantly of his favour, and not at all from badness of heart. Beggars, especially genteel beggars, ought never to show themselves, but to ask for charity through the newspapers. One can love one's neighbours in the abstract, or even at a distance, but at close quarters it's almost impossible. If it were as on the stage, in the ballet, where if beggars come in, they wear silken rags and tattered lace and beg for alms dancing gracefully, then one might like looking at them. But even then we should not love them. But enough of that. I simply wanted to show you my point of view. I meant to speak of the suffering of mankind generally, but we had better confine ourselves to the sufferings of the children. That reduces the scope of my argument to a tenth of what it would be. Still we'd better keep to the children, though it does weaken my case. But, in the first place, children can be loved even at close quarters, even when they are dirty, even when they are ugly (I fancy, though, children never are ugly). The second reason why I won't speak of grown-up people is that, besides being disgusting and unworthy of love, they have a compensation—they've eaten the apple and know good and evil, and they have become 'like god.' They go on eating it still. But the children haven't eaten anything, and are so far innocent. Are you fond of children, Alyosha? I know you are, and you will understand why I prefer to speak of them. If they, too, suffer horribly on earth, they must suffer for their fathers' sins, they must be punished for their fathers, who have eaten the apple; but that reasoning is of the other world and is incomprehensible for the heart of man here on earth. The innocent must not suffer for another's sins, and especially such innocents! You may be surprised at me, Alyosha, but I am awfully fond of children, too. And observe, cruel people, the violent, the rapacious, the Karamazovs are sometimes very fond of

children. Children while they are quite little—up to seven, for instance
—are so remote from grown-up people; they are different creatures,
as it were, of a different species. I knew a criminal in prison who had,
in the course of his career as a burglar, murdered whole families,
including several children. But when he was in prison, he had a strange
affection for them. He spent all his time at his window, watching the
children playing in the prison yard. He trained one little boy to come
up to his window and made great friends with him. . . . You don't know
why I am telling you all this, Alyosha? My head aches and I am sad."

"You speak with a strange air," observed Alyosha uneasily, "as
though you were not quite yourself."

"By the way, a Bulgarian I met lately in Moscow," Ivan went on,
seeming not to hear his brother's words, "told me about the crimes
committed by Turks and Circassians in all parts of Bulgaria through
fear of a general rising of the Slavs. They burn villages, murder, outrage women and children, they nail their prisoners by the ears to the
fences, leave them so till morning, and in the morning they hang them
—all sorts of things you can't imagine. People talk sometimes of bestial
cruelty, but that's a great injustice and insult to the beasts; a beast can
never be so cruel as a man, so artistically cruel. The tiger only tears
and gnaws, that's all he can do. He would never think of nailing people
by the ears, even if he were able to do it. These Turks took a pleasure
in torturing children, too; cutting the unborn child from the mother's
womb, and tossing babies up in the air and catching them on the points
of their bayonets before their mother's eyes. Doing it before the mother's eyes was what gave zest to the amusement. Here is another scene
that I thought very interesting. Imagine a trembling mother with her
baby in her arms, a circle of invading Turks around her. They've
planned a diversion; they pet the baby, laugh to make it laugh. They
succeed, the baby laughs. At that moment a Turk points a pistol four
inches from the baby's face. The baby laughs with glee, holds out its
little hands to the pistol, and he pulls the trigger in the baby's face and
blows out its brains. Artistic, wasn't it? By the way, Turks are particularly fond of sweet things, they say."

"Brother, what are you driving at?" asked Alyosha.

"I think if the devil doesn't exist, but man has created him, he has
created him in his own image and likeness."

"Just as he did God, then?" observed Alyosha.

" 'It's wonderful how you can turn words,' as Polonius says in *Hamlet,*" laughed Ivan. "You turn my words against me. Well, I am glad.
Yours must be a fine God, if man created Him in His image and
likeness. You asked just now what I was driving at. You see, I am fond

of collecting certain facts, and, would you believe, I even copy anecdotes of a certain sort from newspapers and books, and I've already got a fine collection. The Turks, of course, have gone into it, but they are foreigners. I have specimens from home that are even better than the Turks. You know we prefer beating—rods and scourges—that's our national institution. Nailing ears is unthinkable for us, for we are, after all, Europeans. But the rod and the scourge we have always with us and they cannot be taken from us. Abroad now they scarcely do any beating. Manners are more humane, or laws have been passed, so that they don't dare to flog men now. But they make up for it in another way just as national as ours. And so national that it would be practically impossible among us, though I believe we are being inoculated with it, since the religious movement began in our aristocracy. I have a charming pamphlet, translated from the French, describing how, quite recently, five years ago, a murderer, Richard, was executed—a young man, I believe, of three and twenty, who repented and was converted to the Christian faith at the very scaffold. This Richard was an illegitimate child who was given as a child of six by his parents to some shepherds on the Swiss mountains. They brought him up to work for them. He grew up like a little wild beast among them. The shepherds taught him nothing, and scarcely fed or clothed him, but sent him out at seven to herd the flock in cold and wet, and no one hesitated or scrupled to treat him so. Quite the contrary, they thought they had every right, for Richard had been given to them as a chattel, and they did not even see the necessity of feeding him. Richard himself describes how in those years, like the Prodigal Son in the Gospel, he longed to eat of the mash given to the pigs, which were fattened for sale. But they wouldn't even give him that, and beat him when he stole from the pigs. And that was how he spent all his childhood and his youth, till he grew up and was strong enough to go away and be a thief. The savage began to earn his living as a day labourer in Geneva. He drank what he earned, he lived like a brute, and finished by killing and robbing an old man. He was caught, tried, and condemned to death. They are not sentimentalists there. And in prison he was immediately surrounded by pastors, members of Christian brotherhoods, philanthropic ladies, and the like. They taught him to read and write in prison, and expounded the Gospel to him. They exhorted him, worked upon him, drummed at him incessantly, till at last he solemnly confessed his crime. He was converted. He wrote to the court himself that he was a monster, but that in the end God had vouchsafed him light and shown grace. All Geneva was in excitement about him—all philanthropic and religious Geneva. All the aristocratic and well-bred society

of the town rushed to the prison, kissed Richard and embraced him;
'You are our brother, you have found grace.' And Richard does nothing but weep with emotion, 'Yes, I've found grace! All my youth and
childhood I was glad of pigs' food, but now even I have found grace.
I am dying in the Lord.' 'Yes, Richard, die in the Lord; you have shed
blood and must die. Though it's not your fault that you knew not the
Lord, when you coveted the pigs' food and were beaten for stealing
it (which was very wrong of you, for stealing is forbidden); but you've
shed blood and you must die.' And on the last day, Richard, perfectly
limp, did nothing but cry and repeat every minute: 'This is my happiest
day. I am going to the Lord.' 'Yes,' cry the pastors and the judges and
philanthropic ladies. 'This is the happiest day of your life, for you are
going to the Lord!' They all walk or drive to the scaffold in procession
behind the prison van. At the scaffold they call to Richard: 'Die,
brother, die in the Lord, for even thou hast found grace!' And so,
covered with his brothers' kisses, Richard is dragged on to the scaffold,
and led to the guillotine. And they chopped off his head in brotherly
fashion, because he had found grace. Yes, that's characteristic. That
pamphlet is translated into Russian by some Russian philanthropists
of aristocratic rank and evangelical aspirations, and has been distributed gratis for the enlightenment of the people. The case of Richard
is interesting because it's national. Though to us it's absurd to cut off
a man's head, because he has become our brother and has found grace,
yet we have our own specialty, which is all but worse. Our historical
pastime is the direct satisfaction of inflicting pain. There are lines in
Nekrassov describing how a peasant lashes a horse on the eyes, 'on its
meek eyes,' every one must have seen it. It's peculiarly Russian. He
describes how a feeble little nag had foundered under too heavy a load
and cannot move. The peasant beats it, beats it savagely, beats it at last
not knowing what he is doing in the intoxication of cruelty, thrashes
it mercilessly over and over again. 'However weak you are, you must
pull, if you die for it.' The nag strains, and then he begins lashing the
poor defenceless creature on its weeping, on its 'meek eyes.' The
frantic beast tugs and draws the load, trembling all over, gasping for
breath, moving sideways, with a sort of unnatural spasmodic action—
it's awful in Nekrassov. But that's only a horse, and God has given
horses to be beaten. So the Tatars have taught us, and they left us the
knout as a remembrance of it. But men, too, can be beaten. A well-
educated, cultured gentleman and his wife beat their own child with
a birch-rod, a girl of seven. I have an exact account of it. The papa was
glad that the birch was covered with twigs. 'It stings more,' said he, and
so he began stinging his daughter. I know for a fact there are people

who at every blow are worked up to sensuality, to literal sensuality, which increases progressively at every blow they inflict. They beat for a minute, for five minutes, for ten minutes, more often and more savagely. The child screams. At last the child cannot scream, it gasps, 'Daddy! daddy!' By some diabolical unseemly chance the case was brought into court. A counsel is engaged. The Russian people have long called a barrister 'a conscience for hire.' The counsel protests in his client's defense. 'It's such a simple thing,' he says, 'an every-day domestic event. A father corrects his child. To our shame be it said, it is brought into court.' The jury, convinced by him, give a favourable verdict. The public roars with delight that the torturer is acquitted. Ah, pity I wasn't there! I would have proposed to raise a subscription in his honour! . . . Charming pictures.

"But I've still better things about children. I've collected a great, great deal about Russian children, Alyosha. There was a little girl of five who was hated by her father and mother, 'most worthy and respectable people, of good education and breeding,' You see, I must repeat again, it is a peculiar characteristic of many people, this love of torturing children and children only. To all other types of humanity these torturers behave mildly and benevolently, like cultivated and humane Europeans; but they are very fond of tormenting children, even fond of children themselves in that sense. It's just their defencelessness that tempts the tormentor, just the angelic confidence of the child who has no refuge and no appeal, that sets his vile blood on fire. In every man, of course, a demon lies hidden—the demon of rage, the demon of lustful heat at the screams of the tortured victim, the demon of lawlessness let off the chain, the demon of diseases that follow on vice, gout, kidney disease, and so on.

"This poor child of five was subjected to every possible torture by those cultivated parents. They beat her, thrashed her, kicked her for no reason till her body was one bruise. Then, they went to greater refinements of cruelty—shut her up all night in the cold and frost in a privy, and because she didn't ask to be taken up at night (as though a child of five sleeping its angelic, sound sleep could be trained to wake and ask), they smeared her face and filled her mouth with excrement, and it was her mother, her mother did this. And that mother could sleep, hearing the poor child's groans! Can you understand why a little creature, who can't even understand what's done to her, should beat her little aching heart with her tiny fist in the dark and the cold, and weep her meek unresentful tears to dear, kind God to protect her? Do you understand that, friend and brother, you pious and humble novice? Do you understand why this infamy must be and is permitted?

Without it, I am told, man could not have existed on earth, for he could not have known good and evil. Why should he know that diabolical good and evil when it costs so much? Why, the whole world of knowledge is not worth that child's prayer to 'dear, kind God'! I say nothing of the sufferings of grown-up people, they have eaten the apple, damn them, and the devil take them all! But these little ones! I am making you suffer, Alyosha, you are not yourself. I'll leave off if you like."

"Never mind. I want to suffer too," muttered Alyosha.

"One picture, only one more, because it's so curious, so characteristic, and I have only just read it in some collection of Russian antiquities. I've forgotten the name. I must look it up. It was in the darkest days of serfdom at the beginning of the century, and long live the Liberator of the People! There was in those days a general of aristocratic connections, the owner of great estates, one of those men— somewhat exceptional, I believe, even then—who, retiring from the service into a life of leisure, are convinced that they've earned absolute power over the lives of their subjects. There were such men then. So our general, settled on his property of two thousand souls, lives in pomp, and domineers over his poor neighbours as though they were dependents and buffoons. He has kennels of hundreds of hounds and nearly a hundred dog-boys—all mounted, and in uniform. One day a serf boy, a little child of eight, threw a stone in play and hurt the paw of the general's favourite hound. 'Why is my favourite dog lame?' He is told that the boy threw a stone that hurt the dog's paw. 'So you did it.' The general looked the child up and down. 'Take him.' He was taken—taken from his mother and kept shut up all night. Early that morning the general comes out on horseback, with the hounds, his dependents, dog-boys, and huntsmen, all mounted around him in full hunting parade. The servants are summoned for their edification, and in front of them all stands the mother of the child. The child is brought from the lock-up. It's a gloomy cold, foggy autumn day, a capital day for hunting. The general orders the child to be undressed; the child is stripped naked. He shivers, numb with terror, not daring to cry. . . . 'Make him run,' commands the general. 'Run! run!' shout the dog-boys. The boy runs. . . . 'At him!' yells the general, and he sets the whole pack of hounds on the child. The hounds catch him, and tear him to pieces before his mother's eyes! . . . I believe the general was afterwards declared incapable of administering his estates. Well—what did he deserve? To be shot? To be shot for the satisfaction of our moral feelings? Speak, Alyosha!"

"To be shot," murmured Alyosha, lifting his eyes to Ivan with a pale, twisted smile.

"Bravo!" cried Ivan delighted. "If even you say so . . . You're a pretty monk! So there is a little devil sitting in your heart, Alyosha Karamazov!"

"What I said was absurd, but—"

"That's just the point that 'but'!" cried Ivan. "Let me tell you, novice, that the absurd is only too necessary on earth. The world stands on absurdities, and perhaps nothing would have come to pass in it without them. We know what we know!"

"What do you know?"

"I understand nothing," Ivan went on, as though in delirium. "I don't want to understand anything now. I want to stick to the fact. I made up my mind long ago not to understand. If I try to understand anything, I shall be false to the fact and I have determined to stick to the fact."

"Why are you trying me?" Alyosha cried, with sudden distress. "Will you say what you mean at last?"

"Of course, I will; that's what I've been leading up to. You are dear to me, I don't want to let you go, and I won't give you up to your Zossima."

Ivan for a minute was silent, his face became all at once very sad.

"Listen! I took the case of children only to make my case clearer. Of the other tears of humanity with which the earth is soaked from its crust to its centre, I will say nothing. I have narrowed my subject on purpose. I am a bug, and I recognise in all humility that I cannot understand why the world is arranged as it is. Men are themselves to blame, I suppose; they were given paradise, they wanted freedom, and stole fire from heaven, though they knew they would become unhappy, so there is no need to pity them. With my pitiful, earthly, Euclidian understanding, all I know is that there is suffering and that there are none guilty; that cause follows effect, simply and directly; that everything flows and finds its level—but that's only Euclidian nonsense, I know that, and I can't consent to live by it! What comfort is it to me that there are none guilty and that cause follows effect simply and directly, and that I know it—I must have justice, or I will destroy myself. And not justice in some remote infinite time and space, but here on earth, and that I could see myself. I have believed in it. I want to see it, and if I am dead by then, let me rise again, for if it all happens without me, it will be too unfair. Surely I haven't suffered, simply that I, my crimes and my sufferings, may manure the soil of the future harmony for somebody else. I want to see with my own eyes the hind lie down with the lion and the victim rise up and embrace his murderer. I want to be there when every one suddenly understands what it has

all been for. All the religions of the world are built on this longing, and
I am a believer. But then there are the children, and what am I to do
about them? That's a question I can't answer. For the hundredth time
I repeat, there are numbers of questions, but I've only taken the children, because in their case what I mean is so unanswerably clear.
Listen! If all must suffer to pay for the eternal harmony, what have
children to do with it, tell me please? It's beyond all comprehension
why they should suffer, and why they should pay for the harmony. Why
should they, too, furnish material to enrich the soil for the harmony
of the future? I understand solidarity in sin among men. I understand
solidarity in retribution, too; but there can be no such solidarity with
children. And if it is really true that they must share responsibility for
all their fathers' crimes, such a truth is not of this world and is beyond
my comprehension. Some jester will say, perhaps, that the child would
have grown up and have sinned, but you see he didn't grow up, he was
torn to pieces by the dogs, at eight years old. Oh, Alyosha, I am not
blaspheming! I understand, of course, what an upheaval of the universe it will be, when everything in heaven and earth blends in one
hymn of praise and everything that lives and has lived cries aloud:
'Thou are just, O Lord, for Thy ways are revealed.' When the mother
embraces the fiend who threw her child to the dogs, and all three cry
aloud with tears, 'Thou are just, O Lord!' then, of course, the crown
of knowledge will be reached and all will be made clear. But what pulls
me up here is that I can't accept that harmony. And while I am on
earth, I make haste to take my own measures. You see, Alyosha, perhaps it really may happen that if I live to that moment, or rise again
to see it, I, too, perhaps, may cry aloud with the rest, looking at the
mother embracing the child's torturer, 'Thou art just, O Lord!' but I
don't want to cry aloud then. While there is still time, I hasten to
protect myself and so I renounce the higher harmony altogether. It's
not worth the tears of that one tortured child who beat itself on the
breast with its little fist and prayed in its stinking outhouse, with its
unexpiated tears to 'dear, kind God'! It's not worth it, because those
tears are unatoned for. They must be atoned for, or there can be no
harmony. But how? How are you going to atone for them? Is it possible? By their being avenged? But what do I care for avenging them?
What do I care for a hell for oppressors? What good can hell do, since
those children have already been tortured? And what becomes of
harmony, if there is hell? I want to forgive. I want to embrace. I don't
want more suffering. And if the sufferings of children go to swell the
sum of sufferings which was necessary to pay for truth, then I protest
that the truth is not worth such a price. I don't want the mother to

embrace the oppressor who threw her son to the dogs! She dare not forgive him! Let her forgive him for herself, if she will, let her forgive the torturer for the immeasurable suffering of her mother's heart. But the sufferings of her tortured child she has no right to forgive; she dare not forgive the torturer, even if the child were to forgive him! And if that is so, if they dare not forgive, what becomes of harmony? Is there in the whole world a being who would have the right to forgive and could forgive? I don't want harmony. From love for humanity I don't want it. I would rather be left with the unavenged suffering. I would rather remain with my unavenged suffering and unsatisfied indignation, *even if I were wrong.* Besides, too high a price is asked for harmony; it's beyond our means to pay so much to enter on it. And so I hasten to give back my entrance ticket, and if I am an honest man I am bound to give it back as soon as possible. And that I am doing. It's not God that I don't accept, Alyosha, only I most respectfully return Him the ticket."

"That's rebellion," murmured Alyosha, looking down.

"Rebellion? I am sorry you call it that," said Ivan earnestly. "One can hardly live in rebellion, and I want to live. Tell me yourself, I challenge you—answer. Imagine that you are creating a fabric of human destiny with the object of making men happy in the end, giving them peace and rest at last, but that it was essential and inevitable to torture to death only one tiny creature—that baby beating its breast with its fist, for instance—and to found that edifice on its unavenged tears, would you consent to be the architect on those conditions? Tell me, and tell the truth."

"No, I wouldn't consent," said Alyosha softly.

"And can you admit the idea that men for whom you are building it would agree to accept their happiness on the foundation of the unexpiated blood of a little victim? And accepting it would remain happy for ever?"

"No, I can't admit it. Brother," said Alyosha suddenly, with flashing eyes, "you said just now, is there a being in the whole world who would have the right to forgive and could forgive? But there is a Being and He can forgive everything, all and for all, because He gave His innocent blood for all and everything. You have forgotten Him, and on Him is built the edifice, and it is to Him they cry aloud, 'Thou are just, O Lord, for Thy ways are revealed!' "

"Ah! the One without sin and His blood! No, I have not forgotten Him; on the contrary I've been wondering all the time how it was you did not bring Him in before, for usually all arguments on your side put Him in the foreground. Do you know, Alyosha—don't laugh! I made a poem about a year ago. If you can waste another ten minutes on me, I'll tell it to you."

"You wrote a poem?"

"Oh, no, I didn't write it," laughed Ivan, "and I've never written two lines of poetry in my life. But I made up this poem in prose and I remembered it. I was carried away when I made it up. You will be my first reader—that is, listener. Why should an author forego even one listener?" smiled Ivan. "Shall I tell it to you?"

"I am all attention," said Alyosha.

"My poem is called 'The Grand Inquisitor'; it's a ridiculous thing, but I want to tell it to you."

II. The Grand Inquisitor

"Even this must have a preface—that is, a literary preface," laughed Ivan, "and I am a poor hand at making one. You see, my action takes place in the sixteenth century, and at that time, as you probably learnt at school, it was customary in poetry to bring down heavenly powers on earth. Not to speak of Dante, in France, clerks, as well as the monks in the monasteries, used to give regular performances in which the Madonna, the saints, the angels, Christ, and God Himself were brought on the stage. In those days it was done in all simplicity. In Victor Hugo's 'Notre Dame de Paris' an edifying and gratuitous spectacle was provided for the people in the Hotel de Ville of Paris in the reign of Louis XI. in honour of the birth of the dauphin. It was called *Le bon jugement de la très sainte et gracieuse Vierge Marie,* and she appears herself on the stage and pronounces her *bon jugement.* Similar plays, chiefly from the Old Testament, were occasionally performed in Moscow too, up to the times of Peter the Great. But besides plays there were all sorts of legends and ballads scattered about the world, in which the saints and angels and all the powers of Heaven took part when required. In our monasteries the monks busied themselves in translating, copying, and even composing such poems—and even under the Tatars. There is, for instance, one such poem (of course, from the Greek), 'The Wanderings of Our Lady through Hell,' with descriptions as bold as Dante's. Our Lady visits Hell, and the Archangel Michael leads her through the torments. She sees the sinners and their punishment. There she sees among others one noteworthy set of sinners in a burning lake; some of them sink to the bottom of the lake so that they can't swim out, and 'these God forgets'—an expression of extraordinary depth and force. And so Our Lady, shocked and weeping, falls before the throne of God and begs for mercy for all in Hell

—for all she has seen there, and indiscriminately. Her conversation with God is immensely interesting. She beseeches Him, she will not desist, and when God points to the hands and feet of her Son, nailed to the Cross, and asks, 'How can I forgive His tormentors?' she bids all the saints, all the martyrs, and the angels and archangels to fall down with her and pray for mercy on all without distinction. It ends by her winning from God a respite of suffering every year from Good Friday till Trinity day, and the sinners at once raise a cry of thankfulness from Hell, chanting, 'Thou are just, O Lord, in this judgment.' Well, my poem would have been of that kind if it had appeared at that time. He comes on the scene in my poem, but He says nothing, only appears and passes on. Fifteen centuries have passed since He promised to come in His glory, fifteen centuries since His prophet wrote, 'Behold, I come quickly'; 'Of that day and that hour knoweth no man, neither the Son, but the Father,' as He Himself predicted on earth. But humanity awaits him with the same faith and with the same love. Oh, with greater faith, for it is fifteen centuries since man has ceased to see signs from Heaven.

> No signs from Heaven come to-day
> To add to what the heart doth say.

There was nothing left but faith in what the heart doth say. It is true there were many miracles in those days. There were saints who performed miraculous cures; some holy people, according to their biographies, were visited by the Queen of Heaven herself. But the devil did not slumber, and doubts were already arising among men of the truth of these miracles. And just then there appeared in the north of Germany a terrible new heresy. 'A huge star like to a torch' (that is, to a church) 'fell on the sources of the waters and they became bitter.' These heretics began blasphemously denying miracles. But those who remained faithful were all the more ardent in their faith. The tears of humanity rose up to Him as before, awaiting His coming, loved Him, hoped for Him, yearned to suffer and die for Him as before. And so many ages mankind had prayed with faith and fervour, 'O Lord our God, hasten Thy coming,' so many ages called upon Him, that in His infinite mercy He deigned to come down to His servants. Before that day He had come down, He had visited some holy men, martyrs and hermits, as is written in their 'Lives.' Among us, Tyutchev, with absolute faith in the truth of his words, bore witness that

> Bearing the Cross, in slavish dress
> Weary and worn, the Heavenly King

> Our mother, Russia, came to bless,
> And through our land went wandering.

And that certainly was so, I assure you.

"And behold, He deigned to appear for a moment to the people, to the tortured, suffering people, sunk in iniquity, but loving Him like children. My story is laid in Spain, in Seville, in the most terrible time of the Inquisition, when fires were lighted every day to the glory of God, and 'in the splendid *auto da fé* the wicked heretics were burnt.' Oh, of course, this was not the coming in which He will appear according to His promise at the end of time in all His heavenly glory, and which will be sudden as lightning flashing from east to west.' No, He visited His children only for a moment, and there where the flames were crackling round the heretics. In His infinite mercy He came once more among men in that human shape in which He walked among men for three years fifteen centuries ago. He came down to the 'hot pavement' of the southern town in which on the day before almost a hundred heretics had, *ad majorem gloriam Dei,* been burnt by the cardinal, the Grand Inquisitor, in a magnificent *auto de fé,* in the presence of the king, the court, the knights, the cardinals, the most charming ladies of the court, and the whole population of Seville.

He came softly, unobserved, and yet, strange to say, every one recognised Him. That might be one of the best passages in the poem. I mean, why they recognised Him. The people are irresistibly drawn to Him, they surround Him, they flock about Him, follow Him. He moves silently in their midst with a gentle smile of infinite compassion. The sun of love burns in His heart, light and power shine from His eyes, and their radiance, shed on the people, stirs their hearts with responsive love. He holds out His hands to them, blesses them, and a healing virtue comes from contact with Him, even with His garments. An old man in the crowd, blind from childhood, cries out, 'O Lord, heal me and I shall see Thee!' and, as it were, scales fall from his eyes and the blind man sees Him. The crowd weeps and kisses the earth under His feet. Children throw flowers before Him, sing, and cry hosannah. 'It is He—it is He!' all repeat. 'It must be He, it can be no one but Him!' He stops at the steps of the Seville cathedral at the moment when the weeping mourners are bringing in a little open white coffin. In it lies a child of seven, the only daughter of a prominent citizen. The dead child lies hidden in flowers. 'He will raise your child,' the crowd shouts to the weeping mother. The priest, coming to meet the coffin, looks perplexed, and frowns, but the mother of the dead child throws herself at His feet with a wail. 'If it is Thou, raise my child!' she cries, holding out her hands to Him. The procession halts, the coffin is laid on the steps at His feet. He looks with compassion, and His lips once more softly pronounce, 'Maiden, arise!' and the maiden arises. The little girl sits up in the coffin and looks round, smiling with wide-open wondering eyes, holding a bunch of white roses they had put in her hand.

"There are cries, sobs, confusion among the people and, at that moment the cardinal himself, the Grand Inquisitor, passes by the cathedral. He is an old man, almost ninety, tall and erect, with a withered face and sunken eyes, in which there is still a gleam of light. He is not dressed in his gorgeous cardinal's robes, as he was the day before, when he was burning the enemies of the Roman Church—at that moment he was wearing his coarse, old, monk's cassock. At a distance behind him come his gloomy assistants and slaves and the 'holy guard.' He stops at the sight of the crowd and watches it from a distance. He sees everything; he sees them set the coffin down at His feet, sees the child rise up, and his face darkens. He knits his thick grey brows and his eyes gleam with a sinister fire. He holds out his finger and bids the guards take Him. And such is his power, so completely are the people cowed into submission and trembling obedience to him, that the crowd immediately make way for the guards, and in the midst of deathlike silence they lay hands on Him and lead Him away. The crowd instantly bows down to the earth, like one man, before the old inquisitor. He blesses the people in silence and passes on. The guards lead their prisoner to the close, gloomy vaulted prison in the ancient palace of the Holy Inquisition and shut Him in it. The day passes and is followed by the dark, burning 'breathless' night of Seville. The air is 'fragrant with laurel and lemon.' In the pitch darkness the iron door of the prison is suddenly opened and the Grand Inquisitor himself comes in with a light in his hand. He is alone; the door is closed at once behind him. He stands in the doorway and for a minute or two gazes into His face. At last he goes up slowly, sets the light on the table and speaks.

" 'Is it Thou? Thou?' but receiving no answer, he adds at once, 'Don't answer, be silent. What canst Thou say, indeed? I know too well what Thou wouldst say. And Thou hast no right to add anything to what Thou hadst said of old. Why, then, art Thou come to hinder us? For Thou hast come to hinder us, and Thou knowest that. But dost Thou know what will be to-morrow? I know not who Thou art and care not to know whether it is Thou or only a semblance of Him, but to-morrow I shall condemn Thee and burn Thee at the stake as the worst of heretics. And the very people who have to-day kissed Thy feet, to-morrow at the faintest sign from me will rush to heap up the embers of Thy fire. Knowest Thou that? Yes, maybe Thou knowest it,' he added with thoughtful penetration, never for a moment taking his eyes off the Prisoner."

"I don't quite understand, Ivan. What does it mean?" Alyosha, who had been listening in silence, said with a smile. "Is it simply a wild fantasy, or a mistake on the part of the old man—some impossible *qui pro quo?*"

"Take it as the last," said Ivan, laughing, "if you are so corrupted by modern realism and can't stand anything fantastic. If you like it to be a case of mistaken identity, let it be so. It is true," he went on, laughing, "the old man was ninety, and he might well be crazy over his set idea. He might have been struck by the appearance of the Prisoner. It might, in fact, be simply his ravings, the delusion of an old man of ninety, over-excited by the *auto da fé* of a hundred heretics the day before. But does it matter to us after all whether it was a mistake of identity or a wild fantasy? All that matters is that the old man should speak out, should speak openly of what he has thought in silence for ninety years."

"And the Prisoner too is silent? Does He look at him and not say a word?"

"That's inevitable in any case," Ivan laughed again. "The old man has told Him He hasn't the right to add anything to what He has said of old. One may say it is the most fundamental feature of Roman Catholicism, in my opinion at least. 'All has been given by Thee to the Pope,' they say, 'and all, therefore, is still in the Pope's hands, and there is no need for Thee to come now at all. Thou must not meddle for the time, at least.' That's how they speak and write too—the Jesuits, at any rate. I have read it myself in the words of their theologians. 'Hast Thou the right to reveal to us one of the mysteries of that world from which Thou hast come?' my old man asks Him, and answers the question for Him. 'No, Thou hast not; that Thou mayest not add to what has been said of old, and mayest not take from men the freedom which Thou didst exalt when Thou wast on earth. Whatsoever Thou revealest anew will encroach on men's freedom of faith; for it will be manifest as a miracle, and the freedom of their faith was dearer to Thee than anything in those days fifteen hundred years ago. Didst Thou not often say then, "I will make you free"? But now Thou has seen these "free" men,' the old man adds suddenly, with a pensive smile. 'Yes, we've paid dearly for it,' he goes on, looking sternly at Him, 'but at last we have completed that work in Thy name. For fifteen centuries we have been wrestling with Thy freedom, but now it is ended and over for good. Dost Thou not believe that it's over for good? Thou lookest meekly at me and deignest not even to be wroth with me. But let me tell Thee that now, to-day, people are more persuaded than ever that they have perfect freedom, yet they have brought their freedom to us and laid it humbly at our feet. But that has been our doing. Was this what Thou didst? Was this Thy freedom?' "

"I don't understand again," Alyosha broke in. "Is he ironical, is he jesting?"

"Not a bit of it! He claims it as a merit for himself and his Chruch that at last they have vanquished freedom and have done so to make men happy. 'For now' (he is speaking of the Inquisition, of course) 'for the first time it has become possible to think of the happiness of men. Man was created a rebel; and how can rebels be happy? Thou wast warned,' he says to Him. 'Thou hast had no lack of admonitions and warnings, but Thou didst not listen to those warnings; Thou didst reject the only way by which men might be made happy. But, fortunately, departing Thou didst hand on the work to us. Thou has promised, Thou hast established by Thy word, Thou has given to us the right to bind and to unbind, and now, of course, Thou canst not think of taking it away. Why, then, hast Thou come to hinder us?' "

"And what's the meaning of 'no lack of admonitions and warnings'?" asked Alyosha.

"Why, that's the chief part of what the old man must say."

" 'The wise and dread Spirit, the spirit of self-destruction and non-existence,' the old man goes on, 'the great spirit talked with Thee in the wilderness, and we are told in the books that he "tempted" Thee. Is that so? And could anything truer be said than what he revealed to Thee in three questions and what Thou didst reject, and what in the books is called "the temptation"? And yet if there has ever been on earth a real stupendous miracle, it took place on that day, on the day of the three temptations. The statement of those three questions was itself the miracle. If it were possible to imagine simply for the sake of argument that those three questions of the dread spirit had perished utterly from the books, and that we had to restore them and to invent them anew, and to do so had gathered together all the wise men of the earth—rulers, chief priests, learned men, philosophers, poets—and had set them the task to invent three questions, such as would not only fit the occasion, but express in three words, three human phrases, the whole future history of the world and of humanity—dost Thou believe that all the wisdom of the earth united could have invented anything in depth and force equal to the three questions which were actually put to Thee then by the wise and mighty spirit in the wilderness? From those questions alone, from the miracle of their statement, we can see that we have here to do not with the fleeting human intelligence, but

with the absolute and eternal. For in those three questions the whole
subsequent history of mankind is, as it were, brought together into one
whole, and foretold, and in them are united all the unsolved historical
contradictions of human nature. At the time it could not be so clear,
since the future was unknown; but now that fifteen hundred years have
passed, we see that everything in those three questions was so justly
divined and foretold, and has been so truly fulfilled, that nothing can
be added to them or taken from them.

" 'Judge Thyself who was right—Thou or he who questioned Thee
then? Remember the first question; its meaning, in other words, was
this: "Thou wouldst go into the world, and art going with empty hands,
with some promise of freedom which men in their simplicity and their
natural unruliness cannot even understand, which they fear and dread
—for nothing has ever been more insupportable for a man and a
human society than freedom. But seest Thou these stones in this
parched and barren wilderness? Turn them into bread, and mankind
will run after Thee like a flock of sheep, grateful and obedient, though
for ever trembling, lest Thou withdraw Thy hand and deny them Thy
bread." But Thou wouldst not deprive man of freedom and didst reject
the offer, thinking, what is that freedom worth, if obedience is bought
with bread? Thou didst reply that man lives not by bread alone. But
dost Thou know that for the sake of that earthly bread the spirit of the
earth will rise up against Thee and will strive with Thee and overcome
Thee, and all will follow him, crying, "Who can compare with this
beast? He has given us fire from heaven!" Dost Thou know that the
ages will pass, and humanity will proclaim by the lips of their sages that
there is no crime, and therefore no sin; there is only hunger? "Feed
men, and then ask of them virtue!" that's what they'll write on the
banner, which they will raise against Thee, and with which they will
destroy Thy temple. Where Thy temple stood will rise a new building;
the terrible tower of Babel will be built again, and though, like the one
of old, it will not be finished, yet Thou mightest have prevented that
new tower and have cut short the sufferings of men for a thousand
years; for they will come back to us after a thousand years of agony with
their tower. They will seek us again, hidden underground in the cata-
combs, for we shall be again persecuted and tortured. They will find
us and cry to us, "Feed us, for those who have promised us fire from
heaven haven't given it!" And then we shall finish building their tower,
for he finishes the building who feeds them. And we alone shall feed
them in Thy name, declaring falsely that it is in Thy name. Oh, never,
never can they feed themselves without us! No science will give them
bread so long as they remain free. In the end they will lay their freedom

at our feet, and say to us, "Make us your slaves, but feed us." They will understand themselves, at last, that freedom and bread enough for all are inconceivable together, for never, never will they be able to share between them! They will be convinced, too, that they can never be free, for they are weak, vicious, worthless and rebellious. Thou didst promise them the bread of Heaven, but, I repeat again, can it compare with earthly bread in the eyes of the weak, ever sinful and ignoble race of man? And if for the sake of the bread of Heaven thousands and tens of thousands shall follow Thee, what is to become of the millions and tens of thousands of millions of creatures who will not have the strength to forego the earthly bread for the sake of the heavenly? Or dost Thou care only for the tens of thousands of the great and strong, while the millions, numerous as the sands of the sea, who are weak but love Thee, must exist only for the sake of the great and strong? No, we care for the weak too. They are sinful and rebellious, but in the end they too will become obedient. They will marvel at us and look on us as gods, because we are ready to endure the freedom which they have found so dreadful and to rule over them—so awful it will seem to them to be free. But we shall tell them that we are Thy servants and rule them in Thy name. We shall deceive them again, for we will not let Thee come to us again. That deception will be our suffering, for we shall be forced to lie.

" 'This is the significance of the first question in the wilderness, and this is what Thou hast rejected for the sake of that freedom which Thou hast exalted above everything. Yet in this question lies hid the great secret of this world. Choosing "bread," Thou wouldst have satisfied the universal and everlasting craving of humanity—to find some one to worship. So long as man remains free he strives for nothing so incessantly and so painfully as to find some one to worship. But man seeks to worship what is established beyond dispute, so that all men would agree at once to worship it. For these pitiful creatures are concerned not only to find what one or the other can worship, but to find something that all would believe in and worship; what is essential is that all may be *together* in it. This craving for *community* of worship is the chief misery of every man individually and of all humanity from the beginning of time. For the sake of common worship they've slain each other with the sword. They have set up gods and challenged one another, "Put away your gods and come and worship ours, or we will kill you and your gods!" And so it will be to the end of the world, even when gods disappear from the earth; they will fall down before idols just the same. Thou didst know, Thou couldst not but have known, this fundamental secret of human nature, but Thou didst reject the one infallible banner which was offered Thee to make all men bow down to Thee alone—the banner of earthly bread; and Thou hast rejected it for the sake of freedom and the bread of Heaven. Behold what Thou didst further. And all again in the name of freedom! I tell Thee that man is tormented by no greater anxiety than to find some one quickly to whom he can hand over the gift of freedom with which the ill-fated creature is born. But only one who can appease their conscience can take over their freedom. In bread there was offered Thee an invincible banner; give bread, and man will worship Thee, for nothing is more certain than bread. But if some one else gains possession of his conscience—oh! then he will cast away Thy bread and follow after him who has ensnared his conscience. In that Thou wast right. For the secret of man's being is not only to live but to have something to live for. Without a stable conception of the object of life, man would not consent to go on living, and would rather destroy himself than remain on earth, though he had bread in abundance. That is true. But what happened? Instead of taking men's freedom from them, Thou didst make it greater than ever! Didst Thou forget that man prefers peace, and even death, to freedom of choice in the knowledge of good and evil? Nothing is more seductive for man than his freedom of conscience, but nothing is a greater cause of suffering. And behold, instead of giving a firm foundation for setting the conscience of man at rest for ever, Thou didst choose all that is exceptional, vague and enigmatic; Thou didst choose what was utterly beyond the strength of men, acting as though Thou didst not love them at all—Thou who didst come to give Thy life for them! Instead of taking possession of men's freedom, Thou didst increase it, and burdened the spiritual kingdom of mankind with its sufferings for ever. Thou didst desire man's free love, that he should follow Thee freely, enticed and taken captive by Thee. In place of the rigid ancient law, man must hereafter with free heart decide for himself what is good and what is evil, having only Thy image before him as his guide. But didst Thou not know he would at last reject even Thy image and Thy truth, if he is weighed down with the fearful burden of free choice? They will cry aloud at last that the truth is not in Thee, for they could not have been left in greater confusion and suffering than Thou hast caused, laying upon them so many cares and unanswerable problems.

" 'So that, in truth, Thou didst Thyself lay the foundation for the destruction of Thy kingdom, and no one is more to blame for it. Yet what was offered Thee? There are three powers, three powers alone, able to conquer and to hold captive for ever the conscience of these impotent rebels for their happiness—those forces are miracle, mystery and authority. Thou hast rejected all three and hast set the example for doing so. When the wise and dread spirit set Thee on the pinnacle of the temple and said to Thee, "If Thou wouldst know whether Thou art the Son of God then cast Thyself down, for it is written: the angels shall hold him up lest he fall and bruise himself, and Thou shalt know then whether Thou art the Son of God and shalt prove then how great is Thy faith in Thy Father." But Thou didst refuse and wouldst not cast Thyself down. Oh! of course, Thou didst proudly and well like God; but the weak, unruly race of men, are they gods? Oh, Thou didst know then that in taking one step, in making one movement to cast Thyself down, Thou wouldst be tempting God and have lost all Thy faith in Him, and wouldst have been dashed to pieces against that earth which Thou didst come to save. And the wise spirit that tempted Thee would have rejoiced. But I ask again, are there many like Thee? And couldst Thou believe for one moment that men, too, could face such a temptation? Is the nature of men such, that they can reject miracle, and at the great moments of their life, the moments of their deepest, most agonising spiritual difficulties, cling only to the free verdict of the heart? Oh, Thou didst know that Thy deed would be recorded in books, would be handed down to remote times and the utmost ends of the earth, and Thou didst hope that man, following Thee, would cling to God and not ask for a miracle. But Thou didst not know that when man rejects miracle he rejects God too; for man seeks not so much God as the miraculous. And as man cannot bear to be without the miraculous, he will create new miracles of his own for himself, and will worship deeds of sorcery and witchcraft, though he might be a hundred times over a rebel, heretic and infidel. Thou didst not come down from the Cross when they shouted to Thee, mocking and reviling Thee, "Come down from the cross and we will believe that Thou art He." Thou didst not come down, for again Thou wouldst not enslave man by a miracle, and didst crave faith given freely, not based on miracle. Thou didst crave for free love and not the base raptures of the slave before the might that has overawed him for ever. But Thou didst think too highly of men therein, for they are slaves, of course, though rebellious by nature. Look round and judge; fifteen centuries have passed, look upon them. Whom hast Thou raised up to Thyself? I swear, man is weaker and baser by nature than Thou hast believed him! Can he, can he do what Thou didst? By showing him so much respect, Thou didst, as it were, cease to feel for him, for Thou didst ask far too much from him—Thou who hast loved him more than Thyself! Respecting him less, Thou wouldst have asked less of him. That would have been more like love, for his burden would have been lighter. He is weak and vile.

What though he is everywhere now rebelling against our power, and proud of his rebellion? It is the pride of a child and a schoolboy. They are little children rioting and barring out the teacher at school. But their childish delight will end; it will cost them dear. They will cast down temples and drench the earth with blood. But they will see at last, the foolish children, that, though they are rebels, they are impotent rebels, unable to keep up their own rebellion. Bathed in their foolish tears, they will recognise at last that He who created them rebels must have meant to mock at them. They will say this in despair, and their utterance will be a blasphemy which will make them more unhappy still, for man's nature cannot bear blasphemy, and in the end always avenges it on itself. And so unrest, confusion and unhappiness—that is the present lot of man after Thou didst bear so much for their freedom! Thy great prophet tells in vision and in image, that he saw all those who took part in the first resurrection and that there were of each tribe twelve thousand. But if there were so many of them, they must have been not men but gods. They had borne Thy cross, they had endured scores of years in the barren, hungry wilderness, living upon locusts and roots—and Thou mayest indeed point with pride at those children of freedom, of free love, of free and splendid sacrifice for Thy name. But remember that they were only some thousands; and what of the rest? And how are the other weak ones to blame, because they could not endure what the strong have endured? How is the weak soul to blame that it is unable to receive such terrible gifts? Canst Thou have simply come to the elect and for the elect? But if so, it is a mystery and we cannot understand it. And if it is a mystery, we too have a right to preach a mystery, and to teach them that it's not the free judgment of their hearts, not love that matters, but a mystery which they must follow blindly, even against their conscience. So we have done. We have corrected Thy work and have founded it upon *miracle, mystery* and *authority*. And men rejoiced that they were again led like sheep, and that the terrible gift that had brought them such suffering, was, at last, lifted from their hearts. Were we right teaching them this? Speak! Did we not love mankind, so meekly acknowledging their feebleness, lovingly lightening their burden, and permitting their weak nature even sin with our sanction? Why hast Thou come now to hinder us? And why dost Thou look silently and searchingly at me with Thy mild eyes? Be angry. I don't want Thy love, for I love Thee not. And what use is it for me to hide anything from Thee? Don't I know to Whom I am speaking? All that I can say is known to Thee already. And is it for me to conceal from Thee our mystery? Perhaps it is Thy will to hear it from my lips. Listen, then. We are not working with Thee, but with *him*—that is our mystery. It's long—eight centuries—since we have been on *his* side and not on Thine. Just eight centuries ago, we took from him what Thou didst reject with scorn, that last gift he offered Thee, showing Thee all the kingdoms of the earth. We took from him Rome and the sword of Caesar, and proclaimed ourselves sole rulers of the earth, though hitherto we have not been able to complete our work. But whose fault is that? Oh, the work is only beginning, but it has begun. It has long to await completion and the earth has yet much to suffer, but we shall triumph and shall be Caesars, and then we shall plan the universal happiness of man. But Thou mightest have taken even then the sword of Caesar. Why didst Thou reject that last gift? Hadst Thou accepted that last counsel of the mighty spirit, Thou wouldst have accomplished all that man seeks on earth—that is, some one to worship, some one to keep his conscience, and some means of uniting all in one unanimous and harmonious ant-heap, for the craving for universal unity is the third and last anguish of men. Mankind as a whole has always striven to organise a universal state. There have been many great nations with great histories, but the more highly they were developed the more unhappy they were, for they felt more acutely than other people the craving for worldwide union. The great conquerors, Timours and Ghenghis-Khans, whirled like hurricanes over the face of the earth striving to subdue its people, and they too were but the unconscious expression of the same craving for universal unity. Hadst Thou taken the world and Caesar's purple, Thou wouldst have founded the universal state and have given universal peace. For who can rule men if not he who holds their conscience and their bread in his hands. We have taken the sword of Caesar, and in taking it, of course, have rjected Thee and followed *him.* Oh, ages are yet to come of the confusion of free thought, of their science and cannibalism. For having begun to build their tower of Babel without us, they will end, of course, with cannibalism. But then the beast will crawl to us and lick our feet and spatter them with tears of blood. And we shall sit upon the beast and raise the cup, and on it will be written, "Mystery." But then, and only then, the reign of peace and happiness will come for men. Thou art proud of Thine elect, but Thou hast only the elect, while we give rest to all. And besides, how many of those elect, those mighty ones who could become elect, have grown weary waiting for Thee, and have transferred and will transfer the powers of their spirit and the warmth of their heart to the other camp, and end by raising their *free* banner against Thee. Thou didst Thyself lift up that banner. But with us all will be happy and will no more rebel nor destroy one another as under Thy freedom. Oh, we shall persuade them that they will only become free when they renounce their freedom to us and submit to us. And shall we be right or shall we be lying? They will be convinced that we are right, for they will remember the horrors of slavery and confusion to which Thy freedom brought them. Freedom, free thought and science, will lead them into such straits and will bring them face to face with such marvels and insoluble mysteries, that some of them, the fierce and rebellious, will destroy themselves, others, rebellious but weak, will destroy one another, while the rest, weak and unhappy, will crawl fawning to our feet and whine to us: "Yes, you were right, you alone possess His mystery, and we come back to you, save us from ourselves!"

" 'Receiving bread from us, they will see clearly that we take the bread made by their hands from them, to give it to them, without any miracle. They will see that we do not change the stones to bread, but in truth they will be more thankful for taking it from our hands than for the bread itself! For they will remember only too well that in old days, without our help, even the bread they made turned to stones in their hands, while since they have come back to us, the very stones have turned to bread in their hands. Too, too well they know the value of complete submission! And until men know that, they will be unhappy. Who is most to blame for their not knowing it, speak? Who scattered the flock and sent it astray on unknown paths? But the flock will come together again and will submit once more, and then it will be once for all. Then we shall give them the quiet humble happiness of weak creatures such as they are by nature. Oh, we shall persuade them at last not to be proud, for Thou didst lift them up and thereby taught them to be proud. We shall show them that they are weak, that they are only pitiful children, but that childlike happiness is the sweetest of all. They will become timid and will look to us and huddle close to us in fear, as chicks to the hen. They will marvel at us and will be awe-stricken before us, and will be proud at our being so powerful and clever, that we have been able to subdue such a turbulent flock of thousands of millions. They will tremble impotently before our wrath, their minds will grow fearful, they will be quick to shed tears like women and children, but they will be just as ready at a sign from us to pass to laughter and rejoicing, to happy mirth and childish song. Yes, we shall set them to work, but in their leisure hours we shall make their life like a child's game, with children's songs and innocent dance. Oh, we shall allow them even sin, they are weak and helpless, and they will love us like children because we allow them to sin. We shall tell them that every sin will be expiated, if it is done with our permission, that we allow them to sin because we love them, and the punishment for these sins we take upon ourselves. And we shall take it upon ourselves, and they will adore us as their saviour who have taken on themselves their sins before God. And they will have no secrets from us. We shall allow or forbid them to live with their wives and mistresses, to have or not to have children—according to whether they have been obedient or disobedient—and they will submit to us gladly and cheerfully. The most painful secrets of their conscience, all, all they will bring to us, and we shall have an answer for all. And they will be glad to believe our answer, for it will save them from the great anxiety and terrible agony they endure at present in making a free decision for themselves. And all will be happy, all the millions of creatures except the hundred thousand who rule over them. For only we, we who guard the mystery, shall be unhappy. There will be thousands of millions of happy babes, and a hundred thousand sufferers who have taken upon themselves the curse of the knowledge of good and evil. Peacefully they will die, peacefully they will expire in Thy name, and beyond the grave they will find nothing but death. But we shall keep the secret, and for their happiness we shall allure them with the reward of heaven and eternity. Though if there were anything in the other world, it certainly would not be for such as they. It is prophesied that Thou wilt come again in victory, Thou wilt come with Thy chosen, the proud and strong, but we will say that they have only saved themselves, but we have saved all. We are told that the harlot who sits upon the beast, and holds in her hands the *mystery,* shall be put to shame, that the weak will rise up again, and will rend her royal purple and will strip naked her loathsome body. But then I will stand up and point out to Thee the thousand millions of happy children who have known no sin. And we who have taken their sins upon us for their happiness will stand up before Thee and say: "Judge us if Thou canst and darest." Know that I fear Thee not. Know that I too have been in the wilderness, I too have lived on roots and locusts, I too prized the freedom with which Thou hast blessed men, and I too was striving to stand among Thy elect, among the strong and powerful, thirsting "to make up the number." But I awakened and would not serve madness. I turned back and joined the ranks of those *who have corrected Thy work.* I left the proud and went back to the humble, for the happiness of the humble. What I say to Thee will come to pass, and our dominion will be built up. I repeat, to-morrow Thou shalt see that obedient flock who at a sign from me will hasten to heap up the hot cinders about the pile on which I shall burn Thee for coming to hinder us. For if any one has ever deserved our fires, it is Thou. To-morrow I shall burn Thee. Dixi.' "

Ivan stopped. He was carried away as he talked and spoke with excitement; when he had finished, he suddenly smiled.

Alyosha had listened in silence; towards the end he was greatly moved and seemed several times on the point of interrupting, but restrained himself. Now his words came with a rush.

"But . . . that's absurd!" he cried, flushing. "Your poem is in praise of Jesus, not in blame of Him—as you meant it to be. And who will believe you about freedom? Is that the way to understand it? That's not the idea of it in the Orthodox Church . . . That's Rome, and not even the whole of Rome, it's false—those are the worst of the Catholics, the Inquisitors, the Jesuits! . . . And there could not be such a fantastic creature as your Inquisitor. What are these sins of mankind they take on themselves? Who are these keepers of the mystery who have taken some curse upon themselves for the happiness of mankind? When have they been seen? We know the Jesuits, they are spoken ill of, but surely they are not what you describe? They are not that at all, not at all. . . . They are simply the Romish army for the earthly sovereignty of the world in the future, with the Pontiff of Rome for Emperor . . . that's their ideal, but there's no sort of mystery or lofty melancholy about it. . . . It's simple lust of power, of filthy earthly gain, of domination—something like a universal serfdom with them as masters—that's all they stand for. They don't even believe in God perhaps. Your suffering inquisitor is a mere fantasy."

"Stay, stay," laughed Ivan, "how hot you are! A fantasy you say, let it be so! Of course it's a fantasy. But allow me to say: do you really think that the Roman Catholic movement of the last centuries is actually nothing but the lust of power, of filthy earthly gain? Is that Father Païssy's teaching?"

"No, no, on the contrary, Father Païssy did once say something rather the same as you . . . but of course it's not the same, not a bit the same," Alyosha hastily corrected himself.

"A precious admission, in spite of your 'not a bit the same.' I ask you why your Jesuits and Inquisitors have united simply for vile material gain? Why can there not be among them one martyr oppressed by great sorrow and loving humanity? You see, only suppose that there was one such man among all those who desire nothing but filthy material gain—if there's only one like my old inquisitor, who had himself eaten roots in the desert and made frenzied efforts to subdue his flesh to make himself free and perfect. But yet all his life he loved humanity, and suddenly his eyes were opened, and he saw that it is no great moral blessedness to attain perfection and freedom, if at the same time one gains the conviction that millions of God's creatures have been created as a mockery, that they will never be capable of using their freedom, that these poor rebels can never turn into giants to complete the tower, that it was not for such geese that the great idealist dreamt his dream of harmony. Seeing all that he turned back and joined—the clever people. Surely that could have happened?"

"Joined whom, what clever people?" cried Alyosha, completely carried away. "They have no such great cleverness and no mysteries and secrets. . . . Perhaps nothing but Atheism, that's all their secret. Your inquisitor does not believe in God, that's his secret!"

"What if it is so! At last you have guessed it. It's perfectly true that that's the whole secret, but isn't that suffering, at least for a man like that, who has wasted his whole life in the desert and yet could not shake off his incurable love of humanity? In his old age he reached the clear conviction that nothing but the advice of the great dread spirit could build up any tolerable sort of life for the feeble, unruly 'incomplete, empirical creatures created in jest.' And so, convinced of this, he sees that he must follow the council of the wise spirit, the dread spirit of death and destruction, and therefore accept lying and deception, and lead men consciously to death and destruction, and yet deceive them all the way so that they may not notice where they are being led, that the poor blind creatures may at least on the way think themselves happy. And note, the deception is in the name of Him in Whose ideal the old man had so fervently believed all his life long. Is not that tragic? And if only one such stood at the head of the whole army 'filled with the lust of power only for the sake of filthy gain'—would not one such be enough to make a tragedy? More than that, one such standing at the head is enough to create the actual leading idea of the Roman Church with all its armies and Jesuits, its highest idea. I tell you frankly that I firmly believe that there has always been such a man among those who stood at the head of the movement. Who knows, there may have been some such even among the Roman Popes. Who knows, perhaps the spirit of that accursed old man who loves mankind so obstinately in his own way, is to be found even now in a whole multitude of such old men, existing not by chance but by agreement, as a secret league formed long ago for the guarding of the mystery, to guard it from the weak and the unhappy, so as to make them happy. No doubt it is so, and so it must be indeed. I fancy that even among the Masons there's something of the same mystery at the bottom, and that that's why the Catholics so detest the Masons as their rivals breaking up the unity of the idea, while it is so essential that there should be one flock and one shepherd. . . . But from the way I defend my idea I might be an author impatient of your criticism. Enough of it."

"You are perhaps a Mason yourself!" broke suddenly from Alyosha. "You don't believe in God," he added, speaking this time very sorrowfully. He fancied besides that his brother was looking at him ironically.

"How does your poem end?" he asked, suddenly looking down. "Or was it the end?"

"I meant to end it like this. When the Inquisitor ceased speaking he waited some time for his Prisoner to answer him. His silence weighed down upon him. He saw that the Prisoner had listened intently all the time, looking gently in his face and evidently not wishing to reply. The old man longed for Him to say something, however bitter and terrible. But He suddenly approached the old man in silence and softly kissed him on his bloodless aged lips. That was all his answer. The old man shuddered. His lips moved. He went to the door, opened it, and said to Him: 'Go, and come no more. . . . Come not at all, never, never!' And he let Him out into the dark alleys of the town. The Prisoner went away."

"And the old man?"

"The kiss glows in his heart, but the old man adheres to his idea."

"And you with him, you too?" cried Alyosha, mournfully.

Ivan laughed.

"Why, it's all nonsense, Alyosha. It's only a senseless poem of a senseless student, who could never write two lines of verse. Why do you take it so seriously? Surely you don't suppose I am going straight off to the Jesuits, to join the men who are correcting His work? Good Lord, it's no business of mine. I told you, all I want is to live on to thirty, and then . . . dash the cup to the ground!"

"But the little sticky leaves, and the precious tombs, and the blue sky, and the woman you love! How will you live, how will you love them?" Alyosha cried sorrowfully. "With such a hell in your heart and your head, how can you? No, that's just what you are going away for, to join them . . . if not, you will kill yourself, you can't endure it!"

"There is a strength to endure everything," Ivan said with a cold smile.

"What strength?"

"The strength of the Karamazovs—the strength of the Karamazov baseness."

"To sink into debauchery, to stifle your soul with corruption, yes?"

"Possibly even that . . . only perhaps till I am thirty I shall escape it, and then."

"How will you escape it? By what will you escape it? That's impossible with your ideas."

"In the Karamazov way, again."

" 'Everything is lawful,' you mean? Everything is lawful, is that it?"

Ivan scowled, and all at once turned strangely pale.

"Ah, you've caught up yesterday's phrase, which so offended Miüsov

—and which Dmitri pounced upon so naïvely and paraphrased!" he smiled queerly. "Yes, if you like. 'everything is lawful' since the word has been said. I won't deny it. And Mitya's version isn't bad."

Alyosha looked at him in silence.

"I thought that going away from here I have you at least," Ivan said suddenly, with unexpected feeling; "but now I see that there is no place for me even in your heart, my dear hermit. The formula 'all is lawful,' I won't renounce—will you renounce me for that, yes?"

Alyosha got up, went to him and softly kissed him on the lips.

"That's plagiarism," cried Ivan, highly delighted. "You stole that from my poem. Thank you though. Get up, Alyosha, it's time we were going, both of us."

They went out, but stopped when they reached the entrance of the restaurant.

"Listen, Alyosha," Ivan began in a resolute voice, "if I am really able to care for the sticky little leaves I shall only love them, remembering you. It's enough for me that you are somewhere here, and I shan't lose my desire for life yet. Is that enough for you? Take it as a declaration of love if you like. And now you go to the right and I to the left. And it's enough, do you hear, enough. I mean even if I don't go away to-morrow (I think I certainly shall go) and we meet again, don't say a word more on these subjects. I beg that particularly. And about Dmitri too, I ask you specially never speak to me again," he added, with sudden irritation; "it's all exhausted, it has all been said over and over again, hasn't it? And I'll make you one promise in return for it. When at thirty, I want to 'dash the cup to the ground,' wherever I may be I'll come to have one more talk with you, even though it were from America, you may be sure of that. I'll come on purpose. It will be very interesting to have a look at you, to see what you'll be by that time. It's rather a solemn promise, you see. And we really may be parting for seven years or ten. Come, go now to your Pater Seraphicus, he is dying. If he dies without you, you will be angry with me for having kept you. Good-bye, kiss me once more; that's right, now go."

Ivan turned suddenly and went his way without looking back. It was just as Dmitri had left Alyosha the day before, though the parting had been very different. The strange resemblance flashed like an arrow through Alyosha's mind in the distress and dejection of that moment. He waited a little, looking after his brother. He suddenly noticed that Ivan swayed as he walked and that his right shoulder looked lower than his left. He had never noticed it before. But all at once he turned too, and almost ran to the monastery. It was nearly dark, and he felt almost frightened; something new was growing up in him for which he could not account. The wind had risen again as on the previous evening, and the ancient pines murmured gloomily about him when he entered the hermitage copse. He almost ran. "Pater Seraphicus—he got that name from somewhere—where from?" Alyosha wondered. "Ivan, poor Ivan, and when shall I see you again? . . . Here is the hermitage. Yes, yes, that he is, Pater Seraphicus, he will save me—from him and for ever!"

Several times afterwards he wondered how he could on leaving Ivan so completely forget his brother Dmitri, though he had that morning, only a few hours before, so firmly resolved to find him and not to give up doing so, even should he be unable to return to the monastery that night.

Friedrich Nietzsche

7. God and Guilt

I

To breed an animal able to promise—is that not precisely the problem set up by nature in regard to man? Is that not the very problem *of* man?

That this problem has been largely solved must seem even more astonishing to anyone who appreciates the opposing power of *forgetfulness*. Forgetfulness is no simple *vis inertiaei,*[1] as the superficial believe, but is much more an active and, in the strictest sense, positive capacity for suppression. Its task is to see to it that what we experience, learn, or take into ourselves, just as little enters consciousness while being digested (one might call this "psychic incorporation") as does the whole thousand-fold process by which the nourishing of our body —the so-called "incorporation"—takes place. The doors and windows of consciousness close for a while, to remain unbothered by the noise and fights of our underworld of service organs working for and against

---

From *The Genealogy of Morals,* Second Essay " 'Guilt', 'Bad Conscience' and Related Matters," trans. Maudemarie Clark for this book. Title supplied by the editors.

1. Inertia.

111

one another. A little quiet, a little *tabula rasa*[2] of consciousness, so that there is room for something new, above all for the noble functions and functionaries, for ruling, foreseeing, predetermining (for our organism is set up as an oligarchy)—that is the use of the above-mentioned active forgetfulness. Like a gate-keeper, it is the guardian of the order of the soul, of peace and etiquette. Thus can be easily imagined the extent to which there could be no happiness, no cheerfulness, no hope, no pride, no *present,* without forgetfulness. The man in whom this apparatus of suppression is injured is figuratively constipated (and not only figuratively). He can not be "through" with anything.

Precisely this necessarily forgetful animal, in whom forgetting is a strength and represents a form of *robust* health, cultivated in himself an opposing capacity, a memory, with the help of which his forgetfulness is suspended in certain cases—in the case where promises are supposed to be given. This memory is in no way simply a passive inability to get rid of an impression once received, not simply the indigestion of a word once given with which one cannot be "through." It is rather an active not-*wanting*-to-be-rid-of, a continued willing of what was once willed, an actual *memory of the will.* So that between the original "I will," "I will do," and the discharging of the will, its *act,* a world of strange new things, conditions, and even acts of the will can undoubtedly come into being without breaking this long chain of willings. But what does all that presuppose? How much man must have learned in order to be able to ordain the future in advance: to differentiate the necessary from the accidental; causal thinking; to see distant things as present and to anticipate; to fix with certainty an end and the means to it; to reckon, to be able to calculate. In order to guarantee his own future, as one who promises does, man himself must first have become *calculable, regular, necessary,* even in his own idea of himself.

2

Precisely this is the long history of the origin of *responsibility.* The problem of breeding an animal able to promise includes as its condition and preparation, as we have just seen, the prior problem of making man to a certain degree necessary, of one form, equal among equals, regular, and consequently, calculable. The monstrous labor of all this, which I have called the "morality of mores" *(The Dawn),*[3] the

---

2. Blank slate.

3. The page numbers in the first edition which usually accompany the references to Nietzsche's own works have been omitted in this translation. For references to the specific sections intended, see Walter Kaufmann's translation in *Basic Writings of Nietzsche* (New York: The Modern Library, 1968).

actual labor of man on himself during his longest period of existence —his whole *prehistorical* labor—has its sense in this, its great justification, despite the hardness, tyranny, stupidity, and idiocy involved: with the help of the morality of mores and the straitjacket of society, man became calculable. If we imagine the end of this monstrous process— where the tree finally bears its fruit, where society and her morality of mores brings to light that *to which* she was only the means—there we find, as the ripest fruit on her tree, the *sovereign individual,* like only unto himself, free from the morality of mores, the autonomous individual beyond morality (for "autonomous" and "moral" are mutually exclusive), in short, the man of the independent long will, who *is able to promise.* And in him is found a proud consciousness, quivering in all his muscles, of what has finally been achieved and is embodied in him—a real consciousness of power and freedom, a feeling of the completion of man.

This one who has become free, who is really *able* to promise, this master of the *free* will, this sovereign—how could he not be aware of his superiority to those who can not promise and stand as security for themselves? How could he not know how much trust, fear, and reverence he awakens—for he "deserves" all three—and that his mastery over himself necessarily gives to him also mastery over circumstances, over nature, and over all unreliable and short-willed creatures? The "free" man, the possessor of the long unbreakable will, has in this possession also his *standard of value.* Looking out at others he feels either respect or contempt; he necessarily respects his equals, the strong and reliable (those who are *able* to promise)—that is, everyone who promises like a sovereign—with difficulty, rarely, slowly—who only grudgingly trusts, who *honors* when he trusts, who gives his word as something that can be trusted because he knows he is strong enough to keep it in the face of circumstances, even "against fate." And just as necessarily he holds ready a kick for those feeble windbags who promise without being able to, and for the liar who breaks his word almost before it is spoken. The proud knowledge of the extraordinary privilege of *responsibility,* the consciousness of this rare freedom, this power over himself and destiny, has sunk into his innermost depths and become instinct, his dominating instinct. And what would he call this, his dominating instinct, in case he should need a word for it? There is no doubt: this sovereign man calls it his *conscience.*

3

His conscience?—It may be guessed beforehand that the concept of "conscience," which we meet here in its highest and almost astonishing form, already has a long history and has undergone transformation. To stand as security for oneself and to do it with pride, and thus to be *able to affirm* oneself, is a ripe fruit, but also a late fruit—how long this fruit must have hung on the tree tart and sour! And for a much longer time there was absolutely nothing of this fruit to be seen —no one could have promised it even though everything on the tree was being readied for it and growing towards it.

"How does one create a memory for this man-animal? How does one stamp something on this in part stupid, in part silly, momentary mind, so that it stays there?"—This ancient problem could hardly be solved with tender answers and means, as one can imagine; perhaps there is nothing more terrible and sinister in the whole prehistory of man than his techniques for creating a memory. "One must burn something in so that it is remembered; only that which continues to cause pain is remembered"—that is the first principle of the oldest of all psychologies on this earth (unfortunately also the most enduring). One might even say that something of that terror in terms of which promising and pledging became possible still has its after-effect wherever there is solemnity, seriousness, secrecy, and gloomy colors in the life of men or peoples; the past, the longest, hardest, deepest past, shows its trace and wells up in us whenever we become "serious." Blood, martyrs, and sacrifices were never denied when man considered it necessary to create a memory for himself. The most gruesome sacrifices and forfeitures (to which the sacrifices of the first-born belong), the most repulsive mutilations (for instance, castration), the cruelest rituals of religious cults (and all religions are, on the deepest level, systems of cruelty)—all of this has its origin in that instinct which recognizes pain as the strongest means for creating a memory.

In a certain sense the whole of asceticism belongs here. A number of ideas shall be made inextinguishable, ever present, unforgetable, "fixed," so that the whole nervous and intellectual system is hypnotized through these "fixed ideas." The ascetic procedures and lifestyles are means for isolating these few ideas from all other ideas in order to make them "unforgettable." The poorer man's memory was, the more terrible were his customs. The severity of the penal code in particular provides a measure of the effort necessary to conquer forgetfulness and to make present to these slaves of momentary affects and desires a few primitive demands of social living.

We Germans certainly do not regard ourselves as an especially cruel or hardhearted people, still less as especially frivolous or living for the day. But one need only look at our old penal codes in order to realize the effort necessary to breed a "nation of thinkers" (one might say: the European nation in which one finds today the maximum of trust, seriousness, tastelessness, and objectivity, and which therefore has the right to breed every kind of European mandarin.) These Germans have used terrible means to create a memory for themselves, in order to become master of their vulgar basic instincts and the brutal clumsiness of these. One thinks of the old German punishments: stoning for instance (even legend has the millstone fall on the head of the guilty), breaking on the wheel (the most characteristic invention and speciality of the German genius in the realm of punishment!), piercing with stakes, drawing or trampling by horses ("quartering"), boiling criminals in oil or wine (still in the fourteenth and fifteenth centuries), the popular flaying ("flaying into strips"), the cutting of flesh from the breast, even smearing the wrongdoer with honey and leaving him in burning sun to the flies.

With the help of such images and procedures man was finally able to remember five or six "I will nots," in relation to which he had given his word in order to live under the advantages of society. And really, with the help of this kind of memory one finally came "to reason"! Ah, the reason, the seriousness, the mastery of affects, this whole gloomy thing called reflection, all these perogatives and showpieces of man— how dearly they have been paid for, how much blood and cruelty lies at the foundation of all "good things."

4

But how did that other gloomy thing, the consciousness of guilt, the whole "bad conscience" come into the world? And here we turn back again to our geneologists of morality. To repeat—or have I not yet said it?—they are good for nothing. Their own limited simply "modern" experience; no knowledge, no will to knowledge of the past; much less an historical instinct, the necessary "second sight"—and then they pursue the history of morality! This necessarily results in conclusions which bear little relation to the truth. Have these geneologists of morality even the slightest idea, for instance, that the principle moral concept "guilt" (Schuld) has its origins in the extremely material concept "debts" (Schulden)?[4] Or that punishment developed to perfec-

---

4. In German, there is only one word—"Schuld"—corresponding to the two English words "guilt" and "debt." Therefore, I have sometimes translated "Schuld" and the plural "Schulden" as "debt(s) or guilt," but the reader should be aware of the double meaning of the German when only one of the English equivalents has been used.

tion as retaliation quite apart from any presupposition of freedom or the lack of it?—to such an extent in fact that a *high* degree of humanization is necessary before the animal "man" begins to make those much more primitive distinctions between "intentional," "negligent," "accidental," "justifiable," and their opposites, and to take account of these in the meting out of punishment. That cheap explanation, today apparently so natural and unavoidable, concerning the origin of the sense of justice—"the criminal deserves punishment *because* he could have acted otherwise"—is actually a refined form of human judgment and reasoning which is found only at a late stage; and whoever transports this to the origin of punishment violates the psychology of primitive man with his clumsy fingers. Throughout the longest period of human history the wrong-doer was *not* punished *because* he was held responsible for his deed—there was, that is, *no* presupposition that only the guilty were to be punished. Rather one punished as parents still punish their children—out of anger at some injury or offense, which is taken out on the offender. This anger is held in check and modified by the idea that every injury has its *equivalent,* and can be "paid for," even if only by the *pain* of the offender. But what is the source of the power of this ancient and deep-rooted idea, which can perhaps no longer be rooted out? I have already betrayed it: in the contractual relation between *creditor* and *debtor,* which is as old as the existence of "legal subjects," which in turn points back to the basic form of buying, selling, barter, trade, and exchange.

5

Reflection on these contractual relationships awakens, as one might expect from the above remarks, a good deal of suspicion and resistence against the primitive men who created or permitted them. It was here that *promising* occurred, here that one was concerned to *create* a memory for those who promised; and it is here, one suspects, that the discovery of so much hardness, cruelty, and pain is to be located. The debtor, in order to inspire trust in his promise of repayment, to guarantee the sacredness of his promise, and to impress the repayment on his own conscience as duty or obligation, pledged to the creditor something that he would still "possess" or have power over in case he did not pay—for instance, his body, his wife, his freedom, or even his life (or under certain religious presuppositions, even his happiness after death, the salvation of his soul, and lastly, even his peace in the grave: thus in Egypt, the corpse of the debtor found no peace from the creditor even in the grave, and such peace was very important to

Egyptians.) The creditor could above all inflict on the body of the debtor all sorts of humiliations and tortures—for instance, cutting out as much as seemed proportional to the debt—and it was in view of this situation that there were, from earliest times and in all places, systems of calculations, often horrifying in their detail and minuteness, *legally* sanctioned calculations, of the value of different limbs and parts of the body. I consider it as already a sign of progress, as proof of a freer, less petty, *more Roman* conception of law when the Twelve Tables of Rome decreed that it did not matter how much or how little the creditor cut out in such cases; "si plus minusve secuerunt, ne fraude esto."[5]

Let us make the logic of this form of compensation clear; it is odd enough. The equivalence consists in this: that in place of an advantage directly related to the injury (thus, in place of a compensation in terms of money, land, or possessions of different sorts) a kind of *pleasure* is due to the creditor—the pleasure of exercising power over one who is powerless, the sensual pleasure *"de faire le mal pour le plaisir de le faire,"*[6] the enjoyment of doing violence. This pleasure will be valued more highly the lower the creditor stands in the ranks of society, for it can easily seem to him a precious bite, a foretaste of a higher rank. "Punishing" the debtor, the creditor participates in the *rights of masters:* finally he too can experience, for once, the feeling of elevation at being able to mistreat and to be contemptuous of a creature who is "lower than" himself—or, in case the actual power of punishing has been handed over to the "authorities," of simply being able to *see* the creature so mistreated. Compensation thus consists in a warrant for and a right to cruelty.

6

In *this* sphere of rights and obligations one finds the origin of the world of moral concepts: "guilt," "conscience," "duty," "the sacredness of duty"—its beginning, like the beginning of everything great on earth, was thoroughly, and for a long time, spattered with blood. And might one not add that at its core this world has never lost a certain smell of blood and torture? (not even with old Kant: the categorical imperative reeks of cruelty.) It was here likewise that the uncanny and perhaps indissoluble union of "guilt and suffering" was first arranged. To ask again: how can suffering be a compensation for debts or guilt

---

5. If they have taken more or less, let that be no crime.
6. Of doing evil for the pleasure of doing it.

("Schulden")? Insofar as causing suffering gives pleasure in the highest degree, insofar as the injured party receives for his loss, including his displeasure over his loss, an extraordinary counter-pleasure. Causing someone to suffer: an actual *festival,* something which, as mentioned, was valued more highly the more it was in contradiction to the rank and social position of the creditor. This is voiced only as a hypothesis, for it is difficult to see to the bottom of such underground things, not to mention the pain involved; and whoever clumsily interjects the idea of "revenge" here has only veiled and clouded his insight rather than making it clearer. ("Revenge" itself leads back to the same question: "how can making someone suffer be a compensation?")

It seems to me to go against the delicacy, and even more the tartuffery, of tame house animals (that is, modern man; that is, ourselves) to imagine in all its vividness the extent to which the festival joys of primitive men consisted in cruelty, which was in fact an ingredient in almost all of their pleasures; and on the other hand, the innocence and naiveté of their need for cruelty, and the way in which precisely this "disinterested malice" (or to speak with Spinoza, the *sympathia malevolens*) appeared to them as a normal human quality—and accordingly, as something that conscience could heartily affirm. For a more profound eye there is still enough of the oldest and most basic joys of the festival to be perceived even today: in *Beyond Good and Evil* (and before that in *The Dawn*) I have already tentatively pointed to the ever-growing spiritualization and deification of cruelty that runs throughout the whole history of higher culture (and in a meaningful sense actually constitutes it). In any case, it is not that long since royal marriages and folk festivals in grand style were unimaginable without executions, tortures, or perhaps an auto-da-fé, and no noble household was without creatures on whom one could vent one's malice and cruel teasing. (One should recall Don Quixote at the court of the Dutchess. Today we read the whole of Don Quixote with a bitter taste in our mouth, and almost as a torture, and would therefore seem very strange and obscure to its author and his contemporaries, who read it with the best of conscience as the merriest of books, practically laughing themselves to death over it.) To see suffering gives pleasure; to cause suffering even more—that is a hard proposition, but a powerful old human, all-too-human principle to which, by the way, even the apes might subscribe. For it is said that in the invention of bizarre cruelties they announce the advent of man and are his "prelude." Without cruelty, no festival—thus teaches the oldest and longest part of human history—and even in punishing there is so much that is festive!

7

With these reflections, by the way, it is not my intention to provide our pessimists with grist for their discordant and creaking mills of life-weariness. On the contrary, it should be made explicit that life was much more cheerful in those days, when man was not ashamed of his cruelty, than it is now that we have pessimists. The heavens above have always darkened in proportion to the growth of man's shame before man. The tired pessimistic look, the mistrust of the riddle of life, the icy *No* of disgust with life—these are not the signs of the *most evil* periods of human history; they first reach the light of day as the swamp plants that they are only when the swamp in which they can grow is already there—I mean the morbid taming and moralization thanks to which the animal "man" finally learned to be ashamed of all his instincts. On the way to becoming an "angel" (not to use a stronger term here) man bred in himself that disturbed stomach and coated tongue which makes the joy and innocence of the animals repugnant to him, and life itself distasteful. Thus he stands before himself now and then, holding his nose, and with Pope Innocent the Third disapprovingly catalogs the elements of his loathsomeness (impure conception, disgusting means of nourishment in the mother's body, baseness of the matter from which he develops, hideous stink, secretions of saliva, urine, and dung).

Since suffering is always marshalled forth today as the first argument *against* existence, as its largest question mark, it does one good to recall those times when men judged in the reverse way, because they did not want to give up *causing* pain, and saw in it instead a fascination of the first rank, an actual seduction *to* life. Perhaps in those days— to provide a word of consolation for the tender—pain did not hurt as much as it does today. At least a doctor might conclude this when he has treated Negroes (taken as representative of prehistoric man) with severe cases of internal inflammation which would have brought the best-constituted European to despair, but do *not* have this effect on the Negro. (The curve of human susceptibility to pain in fact appears to sink rapidly and almost suddenly as soon as one gets beyond the first ten thousand or ten million representatives of the top level of culture; and for myself, I do not doubt that the combined suffering of all the animals on which the knife has been used for research purposes simply cannot compare to *one* painful night of a single hysterical educated woman.) One might even concede the possibility that it was actually not necessary for the pleasure in cruelty to die out. All that was needed, in view of the fact that pain hurts more today, was that it appear translated into the realm of the imagination and the psyche, adorned with such innocent-sounding names that even the most hypocritical and tender conscience would not be suspicious of them ("tragic pity" is such a name; another is *"les nostalgies dela croix"*).[7]

What really arouses indignation against suffering is not suffering itself, but the senselessness of suffering. But there never was any such *senseless* suffering for the Christian, who read into suffering a whole hidden holy-machinery, or for the naive man of ancient times, who knew how to interpret all suffering in terms of someone who had caused it or a spectator. So that hidden, undiscovered, unwitnessed suffering could be banished from the earth, and honestly denied, one was almost forced to invent gods and intermediary figures of all kinds —in short, someone who roams even into hidden regions, who sees even in the dark, and who would not easily let an interesting and painful spectacle escape him.

With the help of such inventions, life in those days knew the clever trick, which it has always known, of justifying itself, justifying its "evil"; today it is perhaps in need of other auxiliary inventions (for instance, life as a riddle, life as an epistemological problem). "Every evil is justified the sight of which edifies a god," thus spoke the primitive logic of the emotions—and actually, was it only the primitive? The gods as friends of the *cruel* spectacle—how far this primitive idea has been projected even into our humanized Europe! One might consult Calvin and Luther a bit here. It is certain in any case that the *Greeks* knew of no more pleasant offering to garnish the happiness of their gods than the joys of cruelty. Why do you suppose Homer had his gods look down on the fortunes of man? What was the fundamental meaning of the Trojan Wars and similar tragic horrors? There can be no doubt: they were intended as festival plays for the gods; and, insofar as the poet is more like the gods than are other men, as festival plays for the poet. Likewise, the Greek moral philosophers later thought that the eyes of the gods looked down on the moral contest, on the heroism and the self-torture of the virtuous. The "Heracles of duty" was on a stage, and he knew it; unwitnessed virtue was totally unthinkable for this theatrical people. That so audacious and fateful philosophic invention of the "free will," of the absolute spontaneity of man in good and evil, which was first created for Europe at that time—was it not created in order to justify the belief that the gods' interest in man, in man's virtue, *could never be exhausted?* If there were never something really new on this earth-stage, never an unprecedented excitement, complication, catastrophe, such a completely determined world would be

---

7. The nostalgia for the cross.

totally predictable for the gods, and hence tiring—reason enough for these *friends of the gods,* the philosophers, not to impute such a deterministic world to their gods! The man of antiquity is full of tender consideration for the "spectator," as part of an essentially open, essentially visible world in which happiness cannot be imagined without spectacles and festivals. And, as already mentioned, even in great *punishment* there is so much that is festive!

8

The feeling of guilt, of personal obligation—to return to the beginning of our investigation—has its origin, as we have seen, in the oldest and most aboriginal relation between buyer and seller, debtor and creditor. It was here that a person first came up against another person, here that he first *measured himself* against another. No level of civilization has been discovered which is so primitive that this relation is not noticeable. Setting prices, gauging values, establishing equivalences, exchanging—all this preoccupied man's first experience of thinking to such an extent that, in a certain sense, it is thinking. It was here that the oldest form of cleverness was cultivated, and here that we might expect to find the beginning of human pride, of man's feeling of superiority to all the other animals. Perhaps our word "man" *(manas)* still expresses something of this feeling of pride: man designated himself as the creature who gauges values, who values and measures, as "*the* evaluating animal."

Buying and selling, together with their psychological appendages, are even older than the beginnings of any form of social organization or alliance. The embryonic feeling of exchange, contract, debt or guilt (Schuld), right, duty, compensation, together with the habit of comparing power with power, of measuring and calculating, were first *carried over* into the crudest and most elementary social complexes (in comparison to similar complexes) from the most rudimentary form of personal contractual rights. Man's eye was now set in this perspective; and with the clumsy consistency characteristic of the thinking of ancient man, which is slow to start moving but inexorable once set in a certain direction, he arrived at that great generalization: "everything has its price; *everything* can be paid off"—the oldest and most naive moral canon of *justice,* the beginning of all "good nature," all "fairness," all "good will," all "objectivity" on this earth. Justice, on this elementary level, is the good will among those of approximately equal power to come to terms with one another, to come to an "understanding" again through some kind of agreement—and to *force* the less powerful to reach an agreement among themselves.

9

Measured by the standard of prehistory (this prehistory is, after all, always present or again possible in all history) the community stands to its members in that same kind of primary relationship found between creditor and debtor. One lives in a community, and enjoys the advantages of a community (oh, and what advantages! we underestimate these at times today); one lives protected, cared for, unconcerned about certain injuries and hostilities to which the "outsider," "the man outside the peace," is exposed. A German will understand the original meaning of "Elend"[8] —and how one pledged and obligated oneself to the community precisely in view of these injuries and hostilities. What would happen if the pledge were not kept? Society, the disappointed creditor, would make one pay—one could count on that. The least important thing here is the direct injury caused by the offender; apart from this, the criminal is above all a "breaker" of his agreement, and of his word, given *to the whole* in relation to all the goods and comforts of community life, in which he has until now participated. The criminal is a debtor who has not made his repayment for the obvious advantages and advance payment he has received; but further, he has even attacked his creditor. Therefore he shall be deprived of these goods and advantages from now on, as is reasonable—but much more importantly, he shall now be reminded of *what he actually had in these advantages.* The anger of the offended creditor, the community, gives him back again to the wild and bird-free condition from which it previously protected him. He is banished—and now every kind of hostility may be vented on him. "Punishment," at this level of culture, is simply the copy, the *mimic,* of the normal relation to any hated, disarmed, defeated enemy who has been deprived not only of all rights and protection, but also of all mercy. Thus the rights of war, and the victory celebration of the *vae victis*[9] in all its relentlessness and cruelty —all of which explains how war itself (including its cult of sacrifice) has given us all of the *forms* in which punishment has appeared in history.

10

When a society becomes more powerful, it does not take the offenses of single individuals as seriously because they are no longer as dangerous or destructive to the existence of the whole. The wrongdoer is no

---

8. "Elend" means "misery" or "misfortune," but originally meant "exile."

9. Woe to the conquered!

longer considered "outside the peace," nor is he banished, and the communal anger may no longer be vented on him in the same unbridled way—from now on in fact, the wrongdoer will be defended and protected by the whole against this anger, especially that of those who have been directly injured. Compromise with the anger of the injured party; an attempt to localize the case and to prevent a wider or even universal participation and unrest; attempts to find equivalences and to settle the whole matter; above all, the increasingly more definite will to find that every offense can be, in some way, *paid off,* and thus, at least to a certain extent, to *isolate* the criminal from his deed—these are the characteristics which are imprinted with increasing clarity on the further development of punishment.

As the power and self-confidence of a society grows, its penal law always becomes less severe. Every weakening and deep endangerment of the former brings with it a more severe form of the latter. The "creditor" becomes more humane to the extent that he becomes richer; and finally the number of wrongs he can endure without suffering even becomes the measure of his richness. It is not unthinkable that a society have a *consciousness of its own power* so great that it could allow itself the noblest luxury of all—to let its offenders go *unpunished.* "What do my parasites matter to me?" it might say. "May they live and flourish: I am strong enough for that." Justice, which begins with "everything is payable, everything must be paid off," ends by looking the other way, and letting those who cannot pay go free— it ends, as does every good thing on earth, by *transcending itself.* The self-transcendence of justice; its beautiful name is well-known—mercy. It remains, as goes without saying, the special right of the most powerful man, or better yet, his "beyond rights."

11

A word of rebuttal here against attempts made recently to establish the origin of justice on totally different ground—namely on the ground of *ressentiment.*[10] A hint to psychologists, assuming they wish to study *ressentiment* up close: today this plant thrives best among anarchists and anti-semites, in the same way it has always thrived, by the way, in hiding—like violets, though of a different scent. And as like always produces like, it should not come as any surprise to find that attempts are being made in these circles, as have been made many times before, to sanctify *revenge* under the name of justice—as if justice were essen-

---

10. Resentment.

tially a development from the feeling of being injured—and to bring revenge together with all of the other *reactive* affects into good repute. I would hardly object to this last point—it seems to me even to constitute a *service* in view of the whole biological problem (in relation to which the values of these affects has been underestimated.) I wish only to call attention to the fact that this new nuance of scientific fairness (to the benefit of hate, envy, jealousy, mistrust, rancour, and revenge) grows out of the spirit of *ressentiment* itself. This "scientific fairness" ceases immediately and makes room for accents of deadly hostility and prejudice as soon as it concerns itself with another group of affects, which seem to me of much greater value than the reactive ones, and consequently, to have a primary claim to *scientific* evaluation and esteem: namely, the really active affects such as the lust for power, greed, and the like. (E. Duhring, *The Value of Life; A Course in Philosophy;* actually, throughout his works). There is so much against this tendency in general: one who wishes to oblige truth must counter Duhring's proposition, that the home of justice is to be found in the realm of the reactive feelings, with its glaring reversal: the *last* realm conquered by the spirit of justice is that of the reactive feelings! When it really happens that the just man remains just even towards those who harm him (and not simply cold, restrained, distant, indifferent: being just is always a *positive* relation), when the elevated, clear, gentle, and profound objectivity of the just and *judging* eye is not clouded even under the assault of personal injury, derision, and suspicion, now this is a piece of perfection, and the highest mastery on earth—so much so, that one would be prudent not to expect it or to believe in it too easily.

On the average certainly a small dose of attack, spite, and insinuation suffices to drive the blood into the eyes, and all fairness out of the eyes, of even the most upright person. The active, attacking, aggressive man is always a hundred steps closer to justice than the reactive man; he does not need to take a false and prejudiced view of his object, in the way the reactive man does, and must do. In fact the aggressive man, as the stronger, more courageous, more noble, has had as a consequence the *freer* eye, the *better* conscience on his side throughout history; conversely, one can already guess who has the invention of the "bad conscience" on his conscience—the man of *ressentiment.*

Finally, if one looks into history, in what sphere do we find the whole administration of law, even the actual need for law? Perhaps in the sphere of the reactive man? Absolutely not: but rather in that of the active, the strong, the spontaneous and aggressive. Considered historically—may it be said to the dismay of the above-mentioned agitator (who once made the confession: "the doctrine of revenge runs through all of my works and efforts as the red flag of justice")—law on earth represents the battle against the reactive feelings, the battle against these feelings on the part of the active and aggressive powers who use their strength in part to impose measure and restraint on the excesses of the reactive pathos, and to force a settlement. Wherever justice is exercised and maintained one sees a stronger power seeking means to end the senseless raging of the *ressentiment* of a weaker subordinate power (be it a group or an individual)—in part by removing the object of *ressentiment* from the hands of revenge, in part by substituting for revenge wars against the enemies of peace and order, in part by inventing, suggesting, and under some circumstances, requiring certain compensations, in part by establishing as the norm certain equivalences for injuries to which *ressentiment* is then directed.

The most decisive action taken by the higher power against the preponderance of hostility and vindictiveness—and it always does this as soon as it is strong enough—is the establishment of *law,* the imperative explanation of what is, in its eyes, allowed as just, and forbidden as unjust. After the establishment of the law, it handles attacks and capricious acts of individuals or groups as crimes against the law, as rebellion against the highest authority, thus diverting the feelings of its subjects away from the direct injury caused by the crime, and in the long run, accomplishing the reverse of what is desired by revenge, which only sees and admits the viewpoint of the injured party. From now on the eye becomes practiced in an increasingly *impersonal* evaluation of the deed—even the eye of the injured party (though this is the last development, as was already mentioned).

Thus understood, "just" and "unjust" have application only after the establishment of law (and *not,* as Duhring would have it, after the first experience of being injured). To speak of something as just or unjust *in itself* makes no sense; cases of injury, violence, exploitation, destruction can not be "unjust" *in themselves* insofar as life is *essentially*—that is, in its basic functions—injuring, violent, exploiting, and destructive, and simply can not be conceived without such characteristics. But one must admit something even more questionable: that from the highest biological viewpoint situations of justice can only be *exceptions;* as partial restrictions of the life-will, which is after power, they are subordinated as individual means to the total goal—that is, as means for the creation of ever larger units of power.

A legal structure thought of as universal and sovereign, not as a means in the fight between power-complexes, but as a means to *end* all fighting—something following Duhring's communist model with every will treating every other will as equal—would be a principle *hostile* to life, a destroyer and disintegrator of mankind, an assault on the future of man, a sign of exhaustion, a secret road to nothingness.

12

A further word on the origin and purpose of punishment—two problems which are, or ought to be, separate: unfortunately, they are rarely distinguished. How do our geneologists of morals handle things in this case? Naively, as usual: they discover some purpose or other in punishment, such as revenge or deterrence, then simply import this purpose into the beginning as the *causa fiendi*[11] of punishment—and they are finished with the matter. The "purpose of law," however, is the last thing that ought be used to gain enlightenment on the history of the origins of law: for all kinds of history, in fact, there is no more important proposition than the one that has been established only with great effort, but which really *ought to be* established—namely, that the origin of a thing and its eventual utility, its actual use and place in a system of purposes, have nothing to do with one another; that any already existing thing or state of affairs will always be interpreted by a superior power in line with new purposes, seized, transformed and redirected for new uses; that every happening in the organic world is a subjugation, *a mastering,* and that all subjugation and mastering yields a new interpretation, a new organization, in terms of which the previous "meaning" and "purpose" are necessarily obscured or totally obliterated.

When one has sufficiently understood the *utility* of any physiological organ (or of a legal institution, a social norm, a political custom, a style in the arts, or a religious ritual), one has so far understood nothing about its origin: as uncomfortable as this may sound to older ears— for it has always been imagined that the origin is understood in the manifest purpose of any thing, pattern, or institution—the eye is made for seeing, the hand for grasping. Thus it was supposed that punishment was invented for punishing. But all purposes, all utilities, are only *signs* that a will to power has conquered something less powerful and has imposed some function upon it. The whole history of a "thing," an organ, a custom, can be represented as a sign-chain of ever new interpretations and organizations whose causes need have no internal connection to each other—in some circumstances, on the contrary, one simply follows a previous one and takes its place.

The "evolution" of a thing, a custom, an organ, is thus in no way

---

11. Originating cause.

its *progressus* towards a goal, still less a rational and economical *progressus* involving the least expenditure of energy—but is rather the succession of more or less profound, more or less mutually independent processes of subjugation, plus the opposing forces of resistance, attempted transformations for the purpose of defense and reaction, and the results of successful counteractions. The form is fluid; the "meaning" even more so. It is the same even within the individual organism: with every essential growth of the whole, the "meaning" of the individual organ also changes. In some cases, a partial atrophy of an organ, or a decrease in the number of functioning organs (for instance, through the disappearance of the middle phalanges) can be an indication of growing strength and perfection. I would even say that the partial *loss of utility,* atrophy and degeneration, the deprivation of meaning and purpose—in short death—belongs to the conditions of a real *progressus,* which always appears in the form of a will and a way to *greater power* and is always achieved at the cost of countless weaker powers. The magnitude of any "progress" is even *measurable* by that which must be sacrificed to it; the whole of mankind sacrificed to the flourishing of a single *stronger* species of men—that *would be* a case of progress.

I emphasize this major viewpoint of historical method all the more because it runs counter to the prevailing temper of our times which would rather live with absolute chance, even with the mechanistic meaninglessness of all events, than with the theory of a *power-will* playing itself out in these events. The democratic idiosyncracy of hostility towards all that rules and wants to rule, this modern *misarchism* (to coin a bad word for a bad thing), has gradually insinuated itself into the realm of the spiritual, the most spiritual, and has masked itself so well there that today it is gradually creeping into the strictest and apparently most objective of the sciences, and is *allowed* to permeate them. It seems to me to be already the ruling overlord of the whole of physiology and the study of life, to their grave harm, as goes without saying, since it deprives them of their fundamental concept, that of a real *activity.* Under the influence of this idosyncrasy "adaptation" is pushed to the fore—that is, an activity of second rank, a pure reaction. Life itself has even been defined as an increasingly efficient internal adaptation to external circumstances (Herbert Spencer). But this is to misconstrue the essence of life, its *will to power,* and to overlook the essential priority of the spontaneous, attacking, aggressive, and form-giving strength which creates new interpertations and directions and whose effects "adaptation" only follows. This is to deny the governing role of the organism's highest functionaries in which the life-will appears active and form-giving. One should recall Huxley's approach to Spencer—Spencer's "administrative nihilism." But much more is at stake than "administration."

13

To return to the matter at hand—namely *punishment*—two different aspects should be distinguished: first,the relatively *enduring* aspect, the custom, the act, the "drama," a certain rigid sequence of procedures; and secondly, the *fluid* aspect, the meaning, the aim, the expectation which accompanies the execution of such procedures. In accord with the viewpoint of historical method already developed, it will be presupposed here that the procedure itself is something older and earlier than its use in punishing, that the latter was first *imported* and read into the procedure (which had existed for a long time, but with a different purpose). Thus it is *not* as our naive geneologists have assumed—that the procedures were *invented* for the purpose of punishing, as men once thought the hand was invented for the purpose of grasping.

Concerning that other aspect of punishment, the fluid element, the "meaning": in the later stages of culture (for instance in today's Europe), "punishment" no longer has a single meaning, but rather a whole synthesis of meanings. The whole history of punishment, the history of its utilization for the more diverse purposes, finally crystalizes into some kind of unity which is difficult to dissolve, difficult to analyze, and—one must emphasize this—totally and absolutely *impossible to define*. (Today it is impossible to say definitely *why* we punish. Every concept in which a whole process is semiotically condensed eludes definition; only that which has no history is definable.) At earlier stages, on the other hand, that synthesis of meanings was more easily dissoluble, and one can still perceive how the different elements of the synthesis changed their relative values in each separate case, re-ordering themselves so that first one and then another element rose to prominence and dominated at the expense of the others—sometimes one element (the aim of deterrence, for instance) even appears to eliminate all the others.

To give a minimal idea of the unstable, supplementary, and accidental nature of the "meaning" of punishment, of how one and the same procedure can be used, organized, and directed to basically different ends, I present here a schema developed on the basis of relatively limited and random materials. Punishment as a means of rendering someone harmless, of preventing further harm. Punishment as compensation to an injured party (including the compensation of certain affects). Punishment as isolation of a disturbance of equilibrium to prevent it from spreading. Punishment as a means for inspiring fear of those who define and execute the punishment. Punishment as a kind of repayment for the advantages which the criminal has enjoyed (for instance, when he is used as a slave in the mines). Punishment as the elimination of a degenerate element (sometimes of a whole line, as under Chinese law—thus as a means to preserve the purity of a race or the strength of a social type.) Punishment as a festival, as the violation and mockery of an enemy who has finally been defeated. Punishment as a means to create a memory—for the one who is punished, the so-called "reforming" of the criminal, or for the witnesses. Punishment as the payment of a fee set by the authority who protects the wrongdoer from the excesses of revenge. Punishment as a compromise with the natural state of revenge, insofar as the latter is still maintained by powerful groups and claimed as a privilege. Punishment as a declaration of war against an enemy of the peace, of law and order, of the authorities, who is fought with all the available means of war as a danger to the community, as a defaulter in relation to the basic conditions of its existence, as a rebel, a traitor, a breaker of the peace.

14

This list is certainly not complete; punishment is obviously overdetermined by utilities of all kinds. There is all the more reason then to discount one supposed utility, the essential one according to popular opinion, and the one from which the faith in punishment—tottering today for various reasons—still draws its strongest support. Punishment is supposed to awaken the *feeling of guilt* in the guilty person —one seeks in it the actual *instrumentum* of that psychic reaction known as the "bad conscience" or the "bite of conscience." But with this notion reality and psychology are radically misunderstood for today—and how much more so for the longest period of man's history, his prehistory! The real bite of conscience is very rare among criminals and those who have been punished. Prisons and houses of correction are *not* the breeding ground for this species of gnawing worm—there is agreement here among all conscientious observers, many of whom reach this kind of conclusion reluctantly enough and counter to their own wishes.

On the whole punishment hardens and makes one cold. It concentrates, it sharpens the feeling of alienation, and strengthens the power of resistance. When it does manage to destroy the energy and bring about a miserable prostration and self-abasement, the result is even less comforting than its usual effect which is characterized by a dry and gloomy seriousness.

Reflecting on those thousands of years *before* the beginning of history, one must conclude that the development of the feeling of guilt was most strongly retarded precisely by the practice of punishing—at least in relation to those on whom the punishing violence was vented. Let us not underestimate how much the criminal is prevented from experiencing his deed and his kind of behavior as objectionable *in itself* precisely by his view of the judicial and executive procedures. For he sees the very same kind of behavior used in the service of justice, and approved, used with a good conscience: thus spying, deception, bribery, entrapment, the whole intricate and cunning art of the police and the prosecutor, and then the robbery, subjugation, verbal abuse, imprisonment, torture, and murder which mark the different forms of punishment, practiced on principle without even the excuse of emotional involvement—none of these actions are condemned by the judges, or seen as objectionable in themselves, but only from a certain viewpoint, and when they have a certain use. The "bad conscience," this most sinister and interesting plant of our earthly vegetation, did *not* grow on this ground. In fact, for a long time, neither the one who judged, nor even the one who punished, was at all conscious of dealing with a "guilty" party, but only with an instigator of some harm, a non-responsible piece of fate. And the one on whom the punishment fell, again as a piece of fate, experienced no other "inner pain" than that of the sudden entry of something unexpected, of a terrible natural event, of a plunging, pulverizing boulder against which there was simply no fighting.

15

This thought came insidiously to Spinoza one afternoon (to the dismay of his interpreters who really *took pains* to misunderstand him on this point, for instance Kuno Fischer) as he became immersed in the question—provoked by, who knows, what kind of memory—of what was actually left for him of the famous *morsus conscientiae*[12] — he who had consigned good and evil to the realm of human imagination and had furiously defended the honor of his "free" God against the blasphemous claim that he did everything *sub ratione boni*[13] ("that

12. Bite of conscience.
13. For a good reason.

however would make God subject to fate and would certainly be the greatest of all absurdities"). The world for Spinoza had gone back to the state of innocence in which it lay before the invention of the bad conscience: what then had happened to the *morsus conscientiae?* "The opposite of *gaudium*"[14] he said finally—"A sadness, accompanied by an image of something from the past that has turned out counter to all expectations." (Eth. III, propos. XVIII, schol. I. II.)

For thousands of years, convicted offenders have felt *no differently* about their "transgressions" than did Spinoza: "something has unexpectedly gone wrong here,"*not* "I should not have done that." They submitted to punishment as one submits to an illness or a stroke of bad luck or to death—with that stouthearted fatalism without revolt in terms of which the Russians even today have the advantage over Westerners in the management of life. If anything criticized the deed in those days, it was prudence; we must unquestionably seek the actual *effect* of punishment in a sharpening of the sense of prudence, in an extended memory, in the resolve to be more careful, more secretive, and less trusting in the future, in the realization that one is simply too weak for many things, in a kind of improvement in self-criticism. The most that one can usually accomplish by punishing men or animals is an increase in fear, a sharpening of the sense of prudence, a mastery of avid desires. Thus punishment *tames* man, but it does not make him "better"—one could more reasonably claim the reverse. ("Injury makes one prudent" say the people: if it makes one prudent however, it also makes one bad. Luckily it often enough makes one stupid.)

16

At this point I can no longer avoid giving preliminary expression to my own hypothesis regarding the origin of the "bad conscience." It will not be heard easily, and needs to be thought about, lived with, and slept on for a long time. I view the bad conscience as the profound sickness to which man had to succumb under the pressure of the most fundamental of all the changes he had ever experienced—the change that took place when he finally found himself locked in by the restraints of society and the state of peace. As it happened with the water-animals when they were forced to become land-animals or to perish, so it was with these half-animals suited for the wilderness, for war, roaming, and adventure—suddenly all of their instincts were devalued and "unhinged." From now on they must go on foot and "carry themselves"

---

14. Joy.

where they were formerly carried by the water: a terrible heaviness fell over them. They felt clumsy performing the simplest task; in this new and unfamiliar world they had lost their old leaders, the regulating, unconscious, trustworthy instincts. They were reduced to thinking, inferring, calculating, thinking out cause and effect—these unlucky ones—reduced to consciousness, to their poorest and more fallible organ. Never on earth had there been such a feeling of misery and leaden discomfort—and the old instincts had not suddenly stopped making their demands. But it was difficult and rarely possible to satisfy them: in the main they had to seek new and, at the same time, underground means of gratification. All instincts that are not discharged outwardly *turn themselves inward*—this is what I call the *internalization* of man—and that which is later called the "soul" begins to grow. The whole inner world, originally as thin as if stretched between two membranes, dispersed and expanded, received depth, height, and breadth, precisely to the extent that the outward discharge of instincts was blocked. The terrible bulwarks with which societies have protected themselves against the old instincts of freedom—punishment above all belongs to these bulwarks—turned back all those instincts of the wild, free, roaming man, *against the man himself.* Hostility, cruelty, joy in persecution, in attack, in change, in destruction—all of this turned against the possessor of the instinct: that is the origin of the "bad conscience."

The man who was forced into the oppressive narrowness and uniformity of custom, who, from a lack of external enemies and resistance, impatiently tore himself apart, persecuted, disturbed, and mistreated himself; this animal who chafed himself on the bars of his cage, who was supposed to be "tamed"; this deprived one consumed by a homesickness for the wilderness, who had to make an adventure, a torture chamber, an uncertain and dangerous wilderness out of himself; this fool, this longing and despairing prisoner—he became the inventor of the "bad conscience." He ushered in that greatest and most sinister sickness from which mankind has not yet recovered—man became sick *of man, of himself*—as a consequence of a violent separation from his animal past, a leap and a plunge into new circumstances and new conditions of existence, a declaration of war against the old instincts which had been the source of his strength, joy, and fearfulness.

Let us immediately add that along with the animal soul turned against itself, siding against itself, something else so new, profound, unprecedented, puzzling, contradictory, and *pregnant with the future* appeared that the face of the earth was essentially changed. In fact, only divine spectators would be worthy of the spectacle which began here—the end of which is not yet in sight—a spectacle too subtle, too wonderful, too paradoxical to play itself out senselessly unnoticed on some laughable planet. Since that time man is to be counted among the most unexpected and exciting throws in the dice games of the "great child" of Heraclitus, called either Zeus or chance. He awakens an interest, a tension, a hope, almost a certainty, as if something announces itself in him, prepares itself, as if man were not a goal, but only a way, an episode, a bridge, a great promise.

17

The first presupposition of this hypothesis regarding the origin of the bad conscience is that the change was neither gradual nor voluntary, that it did not take place as an organic growth into new conditions, but as a break, a leap, a compulsion, an irresistable fate, against which there was no fighting, and not even any *ressentiment.* A second presupposition is that just as the binding together of a previously unbridled and unformed people into a stable form could begin only with an act of violence, it could be completed only with continuing acts of violence—thus that the earliest "state" began and continued as a terrible tyranny, as a crushing and ruthless machine, until the raw stuff of people and half-animals was not only kneaded and made flexible, but also *moulded.*

I used the word "state," but it is obvious what is intended here: a pack of blond beasts of prey, a conquering master-race, organized for war and possessing the strength to organize, lay its terrible claws on a formless, roaming, perhaps numerically superior people. This is how the "state" began on this earth: I think we have disposed of that nonsense about an original "contract." He who can command, who is "master" by nature, who appears forceful in action and manner—what would he want with contracts! One can not count on such beings; they arrive like fate, without cause, reason, consideration, excuse. They come like lightning, too terrible, sudden, forceful, too "different" even to be hated. Their work is an instinctive creation and imposition of form; they are the most involuntary and unconscious artist that there are—in short, something new begins where they appear, a governing organization that *lives,* limited and harmonious in its various parts and functions, in which nothing finds a place that does not first receive its "meaning" through its relation to the whole. They do not know the meaning of guilt, responsibility, or consideration—these born organizers. They are ruled by that terrible artist's egoism, which shines like bronze and knows itself to be justified to all eternity in its "work," like the mother in her child. These are not the ones in whom the bad conscience grew, that is obvious from the beginning—but that hateful growth would not have developed *without them,* without the force of their hammers, of their artistic violence which ran a tremendous quantum of freedom out of the world, or at least out of sight, at the same time making it *latent.* This *instinct for freedom* forcefully made latent —we have already grasped it—this instinct of freedom forced back and withdrawn, imprisoned in itself, and finally able to discharge and vent itself only on itself: that, and only that, is the *bad conscience* in its beginning.

<h2 style="text-align:center">18</h2>

One should guard against thinking too lightly of this phenomenon merely because it is painful and ugly from the beginning. Fundamentally it is the very same active force that is at work on a larger scale in those artists of domination and organizers who build states, that here —internal, smaller and less significant, and turned back toward the "labyrinth of the breast," to speak with Goethe—creates the bad conscience and builds negative ideals: that same *instinct for freedom* (or in my terms: the will to power). But in this case the matter on which the form-giving and violating nature of the force is vented is man himself, his whole animal self, and *not,* as in the greater and more conspicuous phenomenon, the *other* man, *other* men. This secret self-violation and artist's cruelty, this joy in giving form to onself, in burning a will, a critique, a contradition, a contempt, a No into a piece of heavy and suffering matter striving in contradictory directions, this sinister and horrendous work of a soul voluntarily divided against itself, which made itself suffer out of joy in causing suffering, this wholly *active* "bad conscience" finally brought to light—you will have guessed it already—as the actual womb of all ideal and imaginative phenomena, a whole world of new forms of beauty and affirmation— and perhaps *beauty* itself.—What would be "beautiful" if its opposite had not first become consicous, if the ugly had not first said to itself "I am ugly"?

This suggestion should at least make it seem less puzzling that such contradictory concepts as *selflessness, self-denial, self-sacrifice* could refer to something beautiful. One thing is immediately obvious—I do not doubt it for a minute—namely the kind of *joy* the selfless, self-denying, self-sacrificing man experienced from the beginning: this joy belongs to cruelty.—So much on the origin of the "unegoistic" as a *moral* value and about the ground from which it grew: only the bad conscience, the will to self-mistreatment, provides the pre-conditions for the *value* of the unegoistic.

19

The bad conscience is a sickness—there is no room for doubt here—but a sickness as pregnancy is a sickness. Let us seek out the conditions under which this sickness reached its most terrible and sublime peak—we shall see what actually accompanied it into the world. But one needs a long breath for that—and we must first of all return to an earlier viewpoint.

The civil-law relationship of a debtor to his creditor, of which we have spoken at length, was read into another relationship in an historically noteworthy and questionable way which may seem incomprehensible to us modern men: namely, into the relationship between living men and their ancestors. Within the original tribes—we are referring to prehistory—the living generation recognized a juridical duty to the earlier generations, and especially to the earliest generation, the founders of the tribe (and in no way was this simply a feeling of being obliged—there are reasons to discount the latter for the longest period of man's existence). The conviction is that the tribe *exists* at all only through the sacrifices and deeds of its ancestors—and that one has to *repay* them with sacrifices and deeds. Thus they recognized a *debt* that grew steadily as these ancestors in their existence as powerful spirits continued to provide advantages and protection for the community. Gratuitously? But there is nothing "gratuitous" for these crude and "poor in spirit" ages. How can one repay them? Offerings (originally for food, in the crudest sense), festivals, choirs, indications of respect, and above all, obedience—for all customs are, as the work of the ancestors, also their rules and commands—but, is all this enough? This suspicion always remains, and continues to increase, forcing from time to time a wholesale discharging, some kind of monstrous repayment to the creditor (the infamous sacrifice of the first-born, for instance; blood, human blood, in any case). The *fear* of the ancestor and his power, the consciousness of indebtedness to him, necessarily increases, following this kind of logic, in proportion to the increase in the power of the tribe, as it becomes increasingly victorious, independent, honored and feared. Not the reverse! Every step towards the demise of the tribe, every unhappy accident, all signs of degeneration and approaching dissolution, always *decrease* the fear of the tribe's founder and leave a decreased impression of his prudence, providence, and power.

If this kind of logic is thought through to the end, it must be concluded that the ancestors of the most powerful tribe would grow to monstrous proportions through the phantasies of growing fear, and would be pushed back into the darkness of the divinely sinister and unrepresentable—until the ancestors are eventually transfigured into gods. Perhaps this is the origin of gods—out of fear. And whoever finds it necessary to add "but also out of piety" would hardly be right for the longest period of human history, its prehistory. He would certainly be more correct for the middle part of human history when the noble tribes were developing—in fact, they returned to their founders, their ancestors (heroes, gods), with interest, all of the qualities that had in the meantime become visible in themselves: the noble qualities. We will return to the ennobling of the gods (which is absolutely not their hallowing); let us now follow the development of the sense of indebtedness to its conclusion.

20

The consciousness of being in debt to the gods did not come to an end with the decline of the blood-related community. In the same way that mankind had inherited the notions of "good and bad" from the noble tribes (together with the basic psychological inclination to establish an order of rank), it also inherited, together with the familial and tribal gods, the pressure of the still unpaid debts, and the demand to discharge them. (The transition was made by the large population of slaves and serfs who adapted themselves to the god-cults of their masters, either through force or subservience and mimicry). The feeling of indebtedness to the gods continued to grow for several millennia, and always in the same measure that the idea of god, and the feeling for the divine grew on earth and was carried to the heights. (The whole history of the ethnic fights, reconciliations, amalgamations —all that precedes the rank-ordering of the different peoples in every great race synthesis—was mirrored in the geneological confusion of the gods, in the tales of their fights, victories, and reconciliations; the road to a universal empire is always the road to a universal god-head. Despotism with its overpowering of the independent nobility paves the way for some form of monotheism.) The rise of the Christian God, the maximization of the idea of a god, was accompanied by the maximum feeling of indebtedness on earth. Assuming that we are now involved in a *reversal* of that movement, one might conclude from the irresistible decline of faith in the Christian God that there is already a considerable decrease in the human consciousness of guilt. We can not discount the view that the complete and final victory of atheism would free mankind from this whole feeling of indebtedness to its origins, its *causa prima.* Atheism and a kind of *second innocence* belong together.

21

So much for these rough and summary remarks on the connection between "guilt" and "duty" and their religious presuppositions: I have deliberately left aside the active moralization of these ideas (their pushing back into conscience, or, more precisely, the involvement of the *bad* conscience with the idea of God), and at the end of the last paragraph, I even spoke as if this moralization had not occurred, and consequently as if these ideas would be disposed of as soon as their presupposition, the faith in our "creditor," in God, is destroyed. The actual facts present a far different picture. The moralization of the ideas of guilt and duty, their pushing back into the *bad* conscience, is actually an attempt to reverse the direction of the development described above, or at least to bring the movement to a standstill. The prospect of a final discharge *shall* now be pessimistically blocked forever, the gaze *shall* now desolately recoil from a brazen impossibility, the ideas of "guilt" and "duty" *shall* now be turned back—against whom then? There can be no doubt: primarily against the "debtor" in whom the bad conscience will now establish itself, eating into and expanding itself, growing like a polyp in all directions until along with the irredeemability of guilt, the impossibility of atonement, the idea of the unpayable ("eternal punishment") is conceptualized. Finally, however, it is even turned back on the "creditor"; here one thinks of the *causa prima* of mankind, the beginnings of the human race, the original ancestor burdened with a curse ("Adam," "original sin," the "bondage of the will"), or of nature, from which man comes and in which he now locates the evil principle (the "diabolization of nature"), or of existence itself, which now becomes the *worthless in itself* (nihilistic withdrawal, desire for the nothingness, or for the "opposite" of what exists, Buddhism and the like)—until we are suddenly standing before the paradoxical and horrible expediency in which tortured mankind found a temporary alleviation, *Christianity's* stroke of genius: God sacrificing himself for the guilt of man, God making reparation to himself, God as the only one who can discharge what mankind cannot discharge, the creditor sacrificing himself for his debtor, out of *love* (is that credible?), out of love for his debtor!

22

One will have already guessed what has actually gone on here: that will to self-torture, that suppressed cruelty of the animal-man who now has an interior, who is afraid of himself and imprisoned in the "state" for purposes of taming, who invented the bad conscience in order to hurt himself after the *more natural* channel for his desire to hurt was blocked—this man of the bad conscience seized upon the religious presuppositions in order to drive his self-torture to its most gruesome harshness and intensity. Guilt before *God:* this thought becomes an instrument of his torture. In "God" he grasps the ultimate contradiction to his own irredeemable animal instincts; he reinterprets these instincts as guilt before God (as hostility, resistence, and rebellion against the "master," the "father," the original ancestor and founder of the world); he tears himself apart on the contradiction "God" and "Satan"; he vomits all his rejection of himself, nature, naturalness, the reality of his own being, out of himself as an affirmation, as something existent, bodily, real, as God, the holiness of God, the judgment of God, the punishment of God, as the beyond, as eternity, as unending torment, as Hell, as the immeasurability of punishment and guilt.

This is a kind of madness of the will in the realm of psychic cruelty which is simply unparalleled: man's *will* to find himself guilty and reprehensible to an inexpiable degree; his *will* to think that no amount of punishment could ever provide compensation for his guilt; his *will* to infect and poison the deepest ground of being with the problem of guilt and punishment in order to eternally block his escape from this labyrinth of "fixed ideas"; his *will* to erect an ideal—that of the "holy God"—and to have in the face of this ideal the manifest certainty of his own worthlessness. Oh this insane and miserable beast—man! What ideas occur to him, what perversions, what paroxyms of insanity, what *bestiality in idea* break out in him when he is prevented from being a *beast in deed.*

All this is of great interest, but it also produces such a black, gloomy, and enervating melancholy that one must forbid oneself to look into this abyss for very long. This is *sickness,* there is no doubt, the most terrible sickness that has ever raged in man—and whoever is capable of hearing (but men no longer have ears for it today) the cry of *love* sounded in the night of torture and insanity, the cry of the passionate rapture, of redemption in *love,* will turn away seized by an unconquerable horror. There is so much that is horrible in man!—The earth has been a madhouse for too long.

23

So much for the origin of the "holy God."

That the conception of gods *in itself* need not lead to this degeneration of the imagination, the brief presentation of which we could not
avoid, that there are more noble purposes for inventing gods than this
self-crucifixion and self-violation of man in which Europe has been a
master for the last few millenia—this can be gathered from a glance
at the *Greek gods,* those reflections of noble and self-mastering men
in whom the *animal* in man felt itself deified and did not rip itself apart
and rage against itself! These Greeks used their gods for the longest
time precisely to keep the "bad conscience" at a distance, in order to
be able to enjoy their freedom of soul: thus, this was the reverse of the
use Christianity made of its God.

They went *very far* in this, these magnificent and lionhearted fools,
and no less an authority than Homer's Zeus let them know here and
there that they took the matter too lightly. "Strange" he once said—
it concerned the case of Agisthos, a very bad case—

> Strange that these mortals complain so loudly of the gods!
> *Evil comes only from us,* they think; but they themselves
> through folly create their own misery, even against fate

But one sees and hears that even this Olympic spectator and judge is
far from being angry with them or thinking ill of them: "How foolish
they are," he thinks as he sees the misdeeds of mortals—and even the
Greeks of the strongest and most courageous period allowed themselves "foolishness," "lack of sense," a little "disturbance in the head"
as the cause of many terrible and fatal deeds. Foolishness, *not* sin! Is
that understood?

Even this disturbance in the head was a problem, however: "how is
it even possible? how could it have happened to heads like ours, to men
of noble birth, of good fortune, of the best society, of nobility, of
virtue?" Thus the noble Greek questioned himself for centuries in the
face of every incomprehensible outrage and crime with which someone
of his kind had contaminated himself. "He must have been deceived
by a *god,"* he finally says to himself shaking his head—this way out is
typical for the Greeks. In this way the gods in those days served to
justify man and, to a certain extent, his evil—they served as the causes
of evil. In those days they took upon themselves not the punishment,
but what is more noble: the guilt.

24

I conclude with three question marks, as is obvious. "Are you erecting an ideal here, or destroying one?"—you might ask me.—But have you ever asked yourself how much it cost to erect *every* ideal on this earth? How much reality had to be slandered and falsified, how many lies sanctified, how much conscience disturbed, how much "god" had to be sacrificed each time? In order to erect a temple, a *temple must be destroyed:* that is the law—show me a case where this is not so!

We modern men are the heirs of the conscience vivisection and self-torture of millenia: in this we have our longest practice, our artistry perhaps, in any case our refined and overindulged taste. Man has much too long regarded his natural inclinations with an "evil eye," so that they are now always connected with the "bad conscience." It would be possible to attempt the reverse—but who is strong enough for it?—namely to associate the bad conscience with all the unnatural inclinations: all those aspirations to the beyond and against the senses, the instincts, the natural, the animal—in short, with all the ideals we have had so far, all of which slander the world and are enemies of life. To whom does one turn today with *such* hopes and demands?

In this one would have precisely the *good* men against him, and, of course, the comfortable, the reconciled, the vain, the fanatical, the exhausted. What insults more deeply, what separates more fundamentally, than to allow others to notice something of the strictness and loftiness with which one treats oneself? And on the other hand—what kindness and love all the world shows us as soon as we act like all the world and "let ourselves go" like all the world!

That goal would require a *different* kind of spirit than we can expect to find in our age: spirits strengthened by war and victory, for whom conquest, adventure, danger, and even pain have become necessities. This would require becoming accustomed to sharp high air, to winter wanderings, to ice and mountains in every sense; it would require a kind of sublime malice, an ultimate, self-assured, mischievousness of knowledge, which belongs to great health—it requires, briefly and unfortunately enough, precisely this *great health.*—Is this even possible today?

But somewhere, in an age stronger than our decaying and self-doubting present, he must come to us, the *redeeming* man of the great love and contempt, the creating spirit, whose pressing strength drives him away from all "beyonds" and "aparts," whose solitude will be misunderstood as if it were a flight from reality—when it is actually his plunge, his penetration, and immersion *into* reality, so that, upon returning, he is able to bring *redemption* to this reality, its redemption from the curse with which our present ideal has burdened it. This man of the future who will redeem us from this ideal and from *that which had to grow out of it,* the great disgust, the will to nothingness, nihilism—this stroke of noon and of the great decision, who will make the will free again, and will give back to the earth its goal, and to man his hopes, this anti-christ, and anti-nihilist, this conqueror of God and nothingness—*he must come one day.*

25

But what am I saying? Enough! Enough! Only silence seems appropriate here: otherwise I would appropriate that which belongs only to someone younger and "of the future," someone stronger than I—which belongs only to *Zarathustra, Zarathustra the godless.*

8. The Death of God and the Eternal Recurrence

I

The Madman. Have you not heard of that madman who lit a lantern in the bright morning hours, ran to the market place, and cried incessantly, "I seek God! I seek God!" As many of those who do not believe in God were standing around just then, he provoked much laughter. Why, did he get lost? said one. Did he lose his way like a child? said another. Or is he hiding? Is he afraid of us? Has he gone on a voyage? or emigrated? Thus they yelled and laughed. The madman jumped into their midst and pierced them with his glances.

"Whither is God" he cried. "I shall tell you. *We have killed him*— you and I. All of us are his murderers. But how have we done this? How were we able to drink up the sea? Who gave us the sponge to wipe away the entire horizon? What did we do when we unchained this earth from its sun? Whither is it moving now? Whither are we moving now? Away from all suns? Are we not plunging continually? Backward, sideward, forward, in all directions? Is there any up or down left? Are we not straying as through an infinite nothing? Do we not feel the breath of

From *The Portable Nietzsche* edited and translated by Walter Kaufmann. Copyright 1954 by The Viking Press Inc. Reprinted by permission of The Viking Press, Inc. Part I is Section 125 of *The Gay Science;* part II is excerpted from the Third Part of *Thus Spoke Zarathrustra.* Title supplied by the editors.

empty space? Has it not become colder? Is not night and more night coming on all the while? Must not lanterns be lit in the morning? Do we not hear anything yet of the noise of the gravediggers who are burying God? Do we not smell anything yet of God's decomposition? Gods too decompose. God is dead. God remains dead. And we have killed him. How shall we, the murderers of all murderers, comfort ourselves? What was holiest and most powerful of all that the world has yet owned has bled to death under our knives. Who will wipe this blood off us? What water is there for us to clean ourselves? What festivals of atonement, what sacred games shall we have to invent? Is not the greatness of this deed too great for us? Must not we ourselves become gods simply to seem worthy of it? There has never been a greater deed; and whoever will be born after us—for the sake of this deed he will be part of a higher history than all history hitherto."

Here the madman fell silent and looked again at his listeners; and they too were silent and stared at him in astonishment. At last he threw his lantern on the ground, and it broke and went out. "I come too early," he said then; "my time has not come yet. This tremendous event is still on its way, still wandering—it has not yet reached the ears of man. Lightning and thunder require time, the light of the stars requires time, deeds require time even after they are done, before they can be seen and heard. This deed is still more distant from them than the most distant stars—*and yet they have done it themselves.*"

It has been related further that on that same day the madman entered divers churches and there sang his *requiem aeternam deo.* Led out and called to account, he is said to have replied each time, "What are these churches now if they are not the tombs and sepulchers of God?"

II

The greatest stress. How, if some day or night a demon were to sneak after you into your loneliest loneliness and say to you, "This life as you now live it and have lived it, you will have to live once more and innumerable times more; and there will be nothing new in it, but every pain and every joy and every thought and sigh and everything immeasurably small or great in your life must return to you—all in the same succession and sequence—even this spider and this moonlight between the trees, and even this moment and I myself. The eternal hourglass of existence is turned over and over, and you with it, a dust grain of dust." Would you not throw yourself down and gnash your teeth and curse the demon who spoke thus? Or did you once experience a tremendous moment when you would have answered him, "You are a god, and never have I heard anything more godly." If this thought were to gain possession of you, it would change you, as you are, or perhaps crush you. The question in each and every thing, "Do you want this once more and innumerable times more?" would weigh upon your actions as the greatest stress. Or how well disposed would you have to become to yourself and to life to *crave nothing more fervently* than this ultimate eternal confirmation and seal?

The Convalescent

1

One morning, not long after his return to the cave, Zarathustra jumped up from his resting place like a madman, roared in a terrible voice, and acted as if somebody else were still lying on his resting place who refused to get up. And Zarathustra's voice resounded so that his animals approached in a fright, while out of all the caves and nooks that were near Zarathustra's cave all animals fled—flying, fluttering, crawling, jumping, according to the kind of feet or wings that were given to them. Zarathustra, however, spoke these words:

Up, abysmal thought, out of my depth! I am your cock and dawn, sleepy worm. Up! Up! My voice shall yet crow you awake! Unfasten the fetters of your ears: listen! For I want to hear you. Up! Up! Here is thunder enough to make even tombs learn to listen. And wipe sleep and all that is purblind and blind out of your eyes! Listen to me even with your eyes: my voice cures even those born blind. And once you are awake, you shall remain awake eternally. It is not my way to awaken great-grandmothers from their sleep to bid them sleep on!

You are stirring, stretching, wheezing? Up! Up! You shall not wheeze but speak to me. Zarathustra, the godless, summons you! I, Zarathustra, the advocate of life, the advocate of suffering, the advocate of the circle; I summon you, my most abysmal thought!

Hail to me! You are coming, I hear you. My abyss speaks, I have turned my ultimate depth inside out into the light. Hail to me! Come here! Give me your hand! Huh! Let go! Huhhuh! Nausea, nausea, nausea—woe unto me!

2

No sooner had Zarathustra spoken these words than he fell down as one dead and long remained as one dead. But when he regained his senses he was pale, and he trembled and remained lying there, and for a long time he wanted neither food nor drink. This behavior lasted seven days; but his animals did not leave him by day or night, except that the eagle flew off to get food. And whatever prey he got together, he laid on Zarathustra's resting place; and eventually Zarathustra lay among yellow and red berries, grapes, rose apples, fragrant herbs, and pine cones. But at his feet two lambs lay spread out which the eagle had with difficulty robbed from their shepherds.

At last, after seven days, Zarathustra raised himself on his resting place, took a rose apple into his hand, smelled it, and found its fragrance lovely. Then his animals thought that the time had come to speak to him.

"O Zarathustra," they said, "it is now seven days that you have been lying like this with heavy eyes; won't you at last get up on your feet again? Step out of your cave: the world awaits you like a garden. The wind is playing with heavy fragrances that want to get to you, and all the brooks would run after you. All things have been longing for you, while you have remained alone for seven days. Step out of your cave! All things would be your physicians. Has perhaps some new knowledge come to you, bitter and hard? Like leavened dough you have been lying; your soul rose and swelled over all its rims."

"O my animals," replied Zarathustra, "chatter on like this and let me listen. It is so refreshing for me to hear you chattering: where there is chattering, there the world lies before me like a garden. How lovely it is that there are words and sounds! Are not words and sounds rainbows and illusive bridges between things which are eternally apart?

"To every soul there belongs another world; for every soul, every other soul is an afterworld. Precisely between what is most similar, illusion lies most beautifully; for the smallest cleft is the hardest to bridge.

"For me—how should there be any outside-myself? There is no outside. But all sounds make us forget this; how lovely it is that we forget. Have not names and sounds been given to things that man might find things refreshing? Speaking is a beautiful folly: with that man dances over all things. How lovely is all talking, and all the deception of sounds! With sounds our love dances on many-hued rainbows."

"O Zarathustra," the animals said, "to those who think as we do, all things themselves are dancing: they come and offer their hands and laugh and flee—and come back. Everything goes, everything comes back; eternally rolls the wheel of being. Everything dies, everything blossoms again; eternally runs the year of being. Everything breaks, everything is joined anew; eternally the same house of being is built. Everything parts, everything greets every other thing again; eternally the ring of being remains faithful to itself. In every Now, being begins; round every Here rolls the sphere There. The center is everywhere. Bent is the path of eternity."

"O you buffoons and barrel organs!" Zarathustra replied and smiled again. "How well you know what had to be fulfilled in seven days, and how that monster crawled down my throat and suffocated me. But I bit off its head and spewed it out. And you, have you already made a hurdy-gurdy song of this? But now I lie here, still weary of this biting and spewing, still sick from my own redemption. *And you watched all this?* O my animals, are even you cruel? Did you want to watch my great pain as men do? For man is the cruelest animal.

"At tragedies, bullfights, and crucifixions he has so far felt best on earth; and when he invented hell for himself, behold, that was his heaven on earth.

"When the great man screams, the small man comes running with his tongue hanging from lasciviousness. But he calls it his 'pity.'

"The small man, especially the poet—how eagerly he accuses life with words! Hear him, but do not fail to hear the delight that is in all accusation. Such accusers of life—life overcomes with a wink. 'Do you love me? she says impudently. 'Wait a little while, just yet I have no time for you.'

"Man is the cruelest animal against himself; and whenever he calls himself 'sinner' and 'cross-bearer' and 'penitent,' do not fail to hear the voluptuous delight that is in all such lamentation and accusation.

"And I myself—do I thus want to be man's accuser? Alas, my animals, only this have I learned so far, that man needs what is most evil in him for what is best in him—that whatever is most evil is his best power and the hardest stone for the highest creator; and that man must become better and more evil.

"My torture was not the knowledge that man is evil—but I cried as no one has yet cried: 'Alas, that his greatest evil is so very small! Alas, that his best is so very small!'

"The great disgust with man—*this* choked me and had crawled into my throat; and what the soothsayer said: 'All is the same, nothing is worth while, knowledge chokes.' A long twilight limped before me, a sadness, weary to death, drunken with death, speaking with a yawning mouth. 'Eternally recurs the man of whom you are weary, the small man'—thus yawned my sadness and dragged its feet and could not go to sleep. Man's earth turned into a cave for me, its chest sunken; all that is living became human mold and bones and musty past to me. My sighing sat on all human tombs and could no longer get up; my sighing and questioning croaked and gagged and gnawed and wailed by day and night: 'Alas, man recurs eternally! The small man recurs eternally!'

"Naked I had once seen both, the greatest man and the smallest man: all-too-similar to each other, even the greatest all-too-human. All-too-small, the greatest!—that was my disgust with man. And the eternal recurrence even of the smallest—that was my disgust with all existence. Alas! Nausea! Nausea! Nausea!"

Thus spoke Zarathustra and sighed and shuddered, for he remembered his sickness. But then his animals would not let him go on.

"Do not speak on, O Convalescent!" thus his animals answered him; "but go out where the world awaits you like a garden. Go out to the roses and bees and dove-cots. But especially to the songbirds, that you may learn from them how to sing! For singing is for the convalescent; the healthy can speak. And when the healthy man also wants songs, he wants different songs from the convalescent."

"O you buffoons and barrel organs, be silent!" Zarathustra replied and smiled at his animals. "How well you know what comfort I invented for myself in seven days! That I must sing again, this comfort and convalescence I invented for myself. Must you immediately turn this too into a hurdy-gurdy song?"

"Do not speak on!" his animals answered him again; "rather even, O convalescent, fashion yourself a lyre first, a new lyre! For behold, Zarathustra, new lyres are needed for your new songs. Sing and overflow, O Zarathustra; cure your soul with new songs that you may bear your great destiny, which has never yet been any man's destiny. For your animals know well, O Zarathustra, who you are and must become: behold, *you are the teacher of the eternal recurrence*—that is your destiny! That you as the first must teach this doctrine—how could this great destiny not be your greatest danger and sickness too?

"Behold, we know what you teach: that all things recur eternally, and we ourselves too; and that we have already existed an eternal number of times, and all things with us. You teach that there is a great year of becoming, a monster of a great year, which must, like an hourglass, turn over again and again so that it may run down and run out again; and all these years are alike in what is greatest as in what is smallest; and we ourselves are alike in every great year, in what is greatest as in what is smallest.

"And if you wanted to die now, O Zarathustra, behold, we also know how you would then speak to yourself. But your animals beg you not to die yet. You would speak, without trembling but breathing deeply

with happiness, for a great weight and sultriness would be taken from
you who are most patient.

" 'Now I die and vanish,' you would say, 'and all at once I am
nothing. The soul is as mortal as the body. But the knot of causes in
which I am entangled recurs and will create me again. I myself belong
to the causes of the eternal recurrence. I come again, with this sun with
this earth, with this eagle, with this serpent—*not* to a new life or a
better life or a similar life: I come back eternally to this same, selfsame
life, in what is greatest as in what is smallest, to teach again the eternal
recurrence of all things, to speak again the word of the great noon of
earth and man, to proclaim the overman again to men. I spoke my
word, I break of my word: thus my eternal lot wants it; as a proclaimer
I perish. The hour has now come when he who goes under should bless
himself. Thus *ends* Zarathustra's going under.' "

When the animals had spoken these words they were silent and
waited for Zarathustra to say something to them; but Zarathustra did
not hear that they were silent. Rather he lay still with his eyes closed,
like one sleeping, although he was not asleep; for he was conversing
with his soul. The serpent, however, and the eagle, when they found
him thus silent, honored the great stillness around him and cautiously
stole away.

9.   My Religion

I have lived in the world for fifty-five years, and, with the exception of fourteen or fifteen years of my childhood, have passed thirty-five years as a nihilist in the full sense of the word, that is, not as a socialist and revolutionist, as which this word is generally understood, but as a nihilist in the sense of an absence of every faith.

Five years ago I came to believe in Christ's teaching, and my life suddenly became changed: I ceased desiring what I had wished before, and began to desire what I had not wished before. What formerly had seemed good to me, appeared bad, and what had seemed bad, appeared good. What took place with me was what takes place with a man who goes out on some business and suddenly decides on his way that he does not need that business, and returns home. And everything which was on the right is now on the left, and what was on the left is now on the right: the former desire—to be as far as possible away from the house—is now changed to a desire to be as close as possible to it. The direction of my life, my desires, became different: what was good and bad changed places. All this was due to the fact that I came to

---

Reprinted from Leo Tolstoy, *My Religion, The Complete Works of Count Tolstoy,* Vol. XVI, trans. Leo Wiener, (Boston: Dana Estes & Co., 1904), introduction and part I.

understand Christ's teaching differently from what I had understood it before.

I do not mean to interpret Christ's teaching, but want to tell only how I came to understand what simple, clear, intelligible, indubitable, universally accessible qualities Christ's teaching possessed, and how that which I now understood upturned my soul and gave me peace and happiness.

I do not wish to interpret Christ's teaching; the one thing I want is to prevent men from interpreting it.

All the Christian churches have always acknowledged that all men, who are not equal in learning and reason,—the wise and the foolish, —are equal before God, that the divine truth is accessible to all. Even Christ said that it is the will of God that what is hidden from the wise be revealed to the unwise.

Not all men can be initiated into the deepest secrets of dogmatics, homiletics, patristics, liturgics, hermeneutics, apologetics, and so forth, but all men can and ought to understand what Christ has told all the millions of simple, unwise men who have lived since his day. So it is this, which Christ told those simple people, who had not yet had the chance of turning to Paul, to Clement, to Chrysostom, and to others, for the elucidations of his teaching, that I had not understood before and came to understand then: and it is this that I wish to communicate to all men.

The robber on the cross believed in Christ, and was saved. Would it really have been bad and harmful for any man, if the robber had not died on the cross, but had come down from it, and had told all men how he came to believe in Christ?

Even so I, like the robber on the cross, believed in Christ, and was saved. This is not a far-fetched comparison, but a very close approximation to that spiritual condition of despair and terror before life and death, in which I was formerly, and of that condition of peace and happiness, in which I now am.

Like the robber, I knew that I lived badly, that the majority of men around me lived as badly. Like the robber, I knew that I was unhappy and suffered, and that around me men were as unhappy and suffered as much, and saw no way out, except death, from this condition. Like the robber on the cross, I was nailed by some power to this life of suffering and of evil.

And as for the robber there was in store the terrible darkness of death after senseless sufferings and the evil of life, so also the same was in store for me.

In all this I was precisely like the robber, but there was this difference between the robber and me, that he was already dead, while I was still living. The robber could believe that his salvation would be there, beyond the grave: but I could not believe that, for besides the life beyond the grave, I still had to live here. And I did not understand this life. It seemed terrible to me. Suddenly I heard Christ's words, and I understood them, and life and death no longer appeared to me as an evil, and instead of despair I experienced the joy and happiness of life, which are not impaired by death.

Can it really harm any one, if I tell how this happened with me?

I have written two large works, the Critique of Dogmatic Theology, and a new translation and harmonization of the four gospels with explanations, in which I explain why I had not comprehended Christ's teaching, and how I came to understand it. In these works I try methodically, step by step, to analyze everything which conceals the truth from men, and verse after verse translate anew, collate, and harmonize the four gospels.

This work has been going on for six years. Every year, every month, I find new explanations and confirmations of the fundamental idea, correct the mistakes which have crept in through hurry and overzeal, and add to what has been done. My life, of which not much is left, will, no doubt, be ended before this work. But I am convinced that this labour is needed, and so I do what I can, while I live.

Such has my assiduous external work been on the theology, on the gospels. But the internal work, of which I wish to tell here, was different. It was not a methodical investigation of the theology and texts of the gospels, but a sudden removal of everything which concealed the very meaning of the teaching, and a sudden illumination by the light of truth. It was an event which was like what would happen to a man who from a false drawing tries to reconstruct a statue out of a heap of small pieces of marble, when suddenly he discovers from one insignificant piece that it is an entirely different statue, and, having begun the new reconstruction, suddenly sees the confirmation of his idea, instead of the former incoherency of the fragments, in every piece, which with all its lines combines with the neighbouring pieces and forms one whole. It was this that happened with me. And of this I wish to tell.

I want to tell how I found this key for the comprehension of the teaching of Christ, who revealed to me the truth with a clearness and a conclusiveness that exclude every doubt.

This discovery was made by me in the following manner: ever since the first period of my childhood, when I began to read the Gospel for myself, I was most touched and affected by that teaching of Christ, where he preaches love, meekness, humility, self-renunciation, and retribution of evil with good. Such always remained for me the essence of the Christian teaching, and I loved it with my heart, and in the name of it I, after despair and unbelief, recognized as true the meaning which the labouring people ascribe to the Christian life, and in the name of it I subjected myself to the beliefs which these people confess, that is to the Orthodox Church.

But, in submitting to the church, I soon observed that I should not find in the church doctrine the confirmation and elucidation of those principles of Christianity which to me seemed to be of greatest importance: I observed that this essence of Christianity, which was so dear to me, did not form the chief point in the church doctrine. I observed that that which to me seemed to be of most importance in Christ's teaching was not regarded as such by the church. The church regarded something else as of greatest importance. At first I did not ascribe any meaning to this peculiarity of the church teaching.

Well, I thought, in addition to the meaning of love, humility, self-renunciation, the church recognizes also the dogmatic, the external meaning. This meaning is foreign to me, even repels me, but there is nothing harmful in it.

But the longer I lived, submitting to the church doctrine, the more obvious it became to me that this peculiarity of the church doctrine was not so immaterial as it had seemed to me to be at first. What repelled me from the church was the strangeness of the church dogmas, and the recognition and approval given by the church to persecutions, capital punishment, and wars, and the mutual rejection of the various creeds; but what shattered my confidence in it was that indifference to what to me seemed to be the essence of Christ's teaching and the bias for what I regarded as inessential. But I could not make out what was wrong; I could not make it out, because the church doctrine, far from denying that which to me seemed to be of prime importance in Christ's teaching, fully recognized it, but it did so in such a way that what was of prime importance in Christ's teaching did not occupy the first place. I could not rebuke the church for denying the essential things, but the church recognized them in such a way that they did not satisfy me. The church did not give me what I expected from it.

I passed from nihilism to the church only because I was conscious of the impossibility of living without faith, without the knowledge of what is good and what bad, in spite of my animal instincts. I hoped to find this knowledge in Christianity. But Christianity, as it presented itself to me at that time, was only a certain, very indefinite mood, from which did not result clear and obligatory rules of life. I turned to the church for these rules. But the church gave me such rules as did not in the least bring me nearer to the Christian mood, which was so dear to me, and only removed me farther from it, and I could not follow it. The life which was based on the Christian truths was necessary and dear to me; but the church gave me rules of life which were entirely foreign to the truths which I valued so highly. I did not need the rules which the church gave me about the belief in dogmas, about the observance of sacraments, fasts, and prayers, and there were none that were based on the Christian truths. Moreover, the church rules weakened, and at times destroyed outright, that Christian mood, which alone gave me the meaning of my life. What troubled me more than anything else was that all the human evil—the condemnation of private individuals, of whole nations, of other creeds, and the executions and wars, which resulted from such condemnations—was all justified by the church. Christ's teaching about meekness, about refraining from condemnations, about forgiveness of offences, self-renunciation, and love, was exalted by the church in words, and yet, in fact, that which was incompatible with this teaching was justified by it.

Could it be that Christ's teaching was such that these contradictions ought to exist? I could not believe it. Besides, it had always seemed strange to me that, in so far as I knew the Gospel, those passages on which the definite rules of the church about the dogmas were based were the most obscure of all, while those from which resulted the execution of the teaching were most definite and clear. And yet, the dogmas and the obligations of a Christian which result from them were defined by the church in a most clear and precise manner; while the execution of the teaching was mentioned by it in most obscure, hazy, mystical terms.

Is it possible Christ had that in mind, when he imparted his teaching to men? The solution of my doubts I could find only in the gospels, and I read and re-read them. Out of all the gospels the sermon on the mount always stood out as something special, and I read it oftenest of all. Nowhere else does Christ speak with such solemnity as in this place; nowhere else does he give so many moral, clear, intelligible rules, which reëcho at once in the hearts of all men; nowhere does he speak to a greater assembly of all kinds of simple people. If there existed clear, definite Christian rules, they must be expressed here. In these three chapters of Matthew I tried to find an explanation of what troubled me. Many, many a time did I read the sermon on the mount, and every time I experienced the same feelings of enthusiasm and meekness of spirit, as I read the verses about offering the cheek, giving up the coat, making peace with all men, and loving our enemies, and the same feeling of dissatisfaction. The words of God, which were directed to all men, were not clear. There was demanded a too impossible renunciation of everything, which destroyed life itself, as I understood it, and so the renunciation of everything, I thought, could not be a peremptory condition of salvation. And as long as it was not a peremptory condition of salvation, there was nothing definite and clear.

I read not only the sermon on the mount, but also all the gospels and all the theological commentaries upon them. The theological explanations, that the utterances of the sermon on the mount were an indication of that perfection toward which man must strive, but that the fallen man was abiding in sin and could not with his powers attain this perfection, and that man's salvation was in faith, prayer, and grace, did not satisfy me.

I could not agree to this, because it had always seemed strange to me why Christ, who knew in advance that the execution of his teaching was impossible with the human powers alone, gave such clear and beautiful rules, which had reference directly to every individual man. As I read these rules, it seemed to me that they had special reference to me and demanded that I, if no one else, should execute them.

As I read these rules, I was always overcome by the joyful certainty that I could henceforth, from that very hour, do all that. I wanted and tried to do it; but the moment I experienced a struggle in the execution, I involuntarily recalled the teaching of the church that man is weak and cannot do it of himself, and I weakened.

I was told that we must believe and pray.

But I felt that I had little faith, and so could not pray. I was told that I must pray so that God might give me faith, that faith which gives prayer, which gives that faith, which gives that prayer, and so on, *ad infinitum.*

But reason and experience showed me that only my efforts to carry out Christ's teaching could be real: and so, after many, many vain searchings and studies of what had been written in proof of the divinity of this teaching and in proof of its un-divinity, after many doubts and sufferings, I was again left alone with my heart and with the mysterious book before me. I could not give it the meaning which others ascribed to it, and could find no other meaning for it, and yet could not reject it. And only after I had lost faith in all the interpretations of both the learned criticism and the learned theology, and had rejected them all, according to Christ's saying, If you receive me not as do the children, you will not enter into the kingdom of God, did I suddenly understand what I had not understood before. I did not understand because I in some way artificially and cunningly transposed, collated, interpreted;

on the contrary, everything was revealed to me because I forgot all interpretations. The passage which for me was the key to the whole was Verses 38 and 39 of the fifth chapter of Matthew. It hath been said, An eye for an eye, and a tooth for a tooth: but I say unto you, That ye resist not evil. I suddenly for the first time understood the last verse in its direct and simple meaning. I understood that Christ said precisely what he said. And immediately, not something new appeared, but there disappeared that which obscured the truth, and truth arose before me in all its significance. Ye have heard that it hath been said, An eye for an eye, and a tooth for a tooth: but I say, Do not resist evil. These words suddenly appeared entirely new to me, as though I had never met them before.

Formerly, when I read this passage, I always, by some strange blindness, omitted the words, But I say, Do not resist evil. It was as though these words did not exist, or had no definite meaning.

Later I frequently had occasion in my conversations with many, very many Christians, who knew the Gospel, to observe the same blindness in respect to these words. Nobody remembered these words, and often, when talking about this passage, Christians would take up the Gospel in order to assure themselves that the words were there. Similarly I used to omit the words, and began to understand only from the next words on, But whosoever shall smite thee on thy right cheek, turn to him, etc. And these words always presented themselves to me as a demand for sufferings and privations which are not proper to human nature. These words affected me, and I felt that it would be nice to fulfil them. At the same time I felt that I should never be able to fulfil them, merely to suffer. I said to myself, Very well, I will turn my other cheek to a man, and he will strike me a second time; I will give them what they ask of me, and they will take everything from me. I shall have no life. Life is given to me, why should I deprive myself of it? Christ could not have asked for this.

Formerly I used to say that to myself, imagining that in these words Christ praised sufferings and privations, and, praising them, was speaking in exaggeration and so without precision or clearness; but now that I came to understand the saying about non-resistance to evil, it became clear to me that Christ did not exaggerate at all and did not demand any suffering for the sake of suffering, but meant very definitely and clearly what he said.

He said, Do not resist evil; and doing so, remember that there will be found people who, having struck you on one cheek and finding no resistance, will strike you on the other also; having taken your coat, will take your cloak also; having made use of your labour, will compel you to work more; who will take without returning. And when this happens, you must still not resist evil. Continue to do good to those who will strike and offend you.

And when I comprehended these words, in the manner in which they were said, everything which had been dark became clear, and what had seemed exaggerated became entirely clear. I understood for the first time that the centre of gravity of the whole thought was in the words, Do not resist evil, and that what follows is only an explanation of the first proposition. I understood that Christ does not at all command us to offer our cheek and give up our coat in order that we may suffer, but commands us not to resist evil, and says that, in doing so, we may also have to suffer. Just as a father, sending his son out on a long journey, does not order him to stay awake nights, go without eating, be drenched, and freeze, when he says, Travel on the road, and even if you are to be drenched and frozen, keep to the road,—so Christ does not say, Offer your cheek, suffer, but, Do not resist evil, and no matter what may happen to you, do not resist evil.

These words, Do not resist evil, understood in their direct sense, were for me indeed the key that opened everything to me, and I marvelled how I could have so perverted the clear, definite words. You have been told, A tooth for a tooth, and I say, Do not resist evil, and no matter what evil persons may do to you, suffer, give up, but do not resist evil. What can be clearer, more intelligible, and more indubitable than this? I needed only to understand these words in a simple and direct manner, just as they were said, and everything in Christ's teaching, not merely in the sermon on the mount, but in all the gospels, everything which had been tangled, became clear; what had been contradictory became concordant; and, above all else, what had seemed superfluous became necessary. Everything welded into one whole and each thing indubitably confirmed everthing else, as pieces of a broken statue, when they are recomposed as they ought to be. In this sermon and in all the gospels the same teaching of non-resistance to evil was confirmed on all sides.

In this sermon, as in all other passages, Christ represents to himself his disciples, that is, the men who carry out the rule of non-resistance to evil, not otherwise than men who offer their cheek and give up their cloak, as persecuted, beaten, and poor.

Christ says again and again that he who has not taken the cross, who has not renounced everything, that is, he who is not prepared for all the consequences arising from the execution of the rule of non-resistance to evil, cannot be his disciple. To his disciples Jesus says, Be mendicants; be prepared, while not resisting evil, to receive persecutions, suffering, and death: he prepares himself for suffering and death, without resisting the evil men, and sends away Peter, who is sorry about it, and dies himself, forbidding men to resist evil, and without becoming untrue to his teaching.

All his first disciples carry out this rule of non-resistance, and pass all their life in poverty and persecutions, and never repay evil with evil.

Consequently Jesus says exactly what he says. We may affirm that the constant execution of this rule is very difficult; we may not agree with this, that every man will be blessed in carrying out this rule; we may say that it is foolish, as the unbelievers say, that Christ was a dreamer and idealist, who uttered impracticable rules, which his disciples in their foolishness carried out; but we cannot fail to admit that Christ very clearly and definitely said what he wanted to say, namely, that man, according to his teaching, must not resist evil, and that, therefore, he who has accepted his teaching cannot resist evil. And yet neither believers, nor unbelievers, understand this simple and clear meaning of Christ's words.

10. The Boundaries of Religious Experience

Most books on the philosophy of religion try to begin with a precise definition of what its essence consists of. Some of these would-be definitions may possibly come before us in later portions of this course, and I shall not be pedantic enough to enumerate any of them to you now. Meanwhile the very fact that they are so many and so different from one another is enough to prove that the word 'religion' cannot stand for any single principle or essence, but is rather a collective name. The theorizing mind tends always to the oversimplification of its materials. This is the root of all that absolutism and one-sided dogmatism by which both philosophy and religion have been infested. Let us not fall immediately into a one-sided view of our subject, but let us rather admit freely at the outset that we may very likely find no one essence, but many characters which may alternately be equally important in religion. If we should inquire for the essence of 'government,' for example, one man might tell us it was authority, another submission, another police, another an army, another an assembly, another a system of laws; yet all the while it would be true that no concrete government can exist without all these things, one of which is more important at one moment and others at another. The man who

---

Reprinted from William James, *The Varieties of Religious Experience* (New York: Longmans Green, 1902), lecture II. Title supplied by the editors.

knows goverments most completely is he who troubles himself least about a definition which shall give their essence. Enjoying an intimate acquaintance with all their particularities in turn, he would naturally regard an abstract conception in which these were unified as a thing more misleading than enlightening. And why may not religion be a conception equally complex?[1]

Consider also the 'religious sentiment' which we see referred to in so many books, as if it were a single sort of mental entity.

In the psychologies and in the philosophies of religion, we find the authors attempting to specify just what entity it is. One man allies it to the feeling of dependence; one makes it a derivative from fear; others connect it with the sexual life; others still identify it with the feeling of the infinite; and so on. Such different ways of conceiving it ought of themselves to arouse doubt as to whether it possibly can be one specific thing; and the moment we are willing to treat the term 'religious sentiment' as a collective name for the many sentiments which religious objects may arouse in alternation, we see that it probably contains nothing whatever of a psychologically specific nature. There is religious fear, religious love, religious awe, religious joy, and so forth. But religious love is only man's natural emotion of love directed to a religious object; religious fear is only the ordinary fear of commerce, so to speak, the common quaking of the human breast, in so far as the notion of divine retribution may arouse it; religious awe is the same organic thrill which we feel in a forest at twilight, or in a mountain gorge; only this time it comes over us at the thought of our supernatural relations; and similarly of all the various sentiments which may be called into play in the lives of religious persons. As concrete states of mind, made up of a feeling *plus* a specific sort of object, religious emotions of course are psychic entities distinguishable from other concrete emotions; but there is no ground for assuming a simple abstract 'religious emotion' to exist as a distinct elementary mental affection by itself, present in ever religious experience without exception.

As there thus seems to be no one elementary religious emotion, but only a common storehouse of emotions upon which religious objects may draw, so there might conceivably also prove to be no one specific and essential kind of religious object, and no one specific and essential kind of religious act.

---

1. I can do no better here than refer my readers to the extended and admirable remarks on the futility of all these definitions of religion, in an article by Professor Leuba, published in the Monist for January, 1901, after my own text was written.

The field of religion being as wide as this, it is manifestly impossible that I should pretend to cover it. My lectures must be limited to a fraction of the subject. And, although it would indeed be foolish to set up an abstract definition of religion's essence, and then proceed to defend that definition against all comers, yet this need not prevent me from taking my own narrow view of what religion shall consist in *for the purpose of these lectures,* or, out of the many meanings of the word, from choosing the one meaning in which I wish to interest you particularly, and proclaiming arbitrarily that when I say 'religion' I mean *that.* This, in fact, is what I must do, and I will now preliminarily seek to mark out the field I choose.

One way to mark it out easily is to say what aspects of the subject we leave out. At the outset we are struck by one great partition which divides the religious field. On the one side of it lies institutional, on the other personal religion. As M. P. Sabatier says, one branch of religion keeps the divinity, another keeps man most in view. Worship and sacrifice, procedures for working on the dispositions of the deity, theology and ceremony and ecclesiastical organization, are the essentials of religion in the institutional branch. Were we to limit our view to it, we should have to define religion as an external art, the art of winning the favor of the gods. In the more personal branch of religion it is on the contrary the inner dispositions of man himself which form the centre of interest, his conscience, his deserts, his helplessness, his incompleteness. And although the favor of the God, as forfeited or gained, is still an essential feature of the story, and theology plays a vital part therein, yet the acts to which this sort of religion prompts are personal not ritual acts, the individual transacts the business by himself alone, and the ecclesiastical organization, with its priests and sacraments and other go-betweens, sinks to an altogether secondary place. The relation goes direct from heart to heart, from soul to soul, between man and his maker.

Now in these lectures I propose to ignore the institutional branch entirely, to say nothing of the ecclesiastical organization, to consider as little as possible the systematic theology and the ideas about the gods themselves, and to confine myself as far as I can to personal religion pure and simple. To some of you personal religion, thus nakedly considered, will no doubt seem too incomplete a thing to wear the general name. "It is a part of religion," you will say, "but only its unorganized rudiment; if we are to name it by itself, we had better call it man's conscience or morality than his religion. The name 'religion' should be reserved for the fully organized system of feeling, thought, and institution, for the Church, in short, of which this personal religion, so called, is but a fractional element."

But if you say this, it will only show the more plainly how much the question of definition tends to become a dispute about names. Rather than prolong such a dispute, I am willing to accept almost any name for the personal religion of which I propose to treat. Call it conscience or morality, if you yourselves prefer, and not religion—under either name it will be equally worthy of our study. As for myself, I think it will prove to contain some elements which morality pure and simple does not contain, and these elements I shall soon seek to point out; so I will myself continue to apply the word 'religion' to it; and in the last lecture of all, I will bring in the theologies and the ecclesiasticisms, and say something of its relation to them.

In one sense at least the personal religion will prove itself more fundamental than either theology or ecclesiasticism. Churches, when once established, live at second-hand upon tradition; but the *founders* of every church owed their power originally to the fact of their direct personal communion with the divine. Not only the superhuman founders, the Christ, the Buddha, Mahomet, but all the originators of Christian sects have been in this case;—so personal religion should still seem the primordial thing, even to those who continue to esteem it incomplete.

There are, it is true, other things in religion chronologically more primordial than personal devoutness in the moral sense. Fetishism and magic seem to have preceded inward piety historically—at least our records of inward piety do not reach back so far. And if fetishism and magic be regarded as stages of religion, one may say that personal religion in the inward sense and the genuinely spiritual ecclesiasticisms which it founds are phenomena of secondary or even tertiary order. But, quite apart from the fact that many anthropologists—for instance, Jevons and Frazer—expressly oppose 'religion' and 'magic' to each other, it is certain that the whole system of thought which leads to magic, fetishism, and the lower superstitions may just as well be called primitive science as called primitive religion. The question thus becomes a verbal one again; and our knowledge of all these early stages of thought and feeling is in any case so conjectural and imperfect that farther discussion would not be worth while.

Religion, therefore, as I now ask you arbitrarily to take it, shall mean for us *the feelings, acts, and experiences of individual men in their solitude, so far as they apprehend themselves to stand in relation to whatever they may consider the divine.* Since the relation may be either moral, physical, or ritual, it is evident that out of religion in the sense in which we take it, theologies, philosophies, and ecclesiastical organizations may secondarily grow. In these lectures, however, as I have already said, the immediate personal experiences will amply fill our time, and we shall hardly consider theology or ecclesiasticism at all.

We escape much controversial matter by this arbitrary definition of our field. But, still, a chance of controversy comes up over the word 'divine,' if we take it in the definition in too narrow a sense. There are systems of thought which the world usually calls religious, and yet which do not positively assume a God. Buddhism is in this case. Popularly, of course, the Buddha himself stands in place of a God; but in strictness the Buddhistic system is atheistic. Modern transcendental idealism, Emersonianism, for instance, also seems to let God evaporate into abstract Ideality. Not a deity *in concreto,* not a superhuman person, but the immanent divinity in things, the essentially spiritual structure of the universe, is the object of the transcendentalist cult. In that address to the graduating class at Divinity College in 1838 which made Emerson famous, the frank expression of this worship of mere abstract laws was what made the scandal of the performance.

"These laws," said the speaker, "execute themselves. They are out of time out of space, and not subject to circumstance: Thus, in the soul of man there is a justice whose retributions are instant and entire. He who does a good deed is instantly ennobled. He who does a mean deed is by the action itself contracted. He who puts off impurity thereby puts on purity. If a man is at heart just, then in so far is he God; the safety of God, the immortality of God, the majesty of God, do enter into that man with justice. If a man dissemble, deceive, he deceives himself, and goes out of acquaintance with his own being. Character is always known. Thefts never enrich; alms never impoverish; murder will speak out of stone walls. The least admixture of a lie—for example, the taint of vanity, any attempt to make a good impression, a favorable appearance—will instantly vitiate the effect. But speak the truth, and all things alive or brute are vouchers, and the very roots of the grass underground there do seem to stir and move to bear your witness. For all things proceed out of the same spirit, which is differently named love, justice, temperance, in its different applications, just as the ocean receives different names on the several shores which it washes. In so far as he roves from these ends, a man bereaves himself of power, of auxiliaries. His being shrinks . . . he becomes less and less, a mote, a point, until absolute badness is absolute death. The perception of this law awakens in the mind a sentiment which we call the religious sentiment, and which makes our highest happiness. Wonderful is its power to charm and to command. It is a mountain air. It is the embalmer of the world. It makes the sky and the hills sublime, and the silent song of the stars is it. It is the beatitude of man. It makes him illimitable. When he says 'I ought'; when love warns him; when he chooses, warned from on high, the good and great deed; then, deep melodies wander through his soul from supreme wisdom. Then he can worship, and be enlarged by his worship; for he can never go behind this sentiment. All the expressions of this sentiment are sacred and permanent in proportion to their purity. [They] affect us more than all other compositions. The sentences of the olden time, which ejaculate this piety, are still fresh and fragrant. And the unique impression of Jesus upon mankind, whose name is not so much written as ploughed into the history of this world, is proof of the subtle virtue of this infusion."[2]

Such is the Emersonian religion. The universe has a divine soul of order, which soul is moral, being also the soul within the soul of man. But whether this soul of the universe be a mere quality like the eye's brilliancy or the skin's softness, or whether it be a self-conscious life like the eye's seeing or the skin's feeling, is a decision that never unmistakably appears in Emerson's pages. It quivers on the boundary of these things, sometimes leaning one way, sometimes the other, to suit the literary rather than the philosophic need. Whatever it is, though, it is active. As much as if it were a God, we can trust it to protect all ideal interests and keep the world's balance straight. The sentences in which Emerson, to the very end, gave utterance to this faith are as fine as anything in literature: "If you love and serve men, you cannot by any hiding or stratagem escape the remuneration. Secret retributions are always restoring the level, when disturbed, of the divine justice. It is impossible to tilt the beam. All the tyrants and proprietors and monopolists of the world in vain set their shoulders to heave the bar. Settles forevermore the ponderous equator to its line, and man and mote, and star and sun, must range to it, or be pulverized by the recoil."[3]

Now it would be too absurd to say that the inner experiences that underlie such expressions of faith as this and impel the writer to their utterance are quite unworthy to be called religious experiences. The sort of appeal that Emersonian optimism, on the one hand, and Buddhistic pessimism, on the other, make to the individual and the sort of response which he makes to them in his life are in fact indistinguishable from, and in many respects identical with, the best Christian appeal and response. We must therefore, from the experiential point of view, call these godless or quasi-godless creeds 'religions'; and accordingly

2. *Miscellanies,* 1868, p. 120 (abridged).
3. Lectures and Biographical Sketches, 1868, p. 186.

when in our definition of religion we speak of the individual's relation to 'what he considers the divine,' we must interpret the term 'divine' very broadly, as denoting any object that is god*like*, whether it be a concrete deity or not.

But the term 'godlike,' if thus treated as a floating general quality, becomes exceedingly vague, for many gods have flourished in religious history, and their attributes have been discrepant enough. What then is that essentially godlike quality—be it embodied in a concrete deity or not—our relation to which determines our character as religious men? It will repay us to seek some answer to this question before we proceed farther.

For one thing, gods are conceived to be first things in the way of being and power. They overarch and envelop, and from them there is no escape. What relates to them is the first and last word in the way of truth. Whatever then were most primal and enveloping and deeply true might at this rate be treated as godlike, and a man's religion might thus be identified with his attitude, whatever it might be, towards what he felt to be the primal truth.

Such a definition as this would in a way be defensible. Religion, whatever it is, is a man's total reaction upon life, so why not say that any total reaction upon life is a religion? Total reactions are different from casual reactions, and total attitudes are different from usual or professional attitudes. To get at them you must go behind the foreground of existence and reach down to that curious sense of the whole residual cosmos as an everlasting presence, intimate or alien, terrible or amusing, lovable or odious, which in some degree every one possesses. This sense of the world's presence, appealing as it does to our peculiar individual temperament, makes us either strenuous or careless, devout or blasphemous, gloomy or exultant, about life at large; and our reaction, involuntary and inarticulate and often half unconscious as it is, is the completest of all our answers to the question, "What is the character of this universe in which we dwell?" It expresses our individual sense of it in the most definite way. Why then not call these reactions our religion, no matter what specific character they may have? Non-religious as some of these reactions may be, in one sense of the word 'religious,' they yet belong to *the general sphere of the religious life,* and so should generically be classed as religious reactions. "He believes in No-God, and he worships him," said a colleague of mine of a student who was manifesting a fine atheistic ardor; and the more fervent opponents of Christian doctrine have often enough shown a temper which, psychologically considered, is indistinguishable from religious zeal.

But so very broad a use of the word 'religion' would be inconvenient, however defensible it might remain on logical grounds. There are trifling, sneering attitudes even towards the whole of life; and in some men these attitudes are final and systematic. It would strain the ordinary use of language too much to call such attitudes religious, even though, from the point of view of an unbiased critical philosophy, they might conceivably be perfectly reasonable ways of looking upon life. Voltaire, for example, writes thus to a friend, at the age of seventy-three: "As for myself," he says, "weak as I am, I carry on the war to the last moment. I get a hundred pike-thrusts, I return two hundred, and I laugh. I see near my door Geneva on fire with quarrels over nothing, and I laugh again; and, thank God, I can look upon the world as a farce even when it becomes as tragic as it sometimes does. All comes out even at the end of the day, and all comes out still more even when all the days are over."

Much as we may admire such a robust old gamecock spirit in a valetudinarian, to call it a religious spirit would be odd. Yet it is for the moment Voltaire's reaction on the whole of life. *Je m'en fiche* is the vulgar French equivalent for our English ejaculation 'Who cares?' And the happy term *je m'en fichisme* recently has been invented to designate the systematic determination not to take anything in life too solemnly. 'All is vanity' is the relieving word in all difficult crises for this mode of thought, which that exquisite literary genius Renan took pleasure, in his later days of sweet decay, in putting into coquettishly sacrilegious forms which remain to us as excellent expressions of the 'all is vanity' state of mind. Take the following passage, for example, —we must hold to duty, even against the evidence, Renan says,—but he then goes on:—

> "There are many chances that the world may be nothing but a fairy pantomime of which no God has care. We must therefore arrange ourselves so that on neither hypothesis we shall be completely wrong. We must listen to the superior voices, but in such a way that if the second hypothesis were true we should not have been too completely duped. If in effect the world be not a serious thing, it is the dogmatic people who will be the shallow ones, and the worldly minded whom the theologians now call frivolous will be those who are really wise.

> *"In utrumque paratus,* then. Be ready for anything—that perhaps is wisdom. Give ourselves up, according to the hour, to confidence, to skepticism, to optimism, to irony, and we may be sure that at certain moments at least we shall be with the truth. . . . Good-humor

is a philosophic state of mind; it seems to say to Nature that we take her no more seriously than she takes us. I maintain that one should always talk of philosophy with a smile. We owe it to the Eternal to be virtuous; but we have the right to add to this tribute our irony as a sort of personal reprisal. In this way we return to the right quarter jest for jest; we play the trick that has been played on us. Saint Augustine's phrase: *Lord, if we are deceived, it is by thee!* remains a fine one, well suited to our modern feeling. Only we wish the Eternal to know that if we accept the fraud, we accept it knowingly and willingly. We are resigned in advance to losing the interest on our investments of virtue, but we wish not to appear ridiculous by having counted on them too securely."[4]

Surely all the usual associations of the word 'religion' would have to be stripped away if such a systematic *parti pris* of irony were also to be denoted by the name. For common men 'religion,' whatever more special meanings it may have, signifies always a *serious* state of mind. If any one phrase could gather its universal message, that phrase would be, "All is *not* vanity in this Universe, whatever the appearances may suggest.' If it can stop anything, religion as commonly apprehended can stop just such chaffing talk as Renan's. It favors gravity, not pertness; it says 'hush' to all vain chatter and smart wit.

But if hostile to light irony, religion is equally hostile to heavy grumbling and complaint. The world appears tragic enough in some religions, but the tragedy is realized as purging, and a way of deliverance is held to exist. We shall see enough of the religious melancholy in a future lecture; but melancholy, according to our ordinary use of language, forfeits all title to be called religious when, in Marcus Aurelius's racy words, the sufferer simply lies kicking and screaming after the fashion of a sacrificed pig. The mood of a Schopenhauer or a Nietzsche,—and in a less degree one may sometimes say the same of our own sad Carlyle,—though often an ennobling sadness, is almost as often only peevishness running away with the bit between its teeth. The sallies of the two German authors remind one, half the time, of the sick shriekings of two dying rats. They lack the purgatorial note which religious sadness gives forth.

There must be something solemn, serious, and tender about any attitude which we denominate religious. If glad, it must not grin or snicker; if sad, it must not scream or curse. It is precisely as being *solemn* experiences that I wish to interest you in religious experiences.

4. *Feuilles détachées*, pp. 394–398 (abridged).

So I propose—arbitrarily again, if you please—to narrow our definition once more by saying that the word 'divine,' as employed therein, shall mean for us not merely the primal and enveloping and real, for that meaning if taken without restriction might well prove too broad. The divine shall mean for us only such a primal reality as the individual feels impelled to respond to solemnly and gravely, and neither by a curse nor a jest.

But solemnity, and gravity, and all such emotional attributes, admit of various shades; and, do what we will with our defining, the truth must at last be confronted that we are dealing with a field of experience where there is not a single conception that can be sharply drawn. The pretension, under such conditions, to be rigorously 'scientific' or 'exact' in our terms would only stamp us as lacking in understanding of our task. Things are more or less divine, states of mind are more or less religious, reactions are more or less total, but the boundaries are always misty, and it is everwhere a question of amount and degree. Nevertheless, at their extreme of development, there can never be any question as to what experiences are religious. The divinity of the object and the solemnity of the reaction are too well marked for doubt. Hesitation as to whether a state of mind is 'religious,' or 'irreligious,' or 'moral,' or 'philosophical,' is only likely to arise when the state of mind is weakly characterized, but in that case it will be hardly worthy of our study at all. With states that can only by courtesy be called religious we need have nothing to do, our only profitable business being with what nobody can possibly feel tempted to call anything else. I said in my former lecture that we learn most about a thing when we view it under a microscope, as it were, or in its most exaggerated form. This is as true of religious phenomena as of any other kind of fact. The only cases likely to be profitable enough to repay our attention will therefore be cases where the religious spirit is unmistakable and extreme. Its fainter manifestations we may tranquilly pass by. Here, for example, is the total reaction upon life of Frederick Locker Lampson, whose autobiography, entitled 'Confidences,' proves him to have been a most amiable man.

> "I am so far resigned to my lot that I feel small pain at the thought of having to part from what has been called the pleasant habit of existence, the sweet fable of life. I would not care to live my wasted life over again, and so to prolong my span. Strange to say, I have but little wish to be younger. I submit with a chill at my heart. I humbly submit because it is the Divine Will, and my appointed destiny. I dread the increase of infirmities that will make me a burden to those around me, those dear to me. No! let me slip away

as quietly and comfortably as I can. Let the end come, if peace come with it.

"I do not know that there is a great deal to be said for this world, or our sojourn here upon it; but it has pleased God so to place us, and it must please me also. I ask you, what is human life? Is not it a maimed happiness—care and weariness, weariness and care, with the baseless expectation, the strange cozenage of a brigher to-mor-row? At best it is but a froward child, that must be played with and humored, to keep it quiet till it falls asleep, and then the care is over."[5]

This is a complex, a tender, a submissive, and a graceful state of mind. For myself, I should have no objection to calling it on the whole a religious state of mind, although I dare say that to many of you it may seem too listless and half-hearted to merit so good a name. But what matters it in the end whether we call such a state of mind religious or not? It is too insignificant for our instruction in any case; and its very possessor wrote it down in terms which he would not have used unless he had been thinking of more energetically religious moods in others, with which he found himself unable to compete. It is with these more energetic states that our sole business lies, and we can perfectly well afford to let the minor notes and the uncertain border go.

It was the extremer cases that I had in mind a little while ago when I said that personal religion, even without theology or ritual, would prove to embody some elements that morality pure and simple does not contain. You may remember that I promised shortly to point out what those elements were. In a general way I can now say what I had in mind.

"I accept the universe" is reported to have been a favorite utterance of our New England transcendentalist, Margaret Fuller; and when some one repeated this phrase to Thomas Carlyle, his sardonic comment is said to have been: "Gad! she'd better!" At bottom the whole concern of both morality and religion is with the manner of our acceptance of the universe. Do we accept it only in part and grudgingly, or heartily and altogether? Shall our protests against certain things in it be radical and unforgiving, or shall we think that, even with evil, there are ways of living that must lead to good? If we accept the whole, shall we do so as if stunned into submission,—as Carlyle would have us— "Gad! we'd better!"—or shall we do so with enthusiastic assent? Mo-rality pure and simple accepts the law of the whole which it finds

5. Op. cit., pp. 314,313.

reigning, so far as to acknowledge and obey it, but it may obey it with the heaviest and coldest heart, and never cease to feel it as a yoke. But for religion, in its strong and fully developed manifestations, the service of the highest never is felt as a yoke. Dull submission is left far behind, and a mood of welcome, which may fill any place on the scale between cheerful serenity and enthusiastic gladness, has taken its place.

It makes a tremendous emotional and practical difference to one whether one accept the universe in the drab discolored way of stoic resignation to necessity, or with the passionate happiness of Christian saints. The difference is as great as that between passivity and activity, as that between the defensive and the aggressive mood. Gradual as are the steps by which an individual may grow from one state into the other, many as are the intermediate stages which different individuals represent, yet when you place the typical extremes beside each other for comparison, you feel that two discontinuous psychological universes confront you, and that in passing from one to the other a 'critical point' has been overcome.

If we compare stoic with Christian ejaculations we see much more than a difference of doctrine; rather is it a difference of emotional mood that parts them. When Marcus Aurelius reflects on the eternal reason that has ordered things, there is a frosty chill about his words which you rarely find in a Jewish, and never in a Christian piece of religious writing. The universe is 'accepted' by all these writers; but how devoid of passion or exultation the spirit of the Roman Emperor is! Compare his fine sentence: "If gods care not for me or my children, here is a reason for it," with Job's cry: "Though he slay me, yet will I trust in him!" and you immediately see the difference I mean. The *anima mundi,* to whose disposal of his own personal destiny the Stoic consents, is there to be respected and submitted to, but the Christian God is there to be loved; and the difference of emotional atmosphere is like that between an arctic climate and the tropics, though the outcome in the way of accepting actual conditions uncomplainingly may seem in abstract terms to be much the same.

> "It is a man's duty," says Marcus Aurelius, "to comfort himself and wait for the natural dissolution, and not to be vexed, but to find refreshment solely in these thoughts—first that nothing will happen to me which is not conformable to the nature of the universe; and secondly that I need do nothing contrary to the God and deity within me; for there is no man who can compel me to transgress."[6]

---

6. Book V., ch. x. (abridged).

He is an abscess on the universe who withdraws and separates himself from the reason of our common nature, through being displeased with the things which happen. For the same nature produces these; and has produced thee too. And so accept everything which happens, even if it seem disagreeable, because it leads to this, the health of the universe and to the prosperity and felicity of Zeus. For he would not have brought on any man what he has brought, if it were not useful for the whole. The integrity of the whole is mutilated if thou cuttest off anything. And thou dost cut off, as far as it is in thy power, when thou art dissatisfied, and in a manner triest to put anything out of the way."[7]

Compare now this mood with that of the old Christian author of the Theologia Germanica:—

"Where men are enlightened with the true light, they renounce all desire and choice, and commit and commend themselves and all things to the eternal Goodness, so that every enlightened man could say: 'I would fain be to the Eternal Goodness what his own hand is to a man.' Such men are in a state of freedom, because they have lost the fear of pain or hell, and the hope of reward or heaven, and are living in pure submission to the eternal Goodness, in the perfect freedom of fervent love. When a man truly perceiveth and considereth himself, who and what he is, and findeth himself utterly vile and wicked and unworthy, he falleth into such a deep abasement that it seemeth to him reasonable that all creatures in heaven and earth should rise up against him. And therefore he will not and dare not desire any consolation and release; but he is willing to be unconsoled and unreleased; and he doth not grieve over his sufferings, for they are right in his eyes, and he hath nothing to say against them. This is what is meant by true repentance for sin; and he who in this present time entereth into this hell, none may console him. Now God hath not forsaken a man in this hell, but He is laying his hand upon him, that the man may not desire nor regard anything but the eternal Good only. And then, when the man neither careth for nor desireth anything but the eternal Good alone, and seeketh not himself nor his own things, but the honour of God only, he is made a partaker of all manner of joy, bliss, peace, rest, and consolation, and so the man is henceforth in the kingdom of heaven. This hell and this heaven are two good safe ways for a man, and happy is he who truly findeth them."[8]

---

7. Book V., ch. ix. (abridged).
8. Chaps. x., xi. (abridged): Winkworth's translation.

How much more active and positive the impulse of the Christian writer to accept his place in the universe is! Marcus Aurelius agrees *to* the scheme—the German theologian agrees *with* it. He literally *abounds* in agreement, he runs out to embrace the divine decrees.

Occasionally, it is true, the Stoic rises to something like a Christian warmth of sentiment, as in the often quoted passage of Marcus Aurelius:—

> "Everything harmonizes with me which is harmonious to thee, O Universe. Nothing for me is too early nor too late, which is in due time for thee. Everthing is fruit to me which thy seasons bring, O Nature: from thee are all things, in thee are all things, to thee all things return. The poet says, Dear City of Cecrops; and wilt thou not say, Dear City of Zeus?"[9]

But compare even as devout a passage as this with a genuine Christian outpouring, and it seems a little cold. Turn, for instance, to the Imitation of Christ:—

> "Lord, thou knowest what is best; let this or that be according as thou wilt. Give what thou wilt, so much as thou wilt, when thou wilt. Do with me as thou knowest best, and as shall be most to thine honour. Place me where thou wilt, and freely work thy will with me in all things. . . . When could it be evil when thou wert near? I had rather be poor for thy sake than rich without thee. I choose rather to be a pilgrim upon the earth with thee, than without thee to possess heaven. Where thou art, there is heaven; and where thou art not, behold there death and hell."[10]

It is a good rule in physiology, when we are studying the meaning of an organ, to ask after its most peculiar and characteristic sort of performance, and to seek its office in that one of its functions which no other organ can possibly exert. Surely the same maxim holds good in our present quest. The essence of religious experiences, the thing by which we finally must judge them, must be that element or quality in them which we can meet nowhere else. And such a quality will be of course most prominent and easy to notice in those religious experiences which are most one-sided, exaggerated, and intense.

---

9. Book IV., §23.

10. Benham's translation: Book III., chaps. xv., lix. Compare Mary Moody Emerson: "Let me be a blot on this fair world, the obscurest, the loneliest sufferer, with one proviso,—that I know it is His agency. I will love Him though He shed frost and darkness on every way of mine." R. W. Emerson: *Lectures and Biographical Sketches,* p. 188.

Now when we compare these intenser experiences with the experiences of tamer minds, so cool and reasonable that we are tempted to call them philosophical rather than religious, we find a character that is perfectly distinct. That character, it seems to me, should be regarded as the practically important *differentia* of religion for our purpose; and just what it is can easily be brought out by comparing the mind of an abstractly conceived Christian with that of a moralist similarly conceived.

A life is manly, stoical, moral, or philosophical, we say, in proportion as it is less swayed by paltry personal considerations and more by objective ends that call for energy, even though that energy bring personal loss and pain. This is the good side of war, in so far as it calls for 'volunteers.' And for morality life is a war, and the service of the highest is a sort of cosmic patriotism which also calls for volunteers. Even a sick man, unable to be militant outwardly, can carry on the moral warfare. He can willfully turn his attention away from his own future, whether in this world or the next. He can train himself to indifference to his present drawbacks and immerse himself in whatever objective interests still remain accessible. He can follow public news, and sympathize with other people's affairs. He can cultivate cheerful manners, and be silent about his miseries. He can contemplate whatever ideal aspects of existence his philosophy is able to present to him, and practice whatever duties, such as patience, resignation, trust, his ethical system requires. Such a man lives on his loftiest, largest plane. He is a high-hearted freeman and no pining slave. And yet he lacks something which the Christian *par excellence,* the mystic and ascetic saint, for example, has in abundant measure, and which makes of him a human being of an altogether different denomination.

The Christian also spurns the pinched and mumping sickroom attitude, and the lives of saints are full of a kind of callousness to diseased conditions of body which probably no other human records show. But whereas the merely moralistic spurning takes an effort of volition, the Christian spurning is the result of the excitement of a higher kind of emotion, in the presence of which no exertion of volition is required. The moralist must hold his breath and keep his muscles tense; and so long as this athletic attitude is possible all goes well—morality suffices. But the athletic attitude tends ever to break down, and it inevitably does break down even in the most stalwart when the organism begins to decay, or when morbid fears invade the mind. To suggest personal will and effort to one all sicklied o'er with the sense of irremediable impotence is to suggest the most impossible of things. What he craves is to be consoled in his very powerlessness, to feel that the spirit of the universe recognizes and secures him, all decaying and failing as he is. Well, we are all such helpless failures in the last resort. The sanest and best of us are of one clay with lunatics and prison inmates, and death finally runs the robustest of us down. And whenever we feel this, such a sense of the vanity and provisionality of our voluntary career comes over us that all our morality appears but as a plaster hiding a sore it can never cure, and all our well-doing as the hollowest substitute for the well-*being* that our lives ought to be grounded in, but, alas! are not.

And here religion comes to our rescue and takes our fate into her hands. There is a state of mind, known to religious men, but to no others, in which the will to assert ourselves and hold our own has been displaced by a willingness to close our mouths and be as nothing in the floods and waterspouts of God. In this state of mind, what we most dreaded has become the habitation of our safety, and the hour of our moral death has turned into our spiritual birthday. The time for tension in our soul is over, and that of happy relaxation, of calm deep breathing, of an eternal present, with no discordant future to be anxious about, has arrived. Fear is not held in abeyance as it is by mere morality, it is positively expunged and washed away.

We shall see abundant examples of this happy state of mind in later lectures of this course. We shall see how infinitely passionate a thing religion at its highest flights can be. Like love, like wrath, like hope, ambition, jealousy, like every other instinctive eagerness and impulse, it adds to life an enchantment which is not rationally or logically deducible from anything else. This enchantment, coming as a gift when it does come,—a gift of our organism, the physiologists will tell us, a gift of God's grace, the theologians say,—is either there or not there for us, and there are persons who can no more become possessed by it than they can fall in love with a given woman by mere word of command. Religious feeling is thus an absolute addition to the Subject's range of life. It gives him a new sphere of power. When the outward battle is lost, and the outer world disowns him, it redeems and vivifies an interior world which otherwise would be an empty waste.

If religion is to mean anything definite for us, it seems to me that we ought to take it as meaning this added dimension of emotion, this enthusiastic temper of espousal, in regions where morality strictly so called can at best but bow its head and acquiesce. It ought to mean nothing short of this new reach of freedom for us, with the struggle over, the keynote of the universe sounding in our ears, and everlasting possession spread before our eyes.[11]

This sort of happiness in the absolute and everlasting is what we find nowhere but in religion. It is parted off from all mere animal happiness, all mere enjoyment of the present, by that element of solemnity of which I have already made so much account. Solemnity is a hard thing to define abstractly, but certain of its marks are patent enough. A solemn state of mind is never crude or simple—it seems to contain a certain measure of its own opposite in solution. A solemn joy preserves a sort of bitter in its sweetness; a solemn sorrow is one to which we intimately consent. But there are writers who, realizing that happiness of a supreme sort is the prerogative of religion, forget this complication, and call all happiness, as such, religious. Mr. Havelock Ellis, for example, identifies religion with the entire field of the soul's liberation from oppressive moods.

> "The simplest functions of physiological life," he writes, "may be its ministers. Every one who is at all acquainted with the Persian mystics knows how wine may be regarded as an instrument of religion. Indeed, in all countries and in all ages, some form of physical enlargement—singing, dancing, drinking, sexual excitement—has been intimately associated with worship. Even the momentary expansion of the soul in laughter is, to however slight an extent, a religious exercise. . . . Whenever an impulse from the world strikes against the organism, and the resultant is not discomfort or pain, not even the muscular contraction of strenuous manhood, but a joyous expansion or aspiration of the whole soul—there is a religion. It is the infinite for which we hunger, and we ride gladly on every little wave that promises to bear us towards it."[12]

But such a straight identification of religion with any and every form of happiness leaves the essential peculiarity of religious happiness out. The more commonplace happinesses which we get are 'reliefs,' occasioned by our momentary escapes from evils either experienced or threatened. But in its most characteristic embodiments, religious happiness is no mere feeling of escape. It cares no longer to escape. It consents to the evil outwardly as a form of sacrifice—inwardly it knows it to be permanently overcome. If you ask *how* religion thus falls on

---

11. Once more, there are plenty of men, constitutionally sombre men, in whose religious life this rapturousness is lacking. They are religious in the wider sense; yet in this acutest of all senses they are not so, and it is religion in the acutest sense that I wish, without disputing about words, to study first, so as to get at its typical *differentia.*

12. *The New Spirit,* p. 232.

the thorns and faces death, and in the very act annuls annihilation, I cannot explain the matter, for it is religion's secret, and to understand it you must yourself have been a religious man of the extremer type. In our future examples, even of the simplest and healthiest-minded type of religious consciousness, we shall find this complex sacrificial constitution, in which a higher happiness holds a lower unhappiness in check. In the Louvre there is a picture, by Guido Reni, of St. Michael with his foot on Satan's neck. The richness of the picture is in large part due to the fiend's figure being there. The richness of its allegorical meaning also is due to his being there—that is, the world is all the richer for having a devil in it, *so long as we keep our foot upon his neck.* In the religious consciousness, that is just the position in which the fiend, the negative or tragic principle, is found; and for that very reason the religious consciousness is so rich from the emotional point of view.[13] We shall see how in certain men and women it takes on a monstrously ascetic form. There are saints who have literally fed on the negative principle, on humiliation and privation, and the thought of suffering and death,—their souls growing in happiness just in proportion as their outward state grew more intolerable. No other emotion than religious emotion can bring a man to this peculiar pass. And it is for that reason that when we ask our question about the value of religion for human life, I think we ought to look for the answer among these violenter examples rather than among those of a more moderate hue.

Having the phenomenon of our study in its acutest possible form to start with, we can shade down as much as we please later. And if in these cases, repulsive as they are to our ordinary worldly way of judging, we find ourselves compelled to acknowledge religion's value and treat it with respect, it will have proved in some way its value for life at large. By subtracting and toning down extravagances we may thereupon proceed to trace the boundaries of its legitimate sway.

To be sure, it makes our task difficult to have to deal so much with eccentricities and extremes. "How *can* religion on the whole be the most important of all human functions," you may ask, "if every several manifestation of it in turn have to be corrected and sobered down and pruned away;" Such a thesis seems a paradox impossible to sustain reasonably,—yet I believe that something like it will have to be our final contention. That personal attitude which the individual finds himself impelled to take up towards what he apprehends to be the

---

13. I owe this allegorical illustration to my lamented colleague and friend, Charles Carroll Everett.

divine—and you will remember that this was our definition—will prove to be both a helpless and a sacrificial attitude. That is, we shall have to confess to at least some amount of dependence on sheer mercy, and to practice some amount of renunciation, great or small, to save our souls alive. The constitution of the world we live in requires it:—

> "Entbehren sollst du! sollst entbehren!
> Das ist der ewige Gesang
> Der jedem an die Ohren klingt,
> Den, unser ganzes Leben lang
> Uns heiser jede Stunde singt."

For when all is said and done, we are in the end absolutely dependent on the universe; and into sacrifices and surrenders of some sort, deliberately looked at and accepted, we are drawn and pressed as into our only permanent positions of repose. Now in those states of mind which fall short of religion, the surrender is submitted to as an imposition of necessity, and the sacrifice is undergone at the very best without complaint. In the religious life, on the contrary, surrender and sacrifice are positively espoused: even unnecessary givings-up are added in order that the happiness may increase. *Religion thus makes easy and felicitous what in any case is necessary;* and if it be the only agency that can accomplish this result, its vital importance as a human faculty stands vindicated beyond dispute. It becomes an essential organ of our life, performing a function which no other portion of our nature can so successfully fulfill. From the merely biological point of view, so to call it, this is a conclusion to which, so far as I can now see, we shall inevitably be led, and led moreover by following the purely empirical method of demonstration which I sketched to you in the first lecture. Of the farther office of religion as a metaphysical revelation I will say nothing now.

But to foreshadow the terminus of one's investigations is one thing, and to arrive there safely is another. In the next lecture, abandoning the extreme generalities which have engrossed us hitherto, I propose that we begin our actual journey by addressing ourselves directly to the concrete facts.

11.   The Sense of Presence

Were one asked to characterize the life of religion in the broadest
and most general terms possible, one might say that it consists of the
belief that there is an unseen order, and that our supreme good lies
in harmoniously adjusting ourselves thereto. This belief and this adjustment are the religious attitude in the soul. I wish during this hour
to call your attention to some of the psychological peculiarities of such
an attitude as this, of belief in an object which we cannot see. All our
attitudes, moral, practical, or emotional, as well as religious, are due
to the 'objects' of our consciousness, the things which we believe to
exist, whether really or ideally, along with ourselves. Such objects may
be present to our senses, or they may be present only to our thought.
In either case they elicit from us a *reaction;* and the reaction due to
things of thought is notoriously in many cases as strong as that due to
sensible presences. It may be even stronger. The memory of an insult
may make us angrier than the insult did when we received it. We are
frequently more ashamed of our blunders afterwards than we were at
the moment of making them; and in general our whole higher pruden-
tial and moral life is based on the fact that material sensations actually

---

Reprinted from William James, *The Varieties of Religious Experience* (New York:
Longmans Green, 1902), lecture III. Title supplied by the editors.

present may have a weaker influence on our action than ideas of remoter facts.

The more concrete objects of most men's religion, the deities whom they worship, are known to them only in idea. It has been vouchsafed, for example, to very few Christian believers to have had a sensible vision of their Savior; though enough appearances of this sort are on record, by way of miraculous exception, to merit our attention later. The whole force of the Christian religion, therefore, so far as belief in the divine personages determines the prevalent attitude of the believer, is in general exerted by the instrumentality of pure ideas, of which nothing in the individual's past experience directly serves as a model.

But in addition to these ideas of the more concrete religious objects, religion is full of abstract objects which prove to have an equal power. God's attributes as such, his holiness, his justice, his mercy, his absoluteness, his infinity, his omniscience, his tri-unity, the various mysteries of the redemptive process, the operation of the sacraments, etc., have proved fertile wells of inspiring meditation for Christian believers.[1] We shall see later that the absence of definite sensible images is positively insisted on by the mystical authorities in all religions as the *sine qua non* of a successful orison, or contemplation of the higher divine truths. Such contemplations are expected (and abundantly verify the expectation, as we shall also see) to influence the believer's subsequent attitude very powerfully for good.

Immanuel Kant held a curious doctrine about such objects of belief as God, the design of creation, the soul, its freedom, and the life hereafter. These things, he said, are properly not objects of knowledge at all. Our conceptions always require a sense-content to work with, and as the words 'soul,' 'God,' 'immortality,' cover no distinctive sense-content whatever, it follows that theoretically speaking they are words devoid of any significance. Yet strangely enough they have a definite meaning *for our practice.* We can act *as if* there were a God; feel *as if* we were free; consider Nature *as if* she were full of special designs; lay plans *as if* we were to be immortal; and we find then that these words do make a genuine difference in our moral life. Our faith *that* these unintelligible objects actually exist proves thus to be a full

---

1. Example: "I have had much comfort lately in meditating on the passages which show the personality of the Holy Ghost, and his distinctness from the Father and the Son. It is a subject that requires searching into to find out, but, when realized, gives one so much more true and lively a sense of the fullness of the Godhead, and its work in us and to us, than when only thinking of the Spirit in its effect on us." Augustus Hare: *Memorials,* i. 244, Maria Hare to Lucy H. Hare.

equivalent in *praktischer Hinsicht,* as Kant calls it, or from the point of view of our action, for a knowledge of *what* they might be, in case we were permitted positively to conceive them. So we have the strange phenomenon, as Kant assures us, of a mind believing with all its strength in the real presence of a set of things of no one of which it can form any notion whatsoever.

My object in thus recalling Kant's doctrine to your mind is not to express any opinion as to the accuracy of this particularly uncouth part of his philosophy, but only to illustrate the characteristic of human nature which we are considering, by an example so classical in its exaggeration. The sentiment of reality can indeed attach itself so strongly to our object of belief that our whole life is polarized through and through, so to speak, by its sense of the existence of the thing believed in, and yet that thing, for purpose of definite description, can hardly be said to be present to our mind at all. It is as if a bar of iron, without touch or sight, with no representative faculty whatever, might nevertheless be strongly endowed with an inner capacity for magnetic feeling; and as if, through the various arousals of its magnetism by magnets coming and going in its neighborhood, it might be consciously determined to different attitudes and tendencies. Such a bar of iron could never give you an outward description of the agencies that had the power of stirring it so strongly; yet of their presence, and of their significance for its life, it would be intensely aware through every fibre of its being.

It is not only the Ideas of pure Reason, as Kant styled them, that have this power of making us vitally feel presences that we are impotent articulately to describe. All sorts of higher abstractions bring with them the same kind of impalpable appeal. Remember those passages from Emerson which I read at my last lecture. The whole universe of concrete objects, as we know them, swims, not only for such a transcendentalist writer, but for all of us, in a wider and higher universe of abstract ideas, that lend it its significance. As time, space, and the ether soak through all things, so (we feel) do abstract and essential goodness, beauty, strength, significance, justice, soak through all things good, strong, significant, and just.

Such ideas, and others equally abstract, form the background for all our facts, the fountain-head of all the possibilities we conceive of. They give its 'nature,' as we call it, to every special thing. Everything we know is 'what' it is by sharing in the nature of one of these abstractions. We can never look directly at them, for they are bodiless and featureless and footless, but we grasp all other things by their means, and in handling the real world we should be stricken with helplessness in just so far forth as we might lose these mental objects, these adjectives and adverbs and predicates and heads of classification and conception.

This absolute determinability of our mind by abstractions is one of the cardinal facts in our human constitution. Polarizing and magnetizing us as they do, we turn towards them and from them, we seek them, hold them, hate them, bless them, just as if they were so many concrete beings. And beings they are, beings as real in the realm which they inhabit as the changing things of sense are in the realm of space.

Plato gave so brilliant and impressive a defense of this common human feeling, that the doctrine of the reality of abstract objects has been known as the platonic theory of ideas ever since. Abstract Beauty, for example, is for Plato a perfectly definite individual being, of which the intellect is aware as of something additional to all the perishing beauties of the earth. "The true order of going," he says, in the often quoted passage in his 'Banquet,' "is to use the beauties of earth as steps along which one mounts upwards for the sake of that other Beauty, going from one to two, and from two to all fair forms, and from fair forms to fair actions, and from fair actions to fair notions, until from fair notions he arrives at the notion of absolute Beauty, and at last knows what the essence of Beauty is."[2] In our last lecture we had a glimpse of the way in which a platonizing writer like Emerson may treat the abstract divineness of things, the moral structure of the universe, as a fact worthy of worship. In those various churches without a God which to-day are spreading through the world under the name of ethical societies, we have a similar worship of the abstract divine, the moral law believed in as an ultimate object. 'Science' in many minds is genuinely taking the place of a religion. Where this is so, the scientist treats the 'Laws of Nature' as objective facts to be revered. A brilliant school of interpretation of Greek mythology would have it that in their origin the Greek gods were only half-metaphoric personifications of those great spheres of abstract law and order into which the natural world falls apart—the sky-sphere, the ocean-sphere, the earth-sphere, and the like; just as even now we may speak of the smile of the morning, the kiss of the breeze, or the bite of the cold, without really meaning that these phenomena of nature actually wear a human face.[3]

As regards the origin of the Greek gods, we need not at present seek

---

2. Symposium, Jowett, 1871, i. 527.

3. Example: "Nature is always so interesting, under whatever aspect she shows herself, that when it rains, I seem to see a beautiful woman weeping. She appears the more beautiful, the more afflicted she is." B. de St. Pierre.

an opinion. But the whole array of our instances leads to a conclusion something like this: It is as if there were in the human consciousness a *sense of reality, a feeling of objective presence, a perception* of what we may call *'something there,'* more deep and more general than any of the special and particular 'senses' by which the current psychology supposes existent realities to be originally revealed. If this were so, we might suppose the senses to waken our attitudes and conduct as they so habitually do, by first exciting this sense of reality; but anything else, any idea, for example, that might similarly excite it, would have that same prerogative of appearing real which objects of sense normally possess. So far as religious conceptions were able to touch this reality-feeling, they would be believed in in spite of criticism, even though they might be so vague and remote as to be almost unimaginable, even though they might be such non-entities in point of *whatness,* as Kant makes the objects of his moral theology to be.

The most curious proofs of the existence of such an undifferentiated sense of reality as this are found in experiences of hallucination. It often happens that an hallucination is imperfectly developed: the person affected will feel a 'presence' in the room, definitely localized, facing in one particular way, real in the most emphatic sense of the word, often coming suddenly, and as suddenly gone; and yet neither seen, heard, touched, nor cognized in any of the usual 'sensible' ways. Let me give you an example of this, before I pass to the objects with whose presence religion is more peculiarly concerned.

An intimate friend of mine, one of the keenest intellects I know, has had several experiences of this sort. He writes as follows in response to my inquiries:—

"I have several times within the past few years felt the so-called 'consciousness of a presence.' The experiences which I have in mind are clearly distinguishable from another kind of experience which I have had very frequently, and which I fancy many persons would also call the 'consciousness of a presence.' But the difference for me between the two sets of experience is as great as the difference between feeling a slight warmth originating I know not where, and standing in the midst of a conflagration with all the ordinary senses alert.

"It was about September, 1884, when I had the first experience. On the previous night I had had, after getting into bed at my rooms in College, a vivid tactile hallucination of being grasped by the arm, which made me get up and search the room for an intruder; but the sense of presence properly so called came on the next night. After

I had got into bed and blown out the candle, I lay awake awhile
thinking on the previous night's experience, when suddenly I *felt*
something come into the room and stay close to my bed. It remained only a minute or two. I did not recognize it by any ordinary
sense, and yet there was a horribly unpleasant 'sensation' connected
with it. It stirred something more at the roots of my being than any
ordinary perception. The feeling had something of the quality of a
very large tearing vital pain spreading chiefly over the chest, but
within the organism—and yet the feeling was not *pain* so much as
abhorrence. At all events, something was present with me, and I
knew its presence far more surely than I have ever known the presence of any fleshly living creature. I was conscious of its departure
as of its coming: an almost instantaneously swift going through the
door, and the 'horrible sensation' disappeared.

"On the third night when I retired my mind was absorbed in some
lectures which I was preparing, and I was still absorbed in these
when I became aware of the actual presence (though not of the
coming) of the thing that was there the night before, and of the
'horrible sensation.' I then mentally concentrated all my effort to
charge this 'thing,' if it was evil, to depart, if it was *not* evil, to tell
me who or what it was, and if it could not explain itself, to go, and
that I would compel it to go. It went as on the previous night, and
my body quickly recovered its normal state.

"On two other occasions in my life I have had precisely the same
'horrible sensation.' Once it lasted a full quarter of an hour. In all
three instances the certainty that there in outward space there stood
something was indescribably *stronger* than the ordinary certainty
of companionship when we are in the close presence of ordinary
living people. The something seemed close to me, and intensely
more real than any ordinary perception. Although I felt it to be like
unto myself, so to speak, or finite, small, and distressful, as it were,
I didn't recognize it as any individual being or person."

Of course such an experience as this does not connect itself with the
religious sphere. Yet it may upon occasion do so; and the same corre-
spondent informs me that at more than one other conjuncture he had
the sense of presence developed with equal intensity and abruptness,
only then it was filled with a quality of joy.

"There was not a mere consciousness of something there, but fused
in the central happiness of it, a startling awareness of some ineffable good. Not vague either, not like the emotional effect of some
poem, or scene, or blossom, of music, but the sure knowledge of the
close presence of a sort of mighty person, and after it went, the

memory persisted as the one perception of reality. Everything else might be a dream, but not that."

My friend, as it oddly happens, does not interpret these latter experiences theistically, as signifying the presence of God. But it would clearly not have been unnatural to interpret them as a revelation of the deity's existence. When we reach the subject of mysticism, we shall have much more to say upon this head.

Lest the oddity of these phenomena should disconcert you, I will venture to read you a couple of similar narratives, much shorter, merely to show that we are dealing with a well-marked natural kind of fact. In the first case, which I take from the Journal of the Society for Psychical Research, the sense of presence developed in a few moments into a distinctly visualized hallucination,—but I leave that part of the story out.

"I had read," the narrator says, "some twenty minutes or so, was thoroughly absorbed in the book, my mind was perfectly quiet, and for the time being my friends were quite forgotten, when suddenly without a moment's warning my whole being seemed roused to the highest state of tension or aliveness, and I was aware, with an intenseness not easily imagined by those who had never experienced it, that another being or presence was not only in the room, but quite close to me. I put my book down, and although my excitement was great, I felt quite collected, and not conscious of any sense of fear. Without changing my position, and looking straight at the fire, I knew somehow that my friend A. H. was standing at my left elbow, but so far behind me as to be hidden by the armchair in which I was leaning back. Moving my eyes round slightly without otherwise changing my position, the lower portion of one leg became visible, and I instantly recognized the gray-blue material of trousers he often wore, but the stuff appeared semi-transparent, reminding me of tobacco smoke in consistency,"[4] —and hereupon the visible hallucination came.

Another informant writes:—

"Quite early in the night I was awakened. . . . I felt as if I had been aroused intentionally, and at first thought some one was breaking into the house. . . . I then turned on my side to go to sleep again, and immediately felt a consciousness of a presence in the room, and singular to state, it was not the consciousness of a live person, but

---

4. *Journal of the S. P. R.,* February, 1895, p. 26.

of a spiritual presence. This may provoke a smile, but I can only tell you the facts as they occurred to me. I do not know how to better describe my sensations than by simply stating that I felt a consciousness of a spiritual presence. . . . I felt also at the same time a strong feeling of superstitious dread, as if something strange and fearful were about to happen."[5]

Professor Flournoy of Geneva gives me the following testimony of a friend of his, a lady, who has the gift of automatic or involuntary writing:—

"Whenever I practice automatic writing, what makes me feel that it is not due to a subconscious self is the feeling I always have of a foreign presence, external to my body. It is sometimes so definitely characterized that I could point to its exact position. This impression of presence is impossible to describe. It varies in intensity and clearness according to the personality from whom the writing professes to come. If it is some one whom I love, I feel it immediately, before any writing has come. My heart seems to recognize it."

In an earlier book of mine I have cited at full length a curious case of presence felt by a blind man. The presence was that of the figure of a gray-bearded man dressed in a pepper and salt suit, squeezing himself under the crack of the door and moving across the floor of the room towards a sofa. The blind subject of this quasi-hallucination is an exceptionally intelligent reporter. He is entirely without internal visual imagery and cannot represent light or colors to himself, and is positive that his other senses, hearing, etc., were not involved in this false perception. It seems to have been an abstract conception rather, with the feelings of reality and spatial outwardness directly attached to it—in other words, a fully objectified and exteriorized *idea.*

Such cases, taken along with others which would be too tedious for quotation, seem sufficiently to prove the existence in our mental machinery of a sense of present reality more diffused and general than that which our special senses yield. For the psychologists the tracing of the organic seat of such a feeling would form a pretty problem— nothing could be more natural than to connect it with the muscular sense, with the feeling that our muscles were innervating themselves for action. Whatsoever thus innervated our activity, or 'made our flesh creep,'—our senses are what do so oftenest,—might then appear real and present, even though it were but an abstract idea. But with such

---

5. E. Gurney: *Phantasms of the Living,* i. 384.

vague conjectures we have no concern at present, for our interest lies with the faculty rather than with its organic seat.

Like all positive affections of consciousness, the sense of reality has its negative counterpart in the shape of a feeling of unreality by which persons may be haunted, and of which one sometimes hears complaint:—

> "When I reflect on the fact that I have made my appearance by accident upon a globe itself whirled through space as the sport of the catastrophes of the heavens," says Madame Ackermann; "when I see myself surrounded by beings as ephemeral and incomprehensible as I am myself, and all excitedly pursuing pure chimeras, I experience a strange feeling of being in a dream. It seems to me as if I have loved and suffered and that erelong I shall die, in a dream. My last word will be, 'I have been dreaming.' "[6]

In another lecture we shall see how in morbid melancholy this sense of the unreality of things may become a carking pain, and even lead to suicide.

We may now lay it down as certain that in the distinctively religious sphere of experience, many persons (how many we cannot tell) possess the objects of their belief, not in the form of mere conceptions which their intellect accepts as true, but rather in the form of quasi-sensible realities directly apprehended. As his sense of the real presence of these objects fluctuates, so the believer alternates between warmth and coldness in his faith. Other examples will bring this home to one better than abstract description, so I proceed immediately to cite some. The first example is a negative one, deploring the loss of the sense in question. I have extracted it from an account given me by a scientific man of my acquaintance, of his religious life. It seems to me to show clearly that the feeling of reality may be something more like a sensation than an intellectual operation properly so-called.

> "Between twenty and thirty I gradually became more and more agnostic and irreligious, yet I cannot say that I ever lost that 'indefinite consciousness' which Herbert Spencer describes so well, of an Absolute Reality behind phenomena. For me this Reality was not the pure Unknowable of Spencer's philosophy, for although I had ceased my childish prayers to God, and never prayed to *It* in a formal manner, yet my more recent experience shows me to have been in a relation to *It* which practically was the same thing as

---

6. *Pensées d'un Solitaire*, p. 66.

prayer. Whenever I had any trouble, especially when I had conflict with other people, either domestically or in the way of business, or when I was depressed in spirits or anxious about affairs, I now recognize that I used to fall back for support upon this curious relation I felt myself to be in to this fundamental cosmical *It*. It was on my side, or I was on Its side, however you please to term it, in the particular trouble, and it always strengthened me and seemed to give me endless vitality to feel its underlying and supporting presence. In fact, it was an unfailing fountain of living justice, truth, and strength, to which I instinctively turned at times of weakness, and it always brought me out. I know now that it was a personal relation I was in to it, because of late years the power of communicating with it has left me, and I am conscious of a perfectly definite loss. I used never to fail to find it when I turned to it. Then came a set of years when sometimes I found it, and then again I would be wholly unable to make connection with it. I remember many occasions on which at night in bed, I would be unable to get to sleep on account of worry. I turned this way and that in the darkness, and groped mentally for the familiar sense of that higher mind of my mind which had always seemed to be close at hand as it were, closing the passage, and yielding support, but there was no electric current. A blank was there instead of *It:* I couldn't find anything. Now, at the age of nearly fifty, my power of getting into connection with it has entirely left me; and I have to confess that a great help has gone out of my life. Life has become curiously dead and indifferent; and I can see now that my old experience was probably exactly the same thing as the prayers of the orthodox, only I did not call them by that name. What I have spoken of as 'It' was practically not Spencer's Unknowable, but just my own instinctive and individual God, whom I relied upon for higher sympathy, but whom somehow I have lost."

Nothing is more common in the pages of religious biography than the way in which seasons of lively and of difficult faith are described as alternating. Probably every religious person has the recollection of particular crises in which a directer vision of the truth, a direct perception, perhaps, of a living God's existence, swept in and overwhelmed the languor of the more ordinary belief. In James Russell Lowell's correspondence there is a brief memorandum of an experience of this kind:—

"I had a revelation last Friday evening. I was at Mary's, and happening to say something of the presence of spirits (of whom, I said, I was often dimly aware), Mr. Putnam entered into an argument with me on spiritual matters. As I was speaking, the whole system rose up before me like a vague destiny looming from the Abyss. I never before so clearly felt the Spirit of God in me and around me. The whole room seemed to me full of God. The air seemed to waver to and fro with the presence of Something I knew not what. I spoke with the calmness and clearness of a prophet. I cannot tell you what this revelation was. I have not yet studied it enough. But I shall perfect it one day, and then you shall hear it and acknowledge its grandeur."[7]

Here is a longer and more developed experience from a manuscript communication by a clergyman,—I take it from Starbuck's manuscript collection:—

"I remember the night, and almost the very spot on the hilltop, where my soul opened out, as it were, into the Infinite, and there was a rushing together of the two worlds, the inner and the outer. It was deep calling unto deep,—the deep that my own struggle had opened up within being answered by the unfathomable deep without, reaching beyond the stars. I stood alone with Him who had made me, and all the beauty of the world, and love, and sorrow, and even temptation. I did not seek Him, but felt the perfect unison of my spirit with His. The ordinary sense of things around me faded. For the moment nothing but an ineffable joy and exaltation remained. It is impossible fully to describe the experience. It was like the effect of some great orchestra when all the separate notes have melted into one swelling harmony that leaves the listener conscious of nothing save that his soul is being wafted upwards, and almost bursting with its own emotion. The perfect stillness of the night was thrilled by a more solemn silence. The darkness held a presence that was all the more felt because it was not seen. I could not any more have doubted that *He* was there than that I was. Indeed, I felt myself to be, if possible, the less real of the two.

"My highest faith in God and truest idea of him were then born in me. I have stood upon the Mount of Vision since, and felt the Eternal round about me. But never since has there come quite the same stirring of the heart. Then, if ever, I believe, I stood face to face with God, and was born anew of his spirit. There was, as I recall it, no sudden change of thought or of belief, except that my early crude conception had, as it were, burst into flower. There was no destruction of the old, but a rapid, wonderful unfolding. Since that time no discussion that I have heard of the proofs of God's existence has been able to shake my faith. Having once felt the presence of

7. *Letters of Lowell,* i. 75.

God's spirit, I have never lost it again for long. My most assuring
evidence of his existence is deeply rooted in that hour of vision, in
the memory of that supreme experience, and in the conviction,
gained from reading and reflection, that something the same has
come to all who have found God. I am aware that it may justly be
called mystical. I am not enough acquainted with philosophy to
defend it from that or any other charge. I feel that in writing of it
I have overlaid it with words rather than put it clearly to your
thought. But, such as it is, I have described it as carefully as I now
am able to do."

Here is another document, even more definite in character, which,
the writer being a Swiss, I translate from the French original.[8]

"I was in perfect health: we were on our sixth day of tramping, and
in good training. We had come the day before from Sixt to Trient
by Buet. I felt neither fatigue, hunger, nor thirst, and my state of
mind was equally healthy. I had had at Forlaz good news from home;
I was subject to no anxiety, either near or remote, for we had a good
guide, and there was not a shadow of uncertainty about the road we
should follow. I can best describe the condition in which I was by
calling it a state of equilibrium. When all at once I experienced a
feeling of being raised above myself, I felt the presence of God—
I tell of the thing just as I was conscious of it—as if his goodness
and his power were penetrating me altogether. The throb of emotion was so violent that I could barely tell the boys to pass on and
not wait for me. I then sat down on a stone, unable to stand any
longer, and my eyes overflowed with tears. I thanked God that in
the course of my life he had taught me to know him, that he sustained my life and took pity both on the insignificant creature and
on the sinner that I was. I begged him ardently that my life might
be consecrated to the doing of his will. I felt his reply, which was
that I should do his will from day to day, in humility and poverty,
leaving him, the Almighty God, to be judge of whether I should
some time be called to bear witness more conspicuously. Then,
slowly, the ecstasy left my heart; that is, I felt that God had withdrawn the communion which he had granted, and I was able to walk
on, but very slowly, so strongly was I still possessed by the interior
emotion. Besides, I had wept uninterruptedly for several minutes,
my eyes were swollen, and I did not wish my companions to see me.
The state of ecstasy may have lasted four or five minutes, although
it seemed at the time to last much longer. My comrades waited for

---

8. I borrow it, with Professor Flournoy's permission, from his rich collection of
psychological documents.

me ten minutes at the cross of Barine, but I took about twenty-five
or thirty minutes to join them, for as well as I can remember, they
said that I had kept them back for about half an hour. The impression had been so profound that in climbing slowly the slope I asked
myself if it were possible that Moses on Sinai could have had a more
intimate communication with God. I think it well to add that in this
ecstasy of mine God had neither form, color, odor, nor taste; moreover, that the feeling of his presence was accompanied with no
determinate localization. It was rather as if my personality had been
transformed by the presence of a *spiritual spirit.* But the more I seek
words to express this intimate intercourse, the more I feel the impossibility of describing the thing by any of our usual images. At
bottom the expression most apt to render what I felt is this: God was
present, though invisible; he fell under no one of my senses, yet my
consciousness perceived him."

The adjective 'mystical' is technically applied, most often, to states
that are of brief duration. Of course such hours of rapture as the last
two persons describe are mystical experiences, of which in a later
lecture I shall have much to say. Meanwhile here is the abridged record
of another mystical or semi-mystical experience, in a mind evidently
framed by nature for ardent piety. I owe it to Starbuck's collection. The
lady who gives the account is the daughter of a man well known in his
time as a writer against Christianity. The suddenness of her conversion
shows well how native the sense of God's presence must be to certain
minds. She relates that she was brought up in entire ignorance of
Christian doctrine, but, when in Germany, after being talked to by
Christian friends, she read the Bible and prayed, and finally the plan
of salvation flashed upon her like a stream of light.

"To this day," she writes, "I cannot understand dallying with reli-
gion and the commands of God. The very instant I heard my Fa-
ther's cry calling unto me, my heart bounded in recognition. I ran,
I stretched forth my arms, I cried aloud, 'Here, here I am, my
Father.' Oh, happy child, what should I do? 'Love me,' answered my
God. 'I do, I do,' I cried passionately. 'Come unto me,' called my
Father. 'I will,' my heart panted. Did I stop to ask a single question?
Not one. It never occurred to me to ask whether I was good enough,
or to hesitate over my unfitness, or to find out what I thought of his
church, or . . . to wait until I should be satisfied. Satisfied! I was
satisfied. Had I not found my God and my Father? Did he not love
me? Had he not called me? Was there not a Church into which I
might enter? . . . Since then I have had direct answers to prayer—
so significant as to be almost like talking with God and hearing his

answer. The idea of God's reality has never left me for one moment."

Here is still another case, the writer being a man aged twenty-seven, in which the experience, probably almost as characteristic, is less vividly described:—

"I have on a number of occasions felt that I had enjoyed a period of intimate communion with the divine. These meetings came unasked and unexpected, and seemed to consist merely in the temporary obliteration of the conventionalities which usually surround and cover my life. . . . Once it was when from the summit of a high mountain I looked over a gashed and corrugated landscape extending to a long convex of ocean that ascended to the horizon, and again from the same point when I could see nothing beneath me but a boundless expanse of white cloud, on the blown surface of which a few high peaks, including the one I was on, seemed plunging about as if they were dragging their anchors. What I felt on these occasions was a temporary loss of my own identity, accompanied by an illumination which revealed to me a deeper significance than I had been wont to attach to life. It is in this that I find my justification for saying that I have enjoyed communication with God. Of course the absence of such a being as this would be chaos. I cannot conceive of life without its presence."

Of the more habitual and so to speak chronic sense of God's presence the following sample from Professor Starbuck's manuscript collection may serve to give an idea. It is from a man aged forty-nine,— probably thousands of unpretending Christians would write an almost identical account.

"God is more real to me than any thought or thing or person. I feel his presence positively, and the more as I live in closer harmony with his laws as written in my body and mind. I feel him in the sunshine or rain; and awe mingled with a delicious restfulness most nearly describes my feelings. I talk to him as to a companion in prayer and praise, and our communion is delightful. He answers me again and again, often in words so clearly spoken that it seems my outer ear must have carried the tone, but generally in strong mental impressions. Usually a text of Scripture, unfolding some new view of him and his love for me, and care for my safety. I could give hundreds of instances, in school matters, social problems, financial difficulties, etc. That he is mine and I am his never leaves me, it is an abiding joy. Without it life would be a blank, a desert, a shoreless, trackless waste."

I subjoin some more examples from writers of different ages and sexes. They are also from Professor Starbuck's collection, and their number might be greatly multiplied. The first is from a man twenty-seven years old:—

"God is quite real to me. I talk to him and often get answers. Thoughts sudden and distinct from any I have been entertaining come to my mind after asking God for his direction. Something over a year ago I was for some weeks in the direst perplexity. When the trouble first appeared before me I was dazed, but before long (two or three hours) I could hear distinctly a passage of Scripture: 'My grace is sufficient for thee.' Every time my thoughts turned to the trouble I could hear this quotation. I don't think I ever doubted the existence of God, or had him drop out of my consciousness. God has frequently stepped into my affairs very perceptibly, and I feel that he directs many little details all the time. But on two or three occasions he has ordered ways for me very contrary to my ambitions and plans."

Another statement (none the less valuable psychologically for being so decidedly childish) is that of a boy of seventeen:—

"Sometimes as I go to church, I sit down, join in the service, and before I go out I feel as if God was with me. . . . And then again I feel as if I could sit beside him, and put my arms around him, kiss him, etc. When I am taking Holy Communion at the altar, I try to get with him and generally feel his presence."

I let a few other cases follow at random:—

"God surrounds me like the physical atmosphere. He is closer to me than my own breath. In him literally I live and move and have my being."—

"There are times when I seem to stand in his very presence, to talk with him. Answers to prayer have come, sometimes direct and overwhelming in their revelation of his presence and powers. There are times when God seems far off, but this is always my own fault."—

"I have the sense of a presence, strong, and at the same time soothing, which hovers over me. Sometimes it seems to enwrap me with sustaining arms."

Such is the human ontological imagination, and such is the convincingness of what it brings to birth. Unpicturable beings are realized, and realized with an intensity almost like that of an hallucination. They determine our vital attitude as decisively as the vital attitude of lovers is determined by the habitual sense, by which each is haunted, of the other being in the world. A lover has notoriously this sense of the continuous being of his idol, even when his attention is addressed to other matters and he no longer represents her features. He cannot forget her; she uninterruptedly affects him through and through.

I spoke of the convincingness of these feelings of reality, and I must dwell a moment longer on that point. They are as convincing to those who have them as any direct sensible experiences can be, and they are, as a rule, much more convincing than results established by mere logic ever are. One may indeed be entirely without them; probably more than one of you here present is without them in any marked degree; but if you do have them, and have them at all strongly, the probability is that you cannot help regarding them as genuine perceptions of truth, as revelations of a kind of reality which no adverse argument, however unanswerable by you in words, can expel from your belief. The opinion opposed to mysticism in philosophy is sometimes spoken of as *rationalism*. Rationalism insists that all our beliefs ought ultimately to find for themselves articulate grounds. Such grounds, for rationalism, must consist of four things: (1) definitely statable abstract principles; (2) definite facts of sensation; (3) definite hypotheses based on such facts; and (4) definite inferences logically drawn. Vague impressions of something indefinable have no place in the rationalistic system, which on its positive side is surely a splendid intellectual tendency, for not only are all our philosophies fruits of it, but physical science (amongst other good things) is its result.

Nevertheless, if we look on man's whole mental life as it exists, on the life of men that lies in them apart from their learning and science, and that they inwardly and privately follow, we have to confess that the part of it of which rationalism can give an account is relatively superficial. It is the part that has the *prestige* undoubtedly, for it has the loquacity, it can challenge you for proofs, and chop logic, and put you down with words. But it will fail to convince or convert you all the same, if your dumb intuitions are opposed to its conclusions. If you have intuitions at all, they come from a deeper level of your nature than the loquacious level which rationalism inhabits. Your whole subconscious life, your impulses, your faiths, your needs, your divinations, have prepared the premises, of which your consciousness now feels the weight of the result; and something in you absolutely *knows* that that result must be truer than any logic-chopping rationalistic talk, however clever, that may contradict it. This inferiority of the rationalistic level in founding belief is just as manifest when rationalism argues for religion as when it argues against it. That vast literature of proofs of God's existence drawn from the order of nature, which a century ago seemed so overwhelmingly convincing, to-day does little more than gather dust in libraries, for the simple reason that our generation has ceased to believe in the kind of God it argued for. Whatever sort of a being God may be, we *know* to-day that he is nevermore that mere external inventor of 'contrivances' intended to make manifest his 'glory' in which our great-grandfathers took such satisfaction, though just how we know this we cannot possibly make clear by words either to others or to ourselves. I defy any of you here fully to account for your persuasion that if a God exist he must be a more cosmic and tragic personage than that Being.

The truth is that in the metaphysical and religious sphere, articulate reasons are cogent for us only when our inarticulate feelings of reality have already been impressed in favor of the same conclusion. Then, indeed, our intuitions and our reason work together, and great world-ruling systems, like that of the Buddhist or of the Catholic philosophy, may grow up. Our impulsive belief is here always what sets up the original body of truth, and our articulately verbalized philosophy is but its showy translation into formulas. The unreasoned and immediate assurance is the deep thing in us, the reasoned argument is but a surface exhibition. Instinct leads, intelligence does but follow. If a person feels the presence of a living God after the fashion shown by my quotations, your critical arguments, be they never so superior, will vainly set themselves to change his faith.

Please observe, however, that I do not yet say that it is *better* that the subconscious and non-rational should thus hold primacy in the religious realm. I confine myself to simply pointing out that they do so hold it as a matter of fact.

So much for our sense of the reality of the religious objects. Let me now say a brief word more about the attitudes they characteristically awaken.

We have already agreed that they are *solemn;* and we have seen reason to think that the most distinctive of them is the sort of joy which may result in extreme cases from absolute self-surrender. The sense of the kind of object to which the surrender is made has much to do with determining the precise complexion of the joy; and the whole phenomenon is more complex than any simple formula allows. In the literature of the subject, sadness and gladness have each been empha-sized in turn. The ancient saying that the first maker of the Gods was fear receives voluminous corroboration from every age of religious history; but none the less does religious history show the part which joy has evermore tended to play. Sometimes the joy has been primary; sometimes secondary, being the gladness of deliverance from the fear. This latter state of things, being the more complex, is also the more complete; and as we proceed, I think we shall have abundant reason for refusing to leave out either the sadness or the gladness, if we look at religion with the breadth of view which it demands. Stated in the completest possible terms, a man's religion involves both moods of contraction and moods of expansion of his being. But the quantitative mixture and order of these moods vary so much from one age of the world, from one system of thought, and from one individual to another, that you may insist either on the dread and the submission, or on the peace and the freedom as the essence of the matter, and still remain materially within the limits of the truth. The constitutionally sombre and the constitutionally sanguine onlooker are bound to emphasize opposite aspects of what lies before their eyes.

The constitutionally sombre religious person makes even of his religious peace a very sober thing. Danger still hovers in the air about it. Flexion and contraction are not wholly checked. It were sparrowlike and childish after our deliverance to explode into twittering laughter and caper-cutting, and utterly to forget the imminent hawk on bough. Lie low, rather, lie low; for you are in the hands of a living God. In the Book of Job, for example, the impotence of man and the omnipotence of God is the exclusive burden of its author's mind. "It is as high as heaven; what canst thou do?—deeper than hell; what canst thou know?" There is an astringent relish about the truth of this conviction which some men can feel, and which for them is as near an approach as can be made to the feeling of religious joy.

> "In Job," says that coldly truthful writer, the author of Mark Rutherford, "God reminds us that man is not the measure of his creation. The world is immense, constructed on no plan or theory which the intellect of man can grasp. It is *transcendent* everywhere. This is the burden of every verse, and is the secret, if there be one, of the poem. Sufficient or insufficient, there is nothing more. . . . God is great, we know not his ways. He takes from us all we have, but yet if we possess our souls in patience, we *may* pass the valley of the shadow, and come out in sunlight again. We may or we may not! . . . What more have we to say now than God said from the whirlwind over two thousand five hundred years ago?"[9]

If we turn to the sanguine onlooker, on the other hand, we find that deliverance is felt as incomplete unless the burden be altogether over-

---

9. *Mark Rutherford's Deliverance,* London, 1885, pp. 196, 198.

come and the danger forgotten. Such onlookers give us definitions that seem to the sombre minds of whom we have just been speaking to leave out all the solemnity that makes religious peace so different from merely animal joys. In the opinion of some writers an attitude might be called religious, though no touch were left in it of sacrifice or submission, no tendency to flexion, no bowing of the head. Any "habitual and regulated admiration," says Professor J. R. Seeley,[10] "is worthy to be called a religion"; and accordingly he thinks that our Music, our Science, and our so-called 'Civilization,' as these things are now organized and admiringly believed in, form the more genuine religions of our time. Certainly the unhesitating and unreasoning way in which we feel that we must inflict our civilization upon 'lower' races, by means of Hotchkiss guns, etc., reminds one of nothing so much as of the early spirit of Islam spreading its religion by the sword.

In my last lecture I quoted to you the ultra-radical opinion of Mr. Havelock Ellis, that laughter of any sort may be considered a religious exercise, for it bears witness to the soul's emancipation. I quoted this opinion in order to deny its adequacy. But we must now settle our scores more carefully with this whole optimistic way of thinking. It is far too complex to be decided off-hand. I propose accordingly that we make of religious optimism the theme of the next two lectures.

---

10. In his book (too little read, I fear), *Natural Religion,* 3d edition, Boston, 1886, pp. 91, 122.

12.   The Future of an Illusion

Human civilization, by which I mean all those respects in which
human life has raised itself above its animal status and differs from the
life of beasts—and I scorn to distinguish between culture and civilization—, presents, as we know, two aspects to the observer. It includes
on the one hand all the knowledge and capacity that men have acquired in order to control the forces of nature and extract its wealth
for the satisfaction of human needs, and, on the other hand, all the
regulations necessary in order to adjust the relations of men to one
another and especially the distribution of the available wealth. The two
trends of civilization are not independent of each other: firstly, because
the mutual relations of men are profoundly influenced by the amount
of instinctual satisfaction which the existing wealth makes possible;
secondly, because an individual man can himself come to function as
wealth in relation to another one, in so far as the other person makes
use of his capacity for work, or chooses him as a sexual object; and
thirdly, moreover, because every individual is virtually an enemy of
civilization, though civilization is supposed to be an object of universal

human interest.[1] It is remarkable that, little as men are able to exist in isolation, they should nevertheless feel as a heavy burden the sacrifices which civilization expects of them in order to make a communal life possible. Thus civilization has to be defended against the individual, and its regulations, institutions and commands are directed to that task. They aim not only at effecting a certain distribution of wealth but at maintaining that distribution; indeed, they have to protect everything that contributes to the conquest of nature and the production of wealth against men's hostile impulses. Human creations are easily destroyed, and science and technology, which have built them up, can also be used for their annihilation.

One thus gets an impression that civilization is something which was imposed on a resisting majority by a minority which understood how to obtain possession of the means to power and coercion. It is, of course, natural to assume that these difficulties are not inherent in the nature of civilization itself but are determined by the imperfections of the cultural forms which have so far been developed. And in fact it is not difficult to indicate those defects. While mankind has made continual advances in its control over nature and may expect to make still greater ones, it is not possible to establish with certainty that a similar advance has been made in the management of human affairs; and probably at all periods, just as now once again, many people have asked themselves whether what little civilization has thus acquired is indeed worth defending at all. One would think that a re-ordering of human relations should be possible, which would remove the sources of dissatisfaction with civilization by renouncing coercion and the suppression of the instincts, so that, undisturbed by internal discord, men might devote themselves to the acquisition of wealth and its enjoyment. That would be the golden age, but it is questionable if such a state of affairs can be realized. It seems rather that every civilization must be built up on coercion and renunciation of instinct; it does not even seem certain that if coercion were to cease the majority of human beings would be prepared to undertake to perform the work necessary for acquiring new wealth. One has, I think, to reckon with the fact that there are present in all men destructive, and therefore anti-social and anti-cultural, trends and that in a great number of people these are strong enough to determine their behavior in human society.

This psychological fact has a decisive importance for our judgement

---

1. [The hostility of human individuals to civilization plays a large part in the earlier chapters of this work. Freud returned to the subject and discussed it still more fully two years later in his *Civilization and Its Discontents* (1930a).]

of human civilization. Whereas we might at first think that its essence
lies in controlling nature for the purpose of acquiring wealth and that
the dangers which threaten it could be eliminated through a suitable
distribution of that wealth among men, it now seems that the emphasis
has moved over from the material to the mental. The decisive question
is whether and to what extent it is possible to lessen the burden of the
instinctual sacrifices imposed on men, to reconcile men to those which
must necessarily remain and to provide a compensation for them. It
is·just as impossible to do without control of the mass[2] by a minority
as it is to dispense with coercion in the work of civilization. For masses
are lazy and unintelligent; they have no love for instinctual renunciation, and they are not to be convinced by argument of its inevitability;
and the individuals composing them support one another in giving
free rein to their indiscipline. It is only through the influence of individuals who can set an example and whom masses recognize as their
leaders that they can be induced to perform the work and undergo the
renunciations on which the existence of civilization depends. All is well
if these leaders are persons who possess superior insight into the
necessities of life and who have risen to the height of mastering their
own instinctual wishes. But there is danger that in order not to lose
their influence they may give way to the mass more than it gives way
to them, and it therefore seems necessary that they shall be independent of the mass by having means to power at their disposal. To put
it briefly, there are two widespread human characteristics which are
responsible for the fact that the regulations of civilization can only be
maintained by a certain degree of coercion—namely, that men are not
spontaneously fond of work and that arguments are of no avail against
their passions

We have slipped unawares out of the economic field into the field of
psychology. At first we were tempted to look for the assets of civilization in the available wealth and in the regulations for its distribution.
But with the recognition that every civilization rests on a compulsion
to work and a renunciation of instinct and therefore inevitably pro-
vokes opposition from those affected by these demands, it has become
clear that civilization cannot consist principally or solely in wealth itself
and the means of acquiring it and the arrangements for its distribution;
for these things are threatened by the rebelliousness and destructive

---

2. [*"Masse."* The German word has a very wide meaning. It is translated "group" for
special reasons in Freud's *Group Psychology* (1921c). See *S.E.,* 18, 69*n;* I.P.L., 6, 1 *n.*
Here "mass" seems more appropriate.]

mania of the participants in civilization. Alongside of wealth we now come upon the means by which civilization can be defended—measures of coercion and other measures that are intended to reconcile men to it and to recompense them for their sacrifices. These latter may be described as the mental assets of civilization.

For the sake of a uniform terminology we will describe the fact that an instinct cannot be satisfied as a "frustration," the regulation by which this frustration is established as a "prohibition" and the condition which is produced by the prohibition as a "privation." The first step is to distinguish between privations which affect everyone and privations which do not affect everyone but only groups, classes or even single individuals. The former are the earliest; with the prohibitions that established them, civilization—who knows how many thousands of years ago?—began to detach man from his primordial animal condition. We have found to our surprise that these privations are still operative and still form the kernel of hostility to civilization. The instinctual wishes that suffer under them are born afresh with every child; there is a class of people, the neurotics, who already react to these frustrations with asocial behavior. Among these instinctual wishes are those of incest, cannibalism and lust for killing. It sounds strange to place alongside one another wishes which everyone seems united in repudiating and others about which there is so much lively dispute in our civilization as to whether they shall be permitted or frustrated; but psychologically it is justifiable to do so. Nor is the attitude of civilization to these oldest instinctual wishes by any means uniform. Cannibalism alone seems to be universally proscribed and— to the non-psychoanalytic view—to have been completely surmounted. The strength of the incestuous wishes can still be detected behind the prohibition against them; and under certain conditions killing is still practised, and indeed commanded, by our civilization. It is possible that cultural developments lie ahead of us in which the satisfaction of yet other wishes, which are entirely permissible today, will appear just as unacceptable as cannibalism does now.

These earliest instinctual renunciations already involve a psychological factor which remains inportant for all further instinctual renunciations as well. It is not true that the human mind has undergone no development since the earliest times and that, in contrast to the advances of science and technology, it is the same to-day as it was at the beginning of history. We can point out one of these mental advances at once. It is in keeping with the course of human development that external coercion gradually becomes internalized; for a special mental agency, man's super-ego, takes it over and includes it among its commandments.[3] Every child presents this process of transformation to us; only by that means does it become a moral and social being. Such a strengthening of the super-ego is a most precious cultural asset in the psychological field. Those in whom it has taken place are turned from being opponents of civilization into being its vehicles. The greater their number is in a cultural unit the more secure is its culture and the more it can dispense with external measures of coercion. Now the degree of this internalization differs greatly between the various instinctual prohibitions. As regards the earliest cultural demands, which I have mentioned, the internalization seems to have been very extensively achieved, if we leave out of account the unwelcome exception of the neurotics. But the case is altered when we turn to the other instinctual claims. Here we observe with surprise and concern that a majority of people obey the cultural prohibitions on these points only under the pressure of external coercion—that is, only where that coercion can make itself effective and so long as it is to be feared. This is also true of what are known as the *moral* demands of civilization, which likewise apply to everyone. Most of one's experiences of man's moral untrustworthiness fall into this category. There are countless civilized people who would shrink from murder or incest but who do not deny themselves the satisfaction of their avarice, their aggressive urges, or their sexual lusts, and who do not hesitate to injure other people by lies, fraud and calumny, so long as they can remain unpunished for it; and this, no doubt, has always been so through many ages of civilization.

. . . We know already how the individual reacts to the injuries which civilization and other men inflict on him: he develops a corresponding degree of resistance to the regulations of civilization and of hostility to it. But how does he defend himself against the superior powers of nature, of Fate, which threaten him as they threaten all the rest?

Civilization relieves him of this task; it performs it in the same way for all alike; and it is noteworthy that in this almost all civilizations act alike. Civilization does not call a halt in the task of defending man against nature, it merely pursues it by other means. The task is a manifold one. Man's self-regard, seriously menaced, calls for consolation; life and the universe must be robbed of their terrors; moreover his curiosity, moved, it is true, by the strongest practical interest, demands an answer.

---

3. [See Chapter III of *The Ego and the Id* (1923b), *Standard Ed.,* 19, 28 ff.; I.P.L., 12, 18 ff.]

A great deal is already gained with the first step: the humanization of nature. Impersonal forces and destinies cannot be approached; they remain eternally remote. But if the elements have passions that rage as they do in our own souls, if death itself is not something spontaneous but the violent act of an evil Will, if everywhere in nature there are Beings around us of a kind that we know in our own society, then we can breathe freely, can feel at home in the uncanny and can deal by psychical means with our senseless anxiety. We are still defenceless, perhaps, but we are no longer helplessly paralysed; we can at least react. Perhaps, indeed, we are not even defenceless. We can apply the same methods against these violent supermen outside that we employ in our own society; we can try to adjure them, to appease them, to bribe them, and, by so influencing them, we may rob them of a part of their power. A replacement like this of natural science by psychology not only provides immediate relief, but also points the way to a further mastering of the situation.

For this situation is nothing new. It has an infantile prototype, of which it is in fact only the continuation. For once before one has found oneself in a similar state of helplessness: as a small child, in relation to one's parents. One had reason to fear them, and especially one's father; and yet one was sure of his protection against the dangers one knew. Thus it was natural to assimilate the two situations. Here, too, wishing played its part, as it does in dream-life. The sleeper may be seized with a presentiment of death, which threatens to place him in the grave. But the dream-work knows how to select a condition that will turn even that dreaded event into a wish-fulfilment: the dreamer sees himself in an ancient Etruscan grave which he has climbed down into, happy to find his archaeological interests satisfied.[4] In the same way, a man makes the forces of nature not simply into persons with whom he can associate as he would with his equals—that would not do justice to the overpowering impression which those forces make on him—but he gives them the character of a father. He turns them into gods, following in this, as I have tried to show,[5] not only an infantile prototype but a phylogenetic one.

In the course of time the first observations were made of regularity and conformity to law in natural phenomena, and with this the forces of nature lost their human traits. But man's helplessness remains and

---

4. [This was an actual dream of Freud's, reported in Chapter VI (G) of *The Interpretation of Dreams* (1900a), *Standard Ed.*, 5, 454–5.]

5. [See Section 6 of the fourth essay in *Totem and Taboo* (1912–13), *Standard Ed.*, 13, 146 ff.]

along with it his longing for his father, and the gods. The gods retain their threefold task: they must exorcize the terrors of nature, they must reconcile men to the cruelty of Fate, particularly as it is shown in death, and they must compensate them for the sufferings and privations which a civilized life in common has imposed on them.

But within these functions there is a gradual displacement of accent. It was observed that the phenomena of nature developed automatically according to internal necessities. Without doubt the gods were the lords of nature; they had arranged it to be as it was and now they could leave it to itself. Only occasionally, in what are known as miracles, did they intervene in its course, as though to make it plain that they had relinquished nothing of their original sphere of power. As regards the apportioning of destinies, an unpleasant suspicion persisted that the perplexity and helplessness of the human race could not be remedied. It was here that the gods were most apt to fail. If they themselves created Fate, then their counsels must be deemed inscrutable. The notion dawned on the most gifted people of antiquity that Moira [Fate] stood above the gods and that the gods themselves had their own destinies. And the more autonomous nature became and the more the gods withdrew from it, the more earnestly were all expectations directed to the third function of the gods—the more did morality become their true domain. It now became the task of the gods to even out the defects and evils of civilization, to attend to the sufferings which men inflict on one another in their life together and to watch over the fulfilment of the precepts of civilization, which men obey so imperfectly. Those precepts themselves were credited with a divine origin; they were elevated beyond human society and were extended to nature and the universe.

And thus a store of ideas is created, born from man's need to make his helplessness tolerable and built up from the material of memories of the helplessness of his own childhood and the childhood of the human race. It can clearly be seen that the possession of these ideas protects him in two directions—against the dangers of nature and Fate, and against the injuries that threaten him from human society itself. Here is the gist of the matter. Life in this world serves a higher purpose; no doubt it is not easy to guess what that purpose is, but it certainly signifies a perfecting of man's nature. It is probably the spiritual part of man, the soul, which in the course of time has so slowly and unwillingly detached itself from the body, that is the object of this elevation and exaltation. Everything that happens in this world is an expression of the intentions of an intelligence superior to us, which in the end, though its ways and byways are difficult to follow, orders everything for the best—that is, to make it enjoyable for us. Over each one of us there watches a benevolent Providence which is only seemingly stern and which will not suffer us to become a plaything of the over-mighty and pitiless forces of nature. Death itself is not extinction, is not a return to inorganic lifelessness, but the beginning of a new kind of existence which lies on the path of development to something higher. And, looking in the other direction, this view announces that the same moral laws which our civilizations have set up govern the whole universe as well, except that they are maintained by a supreme court of justice with incomparably more power and consistency. In the end all good is rewarded and all evil punished, if not actually in this form of life then in the later existences that begin after death. In this way all the terrors, the sufferings and the hardships of life are destined to be obliterated. Life after death, which continues life on earth just as the invisible part of the spectrum joins on to the visible part, brings us all the perfection that we may perhaps have missed here. And the superior wisdom which directs this course of things, the infinite goodness that expresses itself in it, the justice that achieves its aim in it— these are the attributes of the divine beings who also created us and the world as a whole, or rather, of the one divine being into which, in our civilization, all the gods of antiquity have been condensed. The people which first succeeded in thus concentrating the divine attributes was not a little proud of the advance. It had laid open to view the father who had all along been hidden behind every divine figure as its nucleus. Fundamentally this was a return to the historical beginnings of the idea of God. Now that God was a single person, man's relations to him could recover the intimacy and intensity of the child's relation to his father. But if one had done so much for one's father, one wanted to have a reward, or at least to be his only beloved child, his Chosen People. Very much later, pious America laid claim to being "God's own Country," and, as regards one of the shapes in which men worship the deity, the claim is undoubtedly valid.

The religious ideas that have been summarized above have of course passed through a long process of development and have been adhered to in various phases by various civilizations. I have singled out one such phase, which roughly corresponds to the final form taken by our present-day white Christian civilization. It is easy to see that not all the parts of this picture tally equally well with one another, that not all the questions that press for an answer receive one, and that it is difficult to dismiss the contradiction of daily experience. Nevertheless, such as they are, those ideas—ideas which are religious in the widest sense— are prized as the most precious possession of civilization, as the most

precious thing it has to offer its participants. It is far more highly prized
than all the devices for winning treasures from the earth or providing
men with sustenance or preventing their illnesses, and so forth. People
feel that life would not be tolerable if they did not attach to these ideas
the value that is claimed for them. And now the question arises: what
are these ideas in the light of psychology? Whence do they derive the
esteem in which they are held? And, to take a further timid step, what
is their real worth?

. . . Religious ideas are teachings and assertions about facts and conditions of external (or internal) reality which tell one something one has
not discovered for oneself and which lay claim to one's belief. . . .

. . . When we ask on what their claim to be believed is founded, we
are met with three answers, which harmonize remarkably badly with
one another. Firstly, these teachings deserve to be believed because
they were already believed by our primal ancestors; secondly, we possess proofs which have been handed down to us from those same
primaeval times; and thirdly, it is forbidden to raise the question of
their authentication at all. In former days anything so presumptuous
was visited with the severest penalties, and even to-day society looks
askance at any attempt to raise the question again.

This third point is bound to rouse our strongest suspicions. After all,
a prohibition like this can only be for one reason—that society is very
well aware of the insecurity of the claim it makes on behalf of its
religious doctrines. . . .

. . . in past times religious ideas, in spite of their incontrovertible lack
of authentication, have exercised the strongest possible influence on
mankind. This is a fresh psychological problem. We must ask where
the inner force of those doctrines lies and to what it is that they owe
their efficacy, independent as it is of recognition by reason.

I think we have prepared the way sufficiently for an answer to both
these questions. It will be found if we turn our attention to the psychical origin of religious ideas. These, which are given out as teachings, are not precipitates of experience or end-results of thinking: they
are illusions, fulfilments of the oldest, strongest and most urgent
wishes of mankind. The secret of their strength lies in the strength of
those wishes. As we already know, the terrifying impression of helplessness in childhood aroused the need for protection—for protection
through love—which was provided by the father; and the recognition
that this helplessness lasts throughout life made it necessary to cling

to the existence of a father, but this time a more powerful one. Thus the benevolent rule of a divine Providence allays our fear of the dangers of life; the establishment of a moral world-order ensures the fulfilment of the demands of justice, which have so often remained unfulfilled in human civilization; and the prolongation of earthly existence in a future life provides the local and temporal framework in which these wish-fulfilments shall take place. Answers to the riddles that tempt the curiosity of man, such as how the universe began or what the relation is between body and mind, are developed in conformity with the underlying assumptions of this system. It is an enormous relief to the individual psyche if the conflicts of its childhood arising from the father-complex—conflicts which it has never wholly overcome—are removed from it and brought to a solution which is universally accepted.

When I say that these things are all illusions, I must define the meaning of the word. An illusion is not the same thing as an error; nor is it necessarily an error. Aristotle's belief that vermin are developed out of dung (a belief to which ignorant people still cling) was an error; so was the belief of a former generation of doctors that *tabes dorsalis* is the result of sexual excess. It would be incorrect to call these errors illusions. On the other hand, it was an illusion of Columbus's that he had discovered a new sea-route to the Indies. The part played by his wish in this error is very clear. One may describe as an illusion the assertion made by certain nationalists that the Indo-Germanic race is the only one capable of civilization; or the belief, which was only destroyed by psycho-analysis, that children are creatures without sexuality. What is characteristic of illusions is that they are derived from human wishes. In this respect they come near to psychiatric delusions. But they differ from them, too, apart from the more complicated structure of delusions. In the case of delusions, we emphasize as essential their being in contradiction with reality. Illusions need not necessarily be false—that is to say, unrealizable or in contradiction to reality. For instance, a middle-class girl may have the illusion that a prince will come and marry her. This is possible; and a few such cases have occurred. That the Messiah will come and found a golden age is much less likely. Whether one classifies this belief as an illusion or as something analogous to a delusion will depend on one's personal attitude. Examples of illusions which have proved true are not easy to find, but the illusion of the alchemists that all metals can be turned into gold might be one of them. The wish to have a great deal of gold, as much gold as possible, has, it is true, been a good deal damped by our present-day knowledge of the determinants of wealth, but chemistry no longer regards the transmutation of metals into gold as impossible.

Thus we call a belief an illusion when a wish-fulfilment is a prominent factor in its motivation, and in doing so we disregard its relations to reality, just as the illusion itself sets no store by verification.

Having thus taken our bearings, let us return once more to the question of religious doctrines. We can now repeat that all of them are illusions and insusceptible of proof. . . .

To assess the truth-value of religious doctrines does not lie within the scope of the present enquiry. It is enough for us that we have recognized them as being, in their psychological nature, illusions. But we do not have to conceal the fact that this discovery also strongly influences our attitude to the question which must appear to many to be the most important of all. We know approximately at what periods and by what kind of men religious doctrines were created. If in addition we discover the motives which led to this, our attitude to the problem of religion will undergo a marked displacement. We shall tell ourselves that it would be very nice if there were a God who created the world and was a benevolent Providence, and if there were a moral order in the universe and an after-life; but it is a very striking fact that all this is exactly as we are bound to wish it to be. And it would be more remarkable still if our wretched, ignorant and downtrodden ancestors had succeeded in solving all these difficult riddles of the universe.

We now observe that the store of religious ideas includes not only wish-fulfilments but important historical recollections. This concurrent influence of past and present must give religion a truly incomparable wealth of power. But perhaps with the help of an analogy yet another discovery may begin to dawn on us. Though it is not a good plan to transplant ideas far from the soil in which they grew up, yet here is a conformity which we cannot avoid pointing out. We know that a human child cannot successfully complete its development to the civilized stage without passing through a phase of neurosis sometimes of greater and sometimes of less distinctness. This is because so many instinctual demands which will later be unserviceable cannot be suppressed by the rational operation of the child's intellect but have to be tamed by acts of repression, behind which, as a rule, lies the motive of anxiety. Most of these infantile neuroses are overcome spontaneously in the course of growing up, and this is especially true of the obsessional neuroses of childhood. The remainder can be cleared up later still by psycho-analytic treatment. In just the same way, one might assume, humanity as a whole, in its development through the ages, fell into states analogous to the neuroses,[6] and for the same reasons—namely because in the times of its ignorance and intellectual weakness the instinctual renunciations indispensable for man's communal existence had only been achieved by it by means of purely affective forces. The precipitates of these processes resembling repression which took place in prehistoric times still remained attached to civilization for long periods. Religion would thus be the universal obsessional neurosis of humanity; like the obsessional neurosis of children, it arose out of the Oedipus complex, out of the relation to the father. If this view is right, it is to be supposed that a turning away from religion is bound to occur with the fatal inevitability of a process of growth, and that we find ourselves at this very juncture in the middle of that phase of development. Our behaviour should therefore be modelled on that of a sensible teacher who does not oppose an impending new development but seeks to ease its path and mitigate the violence of its irruption. . . .

. . . Think of the depressing contrast between the radiant intelligence of a healthy child and the feeble intellectual powers of the average adult. Can we be quite certain that it is not precisely religious education which bears a large share of the blame for this relative atrophy? I think it would be a very long time before a child who was not influenced began to trouble himself about God and things in another world. Perhaps his thoughts on these matters would then take the same paths as they did with is forefathers. But we do not wait for such a development; we introduce him to the doctrines of religion at an age when he is neither interested in them nor capable of grasping their import. Is it not true that the two main points in the programme for the education of children to-day are retardation of sexual development and premature religious influence? Thus by the time the child's intellect awakens, the doctrines of religion have already become unassailable. But are you of opinion that it is very conducive to the strengthening of the intellectual function that so important a field should be closed against it by the threat of Hell-fire? When a man has once brought himself to accept uncritically all the absurdities that religious doctrines put before him and even to overlook the contradictions between them, we need not be greatly surprised at the weakness of his intellect. But we have no other means of controlling our instinc-

6. [Freud returned to this question at the end of his *Civilization and Its Discontents* (1930a), *S.E.*, 21, 144, in the last of the *New Introductory Lectures* (1933a) and in Chapter III of *Moses and Monotheism* (1939a).]

tual nature but our intelligence. How can we expect people who are under the dominance of prohibitions of thought to attain the psychological ideal, the primacy of the intelligence? You know, too, that women in general are said to suffer from "physiological feeble-mindedness"[7] —that is, from a lesser intelligence than men. The fact itself is disputable and its interpretation doubtful, but one argument in favour of this intellectual atrophy being of a secondary nature is that women labour under the harshness of an early prohibition against turning their thoughts to what would most have interested them—namely, the problems of sexual life. So long as a person's early years are influenced not only by a sexual inhibition of thought but also by a religious inhibition and by a loyal inhibition[8] derived from this, we cannot really tell what in fact he is like.

But I will moderate my zeal and admit the possibility that I, too, am chasing an illusion. Perhaps the effect of the religious prohibition of thought may not be so bad as I suppose; perhaps it will turn out that human nature remains the same even if education is not abused in order to subject people to religion. I do not know and you cannot know either. It is not only the great problems of this life that seem insoluble at the present time; many lesser questions too are difficult to answer. But you must admit that here we are justified in having a hope for the future—that perhaps there is a treasure to be dug up capable of enriching civilization and that it is worth making the experiment of an irreligious education. Should the experiment prove unsatisfactory I am ready to give up the reform and to return to my earlier, purely descriptive judgement that man is a creature of weak intelligence who is ruled by his instinctual wishes.

On another point I agree with you unreservedly. It is certainly senseless to begin by trying to do away with religion by force and at a single blow. Above all, because it would be hopeless. The believer will not let his belief be torn from him, either by arguments or prohibitions. And even if this did succeed with some it would be cruelty. A man who has been taking sleeping draughts for tens of years is naturally unable to sleep if his sleeping draught is taken away from him. That the effect of religious consolations may be likened to that of a narcotic is well illustrated by what is happening in America. There they are now trying —obviously under the influence of petticoat government—to deprive

---

7. [The phrase was used by Moebius (1903). Cf. Freud's early paper on "civilized" sexual morality (1908*d*), *Standard Ed.*, 9, 199, where the present argument is anticipated.]

8. [I.e. in regard to the Monarchy.]

people of all stimulants, intoxicants, and other pleasure-producing substances, and instead, by way of compensation, are surfeiting them with piety. This is another experiment as to whose outcome we need not feel curious.

Thus I must contradict you when you go on to argue that men are completely unable to do without the consolation of the religious illusion, that without it they could not bear the troubles of life and the cruelties of reality. That is true, certainly, of the men into whom you have instilled the sweet—or bitter-sweet—poison from childhood onwards. But what of the other men, who have been sensibly brought up? Perhaps those who do not suffer from the neurosis will need no intoxicant to deaden it. They will, it is true, find themselves in a difficult situation. They will have to admit to themselves the full extent of their helplessness and their insignificance in the machinery of the universe; they can no longer be the centre of creation, no longer the object of tender care on the part of a beneficent Providence. They will be in the same position as a child who has left the parental house where he was so warm and comfortable. But surely infantilism is destined to be surmounted. Men cannot remain children for ever; they must in the end go out into "hostile life." We may call this *"education to reality."* Need I confess to you that the sole purpose of my book is to point out the necessity for this forward step?

Alfred J. Ayer

13. Critique of Theology

This mention of God brings us to the question of the possibility of religious knowledge. We shall see that this possibility has already been ruled out by our treatment of metaphysics. But, as this is a point of considerable interest, we may be permitted to discuss it at some length.

It is now generally admitted, at any rate by philosophers, that the existence of a being having the attributes which define the god of any non-animistic religion cannot be demonstratively proved. To see that this is so, we have only to ask ourselves what are the premises from which the existence of such a god could be deduced. If the conclusion that a god exists is to be demonstratively certain, then these premises must be certain; for, as the conclusion of a deductive argument is already contained in the premises, any uncertainty there may be about the truth of the premises is necessarily shared by it. But we know that no empirical proposition can ever be anything more than probable. It is only *a priori* propositions that are logically certain. But we cannot deduce the existence of a god from an *a priori* proposition. For we know that the reason why *a priori* propositions are certain is that they

Reprinted from Alfred J. Ayer, *Language, Truth and Logic,* 2d ed. (New York: Dover Publications; London: Victor Gollancz, Ltd., 1946), by permission of the publishers. Title supplied by the editors.

are tautologies. And from a set of tautologies nothing but a further tautology can be validly deduced. It follows that there is no possibility of demonstrating the existence of a god.

What is not so generally recognized is that there can be no way of proving that the existence of a god, such as the God of Christianity, is even probable. Yet this also is easily shown. For if the existence of such a god were probable, then the proposition that he existed would be an empirical hypothesis. And in that case it would be possible to deduce from it, and other empirical hypotheses, certain experiential propositions which were not deducible from those other hypotheses alone. But in fact this is not possible. It is sometimes claimed, indeed, that the existence of a certain sort of regularity in nature constitutes sufficient evidence for the existence of a god. But if the sentence "God exists" entails no more than that certain types of phenomena occur in certain sequences, then to assert the existence of a god will be simply equivalent to asserting that there is the requisite regularity in nature; and no religious man would admit that this was all he intended to assert in asserting the existence of a god. He would say that in talking about God, he was talking about a transcendent being who might be known through certain empirical manifestations, but certainly could not be defined in terms of those manifestations. But in that case the term "god" is a metaphysical term. And if "god" is a metaphysical term, then it cannot be even probable that a god exists. For to say that "God exists" is to make a metaphysical utterance which cannot be either true or false. And by the same criterion, no sentence which purports to describe the nature of a transcendent god can possess any literal significance.

It is important not to confuse this view of religious assertions with the view that is adopted by atheists, or agnostics.[1] For it is characteristic of an agnostic to hold that the existence of a god is a possibility in which there is no good reason either to believe or disbelieve; and it is characteristic of an atheist to hold that it is at least probable that no god exists. And our view that all utterances about the nature of God are nonsensical, so far from being identical with, or even lending any support to, either of these familiar contentions, is actually incompatible with them. For if the assertion that there is a god is nonsensical, then the atheist's assertion that there is no god is equally nonsensical, since it is only a significant proposition that can be significantly contradicted. As for the agnostic, although he refrains from saying either that there is or that there is not a god, he does not deny that the question

---

1. This point was suggested to me by Professor H. H. Price.

whether a transcendent god exists is a genuine question. He does not deny that the two sentences "There is a transcendent god" and "There is no transcendent god" express propositions one of which is actually true and the other false. All he says is that we have no means of telling which of them is true, and therefore ought not to commit ourselves to either. But we have seen that the sentences in question do not express propositions at all. And this means that agnosticism also is ruled out.

Thus we offer the theist the same comfort as we gave to the moralist. His assertions cannot possibly be valid, but they cannot be invalid either. As he says nothing at all about the world, he cannot justly be accused of saying anything false, or anything for which he has insufficient grounds. It is only when the theist claims that in asserting the existence of a transcendent god he is expressing a genuine proposition that we are entitled to disagree with him.

It is to be remarked that in cases where deities are identified with natural objects, assertions concerning them may be allowed to be significant. If, for example, a man tells me that the occurence of thunder is alone both necessary and sufficient to establish the truth of the proposition that Jehovah is angry, I may conclude that, in his usage of the words, the sentence "Jehovah is angry" is equivalent to "It is thundering." But in sophisticated religions, though they may be to some extent based on men's awe of natural process which they cannot sufficiently understand, the "person" who is supposed to control the empirical world is not himself located in it; he is held to be superior to the empirical world, and so outside it; and he is endowed with super-empirical attributes. But the notion of a person whose essential attributes are non-empirical is not an intelligible notion at all. We may have a word which is used as if it named this "person," but, unless the sentences in which it occurs express propositions which are empirically verifiable, it cannot be said to symbolize anything. And this is the case with regard to the word "god," in the usage in which it is intended to refer to a transcendent object. The mere existence of the noun is enough to foster the illusion that there is a real, or any any rate a possible entity corresponding to it. It is only when we enquire what God's attributes are that we discover that "God," in this usage, is not a genuine name.

It is common to find belief in a transcendent god conjoined with belief in an after-life. But, in the form which it usually takes, the content of this belief is not a genuine hypothesis. To say that men do not ever die, or that the state of death is merely a state of prolonged insensibility, is indeed to express a significant proposition, though all the available evidence goes to show that it is false. But to say that there is something imperceptible inside a man, which is his soul or his real self, and that it goes on living after he is dead, is to make a metaphysical assertion which has no more factual content than the assertion that there is a transcendent god.

It is worth mentioning that, according to the account which we have given of religious assertions, there is no logical ground for antagonism between religion and natural science. As far as the question of truth or falsehood is concerned, there is no opposition between the natural scientist and the theist who believes in a transcendent god. For since the religious utterances of the theist are not genuine propositions at all, they cannot stand in any logical relation to the propositions of science. Such antagonism as there is between religion and science appears to consist in the fact that science takes away one of the motives which make men religious. For it is acknowledged that one of the ultimate sources of religious feeling lies in the inability of men to determine their own destiny; and science tends to destroy the feeling of awe with which men regard an alien world, by making them believe that they can understand and anticipate the course of natural phenomena, and even to some extent control it. The fact that it has recently become fashionable for physicists themselves to be sympathetic towards religion is a point in favour of this hypothesis. For this sympathy towards religion marks the physicists' own lack of confidence in the validity of their hypotheses, which is a reaction on their part from the anti-religious dogmatism of nineteenth-century scientists, and a natural outcome of the crisis through which physics has just passed.

It is not within the scope of this enquiry to enter more deeply into the causes of religious feeling, or to discuss the probability of the continuance of religious belief. We are concerned only to answer those questions which arise out of our discussion of the possibility of religious knowledge. The point which we wish to establish is that there cannot be any transcendent truths of religion. For the sentences which the theist uses to express such "truths" are not literally significant.

An interesting feature of this conclusion is that it accords with what many theists are accustomed to say themselves. For we are often told that the nature of God is a mystery which transcends the human understanding. But to say that something transcends the human understanding is to say that it is unintelligible. And what is unintelligible cannot significantly be described. Again, we are told that God is not an object of reason but an object of faith. This may be nothing more than an admission that the existence of God must be taken on trust, since it cannot be proved. But it may also be an assertion that God is the object of a purely mystical intuition, and cannot therefore be defined in terms which are intelligible to the reason. And I think there are many theists who would assert this. But if one allows that it is impossible to define God in intelligible terms, then one is allowing that it is impossible for a sentence both to be significant and to be about God. If a mystic admits that the object of his vision is something which cannot be described, then he must also admit that he is bound to talk nonsense when he describes it.

For his part, the mystic may protest that his intuition does reveal truths to him, even though he cannot explain to others what these truths are; and that we who do not possess this faculty of intuition can have no ground for denying that it is a cognitive faculty. For we can hardly maintain *a priori* that there are no ways of discovering true propositions except those which we ourselves employ. The answer is that we set no limit to the number of ways in which one may come to formulate a true proposition. We do not in any way deny that a synthetic truth may be discovered by purely intuitive methods as well as by the rational method of induction. But we do say that every synthetic proposition, however it may have been arrived at, must be subject to the test of actual experience. We do not deny *a priori* that the mystic is able to discover truths by his own special methods. We wait to hear what are the propositions which embody his discoveries, in order to see whether they are verified or confuted by our empirical observations. But the mystic, so far from producing propositions which are empirically verified, is unable to produce any intelligible propositions at all. And therefore we say that his intuition has not revealed to him any facts. It is no use his saying that he has apprehended facts but is unable to express them. For we know that if he really had acquired any information, he would be able to express it. He would be able to indicate in some way or other how the genuineness of his discovery might be empirically determined. The fact that he cannot reveal what he "knows," or even himself devise an empirical test to validate his "knowledge," shows that his state of mystical intuition is not a genuinely cognitive state. So that in describing his vision the mystic does not give us any information about the external world; he merely gives us indirect information about the condition of his own mind.

These considerations dispose of the argument from religious experience, which many philosophers still regard as a valid argument in favour of the existence of a god. They say that it is logically possible for men to be immediately acquainted with God, as they are immediately acquainted with a sense-content, and that there is no reason why one should be prepared to believe a man when he says that he is seeing a yellow patch, and refuse to believe him when he says that he is seeing

God. The answer to this is that if the man who asserts that he is seeing God is merely asserting that he is experiencing a peculiar kind of sense-content, then we do not for a moment deny that his assertion may be true. But, ordinarily, the man who says that he is seeing God is saying not merely that he is experiencing a religious emotion, but also that there exists a transcendent being who is the object of this emotion; just as the man who says that he sees a yellow patch is ordinarily saying not merely that his visual sense-field contains a yellow sense-content, but also that there exists a yellow object to which the sense-content belongs. And it is not irrational to be prepared to believe a man when he asserts the existence of a yellow object, and to refuse to believe him when he asserts the existence of a transcendent god. For whereas the sentence "There exists here a yellow-coloured material thing" expresses a genuine synthetic proposition which could be empirically verified, the sentence "There exists a transcendent god" has, as we have seen, no literal significance.

We conclude, therefore, that the argument from religious experience is altogether fallacious. The fact that people have religious experiences is interesting from the psychological point of view, but it does not in any way imply that there is such a thing as religious knowledge, any more than our having moral experiences implies that there is such a thing as moral knowledge. The theist, like the moralist, may believe that his experiences are cognitive experiences, but, unless he can formulate his "knowledge" in propositions that are empirically verifiable, we may be sure that he is deceiving himself. It follows that those philosophers who fill their books with assertions that they intuitively "know" this or that moral or religious "truth" are merely providing material for the psycho-analyst. For no act of intuition can be said to reveal a truth about any matter of fact unless it issues in verifiable propositions. And all such propositions are to be incorporated in the system of empirical propositions which constitutes science.

14. Gods

1. *The existence of God is not an experimental issue in the way it was.* An atheist or agnostic might say to a theist "You still think there are spirits in the trees, nymphs in the streams, a God of the world." He might say this because he noticed the theist in time of drought pray for rain and make a sacrifice and in the morning look for rain. But disagreement about whether there are gods is now less of this experimental or betting sort than it used to be. This is due in part, if not wholly, to our better knowledge of why things happen as they do.

It is true that even in these days it is seldom that one who believes in God has no hopes or fears which an atheist has not. Few believers now expect prayer to still the waves, but some think it makes a difference to people and not merely in ways the atheist would admit. Of course with people, as opposed to waves and machines, one never knows what they won't do next, so that expecting prayer to make a difference to them is not so definite a thing as believing in its mechanical efficacy. Still, just as primitive people pray in a business-like way for rain so some people still pray for others with a real feeling of doing something to help. However, in spite of this persistence of an experimental element in some theistic belief, it remains true that Elijah's

From *Proceedings of the Aristotelian Society,* vol. XLV (1944/45):185–206, reprinted by courtesy of the Editor of The Aristotelian Society. © 1945 The Aristotelian Society.

method on Mount Carmel of settling the matter of what god or gods exist would be far less appropriate to-day than it was then.

2. *Belief in gods is not merely a matter of expectation of a world to come.* Someone may say "The fact that a theist no more than an atheist expects prayer to bring down fire from heaven or cure the sick does not mean that there is no difference between them as to the facts, it does not mean that the theist has no expectations different from the atheist's. For very often those who believe in God believe in another world and believe that God is there and that we shall go to that world when we die."

This is true, but I do not want to consider here expectations as to what one will see and feel after death nor what sort of reasons these logically unique expectations could have. So I want to consider those theists who do not believe in a future life, or rather, I want to consider the differences between atheists and theists in so far as these differences are not a matter of belief in a future life.

3. *What are these differences? And is it that theists are superstitious or that atheists are blind?* A child may wish to sit a while with his father and he may, when he has done what his father dislikes, fear punishment and feel distress at causing vexation, and while his father is alive he may feel sure of help when danger threatens and feel that there is sympathy for him when disaster has come. When his father is dead he will no longer expect punishment or help. Maybe for a moment an old fear will come or a cry for help escape him, but he will at once remember that this is no good now. He may feel that his father is no more until perhaps someone says to him that his father is still alive though he lives now in another world and one so far away that there is no hope of seeing him or hearing his voice again. The child may be told that nevertheless his father can see him and hear all he says. When he has been told this the child will still fear no punishment nor expect any sign of his father, but now, even more than he did when his father was alive, he will feel that his father sees him all the time and will dread distressing him and when he has done something wrong he will feel separated from his father until he has felt sorry for what he has done. Maybe when he himself comes to die he will be like a man who expects to find a friend in the strange country where he is going, but even when this is so, it is by no means all of what makes the difference between a child who believes that his father lives still in another world and one who does not.

Likewise one who believes in God may face death differently from one who does not, but there is another difference between them besides this. This other difference may still be described as belief in another world, only this belief is not a matter of expecting one thing rather than another here or hereafter, it is not a matter of a world to come but of a world that now is, though beyond our senses.

We are at once reminded of those other unseen worlds which some philosophers "believe in" and others "deny," while non-philosophers unconsciously "accept" them by using them as models with which to "get the hang of" the patterns in the flux of experience. We recall the timeless entities whose changeless connections we seek to represent in symbols, and the values which stand firm[1] amidst our flickering satisfaction and remorse, and the physical things which, though not beyond the corruption of moth and rust, are yet more permanent than the shadows they throw upon the screen before our minds. We recall, too, our talk of souls and of what lies in their depths and is manifested to us partially and intermittently in our own feelings and the behaviour of others. The hypothesis of mind, of other human minds and of animal minds, is reasonable because it explains for each of us why certain things behave so cunningly all by themselves unlike even the most ingenious machines. Is the hypothesis of minds in flowers and trees reasonable for like reasons? Is the hypothesis of a world mind reasonable for like reasons—someone who adjusts the blossom to the bees, someone whose presence may at times be felt—in a garden in high summer, in the hills when clouds are gathering, but not, perhaps, in a cholera epidemic?

4. *The question "Is belief in gods reasonable?" has more than one source.* It is clear now that in order to grasp fully the logic of belief in divine minds we need to examine the logic of belief in animal and human minds. But we cannot do that here and so for the purposes of this discussion about divine minds let us acknowledge the reasonableness of our belief in human minds without troubling ourselves about its logic. The question of the reasonableness of belief in divine minds then becomes a matter of whether there are facts in nature which support claims about divine minds in the way facts in nature support our claims about human minds.

In this way we resolve the force behind the problem of the existence of gods into two components, one metaphysical and the same which prompts the question "Is there *ever any* behaviour which gives reason to believe in *any* sort of mind?" and one which finds expression in "Are there other mind-patterns in nature beside the human and animal patterns which we can all easily detect, and are these other mind-patterns super-human?"

---

1. In another world, Dr. Joad says in the *New Statesman* recently.

Such over-determination of a question syndrome is common. Thus, the puzzling questions "Do dogs think?", "Do animals feel?" are partly metaphysical puzzles and partly scientific questions. They are not purely metaphysical; for the reports of scientists about the poor performances of cats in cages and old ladies' stories about the remarkable performances of their pets are not irrelevant. But nor are these questions purely scientific; for the stories never settle them and therefore they have other sources. One other source is the metaphysical source we have already noticed, namely, the difficulty about getting behind an animal's behaviour to its mind, whether it is a nonhuman animal or a human one.

But there's a third component in the force behind these questions. These disputes have a third source, and it is one which is important in the dispute which finds expression in the words "I believe in God." "I do not." This source comes out well if we consider the question "Do flowers feel?" Like the questions about dogs and animals this question about flowers comes partly from the difficulty we sometimes feel over inference from *any* behaviour to thought or feeling and partly from ignorance as to what behaviour is to be found. But these questions, as opposed to a like question about human beings, come also from hesitation as to whether the behaviour in question is *enough* mind-like, that is, is it enough similar to or superior to human behaviour to be called "mind-proving"? Likewise, even when we are satisfied that human behaviour shows mind and even when we have learned whatever mind-suggesting things there are in nature which are not explained by human and animal minds, we may still ask "But are these things sufficiently striking to be called a mind-pattern? Can we fairly call them manifestations of a divine being?"

"The question," someone may say, "has then become merely a matter of the application of a name. And 'What's in a name?'"

5. *But the line between a question of fact and a question or decision as to the application of a name is not so simple as this way of putting things suggests.* The question "What's in a name?" is engaging because we are inclined to answer both "Nothing" and "Very much." And this "Very much" has more than one source. We might have tried to comfort Heloise by saying "It isn't that Abelard no longer loves you, for this man isn't Abelard"; we might have said to poor Mr. Tebrick in Mr. Garnet's *Lady into Fox* "But this is no longer Silvia." But if Mr. Tebrick replied "Ah, but it is!" this might come not at all from observing facts about the fox which we have not observed, but from noticing facts about the fox which we had missed, although we had in a sense observed all that Mr. Tebrick had observed. It is possible to have

before one's eyes all the items of a pattern and still to miss the pattern. Consider the following conversation:

" 'And I think Kay and I are pretty happy. We've always been happy.'

"Bill lifted up his glass and put it down without drinking.

" 'Would you mind saying that again?' he asked.

" 'I don't see what's so queer about it. Taken all in all, Kay and I have really been happy.'

" 'All right,' Bill said gently, 'Just tell me how you and Kay have been happy.'

"Bill had a way of being amused by things which I could not understand.

" 'It's a little hard to explain,' I said. 'It's like taking a lot of numbers that don't look alike and that don't mean anything until you add them all together.'

"I stopped, because I hadn't meant to talk to him about Kay and me.

" 'Go ahead,' Bill said. 'What about the numbers.' And he began to smile.

" 'I don't know why you think it's so funny," I said. 'All the things that two people do together, two people like Kay and me, add up to something. There are the kids and the house and the dog and all the people we have known and all the times we've been out to dinner. Of course, Kay and I do quarrel sometimes but when you add it all together, all of it isn't as bad as the parts of it seem. I mean, maybe that's all there is to anybody's life.'

"Bill poured himself another drink. He seemed about to say something and checked himself. He kept looking at me."[2]

Or again, suppose two people are speaking of two characters in a story which both have read[3] or of two friends which both have known, and one says "Really she hated him," and the other says "She didn't, she loved him." Then the first may have noticed what the other has not although he knows no incident in the lives of the people they are talking about which the other doesn't know too, and the second speaker may say "She didn't, she loved him" because he hasn't noticed what the first noticed, although he can remember every incident the first can remember. But then again he may say "She didn't, she loved him" not because he hasn't noticed the patterns in time which the first has noticed but because though he has noticed them he doesn't feel he still needs to emphasize them with "Really she hated him." The line

---

2. John P. Marquand, *H. M. Pulham, Esq.,* p. 320.

3. E.g. Havelock Ellis's autobiography.

between using a name because of how we feel and because of what we have noticed isn't sharp. "A difference as to the facts," "a discovery," "a revelation," these phrases cover many things. Discoveries have been made not only by Christopher Columbus and Pasteur, but also by Tolstoy and Dostoievsky and Freud. Things are revealed to us not only by the scientists with microscopes, but also by the poets, the prophets, and the painters. What is so isn't merely a matter of "the facts." For sometimes when there is agreement as to the facts there is still argument as to whether defendant did or did not "exercise reasonable care," was or was not "negligent."

And though we shall need to emphasize how much "There is a God" evinces an attitude to the familiar[4] we shall find in the end that it also evinces some recognition of patterns in time easily missed and that, therefore, difference as to there being any gods is in part a difference as to what is so and therefore as to the facts, though not in the simple ways which first occurred to us.

6. *Let us now approach these same points by a different road.*

6.1. *How it is that an explanatory hypothesis, such as the existence of God, may start by being experimental and gradually become something quite different can be seen from the following story:*

Two people return to their long neglected garden and find among the weeds a few of the old plants surprisingly vigorous. One says to the other "It must be that a gardener has been coming and doing something about these plants." Upon inquiry they find that no neighbour has ever seen anyone at work in their garden. The first man says to the other "He must have worked while people slept." The other says "No, someone would have heard him and besides, anybody who cared about the plants would have kept down these weeds." The first man says "Look at the way these are arranged. There is purpose and a feeling for beauty here. I believe that someone comes, someone invisible to mortal eyes. I believe that the more carefully we look the more we shall find confirmation of this." They examine the garden ever so carefully and sometimes they come on new things suggesting that a gardener comes and sometimes they come on new things suggesting the contrary and even that a malicious person has been at work. Besides examining the garden carefully they also study what happens to gardens left without attention. Each learns all the other learns about this and about the garden. Consequently, when after all this, one says

---

4. Charles Leslie Stevenson, "Persuasive Definitions," *Mind,* July, 1938, should be read here. It is very good. [Also in his *Ethics and Language,* Yale, 1945.—Editor.]

"I still believe a gardener comes" while the other says "I don't" their different words now reflect no difference as to what they have found in the garden, no difference as to what they would find in the garden if they looked further and no difference about how fast untended gardens fall into disorder. At this stage, in this context, the gardener hypothesis has ceased to be experimental, the difference between one who accepts and one who rejects it is now not a matter of the one expecting something the other does not expect. What is the difference between them? The one says "A gardener comes unseen and unheard. He is manifested only in his works with which we are all familiar," the other says "There is no gardener" and with this difference in what they say about the gardener goes a difference in how they feel towards the garden, in spite of the fact that neither expects anything of it which the other does not expect.

But is this the whole difference between them—that the one calls the garden by one name and feels one way towards it, while the other calls it by another name and feels in another way towards it? And if this is what the difference has become then is it any longer appropriate to ask "Which is right?" or "Which is reasonable?"

And yet surely such questions *are* appropriate when one person says to another "You still think the world's a garden and not a wilderness, and that the gardener has not forsaken it" or "You still think there are nymphs of the streams, a presence in the hills, a spirit of the world." Perhaps when a man sings "God's in His heaven" we need not take this as more than an expression of how he feels. But when Bishop Gore or Dr. Joad writes about belief in God and young men read them in order to settle their religious doubts the impression is not simply that of persons choosing exclamations with which to face nature and the "changes and chances in this mortal life." The disputants speak as if they are concerned with a matter of scientific fact, or of trans-sensual, trans-scientific and metaphysical fact, but still of fact and still a matter about which reasons for and against may be offered, although no scientific reasons in the sense of field surveys for fossils or experiments on delinquents are to the point.

6.2. *Now can an interjection have a logic?* Can the manifestation of an attitude in the utterance of a word, in the application of a name, have a logic? When all the facts are known how can there still be a question? Surely as Hume says ". . . after every circumstance, every relation is known, the understanding has no further room to operate"?[5]

---

5. Hume, *An Enquiry concerning the Principles of Morals.* Appendix I.

6.3. When the madness of these questions leaves us for a moment *we can all easily recollect disputes which though they cannot be settled by experiment are yet disputes in which one party may be right and the other wrong* and in which both parties may offer reasons and the one better reasons than the other. *This may happen in pure and applied mathematics and logic.* Two accountants or two engineers provided with the same data may reach different results and this difference is resolved not by collecting further data but by going over the calculations again. Such differences indeed share with differences as to what will win a race, the honour of being among the most "settlable" disputes in the language.

6.4. *But it won't do to describe the theistic issue as one settlable by such calculation,* or as one about what can be deduced in this *vertical* fashion from the facts we know. No doubt dispute about God has sometimes, perhaps especially in mediaeval times, been carried on in this fashion. But nowadays it is not and we must look for some other analogy, some other case in which a dispute is settled but not by experiment.

6.5. *In courts of law* it sometimes happens that opposing counsel are agreed as to the facts and are not trying to settle a question of further fact, are not trying to settle whether the man who admittedly had quarrelled with the deceased did or did not murder him, but are concerned with whether Mr. A who admittedly handed his long-trusted clerk signed blank cheques did or did not exercise reasonable care, whether a ledger is or is not a document,[6] whether a certain body was or was not a public authority.

In such cases we notice that the process of argument is not a *chain* of demonstrative reasoning. It is a presenting and representing of those features of the case which *severally co-operate* in favour of the conclusion, in favour of saying what the reasoner wishes said, in favour of calling the situation by the name by which he wishes to call it. The reasons are like the legs of a chair, not the links of a chain. Consequently although the discussion is *a priori* and the steps are not a matter of experience, the procedure resembles scientific argument in that the reasoning is not *vertically* extensive but *horizontally* extensive

---

6. *The Times,* March 2, 1945. Also in *The Times* of June 13, 1945, contrast the case of Hannah v. Peel with that of the cruiser cut in two by a liner. In the latter case there is not agreement as to the facts. See also the excellent articles by Dr. Glanville L. Williams in the *Law Quarterly Review,* "Language and the Law," January, and April, 1945, and "The Doctrine of Repugnancy," October, 1943, January, 1944, and April, 1944. The author, having set out how arbitrary are many legal decisions, needs now to set out how far from arbitrary they are—if his readers are ready for the next phase in the dialectic process.

—it is a matter of the cumulative effect of several independent premises, not of the repeated transformation of one or two. And because the premises are severally inconclusive the process of deciding the issue becomes a matter of weighing the cumulative effect of one group of severally inconclusive items against the cumulative effect of another group of severally inconclusive items, and thus lends itself to description in terms of conflicting "probabilities." This encourages the feeling that the issue is one of fact—that it is a matter of guessing from the premises at a further fact, at what is to come. But this is a muddle. *The dispute does not cease to be* a priori *because it is a matter of the cumulative effect of severally inconclusive premises.* The logic of the dispute is not that of a chain of deductive reasoning as in a mathematic calculation. But nor is it a matter of collecting from several inconclusive items of information an expectation as to something further, as when a doctor from a patient's symptoms guesses at what is wrong, or a detective from many clues guesses the criminal. It has its own sort of logic and its own sort of end—the solution of the question at issue is a decision, a ruling by the judge. But it is not an arbitrary decision though the rational connections are neither quite like those in vertical deductions or like those in inductions in which from many signs we guess at what is to come; and though the decision manifests itself in the application of a name it is no more merely the application of a name than is the pinning on of a medal merely the pinning on of a bit of metal. Whether a lion with stripes is a tiger or a lion is, if you like, merely a matter of the application of a name. Whether Mr. So-and-So of whose conduct we have so complete a record did or did not exercise reasonable care is not merely a matter of the application of a name or, if we choose to say it is, then we must remember that with this name a game is lost and won and a game with very heavy stakes. With the judges' choice of a name for the facts goes an attitude, and the declaration, the ruling, is an exclamation evincing that attitude. But *it is an exclamation which not only has a purpose but also has a logic,* a logic surprisingly like that of "futile," "deplorable," "graceful," "grand," "divine."

6.6. *Suppose two people are looking at a picture or natural scene.* One says "Excellent" or "Beautiful" or "Divine"; the other says "I don't see it." He means he doesn't see the beauty. And this reminds us of how we felt the theist accuse the atheist of blindness and the atheist accuse the theist of seeing what isn't there. And yet surely each sees what the other sees. It isn't that one can see part of the picture which the other can't see. So the difference is in a sense not one as to the facts. And so it cannot be removed by the one disputant discovering to the other what so far he hasn't seen. It isn't that the one sees the picture in a different light and so, as we might say, sees a different picture. Consequently the difference between them cannot be resolved by putting the picture in a different light. And yet surely this is just what can be done in such a case—not by moving the picture but by talk perhaps. To settle a dispute as to whether a piece of music is good or better than another we listen again, with a picture we look again. Someone perhaps points to emphasize certain features and we see it in a different light. Shall we call this "field work" and "the last of observation" or shall we call it "reviewing the premises" and "the beginning of deduction (horizontal)"?

If in spite of all this we choose to say that a difference as to whether a thing is beautiful is not a factual difference we must be careful to remember that there is a procedure for settling these differences and that this consists not only in reasoning and redescription as in the legal case, but also in a more literal re-setting-before with re-looking or re-listening.

6.7. *And if we say as we did at the beginning that when a difference as to the existence of a God is not one as to future happenings then it is not experimental and therefore not as to the facts, we must not forthwith assume that there is no right and wrong about it,* no rationality or irrationality, no appropriateness or inappropriateness, no procedure which tends to settle it, *nor even that this procedure is in no sense a discovery of new facts.* After all even in science this is not so. Our two gardeners even when they had reached the stage when neither expected any experimental result which the other did not, might yet have continued the dispute, each presenting and re-presenting the features of the garden favouring his hypothesis, that is, fitting his model for describing the accepted fact; each emphasizing the pattern he wishes to emphasize. True, in science, there is seldom or never a pure instance of this sort of dispute, for nearly always with difference of hypothesis goes some difference of expectation as to the facts. But scientists argue about rival hypotheses with a vigour which is not exactly proportioned to difference in expectations of experimental results.

The difference as to whether a God exists involves our feelings more than most scientific disputes and in this respect is more like a difference as to whether there is beauty in a thing.

7. *The Connecting Technique.* Let us consider again the technique used in revealing or proving beauty, in removing a blindness, in induc-

ing an attitude which is lacking, in reducing a reaction that is inappropriate. Besides running over in a special way the features of the picture, tracing the rhythms, making sure that this and that are not only seen but noticed, and their relation to each other—besides all this—there are other things we can do to justify our attitude and alter that of the man who cannot see. For features of the picture may be brought out by setting beside it other pictures; just as the merits of an argument may be brought out, proved, by setting beside it other arguments, in which striking but irrelevant features of the original are changed and relevant features emphasized; just as the merits and demerits of a line of action may be brought out by setting beside it other actions. To use Susan Stebbing's example: Nathan brought out for David certain features of what David had done in the matter of Uriah the Hittite by telling him a story about two sheepowners. This is the kind of thing we very often do when someone is "inconsistent" or "unreasonable." This is what we do in referring to other cases in law. The paths we need to trace from other cases to the case in question are often numerous and difficult to detect and the person with whom we are discussing the matter may well draw attention to connections which, while not incompatible with those we have tried to emphasize, are of an opposite inclination. A may have noticed in B subtle and hidden likenesses to an angel and reveal these to C, while C has noticed in B subtle and hidden likenesses to a devil which he reveals to A.

Imagine that a man picks up some flowers that lie half withered on a table and gently puts them in water. Another man says to him "You believe flowers feel." He says this although he knows that the man who helps the flowers doesn't expect anything of them which he himself doesn't expect; for he himself expects the flowers to be "refreshed" and to be easily hurt, injured, I mean, by rough handling, while the man who puts them in water does not expect them to whisper "Thank you." The Sceptic says "You believe flowers feel" because something about the way the other man lifts the flowers and puts them in water suggests an attitude to the flowers which he feels inappropriate although perhaps he would not feel it inappropriate to butterflies. He feels that this attitude to flowers is somewhat crazy *just as it is sometimes felt that a lover's attitude is somewhat crazy even when this is not a matter of his having false hopes about how the person he is in love with will act.* It is often said in such cases that reasoning is useless. But the very person who says this feels that the lover's attitude is crazy, is inappropriate like some dreads and hatreds, such as some horrors of enclosed places. And often one who says "It is useless to reason" proceeds at once to reason with the lover, nor is this reasoning always quite without effect. We may draw the lover's attention to certain things done by her he is in love with and trace for him a path to these from things done by others at other times[7] which have disgusted and infuriated him. And by this means we may weaken his admiration and confidence, make him feel it unjustified and arouse his suspicion and contempt and make him feel our suspicion and contempt reasonable. It is possible, of course, that he has already noticed the analogies, the connections, we point out and that he has accepted them—that is, he has not denied them nor passed them off. He has recognized them and they have altered his attitude, altered his love, but he still loves. We then feel that perhaps it is we who are blind and cannot see what he can see.

8. *Connecting and Disconnecting.* But before we confess ourselves thus inadequate there are other fires his admiration must pass through. For when a man has an attitude which it seems to us he should not have or lacks one which it seems to us he should have then, not only do we suspect that he is not influenced by connections which we feel should influence him and draw his attention to these, but also we suspect he is influenced by connections which should not influence him and draw his attention to these. It may, for a moment, seem strange that we should draw his attention to connections which we feel should not influence him, and which, since they do influence him, he has in a sense already noticed. But we do—such is our confidence in "the light of reason."

Sometimes the power of these connections comes mainly from a man's mismanagement of the language he is using. This is what happens in the Monte Carlo fallacy, where by mismanaging the laws of chance a man passes from noticing that a certain colour or number has not turned up for a long while to an improper confidence that now it soon will turn up. In such cases our showing up of the false connections is a process we call "explaining a fallacy in reasoning." To remove fallacies in reasoning we urge a man to call a spade a spade, ask him what he means by "the State" and having pointed out ambiguities and vaguenesses ask him to reconsider the steps in his argument.

9. *Unspoken Connections. Usually, however, wrongheadedness or wrongheartedness in a situation, blindness to what is there or seeing what is not, does not arise merely from mismanagement of language but is more due to connections which are not mishandled in language, for the reason that they are not put into language at all.* And often

---

7. Thus, like the scientist, the critic is concerned to show up the irrelevance of time and space.

these misconnections too, weaken in the light of reason, if only we can guess where they lie and turn in on them. In so far as these connections are not presented in language the process of removing their power is not a process of correcting the mismanagement of language. But it is still akin to such a process; for though it is not a process of setting out fairly what has been set out unfairly, it is a process of setting out fairly what has not been set out at all. And we must remember that the line between connections ill-presented or half-presented in language and connections operative but not presented in language, or only hinted at, is not a sharp one.

Whether or not we call the process of showing up these connections "reasoning to remove bad unconscious reasoning" or not, it is certain that in order to settle in ourselves what weight we shall attach to someone's confidence or attitude we not only ask him for his reasons but also look for unconscious reasons both good and bad; that is, for reasons which he can't put into words, isn't explicitly aware of, is hardly aware of, isn't aware of at all—perhaps it's long experience which he *doesn't* recall which lets him know a squall is coming, perhaps it's old experience which he *can't* recall which makes the cake in the tea mean so much and makes Odette so fascinating.[8]

I am well aware of the distinction between the question "What reasons are there for the belief that S is P?" and the question "What are the sources of beliefs that S is P?" There are cases where investigation of the rationality of a claim which certain persons make is done with very little inquiry into why they say what they do, into the causes of their beliefs. This is so when we have very definite ideas about what is really logically relevant to their claim and what is not. Offered a mathematical theorem we ask for the proof; offered the generalization that parental discord causes crime we ask for the correlation coefficients. But even in this last case, if we fancy that only the figures are reasons we underestimate the complexity of the logic of our conclusion; and yet it is difficult to describe the other features of the evidence which have weight and there is apt to be disagreement about the weight they should have. In criticizing other conclusions and especially conclusions which are largely the expression of an attitude, we have not only to ascertain what reasons there are for them but also to decide what things are reasons and how much. This latter process of sifting reasons from causes is part of the critical process for every belief, but in some spheres it has been done pretty fully already. In these spheres we don't need to examine the actual processes to belief and distil from

8. Proust, *Swann's Way,* Vol. I, p. 58, Vol. II. Phoenix ed.

them a logic. But in other spheres this remains to be done. Even in science or on the stock exchange or in ordinary life we sometimes hesitate to condemn a belief or a hunch[9] merely because those who believe it cannot offer the sort of reasons we had hoped for. And now suppose Miss Gertrude Stein finds excellent the work of a new artist while we see nothing in it. We nervously recall, perhaps, how pictures by Picasso, which Miss Stein admired and others rejected, later came to be admired by many who gave attention to them, and we wonder whether the case is not a new instance of her perspicacity and our blindness. But if, upon giving all our attention to the work in question, we still do not respond to it, and we notice that the subject matter of the new pictures is perhaps birds in wild places and learn that Miss Stein is a birdwatcher, then we begin to trouble ourselves less about her admiration.

It must not be forgotten that our attempt to show up misconnections in Miss Stein may have an opposite result and reveal to us connections we had missed. Thinking to remove the spell exercised upon his patient by the old stories of the Greeks, the psycho-analyst may himself fall under that spell and find in them what his patient has found and, incidentally, what made the Greeks tell those tales.

10. *Now what happens, what should happen, when we inquire in this way into the reasonableness, the propriety of belief in gods?* The answer is: A double and opposite-phased change. Wordsworth writes:

> . . . And I have felt
> A presence that disturbs me with the joy
> Of elevated thoughts; a sense sublime
> Of something far more deeply interfused,
> Whose dwelling is the light of setting suns,
> And the round ocean and the living air,
> And the blue sky, and in the mind of man:
> A motion and a spirit, that impels
> All thinking things, all objects of all thought,
> And rolls through all things . . .[10]

We most of us know this feeling. But is it well placed like the feeling that here is first-rate work, which we sometimes rightly have even before we have fully grasped the picture we are looking at or the book we are reading? Or is it misplaced like the feeling in a house that has

---

9. Here I think of Mr. Stace's interesting reflections in *Mind,* January, 1945, "The Problems of Unreasoned Beliefs."

10. *Tintern Abbey.*

long been empty that someone secretly lives there still. Wordsworth's feeling *is* the feeling that the world is haunted, that something watches in the hills and manages the stars. The child feels that the stone tripped him when he stumbled, that the bough struck him when it flew back in his face. He has to learn that the wind isn't buffeting him, that there is not a devil in it, that he was wrong, that his attitude was inappropriate. And as he learns that the wind wasn't hindering him so he also learns it wasn't helping him. But we know how, though he learns, his attitude lingers. It is plain that Wordsworth's feeling is of this family.

Belief in gods, it is true, is often very different from belief that stones are spiteful, the sun kindly. For the gods appear in human form and from the waves and control these things and by so doing reward and punish us. But varied as are the stories of the gods they have a family likeness and we have only to recall them to feel sure of the other main sources which co-operate with animism to produce them.

What are the stories of the gods? What are our feelings when we believe in God? They are feelings of awe before power, dread of the thunderbolts of Zeus, confidence in the everlasting arms, unease beneath the all-seeing eye. They are feelings of guilt and inescapable vengeance, of smothered hate and of a security we can hardly do without. We have only to remind ourselves of these feelings and the stories of the gods and goddesses and heros in which these feelings find expression, to be reminded of how we felt as children to our parents and the big people of our childhood. Writing of a first telephone call from his grandmother, Proust says: ". . . it was rather that this isolation of the voice was like a symbol, a presentation, a direct consequence of another isolation, that of my grandmother, separated for the first time in my life, from myself. The orders or prohibitions which she addressed to me at every moment in the ordinary course of my life, the tedium of obedience or the fire of rebellion which neutralized the affection that I felt for her were at this moment eliminated. . . . "Granny!" I cried to her . . . but I had beside me only that voice, a phantom, as unpalpable as that which would come to revisit me when my grandmother was dead. 'Speak to me!' but then it happened that, left more solitary still, I ceased to catch the sound of her voice. My grandmother could no longer hear me . . . I continued to call her, sounding the empty night, in which I felt that her appeals also must be straying. I was shaken by the same anguish which, in the distant past, I had felt once before, one day when, a little child, in a crowd, I had lost her."

Giorgio do Chirico, writing of Courbet, says: "The word yesterday envelops us with its yearning echo, just as, on waking, when the sense of time and the logic of things remain a while confused, the memory of a happy hour we spent the day before may sometimes linger reverberating within us. At times we think of Courbet and his work as we do of our own father's youth."

When a man's father fails him by death or weakness how much he needs another father, one in the heavens with whom is "no variableness nor shadow of turning."

We understood Mr. Kenneth Graham when he wrote of the Golden Age we feel we have lived in under the Olympians. Freud says: "The ordinary man cannot imagine this Providence in any other form but that of a greatly exalted father, for only such a one could understand the needs of the sons of men, or be softened by their prayers and be placated by the signs of their remorse. The whole thing is so patently infantile, so incongruous with reality. . . ." "So incongruous with reality"! It cannot be denied.

But here a new aspect of the matter may strike us.[11] For the very facts which make us feel that now we can recognize systems of superhuman, sub-human, elusive, beings for what they are—the persistent projections of infantile phantasies—include facts which make these systems less fantastic. What are these facts? They are patterns in human reactions which are well described by saying that we are as if there were hidden within us powers, persons, not ourselves and stronger than ourselves. That this is so may perhaps be said to have been common knowledge yielded by ordinary observation of people,[12] but we did not know the degree in which this is so until recent study of extraordinary cases in extraordinary conditions had revealed it. I refer, of course, to the study of multiple personalities and the wider studies of psycho-analysts. Even when the results of this work are reported to us that is not the same as tracing the patterns in the details of the cases on which the results are based; and even that is not the same as taking part in the studies oneself. One thing not sufficiently realized is that some of the things shut within us are not bad but good.

Now the gods, good and evil and mixed, have always been mysterious powers outside us rather than within. But they have also been within. It is not a modern theory but an old saying that in each of us

---

11. I owe to the late Dr. Susan Isaacs the thought of this different aspect of the matter, of this connection between the heavenly Father and "the good father" spoken of in psycho-analysis.

12. Consider Tolstoy and Dostoievsky—I do not mean, of course, that their observation was ordinary.

a devil sleeps. Eve said: "The serpent beguiled me." Helen says to
Menelaus:

> . . . And yet how strange it is!
> I ask not thee; I ask my own sad thought,
> What was there in my heart, that I forgot
> My home and land and all I loved, to fly
> With a strange man? Surely it was not I,
> But Cypris there![13]

Elijah found that God was not in the wind, nor in the thunder, but in
a still small voice. The kingdom of Heaven is within us, Christ insisted,
though usually about the size of a grain of mustard seed, and he prayed
that we should become one with the Father in Heaven.

New knowledge made it necessary either to give up saying "The sun
is sinking" or to give the words a new meaning. In many contexts we
preferred to stick to the old words and give them a new meaning which
was not entirely new but, on the contrary, *practically* the same as the
old. The Greeks did not speak of the dangers of repressing instincts
but they did speak of the dangers of thwarting Dionysos, of neglecting
Cypris for Diana, of forgetting Poseidon for Athena. We have eaten of
the fruit of a garden we can't forget though we were never there, a
garden we still look for though we can never find it. Maybe we look
for too simple a likeness to what we dreamed. Maybe we are not as free
as we fancy from the old idea that Heaven is a happy hunting ground,
or a city with streets of gold. Lately Mr. Aldous Huxley has recommended our seeking not somewhere beyond the sky or late in time but
a timeless state not made of the stuff of this world, which he rejects,
picking it into worthless pieces. But this sounds to me still too much
a looking for another place, not indeed one filled, with sweets but
instead so empty that some of us would rather remain in the Lamb or

---

13. Euripides: *The Trojan Women,* Gilbert Murray's translation. Roger Hinks in
Myth and Allegory in Ancient Art writes (p. 108): "Personifications made their appearance very early in Greek poetry. . . . It is out of the question to call these terrible beings
'abstractions'. . . . They are real daemons to be worshipped and propitiated. . . . These
beings we observe correspond to states of mind. The experience of man teaches him
that from time to time his composure is invaded and overturned by some power from
outside, panic, intoxication, sexual desire."

> "What use to shoot off guns at unicorns?
> Where one horn's hit another fierce horn grows.
> These beasts are fabulous, and none were born
> Of woman who could lay a fable low."

The Glass Tower, Nicholas Moore, p. 100.

the Elephant, where, as we know, they stop whimpering with another bitter and so far from sneering at all things, hang pictures of winners at Kempton and stars of the 'nineties. Something good we have for each other if freed there, and in some degree and for a while the miasma of time is rolled back without obliging us to deny the present.

The artists who do most for us don't tell us only of fairylands. Proust, Manet, Breughel, even Botticelli and Vermeer show us reality. And yet they give us for a moment exhilaration without anxiety, peace without boredom. And those who, like Freud, work in a different way against that which too often comes over us and forces us into deadness or despair,[14] also deserve critical, patient and courageous attention. For they, too, work to release us from human bondage into human freedom.

Many have tried to find ways of salvation. The reports they bring back are always incomplete and apt to mislead even when they are not in words but in music or paint. But they are by no means useless; and not the worst of them are those which speak of oneness with God. But in so far as we become one with Him He becomes one with us. St. John says he is in us as we love one another.

This love, I suppose, is not benevolence but something that comes of the oneness with one another of which Christ spoke.[15] Sometimes it momentarily gains strength.[16] Hate and the Devil do too. And what is oneness without otherness?

---

14. Matthew Arnold, *Summer Night*.
15. St. John 16:21.
16. "The Harvesters," in Kenneth Graham, *The Golden Age*.

Rudolf Bultmann

15. Kerygma and Myth

The Task of Demythologizing
the New Testament Proclamation

A. THE PROBLEM

1. *The Mythical View of the World and the Mythical Event of Redemption*

The cosmology of the New Testament is essentially mythical in character. The world is viewed as a three-storied structure, with the earth in the centre, the heaven above, and the underworld beneath. Heaven is the abode of God and of celestial beings—the angels. The underworld is hell, the place of torment. Even the earth is more than the scene of natural, everyday events, of the trivial round and common task. It is the scene of the supernatural activity of God and his angels on the one hand, and of Satan and his daemons on the other. These supernatural forces intervene in the course of nature and in all that men think and will and do. Miracles are by no means rare. Man is not in control of his own life. Evil spirits may take possession of him. Satan

Reprinted from Rudolf Bultmann, *Kerygma and Myth: A Theological Debate,* edited by Hans-Werner Bartsch, trans. Reginald H. Fuller (London: The Society for Promoting Christian Knowledge, 1953; New York: Harper and Row, 1961), by permission of S. P. C. K. Title supplied by the editors.

may inspire him with evil thoughts. Alternatively, God may inspire his thought and guide his purposes. He may grant him heavenly visions. He may allow him to hear his word of succour or demand. He may give him the supernatural power of his Spirit. History does not follow a smooth unbroken course; it is set in motion and controlled by these supernatural powers. This aeon is held in bondage by Satan, sin, and death (for "powers" is precisely what they are), and hastens towards its end. That end will come very soon, and will take the form of a cosmic catastrophe. It will be inaugurated by the "woes" of the last time. Then the Judge will come from heaven, the dead will rise, the last judgment will take place, and men will enter into eternal salvation or damnation.

This then is the mythical view of the world which the New Testament presupposes when it presents the event of redemption which is the subject of its preaching. It proclaims in the language of mythology that the last time has now come. "In the fulness of time" God sent forth his Son, a pre-existent divine Being, who appears on earth as a man.[1] He dies the death of a sinner[2] on the cross and makes atonement for the sins of men.[3] His ressurection marks the beginning of the cosmic catastrophe. Death, the consequence of Adam's sin, is abolished,[4] and the daemonic forces are deprived of their power.[5] The risen Christ is exalted to the right hand of God in heaven[6] and made "Lord" and "King."[7] He will come again on the clouds of heaven to complete the work of redemption, and the resurrection and judgement of men will follow.[8] Sin, suffering and death will then be finally abolished.[9] All this is to happen very soon; indeed, St Paul thinks that he himself will live to see it.[10]

All who belong to Christ's Church and are joined to the Lord by Baptism and the Eucharist are certain of resurrection to salvation,[11] unless they forfeit it by unworthy behavior. Christian believers already

---

1. Gal. 4. 4; Phil. 2. 6ff.; 2 Cor. 8. 9; John 1. 14, etc.
2. 2 Cor. 5. 21; Rom. 8. 3.
3. Rom. 3. 23–26; 4. 25; 8. 3; 2 Cor. 5. 14, 19; John 1. 29; I John 2. 2, etc.
4. I Cor. 15. 21f.; Rom. 5. 12ff.
5. I Cor. 2. 6; Col. 2. 15; Rev. 12. 7ff., etc.
6. Acts 1. 6f.; 2. 33; Rom. 8. 34, etc.
7. Phil. 2. 9–11; I Cor. 15. 25.
8. I Cor. 15. 23f., 50ff., etc.
9. Rev. 21. 4, etc.
10. I Thess. 4. 15ff.; I Cor. 15. 51f.; cf. Mark 9. 1.
11. Rom. 5. 12ff.; I Cor. 15. 21ff., 44b, ff.

enjoy the first instalment of salvation, for the Spirit[12] is at work within them, bearing witness to their adoption as sons of God,[13] and guaranteeing their final resurrection.[14]

2. *The Mythological View of the World Obsolete*

All this is the language of mythology, and the origin of the various themes can be easily traced in the contemporary mythology of Jewish Apocalyptic and in the redemption myths of Gnosticism. To this extent *the kerygma is incredible to modern man, for he is convinced that the mythical view of the world is obsolete.* We are therefore bound to ask whether, when we preach the Gospel to-day, we expect our converts to accept not only the Gospel message, but also the mythical view of the world in which it is set. If not, does the New Testament embody a truth which is quite independent of its mythical setting? If it does, theology must undertake the task of stripping the Kerygma from its mythical framework, of "demythologizing" it.

Can Christian preaching expect modern man *to accept the mythical view of the world as true?* To do so would be both senseless and impossible. It would be senseless, because there is nothing specifically Christian in the mythical view of the world as such. It is simply the cosmology of a pre-scientific age. Again, it would be impossible, because no man can adopt a view of the world by his own volition—it is already determined for him by his place in history. Of course such a view is not absolutely unalterable, and the individual may even contribute to its change. But he can do so only when he is faced by a new set of facts so compelling as to make his previous view of the world untenable. He has then no alternative but to modify his view of the world or produce a new one. The discoveries of Copernicus and the atomic theory are instances of this, and so was romanticism, with its discovery that the human subject is richer and more complex than enlightenment or idealism had allowed, and nationalism, with its new realization of the importance of history and the tradition of peoples.

It may equally well happen that truths which a shallow enlightenment had failed to perceive are later rediscovered in ancient myths. Theologians are perfectly justified in asking whether this is not exactly what has happened with the New Testament. At the same time it is impossible to revive an obsolete view of the world by a mere fiat, and certainly not a mythical view. For all our thinking to-day is shaped irrevocably by modern science. A blind acceptance of the New Testa-

---

12. 'Απαρχή: Rom. 8. 23, ἀρραβών: 2 Cor. 1. 22; 5. 5.

13. Rom. 8. 15; Gal. 4. 6.

14. Rom. 8. 11.

ment mythology would be arbitrary, and to press for its acceptance as an article of faith would be to reduce faith to works. Wilhelm Herrmann pointed this out, and one would have thought that his demonstration was conclusive. It would involve a sacrifice of the intellect which could have only one result—a curious form of schizophrenia and insincerity. It would mean accepting a view of the world in our faith and religion which we should deny in our everyday life. Modern thought as we have inherited it brings with it criticism of the *New Testament view of the world.*

Man's knowledge and mastery of the world have advanced to such an extent through science and technology that it is no longer possible for anyone seriously to hold the New Testament view of the world—in fact, there is no one who does. What meaning, for instance, can we attach to such phrases in the creed as "descended into hell" or "ascended into heaven"? We no longer believe in the three-storied universe which the creeds take for granted. The only honest way of reciting the creeds is to strip the mythological framework from the truth they enshrine—that is, assuming that they contain any truth at all, which is just the question that theology has to ask. No one who is old enough to think for himself supposes that God lives in a local heaven. There is no longer any heaven in the traditional sense of the word. The same applies to hell in the sense of a mythical underworld beneath our feet. And if this is so, the story of Christ's descent into hell and of his Ascension into heaven is done with. We can no longer look for the return of the Son of Man on the clouds of heaven or hope that the faithful will meet him in the air (1 Thess. 4. 15ff.).

Now that the forces and the laws of nature have been discovered, we can no longer believe in *spirits, whether good or evil.* We know that the stars are physical bodies whose motions are controlled by the laws of the universe, and not daemonic beings which enslave mankind to their service. Any influence they may have over human life must be explicable in terms of the ordinary laws of nature; it cannot in any way be attributed to their malevolence. Sickness and the cure of disease are likewise attributable to natural causation; they are not the result of daemonic activity or of evil spells.[15] The *miracles of the New Testa-*

---

15. It may of course be argued that there are people alive to-day whose confidence in the traditional scientific view of the world has been shaken, and others who are primitive enough to qualify for an age of mythical thought. And there are also many varieties of superstition. But when belief in spirits and miracles has degenerated into superstition, it has become something entirely different from what it was when it was genuine faith. The various impressions and speculations which influence credulous people here and there are of little importance, nor does it matter to what extent cheap slogans have spread an atmosphere inimical to science. What matters is the world view which men imbibe from their environment, and it is science which determines that view of the world through the school, the press, the wireless, the cinema, and all the other fruits of technical progress.

ment have ceased to be miraculous, and to defend their historicity by recourse to nervous disorders or hypnotic effects only serves to underline the fact. And if we are still left with certain physiological and psychological phenomena which we can only assign to mysterious and enigmatic causes, we are still assigning them to causes, and thus far are trying to make them scientifically intelligible. Even occultism pretends to be a science.

It is impossible to use electric light and the wireless and to avail ourselves of modern medical and surgical discoveries, and at the same time to believe in the New Testament world of spirits and miracles.[16] We may think we can manage it in our own lives, but to expect others to do so is to make the Christian faith unintelligible and unacceptable to the modern world.

The mythical eschatology is untenable for the simple reason that the parousia of Christ never took place as the New Testament expected. History did not come to an end, and, as every schoolboy knows, it will continue to run its course. Even if we believe that the world as we know it will come to an end in time, we expect the end to take the form of a natural catastrophe, not of a mythical event such as the New Testament expects. And if we explain the parousia in terms of modern scientific theory, we are applying criticism to the New Testament, albeit unconsciously.

But natural science is not the only challenge which the mythology of the New Testament has to face. There is the still more serious challenge presented by *modern man's understanding of himself.*

Modern man is confronted by a curious dilemma. He may regard himself as pure nature, or as pure spirit. In the latter case he distinguishes the essential part of his being from nature. In either case, however, *man is essentially a unity.* He bears the sole responsibility for his own feeling, thinking, and willing.[17] He is not, as the New Testament regards him, the victim of a strange dichotomy which exposes him to the interference of powers outside himself. If his exterior behavior and his interior condition are in perfect harmony, it is something he has achieved himself, and if other people think their interior unity is torn asunder by daemonic or divine interference, he calls it schizophrenia.

Although biology and psychology recognize that man is a highly dependent being, that does not mean that he has been handed over

---

16. Cp. the observations of Paul Schütz on the decay of mythical religion in the East through the introduction of modern hygiene and medicine.

17. Cp. Gerhardt Krüger, *Einsicht und Leidenschaft, Das Wesen des platonischen Denkens,* Frankfort, 1939, p. 11f.

to powers outside of and distinct from himself. This dependence is inseparable from human nature, and he needs only to understand it in order to recover his self-mastery and organize his life on a rational basis. If he regards himself as spirit, he knows that he is permanently conditioned by the physical, bodily part of his being, but he distinguishes his true self from it, and knows that he is independent and responsible for his mastery over nature.

In either case he finds *what the New Testament has to say about the "Spirit"* ($\pi\nu\epsilon\tilde{v}\mu\alpha$) *and the sacraments utterly strange and incomprehensible.* Biological man cannot see how a supernatural entity like the $\pi\nu\epsilon\tilde{v}\mu\alpha$ can penetrate within the close texture of his natural powers and set to work within him. Nor can the idealist understand how a $\pi\nu\epsilon\tilde{v}\mu\alpha$ working like a natural power can touch and influence his mind and spirit. Conscious as he is of his own moral responsibility, he cannot conceive how baptism in water can convey a mysterious something which is henceforth the agent of all his decisions and actions. He cannot see how physical food can convey spiritual strength, and how the unworthy receiving of the Eucharist can result in physical sickness and death (I Cor. 11. 30). The only possible explanation is that it is due to suggestion. He cannot understand how anyone can be baptized for the dead (I Cor. 15. 29).

We need not examine in detail the various forms of modern *Weltanschauung,* whether idealist or naturalist. For the only criticism of the New Testament which is theologically relevant is that which arises *necessarily* out of the situation of modern man. The biological *Weltanschauung* does not, for instance, arise necessarily out of the contemporary situation. We are still free to adopt it or not as we choose. The only relevant question for the theologian is the basic assumption on which the adoption of a biological as of every other *Weltanschauung* rests, and that assumption is the view of the world which has been moulded by modern science and the modern conception of human nature as a self-subsistent unity immune from the interference of supernatural powers.

Again, the biblical doctrine that *death is the punishment of sin* is equally abhorrent to naturalism and idealism, since they both regard death as a simple and necessary process of nature. To the naturalist death is no problem at all, and to the idealist it is a problem for that very reason, for so far from arising out of man's essential spiritual being it actually destroys it. The idealist is faced with a paradox. On the one hand man is a spiritual being, and therefore essentially different from plants and animals, and on the other hand he is the prisoner of nature, whose birth, life, and death are just the same as those of the animals. Death may present him with a problem, but he cannot see how it can be a punishment for sin. Human beings are subject to death even before they have committed any sin. And to attribute human mortality to the fall of Adam is sheer nonsense, for guilt implies personal responsibility, and the idea of original sin as an inherited infection is sub-ethical, irrational, and absurd.

The same objections apply to *the doctrine of the atonement.* How can the guilt of one man be expiated by the death of another who is sinless—if indeed one may speak of a sinless man at all? What primitive notions of guilt and righteousness does this imply? And what primitive idea of God? The rationale of sacrifice in general may of course throw some light on the theory of the atonement, but even so, what a primitive mythology it is, that a divine Being should become incarnate, and atone for the sins of men through his own blood! Or again, one might adopt an analogy from the law courts, and explain the death of Christ as a transaction between God and man through which God's claims on man were satisfied. But that would make sin a juridical matter; it would be no more than an external transgression of a commandment, and it would make nonsense of all our ethical standards. Moreover, if the Christ who died such a death was the pre-existent Son of God, what could death mean for him? Obviously very little, if he knew that he would rise again in three days!

The *resurrection of Jesus* is just as difficult for modern man, if it means an event whereby a living supernatural power is released which can henceforth be appropriated through the sacraments. To the biologist such language is meaningless, for he does not regard death as a problem at all. The idealist would not object to the idea of a life immune from death, but he could not believe that such a life is made available by the resuscitation of a dead person. If that is the way God makes life available for man, his action is inextricably involved in a nature miracle. Such a notion he finds incomprehensible, for he can see God at work only in the reality of his personal life and in his transformation. But, quite apart from the incredibility of such a miracle, he cannot see how an event like this could be the act of God, or how it could affect his own life.

Gnostic influence suggests that this Christ, who died and rose again, was not a mere human being but a God-man. His death and resurrection were not isolated facts which concerned him alone, but a cosmic event in which we are all involved.[18] It is only with effort that modern man can think himself back into such an intellectual atmosphere, and

18. Rom. 5. 12ff.; I Cor. 15. 21ff., 44b.

even then he could never accept it himself, because it regards man's essential being as nature and redemption as a process of nature. And as for the pre-existence of Christ, with its corollary of man's translation into a celestial realm of light, and the clothing of the human personality in heavenly robes and a spiritual body—all this is not only irrational but utterly meaningless. Why should salvation take this particular form? Why should this be the fulfilment of human life and the realization of man's true being?

B. THE TASK BEFORE US

1. *Not Selection or Subtraction*

Does this drastic criticism of the New Testament mythology mean the complete elimination of the kerygma?

Whatever else may be true, we cannot save the kerygma by selecting some of its features and subtracting others, and thus reduce the amount of mythology in it. For instance, it is impossible to dismiss St Paul's teaching about the unworthy reception of Holy Communion or about baptism for the dead, and yet cling to the belief that physical eating and drinking can have a spiritual effect. If we accept *one* idea, we must accept everything which the New Testament has to say about Baptism and Holy Communion, and it is just this one idea which we cannot accept.

It may of course be argued that some features of the New Testament mythology are given greater prominence than others: not all of them appear with the same regularity in the various books. There is for example only one occurrence of the legends of the Virgin birth and the Ascension; St Paul and St John appear to be totally unaware of them. But, even if we take them to be later accretions, it does not affect the mythical character of the event of redemption as a whole. And if we once start subtracting from the kerygma, where are we to draw the line? The mythical view of the world must be accepted or rejected in its entirety.

At this point absolute clarity and ruthless honesty are essential both for the academic theologian and for the parish priest. It is a duty they owe to themselves, to the Church they serve, and to those whom they seek to win for the Church. They must make it quite clear what their hearers are expected to accept and what they are not. At all costs the preacher must not leave his people in the dark about what he secretly eliminates, nor must he be in the dark about it himself. In Karl Barth's book *The Resurrection of the Dead* the cosmic eschatology in the sense of "chronologically final history" is eliminated in favour of what he intends to be a non-mythological "ultimate history." He is able to delude himself into thinking that this is exegesis of St Paul and of the New Testament generally only because he gets rid of everything mythological in I Corinthians by subjecting it to an interpretation which does violence to its meaning. But that is an impossible procedure.

If the truth of the New Testament proclamation is to be preserved, the only way is to demythologize it. But our motive in so doing must not be to make the New Testament relevant to the modern world at all costs. The question is simply whether the New Testament message consists exclusively of mythology, or whether it actually demands the elimination of myth if it is to be understood as it is meant to be. This question is forced upon us from two sides. First there is the nature of myth in general, and then there is the New Testament itself.

2. *The Nature of Myth*

The real purpose of myth is not to present an objective picture of the world as it is, but to express man's understanding of himself in the world in which he lives. Myth should be interpreted not cosmologically, but anthropologically, or better still, existentially.[19] Myth speaks of the power or the powers which man supposes he experiences as the ground and limit of his world and of his own activity and suffering. He describes these powers in terms derived from the visible world, with its tangible objects and forces, and from human life, with its feelings, motives, and potentialities. He may, for instance, explain the origin of the world by speaking of a world egg or a world tree. Similarly he may account for the present state and order of the world by speaking of a primeval war between the gods. He speaks of the other world in terms of this world, and of the gods in terms derived from human life.[20]

Myth is an expression of man's conviction that the origin and purpose of the world in which he lives are to be sought not within it but beyond it—that is, beyond the realm of known and tangible reality—and that this realm is perpetually dominated and menaced by those mysterious powers which are its source and limit. Myth is also an expression of man's awareness that he is not lord of his own being. It

---

19. Cp. Gerhardt Krüger, *Einsicht und Leidenschaft,* esp. p. 17f., 56f.

20. Myth is here used in the sense popularized by the 'History of Religions' school. Mythology is the use of imagery to express the other worldly in terms of this world and the divine in terms of human life, the other side in terms of this side. For instance, divine transcendence is expressed as spatial distance. It is a mode of expression which makes it easy to understand the cultus as an action in which material means are used to convey immaterial power. Myth is not used in that modern sense, according to which it is practically equivalent to ideology.

expresses his sense of dependence not only within the visible world, but more especially on those forces which hold sway beyond the confines of the known. Finally, myth expresses man's belief that in this state of dependence he can be delivered from the forces within the visible world.

Thus myth contains elements which demand its own criticism— namely, its imagery with its apparent claim to objective validity. The real purpose of myth is to speak of a transcendent power which controls the world and man, but that purpose is impeded and obscured by the terms in which it is expressed.

Hence the importance of the New Testament mythology lies not in its imagery but in the understanding of existence which it enshrines. The real question is whether this understanding of existence is true. Faith claims that it is, and faith ought not to be tied down to the imagery of New Testament mythology.

3. *The New Testament Itself*

The New Testament itself invites this kind of criticism. Not only are there rough edges in its mythology, but some of its features are actually contradictory. For example, the death of Christ is sometimes a sacrifice and sometimes a cosmic event. Sometimes his person is interpreted as the Messiah and sometimes as the Second Adam. The kenosis of the pre-existent Son (Phil. 2. 6ff.) is incompatible with the miracle narratives as proofs of his messianic claims. The Virgin birth is inconsistent with the assertion of his pre-existence. The doctrine of the Creation is incompatible with the conception of the "rulers of this world" (1 Cor. 2. 6ff.), the "god of this world" (2 Cor. 4. 4) and the "elements of this world" $\sigma\tau o\iota\chi\epsilon\tilde{\iota}\alpha$ $\tau o\tilde{\upsilon}$ $\kappa\acute{o}\sigma\mu o\upsilon$, Gal. 4. 3). It is impossible to square the belief that the law was given by God with the theory that it comes from the angels (Gal. 3. 19f.).

But the principal demand for the criticism of mythology comes from a curious contradiction which runs right through the New Testament. Sometimes we are told that human life is determined by cosmic forces, at others we are challenged to a decision. Side by side with the Pauline indicative stands the Pauline imperative. In short, man is sometimes regarded as a cosmic being, sometimes as an independent "I" for whom decision is a matter of life or death. Incidentally, this explains why so many sayings in the New Testament speak directly to modern man's condition while others remain enigmatic and obscure. Finally, attempts at demythologization are sometimes made even within the New Testament itself. But more will be said on this point later.

4. *Previous Attempts at Demythologizing*

How then is the mythology of the New Testament to be reinter-
preted? This is not the first time that theologians have approached this
task. Indeed, all we have said so far might have been said in much the
same way thirty or forty years ago, and it is a sign of the bankruptcy
of contemporary theology that it has been necessary to go all over the
same ground again. The reason for this is not far to seek. The liberal
theologians of the last century were working on the wrong lines. They
threw away not only the mythology but also the kerygma itself. Were
they right? Is that the treatment the New Testament itself required?
That is the question we must face to-day. The last twenty years have
witnessed a movement away from criticism and a return to a naïve
acceptance of the kerygma. The danger both for theological scholarship and for the Church is that this uncritical resuscitation of the New
Testament mythology may make the Gospel message unintelligible to
the modern world. We cannot dismiss the critical labours of earlier
generations without further ado. We must take them up and put them
to constructive use. Failure to do so will mean that the old battles
between orthodoxy and liberalism will have to be fought out all over
again, that is assuming that there will be any Church or any theologians
to fight them at all! Perhaps we may put it schematically like this:
whereas the older liberals used criticism to *eliminate* the mythology
of the New Testament, our task to-day is to use criticism to *interpret*
it. Of course it may still be necessary to eliminate mythology here and
there. But the criterion adopted must be taken not from modern
thought, but from the understanding of human existence which the
New Testament itself enshrines.[21]

To begin with, let us review some of these earlier attempts at demythologizing. We need only mention briefly the allegorical interpretation of the New Testament which has dogged the Church throughout
its history. This method spiritualizes the mythical events so that they
become symbols of processes going on in the soul. This is certainly the
most comfortable way of avoiding the critical question. The literal
meaning is allowed to stand and is dispensed with only for the individual believer, who can escape into the realm of the soul.

It was characteristic of the older liberal theologians that they regarded mythology as relative and temporary. Hence they thought they
could safely eliminate it altogether, and retain only the broad, basic
principles of religion and ethics. They distinguished between what
they took to be the essence of religion and the temporary garb which
it assumed. Listen to what Harnack has to say about the essence of

---

21. As an illustration of this critical re-interpretation of myth cf. Hans Jonas, *Augustin
und das paulinische Freiheitsproblem*, 1930, pp. 66–76.

Jesus' preaching of the Kingdom of God and its coming: "The king-dom has a triple meaning. Firstly, it is something supernatural, a gift from above, not a product of ordinary life. Secondly, it is a purely religious blessing, the inner link with the living God; thirdly, it is the most important experience that a man can have, that on which every-thing else depends; it permeates and dominates his whole existence, because sin is forgiven and misery banished." Note how completely the mythology is eliminated: "The kingdom of God comes by coming to the individual, by entering into his *soul* and laying hold of it."[22]

It will be noticed how Harnack reduces the kerygma to a few basic principles of religion and ethics. Unfortunately this means that *the kerygma has ceased to be kerygma:* it is no longer the proclamation of the decisive act of God in Christ. For the liberals the great truths of religion and ethics are timeless and eternal, though it is only within human history that they are realized, and only in concrete historical processes that they are given clear expression. But the apprehension and acceptance of these principles does not depend on the knowledge and acceptance of the age in which they first took shape, or of the historical persons who first discovered them. We are all capable of verifying them in our own experience at whatever period we happen to live. History may be of academic interest, but never of paramount importance for religion.

But the New Testament speaks of an *event* through which God has wrought man's redemption. For it, Jesus is not primarily the teacher, who certainly had extremely important things to say and will always be honoured for saying them, but whose person in the last analysis is immaterial for those who have assimilated his teaching. On the con-trary, his person is just what the New Testament proclaims as the decisive event of redemption. It speaks of this person in mythological terms, but does this mean that we can reject the kerygma altogether on the ground that it is nothing more than mythology? That is the question.

Next came the History of Religions school. Its representatives were the first to discover the extent to which the New Testament is perme-ated by mythology. The importance of the New Testament, they saw, lay not in its teaching about religion and ethics but in its actual religion and piety; in comparison with that all the dogma it contains, and therefore all the mythological imagery with its apparent objectivity, was of secondary importance or completely negligible. The essence of the New Testament lay in the religious life it portrayed; its high-watermark was the experience of mystical union with Christ, in whom God took symbolic form.

---

22. *What is Christianity?* Williams and Norgate, 1904, pp. 63–4 and 57.

These critics grasped one important truth. Christian faith is not the same as religious idealism; the Christian life does not consist in developing the individual personality, in the improvement of society, or in making the world a better place. The Christian life means a turning away from the world, a detachment from it. But the critics of the History of Religions school failed to see that in the New Testament this detachment is essentially eschatological and not mystical. Religion for them was an expression of the human yearning to rise above the world and transcend it: it was the discovery of a supramundane sphere where the soul could detach itself from all earthly care and find its rest. Hence the supreme manifestation of religion was to be found not in personal ethics or in social idealism but in the cultus regarded as an end in itself. This was just the kind of religious life portrayed in the New Testament, not only as a model and pattern, but as a challenge and inspiration. The New Testament was thus the abiding source of power which enabled man to realize the true life of religion, and Christ was the eternal symbol for the cultus of the Christian Church.[23] It will be noticed how the Church is here defined exclusively as a worshipping community, and this represents a great advance on the older liberalism. This school rediscovered the Church as a *religious* institution. For the idealist there was really no place for the Church at all. But did they succeed in recovering the meaning of the Ecclesia in the full, New Testament sense of the word? For in the New Testament the Ecclesia is invariably a phenomenon of salvation history and eschatology.

Moreover, if the History of Religions school is right, the kerygma has once more ceased to be kerygma. Like the liberals, they are silent about a decisive act of God in Christ proclaimed as the event of redemption. So we are still left with the question whether this event and the person of Jesus, both of which are described in the New Testament in mythological terms, are nothing more than mythology. Can the kerygma be interpreted apart from mythology? Can we recover the truth of the kerygma for men who do not think in mythological terms without forfeiting its character as kerygma?

5. *An Existentialist Interpretation the Only Solution*

The theological work which such an interpretation involves can be sketched only in the broadest outline and with only a few examples. We must avoid the impression that this is a light and easy task, as if all we have to do is to discover the right formula and finish the job on

---

23. Cp. e.g. Troeltsch, *Die Bedeutung der Geschichtlichkeit Jesu für den Glauben*, Tübingen, 1911.

the spot. It is much more formidable than that. It cannot be done single-handed. It will tax the time and strength of a whole theological generation.

The mythology of the New Testament is in essence that of Jewish apocalyptic and the Gnostic redemption myths. A common feature of them both is their basic dualism, according to which the present world and its human inhabitants are under the control of daemonic, satanic powers, and stand in need of redemption. Man cannot achieve this redemption by his own efforts; it must come as a gift through a divine intervention. Both types of mythology speak of such an intervention: Jewish apocalyptic of an imminent world crisis in which this present aeon will be brought to an end and the new aeon ushered in by the coming of the Messiah, and Gnosticism of a Son of God sent down from the realm of light, entering into this world in the guise of a man, and by his fate and teaching delivering the elect and opening up the way for their return to their heavenly home.

The meaning of these two types of mythology lies once more not in their imagery with its apparent objectivity but in the understanding of human existence which both are trying to express. In other words, they need to be interpreted existentially. A good example of such treatment is to be found in Hans Jonas's book on Gnosticism.[24]

Our task is to produce an existentialist interpretation of the dualistic mythology of the New Testament along similar lines. When, for instance, we read of daemonic powers ruling the world and holding mankind in bondage, does the understanding of human existence which underlies such language offer a solution to the riddle of human life which will be acceptable even to the non-mythological mind of to-day? Of course we must not take this to imply that the New Testament presents us with an anthropology like that which modern science can give us. It cannot be proved by logic or demonstrated by an appeal to factual evidence. Scientific anthropologies always take for granted a definite understanding of existence, which is invariably the consequence of a deliberate decision of the scientist, whether he makes it consciously or not. And that is why we have to discover whether the New Testament offers man an understanding of himself which will challenge him to a genuine existential decision.

THE "ACT OF GOD"

Perhaps we may say that behind all the objectives raised against demythologizing there lurks a fear that if it were carried to its logical

24. *Gnosis und spätantiker Geist.* I. *Die mythologische Gnosis,* 1934.

conclusion it would make it impossible for us to speak of an act of God, or if we did it would only be the symbolic description of a subjective experience. For is it not mythology to speak of an act of God as though it were an objective event in which the grace of God encounters God?

In the first place, we must reply that if such language is to have any meaning at all it must denote an act in a real, objective sense, and not just a symbolical or pictorial expression. On the other hand, if the action of God is not to be conceived as a worldly phenomenon capable of being apprehended apart from its existential reference, it can only be spoken of by speaking simultaneously of myself as the person who is existentially concerned. To speak of the act of God means to speak at the same time of my existence. Since human life is lived out in time and space, man's encounter with God can only be a specific event here and now. This event, our being addressed by God here and now, our being questioned, judged, and blessed by him, is what we mean when we speak of an act of God.

Such language is therefore neither symbolical nor pictorial, though it is certainly analogical,[25] for it assumes an analogy between the activity of God and that of man and between the fellowship of God and man and that of man with man.

The meaning of this language requires further clarification. Mythological thought regards the divine activity, whether in nature or in history, as an interference with the course of nature, history, or the life of the soul, a tearing of it asunder—a miracle, in fact. Thus it objectifies the divine activity and projects it on to the plane of worldly happenings. A miracle—i.e. an act of God—is not visible or ascertainable like worldly events. The only way to preserve the unworldly, transcendental character of the divine activity is to regard it not as an interference in worldly happenings, but something accomplished *in* them in such a way that the closed weft of history as it presents itself to objective observation is left undisturbed. To every other eye than the eye of faith the action of God is hidden. Only the "natural" happening is generally visible and ascertainable. In it is accomplished the hidden act of God.

It is easy to object that this is to transform Christian faith into a pantheistic piety. But pantheism believes in a direct identity of worldly happening with the divine activity, whereas faith asserts their paradoxical identity, which can only be believed on in the concrete here and now and in the teeth of outward appearance. When I am encountered

---

25. On the subject of analogy cp. Erich Frank, *Philosophical Language and Religious Truth,* 1945, pp. 44, 161–4, 179, etc.

by such an event, I can in faith accept it as the gift of God or as his judgement, although I can also see it within its context in nature or history. In faith I can understand a thought or a resolve as something which is the work of God without necessarily removing it from its place in the chain of cause and effect.

Christian faith is not a *Weltanschauung* like pantheism. Pantheism is an anterior conviction that everything that happens is the work of God, since God is thought to be immanent in the world. Christian faith, on the other hand, believes that God acts upon us and addresses us in the specific here and now. This belief springs from an awareness of being addressed by the grace of God which confronts us in Jesus Christ. By this grace we are enabled to see that God makes all things work together for good to them that love him (Rom. 8. 28). This kind of faith, however, is not a knowledge possessed once and for all, not a *Weltanschauung.* It can only be an event occurring on specific occasions, and it can remain alive only when the believer is constantly asking himself what God is saying to him here and now. God is generally just as hidden for him as he is for everyone else. But from time to time the believer sees concrete happenings in the light of the world of grace which is addressed to him, and then faith can and ought to apprehend it as the act of God, even if its meaning is still enigmatic. If pantheism can say that any event it likes is the work of the Godhead, quite apart from its meaning in personal encounter, Christian faith can only say that in such-and-such an event God is acting in a hidden way. What God is doing now—it is of course not to be identified *tout court* with the visible occurrence—I may not know as yet, and perhaps I shall never know. But still I must ask what he is trying to say to me through it, even if all he has to say is that I must just grin and bear it.

Similarly, faith in God as Creator is not a piece of knowledge given in advance, in virtue of which every happening may be designated an act of God. Such faith is genuine only when I understand myself here and now existentially to be the creature of God, though it need not necessarily take the form of knowledge consciously acquired as the result of reflection. Faith in the divine omnipotence is not an anterior conviction that there is a Being who can do everything: it can only be attained existentially by submitting to the power of God exercising pressure upon me here and now, and this too need not necessarily be raised to the level of consciousness. The propositions of faith are not abstract truths. Those who have endured the hardships of a Russian prison camp know better than anyone else that you cannot say "*Terra ubique Domini*" as an explicit dogma: it is something which can be uttered only on specific occasions in existential decision.

Hence it is clear that for my existential life, realized as it is in decision in face of encounter, the world is no longer a closed weft of cause and effect. In faith the closed weft presented or produced by objective observation is transcended, though not as in mythological thought. For mythology imagines it to be torn asunder, whereas faith transcends it as a whole when it speaks of the activity of God. In the last resort it is already transcended when I speak of myself, for I myself, my real self, am no more visible or ascertainable than an act of God. When worldly happenings are viewed as a closed series, as not only scientific understanding but even workaday life requires, there is certainly no room for any act of God. But this is just the paradox of faith: it understands an ascertainable event in its context in nature and history as the act of God. Faith cannot dispense with its "nevertheless."

This is the only genuine faith in miracle.[26]   The conception of miracles as ascertainable processes is incompatible with the hidden character of God's activity. It surrenders the acts of God to objective observation, and thus makes belief in miracles (or rather superstition) susceptible to the justifiable criticisms of science.

If then it be true that we cannot speak of an act of God without speaking simultaneously of our own existence, if such an act cannot be established apart from its existential reference, if it dispenses with the objectivity attainable by impartial scientific investigation (e.g. by experiment), we inevitably ask whether divine activity has any objective reality at all. Does it exist apart from our own subjective experience? Is not faith reduced to experience pure and simple? Is God no more than an experience in the soul, despite the fact that faith only makes sense when it is directed towards a God with a real existence outside the believer?

This objection rests upon a psychological misconception of what is meant by the existential life of man.[27]   When we say that faith alone, the faith which is aware of the divine encounter, can speak of God, and that therefore when the believer speaks of an act of God he is *ipso facto* speaking of himself as well, it by no means follows that God has no real existence apart from the believer or the act of believing. It follows only

---

26. Cp. *Glauben und Verstehen,* pp. 214–28, esp. p. 224f.; W. Herrmann, *Offenbarung und Wunder,* 1908, esp. pp. 33ff. Herrmann rightly observes that faith in prayer, like belief in miracles, transcends the idea of nature.

27. I might also say "by human subjectivity," provided this is understood in Kierkegaard's sense as "being subject"—i.e., the personal being of man.

if faith and experience are interpreted in a psychologizing sense.[28] If human Being is properly understood as historic Being, whose experiences consist of encounters, it is clear that faith, which speaks of its encounter with the acts of God, cannot defend itself against the charge of illusion, for the encounter with God is not objective like a worldly event. Yet there is no need for faith, in the sense of an existential encounter, to refute that charge, and indeed it could not do so without misunderstanding its own meaning.

What encounter means as such may be illustrated from our own life in history. The love of another is an encounter whose essential character depends upon its being an event. For it cannot be apprehended as love by objective observation, but only by myself who am encountered by it.[29] Looked at from the outside, it is certainly not visible as love in the real sense of the word, but only as a phenomenon of spiritual or psychic history which is open to various interpretations. Of course the love with which a man loves me does not depend for its reality upon my understanding or reciprocating it.[30] This is just what we learn when we do reciprocate another's love. Even if we fail to understand it or open our hearts to it, it still evokes a kind of existential reaction. For to fail to understand it, to close our hearts to it, to respond by hatred —all these are still existential reactions. In each case we are no longer the same after the encounter as we were before it, though that does not for a moment alter the fact that it is only in encounter that it can be seen as love.

That God cannot be seen apart from faith does not mean that he does not exist apart from it. That an encounter with the Word of God makes a difference to man, whether he opens his heart to it or not, is a fact which only faith can know, the faith which understands that unbelief is a token of God's judgement.

---

28. When W. Herrmann and A. Schlatter speak of experience, neither of them means a bare psychic phenomenon.

29. I cannot see why E. Schweizer calls the love awakened by another an "inner-psychic" process. For love can only exist in encounter or mutual relationship. He completely fails to grasp the existential meaning of love when he writes: "Love awakens more in man than does an ideal. It awakens the desire for fellowship, a concern of the I for the Thou, sexuality, or what you will (!). But it is still an inner-psychic process, for the love of the other is only an external stimulus. Admittedly it affects the whole range of our emotional life, and not only the mind, as when we receive instruction, or our enthusiasm, as when we are presented with an ideal."

30. E. Schweizer, "Zur Interpretation des Kreuzes bei R. Bultmann" *(Festschrift für Maurice Goguel,* 1950).

True faith is not demonstrable in relation to its object. But, as Herrmann taught us long ago, it is just here that its strength lies. For if it were susceptible to proof it would mean that we could know and establish God apart from faith, and that would be placing him on a level with the world of tangible, objective reality.[31] In that realm we are certainly justified in demanding proof.

If faith is man's response to the proclamation of the word of God's grace, a word whose origin and credentials are to be found in the New Testament, must we say that it cannot be proved by the appeal to Scripture? Is not faith simply the hearing of Scripture as the Word of God? That is indeed so, but only when Scripture is understood neither as a compendium of doctrines nor as a document enshrining the beliefs of other people, yet inspiring enough to evoke religious experience in us. It is so only when Scripture is heard as a word addressed personally to ourselves, as kerygma—i.e. when the experience consists in encounter and response to the address. That Scripture is the Word of God is something which happens only in the here and now of encounter; it is not a fact susceptible to objective proof. The Word of God is hidden in Scripture, just like any other act of his.[32]

Nor has God offered a proof of himself in the so-called facts of salvation. For these too are objects of faith, and as facts of salvation are ascertainable and visible to faith alone. Our knowledge of them does not precede our faith or provide a basis for it, as other convictions are based on proven facts. In a sense, of course, they do provide a basis for faith, but only as facts which are themselves apprehended in faith. It is just the same with human trust and love. These too are not based on any trustworthiness or lovableness in another which could be objectively ascertained, but upon the nature of the other apprehended *in* the love and *in* the trust. There can be no trust and no love without this element of risk. Hence, as Herrmann used to say, the ground and object of faith do not fall apart, but are identical, for the very reason that we cannot say what God is like in himself, but only what he does to us.

If then the activity of God is not visible or open to proof like worldly entities, if the event of redemption is not an ascertainable process, if, we may add, the Spirit granted to the believer is not a phenomenon

31. This does not of course imply that the idea of God is properly inconceivable apart from faith. The idea of God is an expression of man's search for him, a search which motivates all human existence. *Vide supra,* p. 192, and cp. my essay, "Die Frage der Natürlichen Offenbarung" in *Offenbarung und Heilsgeschehen,* pp. 1–26.

32. Cp. H. Diem's criticism of the view that the Word of God is available in the Bible *ante et extra usum* (ibid., p. 5).

susceptible to worldly apprehension, if we cannot speak of these things without speaking of our own existence, it follows that faith is a new understanding of existence, and that the activity of God vouchsafes to us a new understanding of self, . . .

If the challenge of demythologiizing was first raised by the conflict between the mythological world-view of the Bible and the modern scientific world view, it at once became evident that the restatement of mythology is a requirement of faith itself. For faith needs to be emancipated from its association with every world view expressed in objective terms, whether it be a mythical or a scientific one. That conflict is a proof that faith has not yet discovered the proper terms in which to express itself, it has not realized that it cannot be logically proven, it has not clearly understood that its basis and its object are identical, it has not clearly apprehended the transcendental and hidden character of the divine activity, and by its failure to perceive its own "Nevertheless" it has tried to project God and his acts into the sphere of objective reality. Starting as it does from the modern world view, and challenging the Biblical mythology and the traditional proclamation of the Church, this new kind of criticism is performing for faith the supreme service of recalling it to a radical consideration of its own nature. It is just this call that our demythologizing seeks to follow.

16. Existentialism Is a Humanism

I should like on this occasion to defend existentialism against some charges which have been brought against it.

First, it has been charged with inviting people to remain in a kind of desperate quietism because, since no solutions are possible, we should have to consider action in this world as quite impossible. We should then end up in a philosophy of contemplation; and since contemplation is a luxury, we come in the end to a bourgeois philosophy. The communists in particular have made these charges.

On the other hand, we have been charged with dwelling on human degradation, with pointing up everywhere the sordid, shady, and slimy, and neglecting the gracious and beautiful, the bright side of human nature; for example, according to Mlle. Mercier, a Catholic critic, with forgetting the smile of the child. Both sides charge us with having ignored human solidarity, with considering man as an isolated being. The communists say that the main reason for this is that we take pure subjectivity, the *Cartesian I think,* as our starting point; in other words, the moment in which man becomes fully aware of what it means to him to be an isolated being; as a result, we are unable to return to

---

Reprinted from Jean-Paul Sartre, *Existentialism* (1947) by permission of The Philosophical Library, Inc. The translation is by Bernard Frechtman.

a state of solidarity with the men who are not ourselves, a state which we can never reach in the *cogito*.

From the Christian standpoint, we are charged with denying the reality and seriousness of human undertakings, since, if we reject God's commandments and the eternal verities, there no longer remains anything but pure caprice, with everyone permitted to do as he pleases and incapable, from his own point of view, of condemning the points of view and acts of others.

I shall try today to answer these different charges. Many people are going to be surprised at what is said here about humanism. We shall try to see in what sense it is to be understood. In any case, what can be said from the very beginning is that by existentialism we mean a doctrine which makes human life possible and, in addition, declares that every truth and every action implies a human setting and a human subjectivity.

As is generally known, the basic charge against us is that we put the emphasis on the dark side of human life. Someone recently told me of a lady who, when she let slip a vulgar word in a moment of irritation, excused herself by saying, "I guess I'm becoming an existentialist." Consequently, existentialism is regarded as something ugly; that is why we are said to be naturalists; and if we are, it is rather surprising that in this day and age we cause so much more alarm and scandal than does naturalism, properly so called. The kind of person who can take in his stride such a novel as Zola's *The Earth* is disgusted as soon as he starts reading an existentialist novel; the kind of person who is resigned to the wisdom of the ages—which is pretty sad—finds us even sadder. Yet, what can be more disillusioning than saying "true charity begins at home" or "a scoundrel will always return evil for good"?

We know the commonplace remarks made when this subject comes up, remarks which always add up to the same thing: we shouldn't struggle against the powers-that-be; we shouldn't resist authority; we shouldn't try to rise above our station; any action which doesn't conform to authority is romantic; any effort not based on past experience is doomed to failure; experience shows that man's bent is always toward trouble, that there must be a strong hand to hold him in check, if not, there will be anarchy. There are still people who go on mumbling these melancholy old saws, the people who say, "It's only human!" whenever a more or less repugnant act is pointed out to them, the people who glut themselves on *chansons réalistes;* these are the people who accuse existentialism of being too gloomy, and to such an extent that I wonder whether they are complaining about it, not for its pessimism, but much rather its optimism. Can it be that what really scares them in the doctrine I shall try to present here is that it leaves to man a possibility of choice? To answer this question, we must re-examine it on a strictly philosophical plane. What is meant by the term *existentialism?*

Most people who use the word would be rather embarrassed if they had to explain it, since, now that the word is all the rage, even the work of a musician or painter is being called existentialist. A gossip columnist in *Clartés* signs himself *The Existentialist,* so that by this time the word has been so stretched and has taken on so broad a meaning, that it no longer means anything at all. It seems that for want of an advance-guard doctrine analogous to surrealism, the kind of people who are eager for scandal and flurry turn to this philosophy which in other respects does not at all serve their purposes in this sphere.

Actually, it is the least scandalous, the most austere of doctrines. It is intended strictly for specialists and philosophers. Yet it can be defined easily. What complicates matters is that there are two kinds of existentialist; first, those who are Christian, among whom I would include Jaspers and Gabriel Marcel, both Catholic; and on the other hand the atheistic existentialists, among whom I class Heidegger, and then the French existentialists and myself. What they have in common is that they think that existence precedes essence, or, if you prefer, that subjectivity must be the starting point.

Just what does that mean? Let us consider some object that is manufactured, for example, a book or a paper-cutter: here is an object which has been made by an artisan whose inspiration came from a concept. He referred to the concept of what a paper-cutter is and likewise to a know method of production, which is part of the concept, something which is, by and large, a routine. Thus, the paper-cutter is at once an object produced in a certain way and, on the other hand, one having a specific use; and one can not postulate a man who produces a paper-cutter but does not know what it is used for. Therefore, let us say that, for the paper-cutter, essence—that is, the ensemble of both the production routines and the properties which enable it to be both produced and defined—precedes existence. Thus, the presence of the paper-cutter or book in front of me is determined. Therefore, we have here a technical view of the world whereby it can be said that production precedes existence.

When we conceive God as the Creator, He is generally thought of as a superior sort of artisan. Whatever doctrine we may be considering, whether one like that of Descartes or that of Leibnitz, we always grant that will more or less follows understanding or, at the very least, accompanies it, and that when God creates He knows exactly what He is creating. Thus, the concept of man in the mind of God is comparable to the concept of paper-cutter in the mind of the manufacturer, and, following certain techniques and a conception, God produces man, just as the artisan, following a definition and a technique, makes a paper-cutter. Thus, the individual man is the realization of a certain concept in the divine intelligence.

In the eighteenth century, the atheism of the *philosophes* discarded the idea of God, but not so much for the notion that essence precedes existence. To a certain extent, this idea is found everywhere; we find it in Diderot, in Voltaire, and even in Kant. Man has a human nature; this human nature, which is the concept of the human, is found in all men, which means that each man is a particular example of a universal concept, man. In Kant, the result of this universality is that the wild-man, the natural man, as well as the bourgeois, are circumscribed by the same definition and have the same basic qualities. Thus, here too the essence of man precedes the historical existence that we find in nature.

Atheistic existentialism, which I represent, is more coherent. It states that if God does not exist, there is at least one being in whom existence precedes essence, a being who exists before he can be defined by any concept, and that this being is man, or, as Heidegger says, human reality. What is meant here by saying that existence precedes essence? It means that, first of all, man exists, turns up, appears on the scene, and, only afterwards, defines himself. If man, as the existentialist conceives him, is indefinable, it is because at first he is nothing. Only afterward will he be something, and he himself will have made what he will be. Thus, there is no human nature, since there is no God to conceive it. Not only is man what he conceives himself to be, but he is also only what he wills himself to be after this thrust toward existence.

Man is nothing else but what he makes of himself. Such is the first principle of existentialism. It is also what is called subjectivity, the name we are labeled with when charges are brought against us. But what do we mean by this, if not that man has a greater dignity than a stone or table? For we mean that man first exists, that is, that man first of all is the being who hurls himself toward a future and who is conscious of imagining himself as being in the future. Man is at the start a plan which is aware of itself, rather than a patch of moss, a piece of garbage, or a cauliflower; nothing exists prior to this plan; there is nothing in heaven; man will be what he will have planned to be. Not what he will want to be. Because by the word "will" we generally mean a conscious decision, which is subsequent to what we have already made of ourselves. I may want to belong to a political party, write a book, get married; but all that is only a manifestation of an earlier, more spontaneous choice that is called "will." But if existence really does precede essence, man is responsible for what he is. Thus, existentialism's first move is to make every man aware of what he is and to make the full responsibility of his existence rest on him. And when we say that a man is responsible for himself, we do not only mean that he is responsible for his own individuality, but that he is responsible for all men.

The word subjectivism has two meanings, and our opponents play on the two. Subjectivism means, on the one hand, that an individual chooses and makes himself; and, on the other, that it is impossible for man to transcend human subjectivity. The second of these is the essential meaning of existentialism. When we say that man chooses his own self, we mean that every one of us does likewise; but we also mean by that that in making this choice he also chooses all men. In fact, in creating the man that we want to be, there is not a single one of our acts which does not at the same time create an image of man as we think he ought to be. To choose to be this or that is to affirm at the same time the value of what we choose, because we can never choose evil. We always choose the good, and nothing can be good for us without being good for all.

If, on the other hand, existence precedes essence, and if we grant that we exist and fashion our image at one and the same time, the image is valid for everybody and for our whole age. Thus, our responsibility is much greater than we might have supposed, because it involves all mankind. If I am a workingman and choose to join a Christian trade-union rather than be a communist, and if by being a member I want to show that the best thing for man is resignation, that the kingdom of man is not of this world, I am not only involving my own case—I want to be resigned for everyone. As a result, my action has involved all humanity. To take a more individual matter, if I want to marry, to have children; even if this marriage depends solely on my own circumstances or passion or wish, I am involving all humanity in monogamy and not merely myself. Therefore, I am responsible for myself and for everyone else. I am creating a certain image of man of my own choosing. In choosing myself, I choose man.

This helps us understand what the actual content is of such rather grandiloquent words as anguish, forlornness, despair. As you will see, it's all quite simple.

First, what is meant by anguish? The existentialists say at once that man is anguish. What that means is this: the man who involves himself and who realizes that he is not only the person he chooses to be, but also a lawmaker who is, at the same time, choosing all mankind as well as himself, can not help escape the feeling of his total and deep responsibility. Of course, there are many people who are not anxious; but we claim that they are hiding their anxiety, that they are fleeing from it. Certainly, many people believe that when they do something, they themselves are the only ones involved, and when someone says to them, "What if everyone acted that way?" they shrug their shoulders and answer, "Everyone doesn't act that way." But really, one should always ask himself, "What would happen if everybody looked at things that way?" There is no escaping this disturbing thought except by a kind of double-dealing. A man who lies and makes excuses for himself by saying "not everybody does that," is someone with an uneasy conscience, because the act of lying implies that a universal value is conferred upon the lie.

Anguish is evident even when it conceals itself. This is the anguish that Kierkegaard called the anguish of Abraham. You know the story: an angel has ordered Abraham to sacrifice his son; if it really were an angel who has come and said, "You are Abraham, you shall sacrifice your son," everything would be all right. But everyone might first wonder, "Is it really an angel, and am I really Abraham? What proof do I have?"

There was a madwoman who had hallucinations; someone used to speak to her on the telephone and give her orders. Her doctor asked her, "Who is it who talks to you?" She answered, "He says it's God." What proof did she really have that it was God? If an angel comes to me, what proof is there that it's an angel? And if I hear voices, what proof is there that they come from heaven and not from hell, or from the subconscious, or a pathological condition? What proves that they are addressed to me? What proof is there that I have been appointed to impose my choice and my conception of man on humanity? I'll never find any proof or sign to convince me of that. If a voice addresses me, it is always for me to decide that this is the angel's voice; if I consider that such an act is a good one, it is I who will choose to say that it is good rather than bad.

Now, I'm not being singled out as an Abraham, and yet at every moment I'm obliged to perform exemplary acts. For every man, everything happens as if all mankind had its eyes fixed on him and were guiding itself by what he does. And every man ought to say to himself,

"Am I really the kind of man who has the right to act in such a way that humanity might guide itself by my actions?" And if he does not say that to himself, he is masking his anguish.

There is no question here of the kind of anguish which would lead to quietism, to inaction. It is a matter of a simple sort of anguish that anybody who has had responsibilities is familiar with. For example, when a military officer takes the responsibility for an attack and sends a certain number of men to death, he chooses to do so, and in the main he alone makes the choice. Doubtless, orders come from above, but they are too broad; he interprets them, and on this interpretation depend the lives of ten or fourteen or twenty men. In making a decision he can not help having a certain anguish. All leaders know this anguish. That doesn't keep them from acting; on the contrary, it is the very condition of their action. For it implies that they envisage a number of possibilities, and when they choose one, they realize that it has value only because it is chosen. We shall see that this kind of anguish, which is the kind that existentialism describes, is explained, in addition, by a direct responsibility to the other men whom it involves. It is not a curtain separating us from action, but is part of action itself.

When we speak of forlornness, a term Heidegger was fond of, we mean only that God does not exist and that we have to face all the consequences of this. The existentialist is strongly opposed to a certain kind of secular ethics which would like to abolish God with the least possible expense. About 1880, some French teachers tried to set up a secular ethics which went something like this: God is a useless and costly hypothesis; we are discarding it; but, meanwhile, in order for there to be an ethics, a society, a civilization, it is essential that certain values be taken seriously and that they be considered as having an *a priori* existence. It must be obligatory, *a priori,* to be honest, not to lie, not to beat your wife, to have children, etc., etc. So we're going to try a little device which will make it possible to show that values exist all the same, inscribed in a heaven of ideas, though otherwise God does not exist. In other words—and this, I believe, is the tendency of everything called reformism in France—nothing will be changed if God does not exist. We shall find ourselves with the same norms of honesty, progress, and humanism, and we shall have made of God an outdated hypothesis which will peacefully die off by itself.

The existentialist, on the contrary, thinks it very distressing that God does not exist, because all possibility of finding values in a heaven of ideas disappears along with Him; there can no longer be an *a priori* Good, since there is no infinite and perfect consciousness to think it. Nowhere is it written that the Good exists, that we must be honest, that we must not lie; because the fact is we are on a plane where there are only men. Dostoievsky said, "If God didn't exist, everything would be possible." That is the very starting point of existentialism. Indeed, everything is permissible if God does not exist, and as a result man is forlorn, because neither within him nor without does he find anything to cling to. He can't start making excuses for himself.

If existence really does precede essence, there is no explaining things away by reference to a fixed and given human nature. In other words, there is no determinism, man is free, man is freedom. On the other hand, if God does not exist, we find no values or commands to turn to which legitimize our conduct. So, in the bright realm of values, we have no excuse behind us, nor justification before us. We are alone, with no excuses.

That is the idea I shall try to convey when I say that man is condemned to be free. Condemned, because he did not create himself, yet, in other respects is free; because, once thrown into the world, he is responsible for everything he does. The existentialist does not believe in the power of passion. He will never agree that a sweeping passion is a ravaging torrent which fatally leads a man to certain acts and is therefore an excuse. He thinks that man is responsible for his passion.

The existentialist does not think that man is going to help himself by finding in the world some omen by which to orient himself. Because he thinks that man will interpret the omen to suit himself. Therefore, he thinks that man, with no support and no aid, is condemned every moment to invent man. Ponge, in a very fine article, has said, "Man is the future of man." That's exactly it. But if it is taken to mean that this future is recorded in heaven, that God sees it, then it is false, because it would really no longer be a future. If it is taken to mean that, whatever a man may be, there is a future to be forged, a virgin future before him, then this remark is sound. But then we are forlorn.

To give you an example which will enable you to understand forlornness better, I shall cite the case of one of my students who came to see me under the following circumstances: his father was on bad terms with his mother, and, moreover, was inclined to be a collaborationist; his older brother had been killed in the German offensive of 1940, and the young man, with somewhat immature but generous feelings, wanted to avenge him. His mother lived alone with him, very much upset by the half-treason of her husband and the death of her older son; the boy was her only consolation.

The boy was faced with the choice of leaving for England and joining the Free French Forces—that is, leaving his mother behind—or remaining with his mother and helping her to carry on. He was fully aware that the woman lived only for him and that his going off—and perhaps his death—would plunge her into despair. He was also aware that every act that he did for his mother's sake was a sure thing, in the sense that it was helping her to carry on, whereas every effort he made toward going off and fighting was an uncertain move which might run aground and prove completely useless; for example, on his way to England he might, while passing through Spain, be detained indefinitely in a Spanish camp; he might reach England or Algiers and be stuck in an office at a desk job. As a result, he was faced with two very different kinds of action: one, concrete, immediate, but concerning only one individual; the other concerned an incomparably vaster group, a national collectivity, but for that very reason was dubious, and might be interrupted en route. And, at the same time, he was wavering between two kinds of ethics. On the one hand, an ethics of sympathy, of personal devotion; on the other, a broader ethics, but one whose efficacy was more dubious. He had to choose between the two.

Who could help him choose? Christian doctrine? No. Christian doctrine says, "Be charitable, love your neighbor, take the more rugged path, etc., etc." But which is the more rugged path? Whom should he love as a brother? The fighting man or his mother? Which does the greater good, the vague act of fighting in a group, or the concrete one of helping a particular human being to go on living? Who can decide *a priori?* Nobody. No book of ethics can tell him. The Kantian ethics says, "Never treat any person as a means, but as an end." Very well, if I stay with my mother, I'll treat her as an end and not as a means; but by virtue of this very fact, I'm running the risk of treating the people around me who are fighting, as means; and, conversely, if I go to join those who are fighting, I'll be treating them as an end, and, by doing that, I run the risk of treating my mother as a means.

If values are vague, and if they are always too broad for the concrete and specific case that we are considering, the only thing left for us is to trust our instincts. That's what this young man tried to do; and when I saw him, he said, "In the end, feeling is what counts. I ought to choose whichever pushes me in one direction. If I feel that I love my mother enough to sacrifice everything else for her—my desire for vengeance, for action, for adventure—then I'll stay with her. If, on the contrary, I feel that my love for my mother isn't enough, I'll leave."

But how is the value of a feeling determined? What gives his feeling for his mother value? Precisely the fact that he remained with her. I may say that I like so-and-so well enough to sacrifice a certain amount of money for him, but I may say so only if I've done it. I may say "I love my mother well enough to remain with her" if I have remained with her. The only way to determine the value of this affection is, precisely, to perform an act which confirms and defines it. But, since I require this affection to justify my act, I find myself caught in a vicious circle.

On the other hand, Gide has well said that a mock feeling and a true feeling are almost indistinguishable; to decide that I love my mother and will remain with her, or to remain with her by putting on an act, amount somewhat to the same thing. In other words, the feeling is formed by the acts one performs; so, I can not refer to it in order to act upon it. Which means that I can neither seek within myself the true condition which will impel me to act, nor apply to a system of ethics for concepts which will permit me to act. You will say, "At least, he did go to a teacher for advice." But if you seek advice from a priest, for example, you have chosen this priest; you already knew, more or less, just about what advice he was going to give you. In other words, choosing your adviser is involving yourself. The proof of this is that if you are a Christian, you will say, "Consult a priest." But some priests are collaborating, some are just marking time, some are resisting. Which to choose? If the young man chooses a priest who is resisting or collaborating, he has already decided on the kind of advice he's going to get. Therefore, in coming to see me he knew the answer I was going to give him, and I had only one answer to give: "You're free, choose, that is, invent." No general ethics can show you what is to be done; there are no omens in the world. The Catholics will reply, "But there are." Granted—but, in any case, I myself choose the meaning they have.

When I was a prisoner, I knew a rather remarkable young man who was a Jesuit. He had entered the Jesuit order in the following way: he had had a number of very bad breaks; in childhood, his father died, leaving him in poverty, and he was a scholarship student at a religious institution where he was constantly made to feel that he was being kept out of charity; then, he failed to get any of the honors and distinctions that children like; later on, at about eighteen, he bungled a love affair; finally, at twenty-two, he failed in military training, a childish enough matter, but it was the last straw.

This young fellow might well have felt that he had botched everything. It was a sign of something, but of what? He might have taken refuge in bitterness or despair. But he very wisely looked upon all this as a sign that he was not made for secular triumphs, and that only the triumphs of religion, holiness, and faith were open to him. He saw the hand of God in all this, and so he entered the order. Who can help seeing that he alone decided what the sign meant?

Some other interpretation might have been drawn from this series of setbacks; for example, that he might have done better to turn carpenter or revolutionist. Therefore, he is fully responsible for the interpretation. Forlornness implies that we ourselves choose our being. Forlornness and anguish go together.

As for despair, the term has a very simple meaning. It means that we shall confine ourselves to reckoning only with what depends upon our will, or on the ensemble of probabilities which make our action possible. When we want something, we always have to reckon with probabilities. I may be counting on the arrival of a friend. The friend is coming by rail or street-car; this supposes that the train will arrive on schedule, or that the street-car will not jump the track. I am left in the realm of possibility; but possibilities are to be reckoned with only to the point where my action comports with the ensemble of these possibilities, and no further. The moment the possibilities I am considering are not rigorously involved by my action, I ought to disengage myself from them, because no God, no scheme, can adapt the world and its possibilities to my will. When Descartes said, "Conquer yourself rather than the world," he meant essentially the same thing.

The Marxists to whom I have spoken reply, "You can rely on the support of others in your action, which obviously has certain limits because you're not going to live forever. That means: rely on both what others are doing elsewhere to help you, in China, in Russia, and what they will do later on, after your death, to carry on the action and lead it to its fulfillment, which will be the revolution. You even *have* to rely upon that, otherwise you're immoral." I reply at once that I will always rely on fellow-fighters insofar as these comrades are involved with me in a common struggle, in the unity of a party or a group in which I can more or less make my weight felt; that is, one whose ranks I am in as a fighter and whose movements I am aware of at every moment. In such a situation, relying on the unity and will of the party is exactly like counting on the fact that the train will arrive on time or that the car won't jump the track. But, given that man is free and that there is no human nature for me to depend on, I can not count on men whom I do not know by relying on human goodness or man's concern for the good of society. I don't know what will become of the Russian revolution; I may make an example of it to the extent that at the present time it is apparent that the proletariat plays a part in Russia that it plays in no other nation. But I can't swear that this will inevitably lead to a triumph of the proletariat. I've got to limit myself to what I see.

Given that men are free and that tomorrow they will freely decide what man will be, I can not be sure that, after my death, fellow-fighters will carry on my work to bring it to its maximum perfection. Tomorrow, after my death, some men may decide to set up Fascism, and the others may be cowardly and muddled enough to let them do it. Fascism will then be the human reality, so much the worse for us.

Actually, things will be as man will have decided they are to be. Does that mean that I should abandon myself to quietism? No. First, I should involve myself; then, act on the old saw, "Nothing ventured, nothing gained." Nor does it mean that I shouldn't belong to a party, but rather that I shall have no illusions and shall do what I can. For example, suppose I ask myself, "Will socialization, as such, ever come about?" I know nothing about it. All I know is that I'm going to do everything in my power to bring it about. Beyond that, I can't count on anything. Quietism is the attitude of people who say, "Let others do what I can't do." The doctrine I am presenting is the very opposite of quietism, since it declares, "There is no reality except in action." Moreover, it goes further, since it adds, "Man is nothing else than his plan; he exists only to the extent that he fulfills himself; he is therefore nothing else than the ensemble of his acts, nothing else than his life."

According to this, we can understand why our doctrine horrifies certain people. Because often the only way they can bear their wretchedness is to think, "Circumstances have been against me. What I've been and done doesn't show my true worth. To be sure, I've had no great love, no great friendship, but that's because I haven't met a man or woman who was worthy. The books I've written haven't been very good because I haven't had the proper leisure. I haven't had children to devote myself to because I didn't find a man with whom I could have spent my life. So there remains within me, unused and quite viable, a host of propensities, inclinations, possibilities, that one wouldn't guess from the mere series of things I've done."

Now, for the existentialist there is really no love other than one which manifests itself in a person's being in love. There is no genius other than one which is expressed in works of art; the genius of Proust is the sum of Proust's works; the genius of Racine is his series of tragedies. Outside of that, there is nothing. Why say that Racine could have written another tragedy, when he didn't write it? A man is involved in life, leaves his impress on it, and outside of that there is nothing. To be sure, this may seem a harsh thought to someone whose life hasn't been a success. But, on the other hand, it prompts people to understand that reality alone is what counts, that dreams, expectations, and hopes warrant no more than to define a man as a disappointed dream, as miscarried hopes, as vain expectations. In other words, to define him negatively and not positively. However, when we say, "You are nothing else than your life," that does not imply that the artist will be judged solely on the basis of his works of art; a thousand other things will contribute toward summing him up. What we mean is that a man is nothing else than a series of undertakings, that he is the sum, the organization, the ensemble of the relationships which make up these undertakings.

When all is said and done, what we are accused of, at bottom, is not our pessimism, but an optimistic toughness. If people throw up to us our works of fiction in which we write about people who are soft, weak, cowardly, and sometimes even downright bad, it's not because these people are soft, weak, cowardly, or bad; because if we were to say, as Zola did, that they are that way because of heredity, the workings of environment, society, because of biological or psychological determinism, people would be reassured. They would say, "Well, that's what we're like, no one can do anything about it." But when the existentialist writes about a coward, he says that this coward is responsible for his cowardice. He's not like that because he has a cowardly heart or lung or brain; he's not like that on account of his physiological make-up; but he's like that because he has made himself a coward by his acts. There's no such thing as a cowardly constitution; there are nervous constitutions; there is poor blood, as the common people say, or strong constitutions. But the man whose blood is poor is not a coward on that account, for what makes cowardice is the act of renouncing our yielding. A constitution is not an act; the coward is defined on the basis of the acts he performs. People feel, in a vague sort of way, that this coward we're talking about is guilty of being a coward, and the thought frightens them. What people would like is that a coward or a hero be born that way.

One of the complaints most frequently made about *The Ways of Freedom** can be summed up as follows: "After all, these people are so spineless, how are you going to make heroes out of them?" This objection almost makes me laugh, for it assumes that people are born heroes. That's what people really want to think. If you're born cowardly, you may set your mind perfectly at rest; there's nothing you can

---

**Les Chemins de la Liberté,* M. Sartre's projected trilogy of novels, two of which, *L'Age de Raison* (The Age of Reason) and *Le Sursis* (The Reprieve) have already appeared.—Translator's note.

do about it; you'll be cowardly all your life, whatever you may do. If you're born a hero, you may set your mind just as much at rest; you'll be a hero all your life; you'll drink like a hero and eat like a hero. What the existentialist says is that the coward makes himself cowardly, that the hero makes himself heroic. There's always a possibility for the coward not to be cowardly any more and for the hero to stop being heroic. What counts is total involvement; some one particular action or set of circumstances is not total involvement.

Thus, I think we have answered a number of the charges concerning existentialism. You see that it can not be taken for a philosophy of quietism, since it defines man in terms of action; nor for a pessimistic description of man—there is no doctrine more optimistic, since man's destiny is within himself; nor for an attempt to discourage man from acting, since it tells him that the only hope is in his acting and that action is the only thing that enables a man to live. Consequently, we are dealing here with an ethics of action and involvement.

17.   An Absurd Reasoning

I. Absurdity and Suicide

There is but one truly serious philosophical problem, and that is
suicide. Judging whether life is or is not worth living amounts to
answering the fundamental question of philosophy. All the rest—
whether or not the world has three dimensions, whether the mind has
nine or twelve categories—comes afterwards. These are games; one
must first answer. And if it is true, as Nietzsche claims, that a philosopher, to deserve our respect, must preach by example, you can appreciate the importance of that reply, for it will precede the definitive act.
These are facts the heart can feel; yet they call for careful study before
they become clear to the intellect.

If I ask myself how to judge that this question is more urgent than
that, I reply that one judges by the actions it entails. I have never seen
anyone die for the ontological argument. Galileo, who held a scientific
truth of great importance, abjured it with the greatest ease as soon as
it endangered his life. In a certain sense, he did right.[1]   That truth was

From *The Myth of Sisyphus,* by Albert Camus, translated by Justin O'Brien. Copyright © 1955 by Alfred A. Knopf, Inc. Reprinted by permission of the publisher. Compare this selection with the discussion of a similar problem by Thomas Nagel in selection
22.

1. From the point of view of the relative value of truth. On the other hand, from the
point of view of virile behavior, this scholar's fragility may well make us smile.

not worth the stake. Whether the earth or the sun revolved around the other is a matter of profound indifference. To tell the truth, it is a futile question. On the other hand, I see many people die because they judge that life is not worth living. I see others paradoxically getting killed for the ideas or illusions that give them a reason for living (what is called a reason for living is also an excellent reason for dying.) I therefore conclude that the meaning of life is the most urgent of questions. How to answer it? On all essential problems (I mean thereby those that run the risk of leading to death or those that intensify the passion of living) there are probably but two methods of thought: the method of La Palisse and the method of Don Quixote. Solely the balance between evidence and lyricism can allow us to achieve simultaneously emotion and lucidity. In a subject at once so humble and so heavy with emotion, the learned and classic dialectic must yield, one can see, to a more modest attitude of mind deriving at one and the same time from common sense and understanding.

Suicide has never been dealt with except as a social phenomenon. On the contrary, we are concerned here, at the outset, with the relation between individual thought and suicide. An act like this is prepared within the silence of the heart, as is a great work of art. The man himself is ignorant of it. One evening he pulls the trigger or jumps. Of an apartment building manager who had killed himself I was told that he had lost his daughter five years before, that he had changed greatly since, and that that experience had "undermined" him. A more exact word cannot be imagined. Beginning to think is beginning to be undermined. Society has but little connection with such beginnings. The worm is in man's heart. That is where it must be sought. One must follow and understand this fatal game that leads from lucidity in the face of existence to flight from light.

There are many causes for a suicide, and generally, the most obvious ones were not the most powerful. Rarely is suicide committed (yet the hypothesis is not excluded) through reflection. What sets off the crisis is almost always unverifiable. Newspapers often speak of "personal sorrows" or of "incurable illness." These explanations are plausible. But one would have to know whether a friend of the desperate man had not that very day addressed him indifferently. He is the guilty one. For that is enough to precipitate all the rancors and all the boredom still in suspension.[2]

---

2. Let us not miss this opportunity to point out the relative character of this essay. Suicide may indeed be related to much more honorable considerations—for example, the political suicides of protest, as they were called during the Chinese revolution.

But if it is hard to fix the precise instant, the subtle step when the mind opted for death, it is easier to deduce from the act itself the consequences it implies. In a sense, and as in melodrama, killing yourself amounts to confessing. It is confessing that life is too much for you or that you do not understand it. Let's not go too far in such analogies, however, but rather return to everyday words. It is merely confessing that that "is not worth the trouble." Living, naturally, is never easy. You continue making the gestures commanded by existence for many reasons, the first of which is habit. Dying voluntarily implies that you have recognized, even instinctively, the ridiculous character of that habit, the absence of any profound reason for living, the insane character of that daily agitation, and the uselessness of suffering.

What, then, is that incalculable feeling that deprives the mind of the sleep necessary to life? A world that can be explained even with bad reasons is a familiar world. But, on the other hand, in a universe suddenly divested of illusions and lights, man feels an alien, a stranger. His exile is without remedy since he is deprived of the memory of a lost home or the hope of a promised land. This divorce between man and his life, the actor and his setting, is properly the feeling of absurdity. All healthy men having thought of their own suicide, it can be seen, without further explanation, that there is a direct connection between this feeling and the longing for death.

The subject of this essay is precisely this relationship between the absurd and suicide, the exact degree to which suicide is a solution to the absurd. . . .

II. Absurd Freedom

Now the main thing is done, I hold certain facts from which I cannot separate. What I know, what is certain, what I cannot deny, what I cannot reject—this is what counts. I can negate everything of that part of me that lives on vague nostalgias, except this desire for unity, this longing to solve, this need for clarity and cohesion. I can refute everything in this world surrounding me that offends or enraptures me, except this chaos, this sovereign chance and this divine equivalence which springs from anarchy. I don't know whether this world has a meaning that transcends it. But I know that I do not know that meaning and that it is impossible for me just now to know it. What can a meaning outside my condition mean to me? I can understand only in human terms. What I touch, what resists me—that is what I understand. And these two certainties—my appetite for the absolute and for unity and the impossibility of reducing this world to a rational and reasonable principle—I also know that I cannot reconcile them. What other truth can I admit without lying, without bringing in a hope I lack and which means nothing within the limits of my condition?

If I were a tree among trees, a cat among animals, this life would have a meaning, or rather this problem would not arise, for I should belong to this world. I should *be* this world to which I am now opposed by my whole consciousness and my whole insistence upon familiarity. This ridiculous reason is what sets me in opposition to all creation. I cannot cross it out with a stroke of the pen. What I believe to be true I must therefore preserve. What seems to me so obvious, even against me, I must support. And what constitutes the basis of that conflict, of that break between the world and my mind, but the awareness of it? If therefore I want to preserve it, I can through a constant awareness, ever revived, ever alert. This is what, for the moment, I must remember. At this moment the absurd, so obvious and yet so hard to win, returns to a man's life and finds its home there. At this moment, too, the mind can leave the arid, dried-up path of lucid effort. That path now emerges in daily life. It encounters the world of the anonymous impersonal pronoun "one," but henceforth man enters in with his revolt and his lucidity. He has forgotten how to hope. This hell of the present is his Kingdom at last. All problems recover their sharp edge. Abstract evidence retreats before the poetry of forms and colors. Spiritual conflicts become embodied and return to the abject and magnificent shelter of man's heart. None of them is settled. But all are transfigured. Is one going to die, escape by the leap, rebuild a mansion of ideas and forms to one's own scale? Is one, on the contrary, going to take up the heart-rending and marvelous wager of the absurd? Let's make a final effort in this regard and draw all our conclusions. The body, affection, creation, action, human nobility will then resume their places in this mad world. At last man will again find there the wine of the absurd and the bread of indifference on which he feeds his greatness.

Let us insist again on the method: it is a matter of persisting. At a certain point on his path the absurd man is tempted. History is not lacking in either religions or prophets, even without gods. He is asked to leap. All he can reply is that he doesn't fully understand, that it is not obvious. Indeed, he does not want to do anything but what he fully understands. He is assured that this is the sin of pride, but he does not understand the notion of sin; that perhaps hell is in store, but he has not enough imagination to visualize that strange future; that he is losing immortal life, but that seems to him an idle consideration. An attempt is made to get him to admit his guilt. He feels innocent. To tell the truth, that is all he feels—his irreparable innocence. This is what allows him everything. Hence, what he demands of himself is to live *solely* with what he knows, to accomodate himself to what is, and to bring in nothing that is not certain. He is told that nothing is. But this at least is a certainty. And it is with this that he is concerned: he wants to find out if it is possible to live *without appeal.*

Now I can broach the notion of suicide. It has already been felt what solution might be given. At this point the problem is reversed. It was previously a question of finding out whether or not life had to have a meaning to be lived. It now becomes clear, on the contrary, that it will be lived all the better if it has no meaning. Living an experience, a particular fate, is accepting it fully. Now, no one will live this fate, knowing it to be absurd, unless he does everything to keep before him that absurd brought to light by consciousness. Negating one of the terms of the opposition on which he lives amounts to escaping it. To abolish conscious revolt is to elude the problem. The theme of permanent revolution is thus carried into individual experience. Living is keeping the absurd alive. Keeping it alive is, above all, contemplating it. Unlike Eurydice, the absurd dies only when we turn away from it. One of the only coherent philosophical positions is thus revolt. It is a constant confrontation between man and his own obscurity. It is an insistence upon an impossible transparency. It challenges the world anew every second. Just as danger provided man the unique opportunity of seizing awareness, so metaphysical revolt extends awareness to the whole of experience. It is that constant presence of man in his own eyes. It is not aspiration, for it is devoid of hope. That revolt is the certainty of a crushing fate, without the resignation that ought to accompany it.

This is where it is seen to what a degree absurd experience is remote from suicide. It may be thought that suicide follows revolt—but wrongly. For it does not represent the logical outcome of revolt. It is just the contrary by the consent it presupposes. Suicide, like the leap, is acceptance at its extreme. Everything is over and man returns to his essential history. His future, his unique and dreadful future—he sees and rushes toward it. In its way, suicide settles the absurd. It engulfs the absurd in the same death. But I know that in order to keep alive, the absurd cannot be settled. It escapes suicide to the extent that it is simultaneously awareness and rejection of death. It is, at the extreme limit of the condemned man's last thought, that shoelace that despite everything he sees a few yards away, on the very brink of his dizzying fall. The contrary of suicide, in fact, is the man condemned to death.

That revolt gives life its value. Spread out over the whole length of a life, it restores its majesty to that life. To a man devoid of blinders, there is no finer sight than that of the intelligence at grips with a reality that transcends it. The sight of human pride is unequaled. No disparagement is of any use. That discipline that the mind imposes on itself, that will conjured up out of nothing, that face-to-face struggle have something exceptional about them. To impoverish that reality whose inhumanity constitutes man's majesty is tantamount to impoverishing him himself. I understand then why the doctrines that explain everything to me also debilitate me at the same time. They relieve me of the weight of my own life, and yet I must carry it alone. At this juncture, I cannot conceive that a skeptical metaphysics can be joined to an ethics of renunciation.

Consciousness and revolt, these rejections are the contrary of renunciation. Everything that is indomitable and passionate in a human heart quickens them, on the contrary, with its own life. It is essential to die unreconciled and not of one's own free will. Suicide is a repudiation. The absurd man can only drain everything to the bitter end, and deplete himself. The absurd is his extreme tension, which he maintains constantly by solitary effort, for he knows that in that consciousness and in that day-to-day revolt he gives proof of his only truth, which is defiance. This is a first consequence.

If I remain in that prearranged position which consists in drawing all the conclusions (and nothing else) involved in a newly discovered notion, I am faced with a second paradox. In order to remain faithful to the method, I have nothing to do with the problem of metaphysical liberty. Knowing whether or not man is free doesn't interest me. I can experience only my own freedom. As to it, I can have no general notions, but merely a few insights. The problem of "freedom as such" has no meaning. For it is linked in quite a different way with the problem of God. Knowing whether or not man is free involves knowing whether he can have a master. The absurdity peculiar to this problem comes from the fact that the very notion that makes the problem of freedom possible also takes away all its meaning. For in the presence of God there is less a problem of freedom than a problem of evil. You know the alternative: either we are not free and God the all-powerful is responsible for evil. Or we are free and responsible but God is not all-powerful. All the scholastic subtleties have neither added anything to nor subtracted anything from the acuteness of this paradox.

This is why I cannot get lost in the glorification or the mere definition of a notion which eludes me and loses its meaning as soon as it goes beyond the frame of reference of my individual experience. I cannot understand what kind of freedom would be given me by a higher being. I have lost the sense of hierarchy. The only conception of freedom I can have is that of the prisoner or the individual in the midst of the State. The only one I know is freedom of thought and action. Now if the absurd cancels all my chances of eternal freedom, it restores and magnifies, on the other hand, my freedom of action. That privation·of hope and future means an increase in man's availability.

Before encountering the absurd, the everyday man lives with aims, a concern for the future or for justification (with regard to whom or what is not the question). He weighs his chances, he counts on "someday," his retirement or the labor of his sons. He still thinks that something in his life can be directed. In truth, he acts as if he were free, even if all the facts make a point of contradicting that liberty. But after the absurd, everything is upset. That idea that "I am," my way of acting as if everything has a meaning (even if, on occasion, I said that nothing has)—all that is given the lie in vertiginous fashion by the absurdity of a possible death. Thinking of the future, establishing aims for oneself, having preferences—all this presupposes a belief in freedom, even if one occasionally ascertains that one doesn't feel it. But at that moment I am well aware that that higher liberty, that freedom *to be,* which alone can serve as basis for a truth, does not exist. Death is there as the only reality. After death the chips are down. I am not even free, either, to perpetuate myself, but a slave, and, above all, a slave without hope of an eternal revolution, without recourse to contempt. And who without revolution and without contempt can remain a slave? What freedom can exist in the fullest sense without assurance of eternity?

But at the same time the absurd man realizes that hitherto he was bound to that postulate of freedom on the illusion of which he was living. In a certain sense, that hampered him. To the extent to which he imagined a purpose to his life, he adapted himself to the demands of a purpose to be achieved and became the slave of his liberty. Thus I could not act otherwise than as the father (or the engineer or the leader of a nation, or the post-office sub-clerk) that I am preparing to be. I think I can choose to be that rather than something else. I think so unconsciously, to be sure. But at the same time I strengthen my postulate with the beliefs of those around me, with the presumptions of my human environment (others are so sure of being free, and that cheerful mood is so contagious!). However far one may remain from any presumption, moral or social, one is partly influenced by them and even, for the best among them (there are good and bad presumptions), one adapts one's life to them. Thus the absurd man realizes that he was not really free. To speak clearly, to the extent to which I hope, to which I worry about a truth that might be individual to me, about a way of being or creating, to the extent to which I arrange my life and prove thereby that I accept its having a meaning, I create for myself barriers between which I confine my life. I do like so many bureaucrats of the mind and heart who only fill me with disgust and whose only vice, I now see clearly, is to take man's freedom seriously.

The absurd enlightens me on this point: there is no future. Henceforth this is the reason for my inner freedom. I shall use two comparisons here. Mystics, to begin with, find freedom in giving themselves. By losing themselves in their god, by accepting his rules, they become secretly free. In spontaneously accepted slavery they recover a deeper independence. But what does that freedom mean? It may be said, above all, that they *feel* free with regard to themselves, and not so much free as liberated. Likewise, completely turned toward death (taken here as the most obvious absurdity), the absurd man feels released from everything outside that passionate attention crystallizing in him. He enjoys a freedom with regard to common rules. It can be seen at this point that the initial themes of existential philosophy keep their entire value. The return to consciousness, the escape from everyday sleep represent the first steps of absurd freedom. But it is existenial *preaching* that is alluded to, and with it that spiritual leap which basically escapes consciousness. In the same way (this is my second comparison) the slaves of antiquity did not belong to themselves. But they knew that freedom which consists in not feeling responsible. Death, too, has patrician hands which, while crushing, also liberate.

Losing oneself in that bottomless certainty, feeling henceforth sufficiently remote from one's own life to increase it and take a broad view of it—this involves the principle of a liberation. Such new independence has a definite time limit, like any freedom of action. It does not write a check on eternity. But it takes the place of the illusions of *freedom,* which all stopped with death. The divine availabiltiy of the condemned man before whom the prison doors open in a certain early dawn, that unbelievable disinterestedness with regard to everything except for the pure flame of life—it is clear that death and the absurd are here the principles of the only reasonable freedom: that which a human heart can experience and live. This is a second consequence. The absurd man thus catches sight of a burning and frigid, transparent and limited universe in which nothing is possible but everything is given, and beyond which all is collapse and nothingness. He can then decide to accept such a universe and draw from it his strength, his refusal to hope, and the unyielding evidence of a life without consolation.

But what does life mean in such a universe? Nothing else for the moment but indifference to the future and a desire to use up everything that is given. Belief in the meaning of life always implies a scale of values, a choice, our preferences. Belief in the absurd, according to our definitions, teaches the contrary. But this is worth examining.

Knowing whether or not one can live *without appeal* is all that interests me. I do not want to get out of my depth. This aspect of life being given me, can I adapt myself to it? Now, faced with this particular concern, belief in the absurd is tantamount to substituting the quantity of experiences for the quality. If I convince myself that this life has no other aspect than that of the absurd, if I feel that its whole equilibrium depends on that perpetual opposition between my conscious revolt and the darkness in which it struggles, if I admit that my freedom has no meaning except in relation to its limited fate, then I must say that what counts is not the best living but the most living. It is not up to me to wonder if this is vulgar or revolting, elegant or deplorable. Once and for all, value judgments are discarded here in favor of factual judgments. I have merely to draw the conclusions from what I can see and to risk nothing that is hypothetical. Supposing that living in this way were not honorable, then true propriety would command me to be dishonorable.

The most living; in the broadest sense, that rule means nothing. It calls for definition. It seems to begin with the fact that the notion of quantity has not been sufficiently explored. For it can account for a large share of human experience. A man's rule of conduct and his scale of values have no meaning except through the quantity and variety of experiences he has been in a position to accumulate. Now, the conditions of modern life impose on the majority of men the same quantity of experiences and consequently the same profound experience. To be sure, there must also be taken into consideration the individual's spontaneous contribution, the "given" element in him. But I cannot judge of that, and let me repeat that my rule here is to get along with the immediate evidence. I see, then, that the individual character of a common code of ethics lies not so much in the ideal importance of its basic principles as in the norm of an experience that it is possible to measure. To stretch a point somewhat, the Greeks had the code of their leisure just as we have the code of our eight-hour day. But already many men among the most tragic cause us to foresee that a longer experience changes this table of values. They make us imagine that adventurer of the everyday who through mere quantity of experiences would break all records (I am purposely using this sports expression) and would thus win his own code of ethics. Yet let's avoid romanticism and just ask ourselves what such an attitude may mean to a man with his mind made up to take up his bet and to observe strictly what he takes to be the rules of the game.

Breaking all the records is first and foremost being faced with the world as often as possible. How can that be done without contradictions and without playing on words? For on the one hand the absurd teaches that all experiences are unimportant, and on the other it urges toward the greatest quantity of experiences. How, then, can one fail to do as so many of those men I was speaking of earlier—choose the form of life that brings us the most possible of that human matter, thereby introducing a scale of values that on the other hand one claims to reject?

But again it is the absurd and its contradictory life that teaches us. For the mistake is thinking that that quantity of experiences depends on the circumstances of our life when it depends solely on us. Here we have to be over-simple. To two men living the same number of years, the world always provides the same sum of experiences. It is up to us to be conscious of them. Being aware of one's life, one's revolt, one's freedom, and to the maximum, is living, and to the maximum. Where lucidity dominates, the scale of values becomes useless. Let's be even more simple. Let us say that the sole obstacle, the sole deficiency to be made good, is constituted by premature death. Thus it is that no depth, no emotion, no passion, and no sacrifice could render equal in the eyes of the absurd man (even if he wished it so) a conscious life of forty years and a lucidity spread over sixty years. Madness and death are his irreparables. Man does not choose. The absurd and the extra life it involves *therefore do not depend on man's will,* but on its contrary, which is death. Weighing words carefully, it is altogether a question of luck. One just has to be able to consent to this. There will never be any substitute for twenty years of life and experience.

By what is an odd inconsistency in such an alert race, the Greeks claimed that those who died young were beloved of the gods. And that is true only if you are willing to believe that entering the ridiculous world of the gods is forever losing the purest of joys, which is feeling, and feeling on this earth. The present and the succession of presents before a constantly conscious soul is the ideal of the absurd man. But the word "ideal" rings false in this connection. It is not even his vocation, but merely the third consequence of his reasoning. Having started from an anguished awareness of the inhuman, the meditation on the absurd returns at the end of its itinerary to the very heart of the passionate flames of human revolt.

Thus I draw from the absurd three consequences, which are my revolt, my freedom, and my passion. By the mere activity of consciousness I transform into a rule of life what was an invitation to death— and I refuse suicide. I know, to be sure, the dull resonance that vibrates throughout these days. Yet I have but a word to say: that it is necessary. When Nietzsche writes: "It clearly seems that the chief thing in heaven and on earth is to *obey* at length and in a single direction: in the long run there results something for which it is worth the trouble of living on this earth as, for example, virtue, art, music, the dance, reason, the mind—something that transfigures, something delicate, mad, or divine," he elucidates the rule of a really distinguished code of ethics. But he also points the way of the absurd man. Obeying the flame is both the easiest and the hardest thing to do. However, it is good for man to judge himself occasionally. He is alone in being able to do so.

"Prayer," says Alain, "is when night descends over thought." "But the mind must meet the night," reply the mystics and the existentials. Yes, indeed, but not that night that is born under closed eyelids and through the mere will of man—dark, impenetrable night that the mind calls up in order to plunge into it. If it must encounter a night, let it be rather that of despair, which remains lucid—polar night, vigil of the mind, whence will arise perhaps that white and virginal brightness which outlines every object in the light of the intelligence. At that degree, equivalence encounters passionate understanding. Then it is no longer even a question of judging the existential leap. It resumes its place amid the age-old fresco of human attitudes. For the spectator, if he is conscious, that leap is still absurd. In so far as it thinks it solves the paradox, it reinstates it intact. On this score, it is stirring. On this score, everything resumes its place and the absurd world is reborn in all its splendor and diversity.

But it is bad to stop, hard to be satisfied with a single way of seeing, to go without contradiction, perhaps the most subtle of all spiritual forces. The preceding merely defines a way of thinking. But the point is to live.

18. The Courage To Be

Guilt and the Courage to Accept Acceptance

In the center of the Protestant courage of confidence stands the courage to accept acceptance in spite of the consciousness of guilt. Luther, and in fact the whole period, experienced the anxiety of guilt and condemnation as the main form of their anxiety. The courage to affirm oneself in spite of this anxiety is the courage which we have called the courage of confidence. It is rooted in the personal, total, and immediate certainty of divine forgiveness. There is belief in forgiveness in all forms of man's courage to be, even in neocollectivism. But there is no interpretation of human existence in which it is so predominant as in genuine Protestantism. And there is no movement in history in which it is equally profound and equally paradoxical. In the Lutheran formula that "he who is unjust is just" (in the view of the divine forgiveness) or in the more modern phrasing that "he who is unacceptable is accepted" the victory over the anxiety of guilt and condemnation is sharply expressed. One could say that the courage to be is the courage to accept oneself as accepted in spite of being unacceptable.

Reprinted from Paul Tillich, *The Courage To Be* (New Haven, Conn: Yale University Press, 1952), pp. 163–90, by permission of Yale University Press.

One does not need to remind the theologians of the fact that this is the genuine meaning of the Pauline-Lutheran doctrine of "justification by faith"(a doctrine which in its original phrasing has become incomprehensible even for students of theology). But one must remind theologians and ministers that in the fight against the anxiety of guilt by psychotherapy the idea of acceptance has received the attention and gained the significance which in the Reformation period was to be seen in phrases like "forgiveness of sins" or "justification through faith." Accepting acceptance though being unacceptable is the basis for the courage of confidence.

Decisive for this self-affirmation is its being independent of any moral, intellectual, or religious precondition: it is not the good or the wise or the pious who are entitled to the courage to accept acceptance but those who are lacking in all these qualities and are aware of being unacceptable. This, however, does not mean acceptance by oneself as oneself. It is not a justification of one's accidental individuality. It is not the Existentialist courage to be as oneself. It is the paradoxical act in which one is accepted by that which infinitely transcends one's individual self. It is in the experience of the Reformers the acceptance of the unacceptable sinner into judging and transforming communion with God.

The courage to be in this respect is the courage to accept the forgiveness of sins, not as an abstract assertion but as the fundamental experience in the encounter with God. Self-affirmation in spite of the anxiety of guilt and condemnation presupposes participation in something which transcends the self. In the communion of healing, for example the psychoanalytic situation, the patient participates in the healing power of the helper by whom he is accepted although he feels himself unacceptable. The healer, in this relationship, does not stand for himself as an individual but represents the objective power of acceptance and self-affirmation. This objective power works through the healer in the patient. Of course, it must be embodied in a person who can realize guilt, who can judge, and who can accept in spite of the judgment. Acceptance by something which is less than personal could never overcome personal self-rejection. A wall to which I confess cannot forgive me. No self-acceptance is possible if one is not accepted in a person-to-person relation. But even if one is personally accepted it needs a self-transcending courage to accept this acceptance, it needs the courage of confidence. For being accepted does not mean that guilt is denied. The healing helper who tried to convince his patient that he was not really guilty would do him a great disservice. He would prevent him from taking his guilt into his self-affirmation. He may help him to transform displaced, neurotic guilt feelings into genuine ones which are, so to speak, put on the right place, but he cannot tell him that there is no guilt in him. He accepts the patient into his communion without condemning anything and without covering up anything.

Here, however, is the point where the religious "acceptance as being accepted" transcends medical healing. Religion asks for the ultimate source of the power which heals by accepting the unacceptable, it asks for God. The acceptance by God, his forgiving or justifying act, is the only and ultimate source of a courage to be which is able to take the anxiety of guilt and condemnation into itself. For the ultimate power of self-affirmation can only be the power of being-itself. Everything less than this, one's own or anybody else's finite power of being, cannot overcome the radical, infinite threat of nonbeing which is experienced in the despair of self-condemnation. This is why the courage of confidence, as it is expressed in man like Luther, emphasizes unceasingly exclusive trust in God and rejects any other foundation for his courage to be, not only as insufficient but as driving him into more guilt and deeper anxiety. The immense liberation brought to the people of the 16th century by the message of the Reformers and the creation of their indomitable courage to accept acceptance was due to the *sola fide* doctrine, namely to the message that the courage of confidence is conditioned not by anything finite but solely by that which is unconditional itself and which we experience as unconditional in a person-to-person encounter.

FATE AND THE COURAGE TO ACCEPT ACCEPTANCE

As the symbolic figures of death and the devil show, the anxiety of this period was not restricted to the anxiety of guilt. It was also an anxiety of death and fate. The astrological ideas of the later ancient world had been revived by the Renaissance and had influenced even those humanists who joined the Reformation. We have already referred to the Neo-Stoic courage, expressed in some Renaissance pictures, where man directs the vessel of his life although it is driven by the winds of fate. Luther faced the anxiety of fate on another level. He experienced the connection between the anxiety of guilt and the anxiety of fate. It is the uneasy conscience which produces innumerable irrational fears in daily life. The rustling of a dry leaf horrifies him who is plagued by guilt. Therefore conquest of the anxiety of guilt is also conquest of the anxiety of fate. The courage of confidence takes the anxiety of fate as well as the anxiety of guilt into itself. It says "in spite of" to both of them. This is the genuine meaning of the doctrine of providence. Providence is not a theory about some activities of God; it is the religious symbol of the courage of confidence with respect to fate and death. For the courage of confidence says "in spite of" even to death.

Like Paul, Luther was well aware of the connection of the anxiety of guilt with the anxiety of death. In Stoicism and Neo-Stoicism the essential self is not threatened by death, because it belongs to being-itself and transcends nonbeing. Socrates, who in the power of his essential self conquered the anxiety of death, has become the symbol for the courage to take death upon oneself. This is the true meaning of Plato's so-called doctrine of immorality of the soul. In discussing this doctrine we should neglect the arguments for immortality, even those in Plato's *Phaedon,* and concentrate on the image of the dying Socrates. All the arguments, skeptically treated by Plato himself, are attempts to interpret the courage of Socrates, the courage to take one's death into one's self-affirmation. Socrates is certain that the self which the executioners will destroy is not the self which affirms itself in his courage to be. He does not say much about the relation of the two selves, and he could not because they are not numerically two, but one in two aspects. But he makes it clear that the courage to die is the test of the courage to be. A self-affirmation which omits taking the affirmation of one's death into itself tries to escape the test of courage, the facing of nonbeing in the most radical way.

The popular belief in immortality which in the Western world has largely replaced the Christian symbol of resurrection is a mixture of courage and escape. It tries to maintain one's self-affirmation even in the face of one's having to die. But it does this by continuing one's finitude, that is one's having to die, infinitely, so that the actual death never will occur. This, however, is an illusion and, logically speaking, a contradiction in terms. It makes endless what, by definition, must come to an end. The "immorality of the soul" is a poor symbol for the courage to be in the face of one's having to die.

The courage of Socrates (in Plato's picture) was based not on a doctrine of the immortality of the soul but on the affirmation of himself in his essential, industructible being. He knows that he belongs to two orders of reality and that the one order is transtemporal. It was the courage of Socrates which more than any philosophical reflection revealed to the ancient world that everyone belongs to two orders.

But there was one presupposition in the Socratic (Stoic and Neo-Stoic) courage to take death upon oneself, namely the ability of every individual to participate in both orders, the temporal and the eternal.

This presupposition is not accepted by Christianity. According to Christianity we are estranged from our essential being. We are not free to realize our essential being, we are bound to contradict it. Therefore death can be accepted only through a state of confidence in which death has ceased to be the "wages of sin." This, however, is the state of being accepted in spite of being unacceptable. Here is the point in which the ancient world was transformed by Christianity and in which Luther's courage to face death was rooted. It is the being accepted into communion with God that underlies this courage, not a questionable theory of immorality. The encounter with God in Luther is not merely the basis for the courage to take upon oneself sin and condemnation, it is also the basis for taking upon oneself fate and death. For encountering God means encountering transcendent security and transcendent eternity. He who participates in God participates in eternity. But in order to participate in him you must be accepted by him and you must have accepted his acceptance of you.

Luther had experiences which he describes as attacks of utter despair *(Anfechtung),* as the frightful threat of a complete meaninglessness. He felt these moments as satanic attacks in which everything was menaced: his Christian faith, the confidence in his work, the Reformation, the forgiveness of sins. Everything broke down in the extreme moments of this despair, nothing was left to the courage to be. Luther in these moments, and in the descriptions he gives of them, anticipated the descriptions of them by modern Existentialism. But for him this was not the last word. The last word was the first commandment, the statement that God is God. It reminded him of the unconditional element in human experience of which one can be aware even in the abyss of meaninglessness. And this awareness saved him.

It should not be forgotten that the great adversary of Luther, Thomas Münzer, the Anabaptist and religious socialist, describes similar experiences. He speaks of the ultimate situation in which everything finite reveals its finitude, in which the finite has come to its end, in which anxiety grips the heart and all previous meanings fall apart, and in which just for this reason the Divine Spirit can make itself felt and can turn the whole situation into a courage to be whose expression is revolutionary action. While Luther represents ecclesiastical Protestantism, Münzer represents evangelical radicalism. Both men have shaped history, and actually Münzer's views had even more influence in America than Luther's. Both men experienced the anxiety of meaninglessness and described it in terms which had been created by Christian mystics. But in doing so they transcended the courage of confidence which is based on a personal encounter with God. They had to receive elements from the courage to be which is based on mystical union. This leads to a last question: whether the two types of the courage to accept acceptance can be united in view of the all-pervasive presence of the anxiety of doubt and meaninglessness in our own period.

ABSOLUTE FAITH AND THE COURAGE TO BE

We have avoided the concept of faith in our description of the courage to be which is based on mystical union with the ground of being as well as in our description of the courage to be which is based on the personal encounter with God. This is partly because the concept of faith has lost its genuine meaning and has received the connotation of "belief in something unbelievable." But this is not the only reason for the use of terms other than faith. The decisive reason is that I do not think either mystical union or personal encounter fulfills the idea of faith. Certainly there is faith in the elevation of the soul above the finite to the infinite, leading to its union with the ground of being. But more than this is included in the concept of faith. And there is faith in the personal encounter with the personal God. But more than this is included in the concept of faith. Faith is the state of being grasped by the power of being-itself. The courage to be is an expression of faith and what "faith" means must be understood through the courage to be. We have defined courage as the self-affirmation of being in spite of nonbeing. The power of this self-affirmation is the power of being which is effective in every act of courage. Faith is the experience of this power.

But it is an experience which has a paradoxical character, the character of accepting acceptance. Being-itself transcends every finite being infinitely; God in the divine-human encounter transcends man unconditionally. Faith bridges this infinite gap by accepting the fact that in spite of it the power of being is present, that he who is separated is accepted. Faith accepts "in spite of"; and out of the "in spite of" of faith the "in spite of" of courage is born. Faith is not a theoretical affirmation of something uncertain, it is the existential acceptance of something transcending ordinary experience. Faith is not an opinion but a state. It is the state of being grasped by the power of being which transcends everything that is and in which everything that is participates. He who is grasped by this power is able to affirm himself because he knows that he is affirmed by the power of being-itself. In this point mystical experience and personal encounter are identical. In both of them faith is the basis of the courage to be.

This is decisive for a period in which, as in our own, the anxiety of doubt and meaninglessness is dominant. Certainly the anxiety of fate and death is not lacking in our time. The anxiety of fate has increased with the degree to which the schizophrenic split of our world has removed the last remnants of former security. And the anxiety of guilt and condemnation is not lacking either. It is surprising how much anxiety of guilt comes to the surface in psychoanalysis and personal counseling. The centuries of puritan and bourgeois repression of vital strivings have produced almost as many guilt feelings as the preaching of hell and purgatory in the Middle Ages.

But in spite of these restricting considerations one must say that the anxiety which determines our period is the anxiety of doubt and meaninglessness. One is afraid of having lost or of having to lose the meaning of one's existence. The expression of this situation is the Existentialism of today.

Which courage is able to take nonbeing into itself in the form of doubt and meaninglessness? This is the most important and most disturbing question in the quest for the courage to be. For the anxiety of meaninglessness undermines what is still unshaken in the anxiety of fate and death and of guilt and condemnation. In the anxiety of guilt and condemnation doubt has not yet undermined the certainty of an ultimate responsibility. We are threatened but we are not destroyed. If, however, doubt and meaninglessness prevail one experiences an abyss in which the meaning of life and the truth of ultimate responsibility disappear. Both the Stoic who conquers the anxiety of fate with the Socratic courage of wisdom and the Christian who conquers the anxiety of guilt with the Protestant courage of accepting forgiveness are in a different situation. Even in the despair of having to die and the despair of self-condemnation meaning is affirmed and certitude preserved. But in the despair of doubt and meaninglessness both are swallowed by nonbeing.

The question then is this: Is there a courage which can conquer the anxiety of meaninglessness and doubts? Or in other words, can the faith which accepts acceptance resist the power of nonbeing in its most radical form? Can faith resist meaninglessness? Is there a kind of faith which can exist together with doubt and meaninglessness? These questions lead to the last aspect of the problem discussed in these lectures and the one most relevant to our time: How is the courage to be possible if all the ways to create it are barred by the experience of their ultimate insufficiency? If life is as meaningless as death, if guilt is as questionable as perfection, if being is no more meaningful than nonbeing, on what can one base the courage to be?

There is an inclination in some Existentialists to answer these questions by a leap from doubt to dogmatic certitude, from meaninglessness to a set of symbols in which the meaning of a special ecclesiastical or political group is embodied. This leap can be interpreted in different ways. It may be the expression of a desire for safety; it may be as arbitrary as, according to Existentialist principles, every decision is; it may be the feeling that the Christian message is the answer to the questions raised by an analysis of human existence; it may be a genuine conversion, independent of the theoretical situation. In any case it is not a solution of the problem of radical doubt. It gives the courage to be to those who are converted but it does not answer the question as to how such a courage is possible in itself. The answer must accept, as its precondition, the state of meaninglessness. It is not an answer if it demands the removal of this state, for that is just what cannot be done. He who is in the grip of doubt and meaninglessness cannot liberate himself from this grip; but he asks for an answer which is valid within and not outside the situation of his despair. He asks for the ultimate foundation of what we have called the "courage of despair." There is only one possible answer, if one does not try to escape the question: namely that the acceptance of despair is in itself faith and on the boundary line of the courage to be. In this situation the meaning of life is reduced to despair about the meaning of life. But as long as this despair is an act of life it is positive in its negativity. Cynically speaking, one could say that it is true to life to be cynical about it. Religiously speaking, one would say that one accepts oneself as accepted in spite of one's despair about the meaning of this acceptance. The paradox of every radical negativity, as long as it is an active negativity, is that it must affirm itself in order to be able to negate itself. No actual negation can be without an implicit affirmation. The hidden pleasure produced by despair witnesses to the paradoxical character of self-negation. The negative lives from the positive it negates.

The faith which makes the courage of despair possible is the acceptance of the power of being, even in the grip of nonbeing. Even in the despair about meaning being affirms itself through us. The act of accepting meaninglessness is in itself a meaningful act. It is an act of faith. We have seen that he who has the courage to affirm his being in spite of fate and guilt has not removed them. He remains threatened and hit by them. But he accepts his acceptance by the power of being-itself in which he participates and which gives him the courage to take the anxieties of fate and guilt upon himself. The same is true of doubt and meaninglessness. The faith which creates the courage to take them into itself has no special content. It is simply faith, undirected, absolute. It is undefinable, since everything defined is dissolved by doubt and meaninglessness. Nevertheless, even absolute faith is not an eruption of subjective emotions or a mood without objective foundation.

An analysis of the nature of absolute faith reveals the following elements in it. The first is the experience of the power of being which is present even in face of the most radical manifestation of nonbeing. If one says that in this experience vitality resists despair one must add that vitality in man is proportional to intentionality. The vitality that can stand the abyss of meaninglessness is aware of a hidden meaning within the destruction of meaning. The second element in absolute faith is the dependence of the experience of nonbeing on the experience of being and the dependence of the experience of meaninglessness on the experience of meaning. Even in the state of despair one has enough being to make despair possible. There is a third element in absolute faith, the acceptance of being accepted. Of course, in the state of despair there is nobody and nothing that accepts. But there is the power of acceptance itself which is experienced. Meaninglessness, as long as it is experienced, includes an experience of the "power of acceptance." To accept this power of acceptance consciously is the religious answer of absolute faith, of a faith which has been deprived by doubt of any concrete content, which nevertheless is faith and the source of the most paradoxical manifestation of the courage to be.

This faith transcends both the mystical experience and the divine-human encounter. The mystical experience seems to be nearer to absolute faith but it is not. Absolute faith includes an element of skepticism which one cannot find in the mystical experience. Certainly mysticism also transcends all specific contents, but not because it doubts them or has found them meaningless; rather it deems them to be preliminary. Mysticism uses the specific contents as grades, stepping on them after having used them. The experience of meaninglessness, however, denies them (and everything that goes with them) without having used them. The experience of meaninglessness is more radical than mysticism. Therefore it transcends the mystical experience.

Absolute faith also transcends the divine-human encounter. In this encounter the subject-object scheme is valid: a definite subject (man) meets a definite object (God). One can reverse this statement and say that a definite subject (God) meets a definite object (man). But in both cases the attack of doubt undercuts the subject-object structure. The theologians who speak so strongly and with such self-certainty about the divine-human encounter should be aware of a situation in which this encounter is prevented by radical doubt and nothing is left but absolute faith. The acceptance of such a situation as religiously valid has, however, the consequence that the concrete contents of ordinary faith must be subjected to criticism and transformation. The courage to be in its radical form is a key to an idea of God which transcends both mysticism and the person-to-person encounter.

The Courage to Be as the Key to Being-Itself

NONBEING OPENING UP BEING

The courage to be in all its forms has, by itself, revelatory character. It shows the nature of being, it shows that the self-affirmation of being is an affirmation that overcomes negation. In a metaphorical statement (and every assertion about being-itself is either metaphorical or symbolic) one could say that being includes nonbeing but nonbeing does not prevail against it. "Including" is a spatial metaphor which indicates that being embraces itself and that which is opposed to it, nonbeing. Nonbeing belongs to being, it cannot be separated from it. We could not even think "being" without a double negation: being must be thought as the negation of the negation of being. This is why we describe being best by the metaphor "power of being." Power is the possibility a being has to actualize itself against the resistance of other beings. If we speak of the power of being-itself we indicate that being affirms itself against nonbeing. In our discussion of courage and life we have mentioned the dynamic understanding of reality by the philosophers of life. Such an understanding is possible only if one accepts the view that nonbeing belongs to being, that being could not be the ground of life without nonbeing. The self-affirmation of being without nonbeing would not even be self-affirmation but an immovable self-identity. Nothing would be manifest, nothing expressed, nothing revealed. But nonbeing drives being out of its seclusion, it forces it to affirm itself dynamically. Philosophy has dealt with the dynamic self-affirmation of being-itself wherever it spoke dialectically, notably in Neoplatonism, Hegel, and the philosophers of life and process. Theology has done the same whenever it took the idea of the living God seriously, most obviously in the trinitarian symbolization of the inner life of God. Spinoza, in spite of his static definition of substance (which is his name for the ultimate power of being), unites philosophical and mystical tendencies when he speaks of the love and knowledge with which God loves and knows himself through the love and knowledge of finite beings. Nonbeing (that in God which makes his self-affirmation dynamic) opens up the divine self-seclusion and reveals him as power and love. Nonbeing makes God a living God. Without the No he has to overcome in himself and in his creature, the divine Yes to himself would be lifeless. There would be no revelation of the ground of being, there would be no life.

But where there is nonbeing there is finitude and anxiety. If we say that nonbeing belongs to being-itself, we say that finitude and anxiety belong to being-itself. Wherever philosophers or theologians have spoken of the divine blessedness they have implicitly (and sometimes explicitly) spoken of the anxiety of finitude which is eternally taken into the blessedness of the divine infinity. The infinite embraces itself and the finite, the Yes includes itself and the No which it takes into itself, blessedness comprises itself and the anxiety of which it is the conquest. All this is implied if one says that being includes nonbeing and that through nonbeing it reveals itself. It is a highly symbolic language which must be used at this point. But its symbolic character does not diminish its truth; on the contrary, it is a condition of its truth. To speak unsymbolically about being-itself is untrue.

The divine self-affirmation is the power that makes the self-affirmation of the finite being, the courage to be, possible. Only because being-itself has the character of self-affirmation in spite of nonbeing is courage possible. Courage participates in the self-affirmation of being-itself, it participates in the power of being which prevails against nonbeing. He who receives this power in an act of mystical or personal or absolute faith is aware of the source of his courage to be.

Man is not necessarily aware of this source. In situations of cynicism and indifference he is not aware of it. But it works in him as long as he maintains the courage to take his anxiety upon himself. In the act of the courage to be the power of being is effective in us, whether we recognize it or not. Every act of courage is a manifestation of the ground of being, however questionable the content of the act may be. The content may hide or distort true being, the courage in it reveals true being. Not arguments but the courage to be reveals the true nature of being-itself. By affirming our being we participate in the self-affirmation of being-itself. There are no valid arguments for the "existence" of God, but there are acts of courage in which we affirm the power of being, whether we know it or not. If we know it, we accept acceptance consciously. If we do not know it, we nevertheless accept it and participate in it. And in our acceptance of that which we do not know the power of being is manifest to us. Courage has revealing power, the courage to be is the key to being-itself.

THEISM TRANSCENDED

The courage to take meaninglessness into itself presupposes a relation to the ground of being which we have called "absolute faith." It is without a *special* content, yet it is not without content. The content of absolute faith is the "God above God." Absolute faith and its consequence, the courage that takes the radical doubt, the doubt about God, into itself, transcends the theistic idea of God.

Theism can mean the unspecified affirmation of God. Theism in this sense does not say what it means if it uses the name of God. Because of the traditional and psychological connotations of the word God such an empty theism can produce a reverent mood if it speaks of God. Politicians, dictators, and other people who wish to use rhetoric to make an impression on their audience like to use the word God in this sense. It produces the feeling in their listeners that the speaker is serious and morally trustworthy. This is especially successful if they can brand their foes as atheistic. On a higher level people without a definite religious commitment like to call themselves theistic, not for special purposes but because they cannot stand a world without God, whatever this God may be. They need some of the connotations of the word God and they are afraid of what they call atheism. On the highest level of this kind of theism the name of God is used as a poetic or practical symbol, expressing a profound emotional state or the highest ethical idea. It is a theism which stands on the boundary line between the second type of theism and what we call "theism transcended." But it is still too indefinite to cross this boundary line. The atheistic negation of this whole type of theism is as vague as the theism itself. It may produce an irreverent mood and angry reaction of those who take their theistic affirmation seriously. It may even be felt as justified against the rhetorical-political abuse of the name God, but it is ultimately as irrelevant as the theism which it negates. It cannot reach the state of despair any more than the theism against which it fights can reach the state of faith.

Theism can have another meaning, quite contrary to the first one: it can be the name of what we have called the divine-human encounter. In this case it points to those elements in the Jewish-Christian tradition which emphasize the person-to-person relationship with God. Theism in this sense emphasizes the personalistic passages in the Bible and the Protestant creeds, the personalistic image of God, the word as the tool of creation and revelation, the ethical and social character of the kingdom of God, the personal nature of human faith and divine forgiveness, the historical vision of the universe, the idea of a divine purpose, the infinite distance between creator and creature, the absolute separation between God and the world, the conflict between holy God and sinful man, the person-to-person character of prayer and practical devotion. Theism in this sense is the nonmystical side of biblical religion and historical Christianity. Atheism from the point of view of this theism is the human attempt to escape the divine-human encounter. It is an existential—not a theoretical—problem.

Theism has a third meaning, a strictly theological one. Theological theism is, like every theology, dependent on the religious substance which it conceptualizes. It is dependent on theism in the first sense insofar as it tries to prove the necessity of affirming God in some way; it usually develops the so-called arguments for the "existence" of God. But it is more dependent on theism in the second sense insofar as it tries to establish a doctrine of God which transforms the person-to-person encounter with God into a doctrine about two persons who may or may not meet but who have a reality independent of each other.

Now theism in the first sense must be transcended because it is irrelevant, and theism in the second sense must be transcended because it is one-sided. But theism in the third sense must be transcended because it is wrong. It is bad theology. This can be shown by a more penetrating analysis. The God of theological theism is a being beside others and as such a part of the whole of reality. He certainly is considered its most important part, but as a part and therefore as subjected to the structure of the whole. He is supposed to be beyond the ontological elements and categories which constitute reality. But every statement subjects him to them. He is seen as a self which has a world, as an ego which is related to a thou, as a cause which is separated from its effect, as having a definite space and an endless time. He is a being, not being-itself. As such he is bound to the subject-object structure of reality, he is an object for us as subjects. At the same time we are objects for him as a subject. And this is decisive for the necessity of transcending theological theism. For God as a subject makes me into an object which is nothing more than an object. He deprives me of my subjectivity because he is all-powerful and all-knowing. I revolt and try to make *him* into an object, but the revolt fails and becomes desperate. God appears as the invincible tyrant, the being in contrast with whom all other beings are without freedom and subjectivity. He is equated with the recent tyrants who with the help of terror try to transform everything into a mere object, a thing among things, a cog in the machine they control. He becomes the model of everything against which existentialism revolted. This is the God Nietzsche said had to be killed because nobody can tolerate being made into a mere object of absolute knowledge and absolute control. This is the deepest root of atheism. It is an atheism which is justified as the reaction against theological theism and its disturbing implications. It is also the deepest root of the Existentialist despair and the widespread anxiety of meaninglessness in our period.

Theism in all its forms is transcended in the experience we have called absolute faith. It is the accepting of the acceptance without somebody or something that accepts. It is the power of being-itself that accepts and gives the courage to be. This is the highest point to which our analysis has brought us. It cannot be described in the way the God of all forms of theism can be described. It cannot be described in mystical terms either. It transcends both mysticism and personal encounter, as it transcends both the courage to be as a part and the courage to be as oneself.

THE GOD ABOVE GOD AND THE COURAGE TO BE

The ultimate source of the courage to be is the "God above God"; this is the result of our demand to transcend theism. Only if the God of theism is transcended can the anxiety of doubt and meaninglessness be taken into the courage to be. The God above God is the object of all mystical longing, but mysticism also must be transcended in order to reach him. Mysticism does not take seriously the concrete and the doubt concerning the concrete. It plunges directly into the ground of being and meaning, and leaves the concrete, the world of finite values and meanings, behind. Therefore it does not solve the problem of meaninglessness. In terms of the present religious situation this means that Eastern mysticism is not the solution of the problems of Western Existentialism, although many people attempt this solution. The God above the God of theism is not the devaluation of the meanings which doubt has thrown into the abyss of meaninglessness; he is their potential restitution. Nevertheless absolute faith agrees with the faith implied in mysticism in that both transcend the theistic objectivation of a God who is a being. For mysticism such a God is not more real than any finite being, for the courage to be such a God has disappeared in the abyss of meaninglessness with every other value and meaning.

The God above the God of theism is present, although hidden, in every divine-human encounter. Biblical religion as well as Protestant theology are aware of the paradoxical character of this encounter. They are aware that if God encounters man God is neither object nor subject and is therefore above the scheme into which theism has forced him. They are aware that personalism with respect to God is balanced by a transpersonal presence of the divine. They are aware that forgiveness can be accepted only if the power of acceptance is effective in man —biblically speaking, if the power of grace is effective in man. They are aware of the paradoxical character of every prayer, of speaking to somebody to whom you cannot speak because he is not "somebody," of asking somebody of whom you cannot ask anything because he gives or gives not before you ask, of saying "thou" to somebody who is nearer to the I than the I is to itself. Each of these paradoxes drives the religious consciousness toward a God above the God of theism.

The courage to be which is rooted in the experience of the God above the God of theism unites and transcends the courage to be as a part and the courage to be as oneself. It avoids both the loss of oneself by participation and the loss of one's world by individualization. The acceptance of the God above the God of theism makes us a part of that which is not also a part but is the ground of the whole. Therefore our self is not lost in a larger whole, which submerges it in the life of a limited group. If the self participates in the power of being-itself it receives itself back. For the power of being acts through the power of the individual selves. It does not swallow them as every limited whole, every collectivism, and every conformism does. This is why the Church, which stands for the power of being-itself or for the God who transcends the God of the religions, claims to be the mediator of the courage to be. A church which is based on the authority of the God of theism cannot make such a claim. It inescapably develops into a collectivist or semicollectivist system itself.

But a church which raises itself in its message and its devotion to the God above the God of theism without sacrificing its concrete symbols can mediate a courage which takes doubt and meaninglessness into itself. It is the Church under the Cross which alone can do this, the Church which preaches the Crucified who cried to God who remained his God after the God of confidence had left him in the darkness of doubt and meaninglessness. To be as a part in such a church is to receive a courage to be in which one cannot lose one's self and in which one receives one's world.

Absolute faith, or the state of being grasped by the God beyond God, is not a state which appears beside other states of the mind. It never is something separated and definite, an event which could be isolated and described. It is always a movement in, with, and under other states of the mind. It is the situation on the boundary of man's possibilities. It *is* this boundary. Therefore it is both the courage of despair and the courage in and above every courage. It is not a place where one can live, it is without the safety of words and concepts, it is without a name, a church, a cult, a theology. But it is moving in the depth of all of them. It is the power of being, in which they participate and of which they are fragmentary expressions.

One can become aware of it in the anxiety of fate and death when the traditional symbols, which enable men to stand the vicissitudes of fate and the horror of death have lost their power. When "providence" has become a superstitition and "immortality" something imaginary that which once was the power in these symbols can still be present and create the courage to be in spite of the experience of a chaotic world and a finite existence. The Stoic courage returns but not as the faith in universal reason. It returns as the absolute faith which says Yes to being without seeing anything concrete which could conquer the nonbeing in fate and death.

And one can become aware of the God above the God of theism in the anxiety of guilt and condemnation when the traditional symbols that enable men to withstand the anxiety of guilt and condemnation have lost their power. When "divine judgment" is interpreted as a psychological complex and forgiveness as a remnant of the "father-image," what once was the power in those symbols can still be present and create the courage to be in spite of the experience of an infinite gap between what we are and what we ought to be. The Lutheran courage returns but not supported by the faith in a judging and forgiving God. It returns in terms of the absolute faith which says Yes although there is no special power that conquers guilt. The courage to take the anxiety of meaninglessness upon oneself is the boundary line up to which the courage to be can go. Beyond it is mere non-being. Within it all forms of courage are re-established in the power of the God above the God of theism. *The courage to be is rooted in the God who appears when God has disappeared in the anxiety of doubt.*

19. Sacred and Secular

A second stumbling block in the way of a psychoanalytical approach to money can be expressed simply, but abstractly, as the absence of a middle term. What has neurosis to do with money? Even if we are prepared to recognize the existence in the domain of the public, the social, the historical, of something that might be called the universal neurosis of mankind, we do not recognize money as part of it. If there is a universal neurosis, it is reasonable to suppose that its core is religion. We might therefore tolerate psychoanalytical investigation of religion and still see no point to a psychoanalytical investigation of money. Is not money essentially secular—not only outside the domain of religion, but even its opposite?

Our common-sense feelings have been articulated by the sociologists, who in various ways contrast the sacred and the secular as polar opposites, always with money and rationality as syndromes in the Gestalt of the secular. In fact the notion of money as essentially secular is interconnected with our notion of its essential rationality. Hence, although sociology has used the antithesis of sacred and secular to probe irrational elements in society, and (e.g., Pareto, Durkheim) has even taken the position that society must always be a secular super-

---

structure on a sacred base—i.e., that society can never get rid of irrational residues—yet sociology has not connected money with the irrational and the sacred. Money remains anchored in the domain of the secular. And since the essence of modern rationalism as a whole is simply autonomy from religion, money as secular is also rational.

But this static contrast of the sacred and the secular as mutually exclusive opposites is misleading, because it is undialectical. The secular is the negation of the sacred, and both Freud's and Hegel's negation affirms its own opposite. The psychological realities here are best grasped in terms of theology, and were already grasped by Luther. Modern secularism, and its companion Protestantism, do not usher in an era in which human consciousness is liberated from inhuman powers, or the natural world is liberated from supernatural manifestations; the essence of the Protestant (or capitalist) era is that the power over this world has passed from God to God's negation, God's ape, the Devil. And already Luther had seen in money the essence of the secular, and therefore of the demonic. The money complex is the demonic, and the demonic is God's ape; the money complex is therefore the heir to and substitute for the religious complex, an attempt to find God in things.

In psychoanalytical terms, modern secularism is no release from the Oedipus complex, from which Freud said religion was derived; it is only the transfer of the projections originating in the Oedipus complex from the world of spirits to the world of things. "The last figure in the series beginning with the parents is that dark supremacy of Fate," says Freud, indicating the residues of the parental complex in secular thought.[1] It still remains true that religion is the middle term connecting psychoanalysis and society. If there is to be a psychoanalysis of money it must start from the hypothesis that the money complex has the essential structure of religion—or, if you will, the negation of religion, the demonic. The psychoanalytical theory of money must start by establishing the proposition that money is, in Shakespeare's words, the "visible god"; in Luther's words, "the God of this world."[2]

The first paradox in the psychoanalytical theory of money is the imputation of irrationality; the second paradox is the imputation of sacredness to the money complex. This paradox also needs careful explanation. Already Marx (again in the "economic-philosophic manu-

---

1. Sigmund Freud, *Collected Papers,* ed. J. Riviere & J. Strachey, 5 vols, New York, London: The International Psycho-Analytical Press, 1924–50. Vol. II, 265. Cf. vol. V, 306.

2. Shakespeare, *Timon of Athens,* IV, iii, 387.

scripts") had compared the money complex with the religious complex, as two forms of human self-alienation. Marx even entertained the hypothesis that the money complex is derived from the religious complex, only to reject it decisively in words well worth considering:

> If my own activity does not belong to me, if it is an alien compulsive activity, to whom does it belong? To a being other than myself. Who is this being? The gods? Certainly it appears that at the earliest times the main production, as for example temple-building in Egypt, India, Mexico, belonged to the service of the gods, as the product belonged to them also. But the gods alone were never masters of labor. Just as little was nature. And what a contradiction indeed would there be if, the more man subjects nature to himself through labor, and the more the miracles of the gods become superfluous because of the miracles of industry, man should renounce in favor of these powers the joy of production and the enjoyment of the product. The alien being, to whom labor and the product of labor belongs, in whose service and for whose enjoyment labor and the product of labor stand, can only be man himself. If the product of work does not belong to the worker, but confronts him as an alien power, this is possible only if it belongs to another man outside of the worker.[3]

Marx comes close to recognizing alienated (compulsive) work as an inner psychological necessity. He seems to recognize that if it is an inner psychological necessity, it amounts to the same thing to say that it is a necessity due to the gods; he is aware that the earliest forms of money-capital fit in with the hypothesis of the religious nature of alienated (compulsive) work. But the psychological implications of this line of thought are too bewildering (cf. "and what a contradiction," etc.); and Marx withdraws to the position that the primary datum is the domination of man over man. In doing so he contradicts his own formulations on the alienated (compulsive) character of all labor as such, as well as his formulation that private property is to be derived from alienated (compulsive) labor and not vice versa.[4] And, of course, the domination of man over man, which itself has to be explained, particularly by one who seeks to abolish it, is left as an ultimate. The ultimate category is presumably force, the force which appropriates another man's labor.

We are here at one of the ultimate crossroads in social theory. We

---

3. K. Marx and F. Engels, *Kleine ökonomische Schriften,* Berlin: Dietz, 1955, pp. 102, 106–108.

4. Marx, Engels, *op. cit.,* pp. 98, 108, 110–11.

have seen elsewhere how Freud himself (with his Primal Father), as well as Hegel (with his Master) and Nietzsche (with his Master Race) are, like Marx in this passage, compelled in the last resort to postulate external domination and its assertion by force in order to explain repression. And we have argued that to take this line is to renounce psychological explanation ("force" being substituted for psychology) and to miss the whole point of the riddle: How can there be an animal which represses itself? And to miss the nature of the human disease is also to miss the nature of the cure. If the cause of the trouble were force, to "expropriate the expropriators" would be enough. But if force did not establish the domination of the master, then perhaps the slave is somehow in love with his own chains. If there is such a deeper psychological malady, then a deeper psychological regeneration is needed.

To take the path of psychological explanation means that the money complex is to be derived from the religious complex. The question then is how such a proposition is to be established. The answer, I think, is that the proposition can be validated only historically; the word "derived" has no verifiable meaning unless it means historically derived. To understand the secular is to understand its relation to the sacred; to understand the civilized is to understand its relation to the primitive, or archaic, as we prefer to call it; to understand modern economics (and money) is to understand its relation to archaic economics (and money). But such a historical, and because historical also philosophical, approach to money is precisely what is lacking in the entire range of modern economic theory.

Classical economic theorists, assuming the basic rationality of economic activity, assumed likewise that archaic economic activity was a core of secular rationalism in an otherwise rude and superstitious milieu. They assumed that economic activity was always and everywhere essentially the same in the fundamental motivation; economic activities were governed by economic motives—that is, by economizing calculation. Assuming the psychology of economizing calculation, they correctly postulated its sociological correlate, the instutition of ownership (property). Again from the psychology of economizing calculation, they deduced the division of labor and its institutional correlate, exchange in a market. Thus Adam Smith:[5]

> In a tribe of hunters or shepherds a particular person makes bows
> and arrows, for example, with more readiness and dexterity than

5. A. Smith, *Wealth of Nations,* London: J. F. Dove, 1826, Book I, chap. II, p. 22.

any other. He frequently exchanges them for cattle or for venison with his companions; and he finds at last that he can in this manner, get more cattle and venison than if he himself went to the field to catch them. From a regard to his own interest, therefore, the making of bows and arrows grows to be his chief business.

And then finally the institution of money was derived from the institution of the market, as medium of exchange or standard of value.

In spite of the cultural relativists' busy warfare against all attempts to generalize (i.e., reach any important conclusion), it is a safe generalization to say that the postulates of classical economic theory have no relation whatever to the anthropological facts. Archaic economics is not governed by the psychology of economizing calculation. We can safely follow Karl Polanyi, the only economist who faces the facts and the problems they pose, when he says, "It is on this one negative point that modern ethnographers agree: the absence of the motive of gain; the absence of the principle of laboring for remuneration; the absence of the principle of least effort; and especially the absence of any separate and distinct institution based on economic motives."[6] (Even the cultural relativist Herskovits cannot avoid generalizations tending in the same direction; he provides much data to support Polanyi's statement and none to contradict it.)[7] And, on the other hand, archaic economics includes often very elaborate systems of ownership, division of labor, and exchange.

Is there money in the ideal type of archaic economy? The radical disjunction between archaic and modern psychology, and therefore terminology, creates difficulties which are only too apparent in the literature on the subject. In a sense Malinowski is right in saying that if we define money as it is defined in modern economic theory, as an object which fulfills the three functions of being a medium of exchange, a standard of value, and a store of wealth, then archaic economics has no money.[8] The classical definition takes the medium-of-exchange function as primary; the reason why there is nothing in the archaic economy that really corresponds to money is not so much that the exchanges are limited in scope, but rather that the psychology of the (often quite elaborate) archaic exchange is not the psychology of self-interest and economizing calculation which the modern defini-

---

6. K. Polanyi, *The Great Transformation,* New York: Rinehart, 1944, p. 47.

7. M. J. Herskovits, *Economic Anthropology,* New York: Knopf, 1952.

8. B. Malinowski, "The Primitive Economics of the Trobriand Islanders," *Economic Journal,* XXXI (1921), p. 13.

tion assumes. But a philosophy of economics cannot leave archaic money flatly distinct from money, just as a philosophy of rationality cannot be satisfied with a flat disjunction between the sacred and the secular. More dialectical thinking is needed. And the fact—recognized by Malinowski himself and the generality of writers on the subject— is that archaic economy does set aside a special class of objects which serve one of the three functions ascribed to modern money, that of being an instrument for condensing and storing wealth.[9] If the study of archaic economics shows that, at least in the historical sense, the prime function of money is to condense and store wealth, it invites modern economic theory to reconsider its traditional emphasis on the medium-of-exchange function. Modern economic theory, with its un- solved problems in the theory of money and the rate of interest, might well profit by accepting the invitation.

This wealth that can be condensed and stored—what is it? It is a well-known fact that the objects characteristically chosen in archaic economies to serve as stores of wealth, and therefore referred to as "primitive money," are, to the modern mind, bizarre in the extreme —shells, dogs' teeth, feather bands, the famous stone money of the island of Yap.[10] That is to say, the condensed wealth of archaic econo- mies is practically useless, and in that sense irrational. We have to stay with common sense here, and avoid the ethical relativism of modern utilitarian economics with its assumption of the "randomness of ends,"[11] as well as the cultural relativism of the anthropologists with its assumption that the law of reason is to do when in Rome what the Romans do. But even official cultural relativists have common sense: Herskovits writes, "There are but few objects employed as money by non-literate peoples that have use value other than to bring prestige to those who display them."[12]

What irrational considerations confer value on shells, dogs' teeth, and feather bands? Herskovits' concept of prestige is certainly not wrong, and it has the advantage of linking up with Veblen's conceptual framework, which the still-to-be-written psychology of economics can- not afford to ignore. But I think we can go further and say that the value conferred on the useless object, and the prestige conferred on the owner, is magical, mystical, religious, and comes from the domain of the sacred. Just as an example, in the Trobriand Islands the "tokens

---

9. Malinowski, *loc. cit.*

10. Herskovits, *op. cit.*, pp. 238–68; R. Firth, "Currency, Primitive," in the *Encyclo- paedia Britannica*, 14th ed., London: Encyclopaedia Britannica, Ltd., 1923.

11. T. Parsons, *The Structure of Social Action*, Glencoe: Free Press, 1949, pp. 59–60.

12. Herskovits, *op. cit.*, p. 214.

of wealth" are "big ceremonial axe-blades," made of a material "rare and difficult to obtain" and fashioned with "much time and labor," but which "are hardly ever put to any real use."[13] Herskovits himself shows the intimate connection between social prestige and supernatural power in nonliterate cultures.[14] The only alternative explanation is to regard these archaic moneys as ornaments and to derive their value from their ornamental purposes;[15] but Laum, in his treatise on the sacral origins of Greek money, correctly argues that ornamentation can hardly be accepted as an ultimate psychological category, and that ornaments in fact are basically magic amulets or tokens.[16] The decisive reason, however, for insisting on the sacred character of archaic money is not so much the object itself as the context of its circulation. All the authorities insist that archaic economic activity is submerged in "noneconomic" relations;[17] and they all emphasize the ceremonial (ritual) character of these noneconomic relations. Hence, when Firth says that primitive money sometimes comprises articles of practical use, his statement cannot be accepted at face value.[18] It is certain that some archaic moneys, which have been taken to be practically useful articles elevated into a standard of value by the process of exchanging utilities as postulated by modern economic theory, became money in no such way. Utility is ambiguous; many useful articles in archaic cultures have also a useless, sacred value. This applies especially to food, which besides serving the useful purpose of satisfying hunger can also be the magic substance of communion or the means for paying religious debts (in the sacrifice). Laum has demonstrated that the famous cattle money in Homer must be derived not from any role of cattle as utilitarian commodities but from the sacred significance of cattle in the sacrifice and in the ceremonial (communion) meal.[19] Compare Herskovits on cattle wealth among the East African Nuer:[20]

> It is striking how non-economic factors enter into every aspect of their ownership. . . . The cattle play an important part in determin-

13. Malinowski, *op. cit.,* p. 9.

14. Herskovits, *op. cit.,* pp. 439–60.

15. Firth, *op. cit.;* G. Simmel, *Philosophie des Geldes,* Munich: Duncker & Humblot, 1922, pp. 116, 162.

16. B. Laum, *Heiliges Geld,* Tübingen: Mohr, 1924, pp. 8–80.

17. Herskovits, *op. cit.,* pp. 11, 155–79.

18. Firth, *op. cit.*

19. Laum, *loc. cit.* Cf. P. Einzig, *Primitive Money,* London: Eyre & Spottiswoode, 1949, pp. 379–86; G. van der Leeuw, *Religion in Essence and Manifestation,* London: G. Allen & Unwin, 1938, p. 353.

20. Herskovits, *op. cit.,* p. 389.

ing affinal relationships. . . . Such facts as these, and the manner in which they enter into the religious life together with their essential place in various rituals, all differentiate them from other kinds of property among this people.

It has been long known that the first markets were sacred markets, the first banks were temples, the first to issue money were priests or priest-kings. But these economic institutions have been interpreted as in themselves secular-rational, though originally sponsored by sacred auspices. The crucial point in Laum's argument is that the institutions are in themselves sacred. Laum derives the very idea of equivalence (equal value) from ritual tariffs of atonement, the very idea of a symbol of value from rituals of symbolic substitution, and the very idea of price from ritual distribution of the sacred food. In other words, the money complex, archaic or modern, is inseparable from symbolism; and symbolism is not, as Simmel thought, the mark of rationality but the mark of the sacred.

If we recognize the essentially sacred character of archaic money, we shall be in a position to recognize the essentially sacred character of certain specific features of modern money—certainly the gold standard, and almost certainly also the rate of interest. As far as gold and silver are concerned it is obvious to the eye of common sense that their salient characteristic is their absolute uselessness for all practical purposes. John Locke put his finger on the essential point with his formula of "mankind having consented to put an *imaginary* value upon gold and silver."[21]

Measured by rational utility and real human needs, there is absolutely no difference between the gold and silver of modern economy and the shells or dogs' teeth of archaic economy. There is no difference between those great stone cartwheels on the island of Yap which, "even though under the sea, continue to symbolize value," and the gold under the ground at Fort Knox.[22] And that the imaginary value placed on gold and silver in the modern economy is derived from the domain of the sacred is a point already fully recognized by Keynes in the *Treatise on Money*. In the chapter entitled *"Auri sacra fames,"* Keynes (correctly, I believe) sees the history of civilized money as continuous from the urban revolution with which civilization began:

---

21. J. Locke, *Some Considerations of the Consequences of the Lowering of Interest and Raising the Value of Money*, in *The Works of John Locke*, 10 vols, London: T. Tegg, 1823, vol. V, 22.

22. Herskovits, *op. cit.*, p. 264.

"The magical properties, with which the Egyptian priestcraft anciently imbued the yellow metal, it has never altogether lost."[23]

Keynes also recognizes that the special attraction of gold and silver is due not to any of the rationalistic considerations generally offered in explanation but to their symbolic identification with Sun and Moon, and to the sacred significance of Sun and Moon in the new astrological theology invented by the earliest civilizations. Heichelheim, the authority on ancient economics, concurs on the essentially magical-religious nature of the value placed on gold and silver in the ancient Near East.[24] Laum states that the value ratio of gold to silver remained stable throughout classical antiquity and into the Middle Ages and even modern times at 1:13½. It is obvious that such a stability in the ratio cannot be explained in terms of rational supply and demand. The explanation, says Laum, lies in the astrological ratio of the cycles of their divine counterparts, the Sun and Moon.[25]

The history of money from this point of view has yet to be written. Greek money, which contributed to modern money the institution of coinage, was recognized by Simmel to be essentially sacred and to have originated not in the market but in the temple.[26] Laum has amplified and established the thesis. But Simmel and Laum are confused by the illusion that modern money is secular, and hence they confuse the past by describing as "secularization" a process which is rather only a metamorphosis of the sacred. Even Keynes perhaps shares this illusion, although he sees the real secularization of money as still lying in the future. The historian must doubt the possibility of having capitalism without gold fetishism in some form or other. At any rate, the historian must conclude that the ideal type of the modern economy retains, at its very heart, the structure of the archaic sacred. And once again the undialectical disjunction of sacred and secular is seen to be inadequate.

The rate of interest is a "highly psychological phenomenon," says Keynes. It presents problems which, I believe, are still unsolved in economics: "A queer beast," says Professor Robertson.[27] Although the notion that the rate of interest is the price of money would be

---

23. J. M. Keynes, *Treatise on Money,* New York: Harcourt, Brace, 1930, II, 289–92.

24. F. M. Heichelheim, *Wirtschaftsgeschichte des Altertums,* Leiden: A. W. Sijthoff, 1938, I, 114–15.

25. Laum, *op. cit.,* pp. 128–29.

26. Simmel, *op. cit.,* p. 176.

27. Keynes, *The General Theory of Employment, Interest and Money,* New York: Harcourt, Brace, 1936, p. 202; D. H. Robertson, *Utility and All That, and Other Essays,* New York: Macmillan, 1952, p. 96.

disputed, it would not be disputed, I think, that there is some close connection between the rate of interest and money. Here I wish to comment on only one of the aspects which puzzle economists, the curious long-range stability of rate of interest. It has been common for economists to go outside of economics for possible explanations; there are theories connecting it with the average rate of growth of animals and plants or with the length of human life. F. H. Knight says the problem can be discussed only as philosophy or theory of history.[28] Keynes postulates the operation of certain "constant psychological characters."[29]

It is possible that the rate of interest is a second sacred residue in the secular world of modern economy. Stability of prices is a general characteristic of the archaic economy, because, as Malinowski says, prices are rigidly prescribed by custom and not by supply and demand.[30] Is there not an essential element or determination by custom, not by supply and demand, in the rate of interest? But if this is granted, the question must be pushed further to inquire what determines the custom. Custom is, in sociological theory, essentially sacred, and why should the custom determinant in the rate of interest be any exception? We remember Laum's solution to the analogous riddle of the stability of the ratio between gold and silver. The institution of interest, like the institution of money based on gold and silver, is coeval with urban civilization. In fact, Heichelheim proposes to take the institution of interest-bearing capital investment as the strategic key factor in the economic development called the urban revolution. Then Heichelheim looks for the source of the new economic institution; he answers only that the source must be sought in the transvaluation of religious values which accompanied the urban revolution.[31]

At a deeper level, the hidden middle term connecting money and the whole domain of the sacred is power (social power). Classical economic theory, with its model of perfect competition, ignores the factor of power. Ruskin was not deceived—Ruskin whom Mumford rightly raised from the dead as the "fundamental economist of the biotechnic order":[32] "Mercantile economy . . . signifies the accumulation, in the hands of individuals, of legal and moral claim upon, or power over, the labour of others"; "What is really desired, under the name of riches,

---

28. F. H. Knight, *The Ethics of Competition,* New York: Harper, 1935, p. 264.

29. Keynes, *General Theory,* p. 356.

30. Malinowski, *op. cit.,* p. 14.

31. Heichelheim, *loc. cit.*

32. L. Mumford, *The Culture of Cities,* New York: Harcourt, Brace, 1938, p. 542.

is, essentially, power over men."[33] Karl Marx' ambiguity on this subject reveals some of the fundamental dilemmas in Marxism. In the first volume of *Capital* he sets out to establish a model of capitalism as a self-contained system governed by the principle of economizing calculation; it was therefore logical for him to incorporate in this system the (to my mind erroneous) notion of classical economic theory that money is basically a medium of exchange originating in a market where economizing calculators meet each other. Even in this first system, however, psychological realities which do not fit in with his basic psychological postulates do not escape his acute eye.

Marx notes the operation of a "desire after hoarding" which clings to the money form, and is therefore a "greed for gold"—and which is an intrinsic factor in capitalism inherited from the precapitalist stage: "With the very earliest development of the circulation of commodities, there is also developed the necessity, and the passionate desire, to hold fast to the product of the first metamorphosis . . . its gold-chrysalis."

Marx also notes the fact, inexplicable by the medium-of-exchange theory of money, that it is intrinsic to the nature of money to get condensed in useless objects, and that this is also an intrinsic feature of capitalism inherited from the precapitalist stage: "In the early stages of the circulation of commodities it is the surplus use-values alone that are converted into money. Gold and silver thus become of themselves social expressions for superfluity of wealth."[34] Here Marx comes close to the notion of money as prestige, and to the connection between prestige and the practically useless, the "surplus use-value." This strange term, "surplus use-value," is so far as I know nowhere elaborated by Marx. It implies that a psychology of money has to be a psychology which can discriminate between useless (irrational) demands and truly human needs; but, as we have seen in another connection, where such a psychology of real human needs should be, there is in Marxism a great gap. The ultimate direction of this other line of thought in the first volume of *Capital* is to make prestige the essential value of money; that is to say, the essence of money is not its function in exchange, but power. And Marx says this: Under capitalism "social power becomes the private power of private persons."[35]

This other line of thought in Marx is elaborated in the third volume

---

33. J. Ruskin, *Unto This Last* in *Works of John Ruskin,* ed. E. T. Cook and A. Wedderburn, 39 vols., London: G. Allen & Unwin, 1903–12, XVII, 44–45, 46.

34. Marx, *Capital,* tr. E. Untermann, 3 vols., Chicago: C. H. Kerr, 1906–1909, I, 146–49.

35. Marx, *Capital,* I, 149.

of *Capital,* which, as a whole, clearly shows that Marx was aware that there were problems not solved in the first volume, especially in the topics of hoarding (and precapitalist accumulation), money, and the rate of interest. There the essence of money and interest emerges more clearly as power: "They represent in this form a command over the labor of others"; "Interest is, therefore, merely the expression of the fact that value in general . . . faces living labor-power as an independent power."[36]

But correlative with this emphasis on power is an explicit recognition that the labor theory of money, which is the automatic consequence of the labor theory of value plus the medium-of-exchange theory of money adopted in his first volume, is wrong. There is the recognition that the price of money in borrowing and lending does not obey the basic law for all commodities laid down there, namely that the price is determined not by use-value but by exchange-value (i.e., amount of labor incorporated into the object, according to the labor theory of value). Hence there is the recognition that there is something irrational about interest: "If interest is to be called the price of money-capital, it will be an irrational form of price, which is quite at variance with the conception of the price of commodities." Interest—again at variance with the labor theory of value—is seen to arise "outside of the process of production," "the fruit of mere ownership."[37] Hence the real essence of money is not disclosed by the labor theory of value but by a theory of ownership—i.e., power. "But how are gold and silver distinguished from other forms of wealth? Not by the magnitude of their value, for this is determined by the quantity of labor materialized in them; but by the fact that they represent independent incarnations, expressions of the social character of wealth."[38] The value of money does not lie in the value with which the labor theory of value is concerned. And conversely—this is the crucial point—the labor theory of value does not contain the answer to the problem of power.

The ultimate category of economics is power; but power is not an economic category. Marx fills up the emergent gap in his theory with the concept of force (violence)—i.e., by conceiving power as a material reality. We have argued elsewhere that this is a crucial mistake; power is in essence a psychological category. And to pursue the tracks of power, we will have to enter the domain of the sacred, and map it: all power is essentially sacred power. Here again the crucial problem is

---

36. Marx, *Capital,* III, 419, 445.
37. Marx, *Capital,* III, 415–16, 439–40, 443, 716.
38. Marx, *Capital,* III, 672–73.

to understand archaic man and the archaic economy. Marxian anthropology, with its assumption of the economic derivation of power and its correlative assumption that the psychology of economics is universally the psychology of appropriation, is committed to deny or belittle the existence of power in the archaic society; "primitive communism" is conceived as in principle egalitarian. But the fact is, to quote Herskovits:[39]

> In the great political groupings of Africa and Indonesia, as well as in the less complex societies in these and other areas, the same mechanisms found to be operative in the cultures of Oceania and the Americas are also active. With but rare exceptions we find that, to the extent to which the economic system, the technological level of achievement, and the natural setting permit, some men enjoy more favored positions than others.

The line of development is continuous from the simplest societies to the great theocratic structures of the first civilizations. If the emergence of social privilege marks the Fall of Man, the Fall took place not in the transition from "primitive communism" to "private property" but in the transition from ape to man. And secondly, the anthropological data—again we can follow Herskovits—show the inherent connection, in the archaic society, between this expanding sector of privilege and the expanding sector of the sacred.[40] Privilege is prestige, and prestige, in its fundamental nature as in the etymology of the word, means deception and enchantment. Again the line of development is continuous from the magician-leader of the simpler societies to the priest-king or god-king of the first civilizations, as indeed Frazer showed fifty years ago.[41]

Power was originally sacred, and it remains so in the modern world. Again we must not be misled by the flat antinomy of the sacred and the secular, and interpret as "secularization" what is only a metamorphosis of the sacred. If there is a class which has nothing to lose but its chains, the chains that bind it are self-imposed, sacred obligations which appear as objective realities with all the force of a neurotic delusion. The perception that class war is sustained by myths underlies Sorel's classic *On Violence.*[42] And on the other side, the perception

39. Herskovits, *op. cit.,* pp. 481–82.

40. Herskovits, *op. cit.,* pp. 439–60.

41. J. G. Frazer, *The Golden Bough,* 3rd ed., 12 vols., New York: Macmillan, 1935, pp. 83–106.

42. G. Sorel, *Réflexions sur la violence,* Paris: M. Rivière, 1925, pp. 32, 132.

that the essence of capitalism is the magnetic leadership of the entre-
preneur was systematically elaborated into an economic theory by
Schumpeter. Already Ruskin wrote in the margin of his copy of Mill
the aphorism "Industry dependent on Will, not Capital."[43] Along
these lines, I believe, a deeper anatomy, a psychological anatomy, of
modern civilization can be pursued. And the underlying phenomenon
of leadership was assimilated into the domain of psychoanalysis when
Freud published his book on mass psychology. Psychoanalysis takes
the final step of showing the origin of the myths which sustain social
power and power struggles in the repression of the human body.

43. Ruskin, *Works,* XVII, 176n; J. A. Schumpeter, *Theory of Economic Development,*
Cambridge: Harvard University Press, 1934; Schumpeter, *Capitalism, Socialism and
Democracy,* New York: Harper, 1942. Cf. O. Spengler, *The Decline of the West,* Lon-
don: G. Allen & Unwin, 1932, II, 492–93.

John Robinson

20.   The Supranaturalist Myth

I. Reluctant Revolution

UP THERE OR OUT THERE?

The bible speaks of a God "up there." No doubt its picture of a three-decker universe, of "the heaven above, the earth beneath and the waters under the earth," was once taken quite literally. No doubt also its more sophisticated writers, if pressed, would have been the first to regard this as symbolic language to represent and convey spiritual realities. Yet clearly they were not pressed. Or at any rate they were not oppressed by it. Even such an educated man of the world as St. Luke can express the conviction of Christ's ascension—the conviction that he is not merely alive but reigns in the might and right of God—in the crudest terms of being "lifted up" into heaven, there to sit down at the right hand of the Most High.[1] He feels no need to offer any apology for this language, even though he of all New Testament writers was commending Christianity to what Schleiermacher called its

---

From *Honest To God,* by John A. T. Robinson. Published in the U.S.A., 1963, by The Westminster Press, Philadelphia. © SCM Press, Ltd., London, 1963. Used by permission. Title supplied by the editors. Excerpts from *The Shaking of the Foundations* by Paul Tillich are used with the permission of Charles Scribner's Sons. Copyright 1948 Charles Scribner's Sons.

1. Acts 1.9–11.

"cultured despisers." This is the more remarkable because, in contrast, he leaves his readers in no doubt that what we might regard as
the scarcely more primitive notions of God entertained by the Atheni-
ans,[2] that the deity lives in temples made by man and needs to be
served by human hands, were utterly superseded by Christianity.

Moreover, it is the two most mature theologians of the New Testament, St John and the later Paul, who write most uninhibitedly of this
"going up" and "coming down."

> No one has ascended into heaven but he who descended from
> heaven, the Son of man.[3]

> Do you take offence at this? Then what if you were to see the Son
> of man ascending where he was before?[4]

> In saying, "He ascended," what does it mean but that he had also
> descended into the lower parts of the earth? He who descended is
> he who also ascended far above all the heavens, that he might fill
> all things.[5]

They are able to use this language without any sense of constraint
because it had not become an embarrassment to them. Everybody
accepted what it meant to speak of a God up there, even though the
groundlings might understand it more grossly than the gnostics. For
St Paul, no doubt, to be "caught up to the third heaven"[6] was as much
a metaphor as it is to us (though for him a considerably more precise
metaphor). But he could use it to the spiritually sophisticated at Cor-
inth with no consciousness that he must "demythologize" if he were
to make it acceptable.

For the New Testament writers the idea of a God "up there" created
no embarrassment—because it had not yet become a difficulty. For us
too it creates little embarrassment—because, for the most part, it has
ceased to be a difficulty. We are scarcely even conscious that the
majority of the words for what we value most are still in terms of
height, though as Edwyn Bevan observed in his Gifford Lectures,[7]
"The proposition: Moral and spiritual worth is greater or less in ratio

---

2. Acts 17.22–31.

3. John 3.13.

4. John 6.61f.

5. Eph. 4.9 f.

6. II Cor. 12.2.

7. *Symbolism and Belief* (1938), p. 30. Chs. II and III on "Height" are a *locus
classicus* for the conception of God "up there."

to the distance outwards from the earth's surface, would certainly seem to be, if stated nakedly like that, an odd proposition." Yet it is one that we have long ago found it unnecessary to explain away. We may indeed continue to have to tell our children that heaven is not in fact over their heads nor God literally "above the bright blue sky." Moreover, whatever we may accept with the top of our minds, most of us still retain deep down the mental image of "an old man in the sky." Nevertheless, for most of us most of the time the traditional language of a three-storeyed universe is not a serious obstacle. It does not worry us intellectually, it is not an "offence" to faith, because we have long since made a remarkable transposition, of which we are hardly aware. In fact, we do not realize how crudely spatial much of the Biblical terminology is, for we have ceased to perceive it that way. It is as though when reading a musical score what we actually saw was not the notes printed but the notes of the key into which mentally we were transposing it. There are some notes, as it were, in the Biblical score which still strike us in the old way (the Ascension story, for instance) and which we have to make a conscious effort to transpose, but in general we assimilate the language without trouble.

For in place of a God who is literally or physically "up there" we have accepted, as part of our mental furniture, a God who is spiritually or metaphysically "out there." There are, of course, those for whom he is almost literally "out there." They may have accepted the Copernican revolution in science, but until recently at any rate they have still been able to think of God as in some way "beyond" outer space. In fact the number of people who instinctively seem to feel that it is no longer possible to believe in God in the space-age shows how crudely physical much of this thinking about a God "out there" has been. Until the last recesses of the cosmos had been explored or were capable of being explored (by radio-telescope if not by rocketry), it was still possible to locate God mentally in some *terra incognita.* But now it seems there is no room for him, not merely in the inn, but in the entire universe: for there are no vacant places left. In reality, of course, our new view of the universe has made not the slightest difference. Indeed, the limit set to "space" by the speed of light (so that beyond a certain point—not all that much further than our present range—everything recedes over the horizon of visibility) is even more severe. And there is nothing to stop us, if we wish to, locating God "beyond" it. And there he would be quite invulnerable—in a "gap" science could never fill. But in fact the coming of the space-age has destroyed this crude projection of God—and for that we should be grateful. For if God is "beyond," he is not *literally* beyond anything.

But the idea of a God spiritually or metaphysically "out there" dies very much harder. Indeed, most people would be seriously disturbed by the thought that it should need to die at all. For it *is* their God, and they have nothing to put in its place. And for the words "they" and "their" it would be more honest to substitute "we" and "our." For it is the God of our own upbringing and conversation, the God of our fathers and of our religion, who is under attack. Every one of us lives with some mental picture of a God "out there," a God who "exists" above and beyond the world he made, a God "to" whom we pray and to to whom we "go" when we die. In traditional Christian theology, the doctrine of the Trinity witnesses to the self-subsistence of this divine Being outside us and apart from us. The doctrine of creation asserts that at a moment of time this God called "the world" into existence over against himself. The Biblical record describes how he proceeds to enter into contact with those whom he has made, how he establishes a "covenant" with them, how he "sends" to them his prophets, and how in the fullness of time he "visits" them in the person of his Son, who must one day "come again" to gather the faithful to himself.

This picture of God "out there" coming to earth like some visitor from outer space underlies every popular presentation of the Christian drama of salvation, whether from the pulpit or the presses. Indeed, it is noticeable that those who have been most successful in communicating it in our day—Dorothy Sayers, C. S. Lewis, J. B. Phillips—have hesitated least in being boldly anthropomorphic in the use of this language. They have not, of course, taken it literally, any more than the New Testament writers take literally the God "up there," but they have not apparently felt it any embarrassment to the setting forth of the Gospel. This is sufficient testimony to the fact that there is a ready-made public for whom this whole frame of reference still presents no difficulties, and their very achievement should make us hesitate to pull it down or call it in question.

Indeed, the last thing I want to do is to appear to criticize from a superior position. I should like to think that it were possible to use this mythological language of the God "out there" and make the same utterly natural and unself-conscious transposition as I have suggested we already do with the language of the God "up there." Indeed, unless we become used to doing this and are able to take this theological notation, as it were, in our stride, we shall cut ourselves off from the classics of the Christian faith, just as we should be unable to read the Bible were we to stumble at *its* way of describing God. I believe, however, that we may have to pass through a century or more of reappraisal before this becomes possible and before this language ceases to be an offence to faith for a great many people. No one wants to live in such a period, and one could heartily wish it were not necessary. But the signs are that we are reaching the point at which the whole conception of a God "out there," which has served us so well since the collapse of the three-decker universe, is itself becoming more of a hindrance than a help.

In a previous age there came a moment when the three-decker likewise proved an embarrassment, even as a piece of mental furniture. But in this case there was a considerable interval between the time when it ceased to be taken literally as a model of the universe and the time when it ceased to perform a useful function as a metaphor. An illustration of this is to be seen in the doctrine of hell. In the old scheme, hell was "down there." By Shakespeare's time no one thought of it as literally under the earth, but still in *Hamlet* it is lively and credible enough as a metaphor. But a localized hell gradually lost more and more of its purchase over the imagination, and revivalist attempts to stoke its flames did not succeed in restoring its power. The tragedy in this instance is that no effective translation into terms of the God "out there" was found for the Devil and his angels, the pit and the lake of fire. This element therefore tended to drop out of popular Christianity altogether—much to the detriment of the depth of the Gospel.

But the point I wish to make here is that the supersession of the old scheme was a gradual one. After it had been discredited scientifically, it continued to serve theologically as an acceptable frame of reference. The image of a God "up there" survived its validity as a literal description of reality by many centuries. But today I believe we may be confronted by a double crisis. The final psychological, if not logical, blow delivered by modern science and technology to the idea that there might *literally* be a God "out there" has *coincided* with an awareness that the *mental* picture of such a God may be more of a stumbling-block than an aid to belief in the Gospel. There is a double pressure to discard this entire construction, and with it any belief in God at all.

Moreover, it is not merely a question of the speed of adjustment required. The abandonment of a God "out there" represents a much more radical break than the transition to this concept from that of a God "up there." For this earlier transposition was largely a matter of verbal notation, of a change in spatial metaphor, important as this undoubtedly was in liberating Christianity from a flat-earth cosmology. But to be asked to give up any idea of a Being "out there" at all will appear to be an outright denial of God. For, to the ordinary way of thinking, to believe in God means to be convinced of the existence

of such a supreme and separate Being. "Theists" are those who believe
that such a Being exists, "atheists" those who deny that he does.

But suppose such a super-Being "out there" is really only a sophisticated version of the Old Man in the sky? Suppose belief in God does
not, indeed cannot, mean being persuaded of the "existence" of some
entity, even a supreme entity, which might or might not be there, like
life on Mars? Suppose the atheists are right—but that this is no more
the end or denial of Christianity than the discrediting of the God "up
there," which must in its time have seemed the contradiction of all that
the Bible said? Suppose that all such atheism does is to destroy an idol,
and that we can and must get on without a God "out there" at all? Have
we seriously faced the possibility that to abandon such an idol may in
the future be the only way of making Christianity meaningful, except
to the few remaining equivalents of flat-earthers (just as to have clung
earlier to the God "up there" would have made it impossible in the
modern world for any but primitive peoples to believe the Gospel)?
Perhaps after all the Freudians are right, that such a God—the God of
traditional popular theology—*is* a projection, and perhaps we are
being called to live without that projection in any form.

That is not an attractive proposition: inevitably it feels like being
orphaned. And it is bound to be misunderstood and resisted as a
denial of the Gospel, as a betrayal of what the Bible says (though
actually the Bible speaks in literal terms of a God whom we have
already abandoned). And it will encounter the opposition not only of
the fundamentalists but of 90 per cent of Church people. Equally it will
be resented by most unthinking non-churchgoers, who tend to be
more jealous of the beliefs they have rejected and deeply shocked that
they should be betrayed. Above all, there is the large percentage of
oneself that finds this revolution unacceptable and wishes it were unnecessary.

This raises again the insistent question, Why? Is it really necessary
to pass through this Copernican revolution? Must we upset what most
people happily believe—or happily choose not to believe? And have
we anything to put in its place?

II. The Ground of Our Being

A DEPTH AT THE CENTRE OF LIFE

The break with traditional thinking to which I believe we are now
summoned is considerably more radical than that which enabled
Christian theology to detach itself from a literal belief in a localized

heaven. The translation from the God "up there" to the God "out there," though of liberating psychological significance, represented, as I have said, no more than a change of direction in spatial symbolism. Both conceptions presuppose fundamentally the same relationship between "God" on the one hand and "the world" on the other: God is a Being existing in his own right to whom the world is related in the sort of way the earth is to the sun. Whether the sun is "above" a flat earth or "beyond" a round one does not fundamentally affect the picture. But suppose there is no Being out there at all? Suppose, to use our analogy, the skies are empty?

Now it would again be possible to present the transposition with which we are concerned as simply a change in spatial metaphor. I quoted earlier the passage from Tillich in which he proposes replacing the images of "height" by those of "depth" in order to express the truth of God. And there is no doubt that this simple substitution can make much religious language suddenly appear more relevant. For we are familiar today with depth psychology, and with the idea that ultimate truth is deep or profound. Moreover, while "spiritual wickedness in high places," and all the mythology of angelic powers which the Biblical writers associate with it, seems to the modern man a fantastic phantasmagoria, similar, equally mythological, language when used by Freud of conflicts in the unconscious appears perfectly acceptable.

And the change of symbolism has real and not merely apparent psychological significance. For the category of "depth" has richer associations than that of height. As Tillich points out:

> "Deep" in its spiritual use has two meanings: it means either the opposite of "shallow," or the opposite of "high." Truth is deep and not shallow; suffering is depth and not height. Both the light of truth and the darkness of suffering are deep. There is a depth in God, and there is a depth out of which the psalmist cries to God.[8]

And this double meaning may explain why "depth" seems to speak to us of concern while "height" so often signifies unconcern. The Epicurean gods, serene in their empyrean above the cares and distractions of this world, are the epitome of "sublime" indifference. And Browning's supreme affirmation of optimism, "God's in his heaven: all's right with the world," strikes the modern man somewhat more cynically. For if God is "above it all" he cannot really be involved.

Yet we are not here dealing simply with a change of symbolism,

---

8. *The Shaking of the Foundations*, p. 60.

important as that may be. This is not just the old system in reverse, with a God "down under" for a God "up there." When Tillich speaks of God in "depth," he is not speaking of another Being *at all*. He is speaking of "the infinite and inexhaustible depth and ground of all being," of our ultimate concern, of what we take seriously without reservation. And after the passage I quoted earlier[9] he goes on to make the same point in relation not only to the depths of our personal life but to the deepest springs of our social and historical existence:

> The name of this infinite and inexhaustible ground of history is *God*. That is what the word means, and it is that to which the words of *Kingdom of God* and *Divine Providence* point. And if these words do not have much meaning for you, translate them, and speak of the depth of history, of the ground and aim of our social life, and of what you take seriously without reservation in your moral and political activities. Perhaps you should call this depth *hope*, simply hope. For if you find hope in the ground of history, you are united with the great prophets who were able to look into the depth of their times, who tried to escape it, because they could not stand the horror of their visions, and who yet had the strength to look to an even deeper level and there to discover hope.[10]

What Tillich is meaning by God is the exact opposite of any *deus ex machina,* a supernatural Being to whom one can turn away from the world and who can be relied upon to intervene from without. God is not "out there." He is in Bonhoeffer's words, "the 'beyond' in the midst of our life," a depth of reality reached "not on the borders of life but at its centre,"[11] not by any flight of the alone to the alone, but, in Kierkegaard's fine phrase, by "a deeper immersion in existence." For the word "God" denotes the ultimate depth of all our being; the creative ground and meaning of all our existence.

So conditioned for us is the word "God" by associations with *a* Being out there that Tillich warns us that to make the necessary transposition, "you must forget everything traditional that you have learned about God, perhaps even that word itself."[12] Indeed, the line between those who believe in God and those who do not bears little relation to their profession of the existence or non-existence of such a Being. It is a question, rather, of their openness to the holy, the sacred, in the

---

9. *Op. cit.,* pp. 63 f; p. 22 above.

10. *Op. cit.,* pp. 65 f.

11. Bonhoeffer, Dietrich, *Letters and Papers from Prison,* ed. E. Bethge; 2nd ed., 1956, p. 124.

12. *Op. cit.,* p. 64.

unfathomable depths of even the most secular relationship. As Martin Buber puts it of the person who professedly denies God,

> When he, too, who abhors the name, and believes himself to be godless, gives his whole being to addressing the *Thou* of his life, as a *Thou* that cannot be limited by another, he addresses God.[13]

For in the conditioned he has seen and responded to the unconditional. He has touched the hem of the eternal.

The difference between the two ways of thought can perhaps best be expressed by asking what is meant by speaking of a *personal* God. Theism, as the term was understood in the previous chapter, understands by this a supreme Person, a self-existent subject of infinite goodness and power, who enters into a relationship with us comparable with that of one human personality with another. The theist is concerned to argue the existence of such a Being as the creator and most sufficient explanation of the world as we know it. Without a Person "out there," the skies would be empty, the heavens as brass, and the world without hope or compassion.

But the way of thinking we are seeking to expound is not concerned to posit, nor, like the antitheists, to depose, such a Being at all. In fact it would not naturally use the phrase "*a* personal God"; for this in itself belongs to an understanding of theology and of what theological statements are about which is alien to it. For this way of thinking, to say that "God is personal" is to say that "reality at its very deepest level is personal," that personality is of *ultimate* significance in the constitution of the universe, that in personal relationships we touch the final meaning of existence as nowhere else. "To predicate personality of God," says Feuerbach, "is nothing else than to declare personality as the absolute essence."[14] To believe in God as love means to believe that in pure personal relationship we encounter, not merely what ought to be, but what is, the deepest, veriest truth about the structure of reality. This, in face of all the evidence, is a tremendous act of faith. But it is not the feat of persuading oneself of the existence of a super-Being beyond this world endowed with personal qualities. Belief in God is the trust, the well-nigh incredible trust, that to give ourselves to the uttermost in love is not to be confounded but to be "accepted," that Love is the ground of our being, to which ultimately we "come home."

If this is true, then theological statements are not a description of "the highest Being" but an analysis of the depths of personal relation-

---

13. *I and Thou* (1937), p. 76; cf. Tillich, *The Protestant Era* (1951), p. 65.
14. *The Essence of Christianity* (Eng. tr. 1854, from the second ed. of 1843), p. 97.

ships—or, rather, an analysis of the depths of *all* experience "interpreted by love." Theology, as Tillich insists, is about "that which concerns us ultimately."[15] A statement is "theological" not because it relates to a particular Being called "God," but because it asks *ultimate* questions about the meaning of existence: it asks what, at the level of *theos,* at the level of its deepest mystery, is the reality and significance of our life. A view of the world which affirms this reality and significance in personal categories is *ipso facto* making an affirmation about the *ultimacy* of personal relationships: it is saying that *God,* the final truth and reality "deep down things," *is* love. And the specifically Christian view of the world is asserting that the final definition of this reality, from which "nothing can separate us," since it is the very ground of our being, is "the love of God in Christ Jesus our Lord."[16]

MAN AND GOD

If statements about God are statements about the "ultimacy" of personal relationships, then we must agree that in a real sense Feuerbach was right in wanting to translate "theology" into "anthropology." He was concerned to restore the divine attributes from heaven to earth, whence, he believed, they had been filched and projected on to a perfect Being, an imaginary Subject before whom impoverished man falls in worship. Feuerbach believed that true religion consists in acknowledging the divinity of the attributes, not in transferring them to an illegitimate subject (dubbed by his Marxist disciple Bakunin "the mirage of God"). "The true atheist," he wrote, "is not the man who denies God, the subject; it is the man for whom the attributes of divinity, such as love, wisdom and justice, are nothing. And denial of the subject is by no means necessarily denial of the attributes."[17] This is, of course, very near to the position we have been taking; and Bultmann, in answer to a challenge from Karl Barth, says, "I would heartily agree: I *am* trying to substitute anthropology for theology, for I am interpreting theological affirmations as assertions about human life."[18]

Yet it is also clear that we are here on very dangerous ground. For, to Feuerbach, to say that "theology is nothing else than anthropology" means that"the knowledge of God is nothing else than a knowledge of

---

15. *Systematic Theology,* vol. i, p. 15.

16. Rom. 8.39.

17. *Op. cit.,* p. 21. I have preferred, for this quotation, the translation in H. de Lubac, *op. cit.,* p. 11.

18. *Kerygma and Myth,* vol. i, p. 107.

man.''[19] And his system runs out into the deification of man, taken to its logical conclusion in the Superman of Nietzsche and Auguste Comte's Religion of Humanity.

The same ambiguity is to be found in the deeply Christian humanism of Professor John Macmurray, whose thought follows similar lines. At the beginning of his Gifford Lectures he says, "The conception of a deity is the conception of a personal ground of all that we experience,"[20] and he concludes them with a chapter, "The Personal Universe,"[21] which argues a position close to that for which we have been contending. But both in these lectures and even more in his earlier book, *The Structure of Religious Experience,* he makes statements which leave one wondering whether there is anything distinctive about religion at all. For instance, "Religion is about fellowship and community,"[22] and, "The task of religion is the maintenance and extension of human community."[23] The question inevitably arises, if theology is translated into anthropology, why do we any longer need the category of God? Is it not "semantically superfluous"? Is not the result of destroying "supranaturalism" simply to end up with naturalism, as the atheists asserted?

The dilemma can be stated in another passage of Macmurray. The question of God is the question of transcendence. It is precisely this that the location of God "up there" or "out there" was to express and safeguard and which its denial appears to imperil. But for Macmurray transcendence is a category that applies equally to humanity:

> We are both transcendent of experience and immanent in it. This union of transcendence and immanence is . . . the full fact about human personality. . . . We are accustomed to find it applied in theology to God, and it is usually assumed to be a peculiar and distinguishing attribute of Deity. We see now that this is a mistake. The union of immanence and transcendence is a peculiar and defining characteristic of all personality, human or divine; but it is primarily a natural, empirical fact of common human experience. Religious reflection applies it to God as a defining characteristic of universal personality because it finds it in experience as a given fact of all finite personal experience.[24]

---

19. *Op. cit.,* p. 206.
20. *The Self as Agent* (1957), p. 17.
21. *Persons in Relation* (1961), Ch. X.
22. *The Structure of Religious Experience* (1936), p. 30 f.
23. *Op. cit.,* p. 43.
24. *Op. cit.,* pp. 27 f.

Macmurray here denies that transcendence is distinctively an attribute of God: he asserts it as a feature of all our experience. I believe that he is wrong in what he denies, but right in what he asserts. Contrary to what he says, our experience of God *is* distinctively and characteristically an awareness of the transcendent, the numinous, the unconditional. Yet that is a feature of *all* our experience—*in depth.* Statements about God are acknowledgements of the transcendent, unconditional element in all our relationships, and supremely in our relationships with other persons. Theological statements are indeed affirmations about human existence—but they are affirmations about the ultimate ground and depth of that existence. It is not enough to say that "religion is about human fellowship and community," any more than one can simply reverse the Biblical statement and say that "love *is* God." And that, significantly, is what Feuerbach thought St John should have said.[25] But it is what the Apostle rather carefully refuses to do. He is clear that *apart from* the relationship of love there is no knowledge of God: "He who does not love does not know God; for God is love."[26] and conversely: "He who abides in love abides in God, and God abides in him."[27] But the premise of this last sentence is not, as we might logically expect, "Love is God," but, "God is love."[28] The most he will say the other way round is that "love is *of* God."[29] It is *ek theou:* it has God as its source and ground. For it is precisely his thesis[30] that our convictions about love and its ultimacy are not projections from human love; rather, our sense of the sacredness of love derives from the fact that in this relationship as nowhere else there is disclosed and laid bare the divine Ground of all our being. And this revelation for St John finds its focus and final vindication in the fact of Jesus Christ—"the humanity of God"[31]—rather than in the divinity of Man.

To assert that *"God* is love" is to believe that in love one comes into touch with the most fundamental reality in the universe, that Being itself ultimately has this character. It is to say, with Buber, that "Every particular *Thou* is a glimpse through to the eternal *Thou,"*[32] that it

---

25. *Op. cit.,* p. 261; cf. p. 47: "Love is God himself, and apart from it there is no God."

26. I John 4.8.

27. I John 4.16.

28. *Ibid.*

29. I John 4.7.

30. I John 4.10, 19.

31. The title of Karl Barth's book (1961) and of the central lecture in it (pp. 37–65). Feuerbach interestingly enough also uses the phase "the human nature of God" (*op. cit.,* p. 49), but as always with a subtly different twist.

32. *I and Thou,* p. 75.

is "between man and man"[33] that we meet God, not, with Feuerbach, that "man with man—the unity of *I* and *Thou*—is God."[34] Nevertheless, as Bonhoeffer insists, "God is the 'beyond' *in the midst*";[35] "The transcendent is not infinitely remote but close at hand."[36] For the eternal *Thou* is met only *in, with and under* the finite *Thou,* whether in the encounter with other persons or in the response to the natural order.

Yet the eternal *Thou* is not to be equated with the finite *Thou,* nor God with man or nature. That is the position of naturalism, whether pantheistic or humanistic. And, Tillich insists, it is necessary to push "beyond naturalism and supranaturalism."[37] The naturalist critique of supranaturalism is valid. It has torn down an idol and Christianity must not be found clinging to it. But equally Christianity must challenge the assumption of naturalism that God is merely a redundant name for nature or for humanity. John Wren-Lewis observes that the naturalist critique of supranaturalism itself points to depths, divine depths, in experience for which it fails to account. He claims that Freud's own analysis of religion indicates as much:

> For it is an integral part of his argument that fantasies about spiritual forces in the occult world are really "projections" or "displacements" of elements in our experience of personal relationships which we seek to avoid recognizing, but it is hard to see why the common projections made by the human race should have a numinous, transcendental character *unless there is something numinous and transcendental in the experience of personal relationshps themselves.*[38]

The necessity for the name "God" lies in the fact that our being has depths which naturalism, whether evolutionary, mechanistic, dialectical or humanistic, cannot or will not recognize. And the nemesis which has overtaken naturalism in our day has revealed the peril of trying to suppress them. As Tillich puts it,

---

33. *Between Man and Man* (1947), pp. 30, 203–5; cf. *I and Thou,* p. 39.

34. *Philosophie der Zukunft, p. 62.*

35. *Op. cit.,* p. 124 (italics mine).

36. *Op. cit.,* p. 175.

37. *Systematic Theology,* vol. ii, p. 5.

38. "The Decline of Magic in Art and Politics," *The Critical Quarterly,* Spring 1960, p. 18. I should add that there is much in Wren-Lewis's writings (for instance, in his subsequent elaboration of this last sentence or in his article "Modern Philosophy and the Doctrine of the Trinity" in *The Philosophical Quarterly,* vol. v (1955), pp. 214–24), which makes me doubt whether in the last analysis he himself is not expounding the thesis "love is God." At any rate he certainly does not guard himself adequately against this interpretation.

Our period has decided for a *secular* world. That was a great and much-needed decision. . . . It gave consecration and holiness to our daily life and work. Yet it excluded those deep things for which religion stands: the feeling for the inexhaustible mystery of life, the grip of an ultimate meaning of existence, and the invincible power of an unconditional devotion. These things *cannot* be excluded. If we try to expel them in their divine images, they re-emerge in daemonic images. Now, in the old age of our secular world, we have seen the most horrible manifestations of these daemonic images; we have looked more deeply into the mystery of evil than most generations before us; we have seen the unconditional devotion of millions to a satanic image; we feel our period's sickness unto death.[39]

There are depths of revelation, intimations of eternity, judgements of the holy and the sacred, awarenesses of the unconditional, the numinous and the ecstatic, which cannot be explained in purely naturalistic categories without being reduced to something else. There is the "Thus saith the Lord" heard by prophet, apostle and martyr for which naturalism cannot account. But neither can it discount it merely by pointing to the fact that "the Lord" is portrayed in the Bible in highly mythological terms, as one who "inhabits eternity" or "walks in the garden in the cool of the evening." The question of God is the question *whether this depth of being is a reality or an illusion,* not whether *a* Being exists beyond the bright blue sky, or anywhere else. Belief in God is a matter of "what you take seriously without any reservation," of what for you is *ultimate* reality.

The man who acknowledges the transcendence of God is the man who *in* the conditioned relationships of life recognizes the unconditional and responds to it in unconditional personal relationship. In Tillich's words again,

> To call God transcendent in this sense does not mean that one must establish a "superworld" of divine objects. It does mean that, within itself, the finite world points beyond itself. In other words, it is self-transcendent.[40]

This, I believe, is Tillich's great contribution to theology—the reinterpretation of transcendence in a way which preserves its reality while detaching it from the projection of supranaturalism. "The Divine, as he sees it, does not inhabit a transcendent world *above nature;* it is found in the 'ecstatic' character of *this* world, as its transcendent

---

39. *The Shaking of the Foundations,* p. 181.
40. *Systematic Theology,* vol. ii, p. 8.

Depth and Ground."[41] Indeed, as a recent commentator has observed, supranaturalism for Tillich actually represents "a loss of transcendence":

> It is the attempt to understand and express God's relation to the world by a literalization of this-worldly categories. . . . The result is a God who *exists* as *a* being, *above* the world. . . . Thus God is described as an entity within the subject-object structures of the spatial-temporal world.[42]

Or, as Tillich puts it himself:

> To criticise such a conditioning of the unconditional, even if it leads to atheistic consequences, is more religious, because it is more aware of the unconditional character of the divine, than a theism that bans God into the supranatural realm.[43]

Nevertheless, the abandonment of any idea of a God "out there" will inevitably appear a denial of his "otherness" and the negation of much in the Biblical assertion of what Kierkegaard called "the infinite qualitative difference between God and man." It will be valuable therefore to look again at what the Bible is saying about the nature of God and see how it can retain, and indeed regain, its deepest significance in the light of this reinterpretation.

---

41. W. M. Horton, "Tillich's Role in Contemporary Theology" in *The Theology of Paul Tillich* (ed. C. W. Kegley and R. W. Bretall, 1952, p. 37). In his "Reply to Interpretation and Criticism" in the same volume, Tillich describes his own position as "self-transcending or ecstatic naturalism" (p. 341).

42. E. Farley, *The Transcendence of God* (1962), p. 77.

43. *The Protestant Era,* p. 92.

21. The Meaning of Theological Language

I. The Problem of Religious Language

Many modern theologians say that one of the major difficulties confronting the Christian who is himself a secular man lies in the nature of religion and the confusion between religion and Christian faith. We have argued that the difficulty lies rather in the character of the language of faith, that the problem is not so much one of bad religion as it is one of bad, or at least unworkable, language. A discussion of the problem of religion and its language will introduce the third element of this study: the method of those who have reflected on the logical structures of various sorts of languages of faith.

Bultmann defines religion as the human longing to escape from this world, fed by the supposed discovery of "a sphere above this world, in which the soul alone, released from all that is worldly, could repose."[1] Such a longing and discovery would undoubtedly be called religious by most people, and a man who entertained such thoughts would be called a religious man, but the concept of religion includes

---

Reprinted with permission of Macmillan Publishing Co., Inc. from *The Secular Meaning of the Gospel* by Paul M. Van Buren. © Paul M. Van Buren 1963. Title supplied by the editors.

1. In *Kerygma und Mythos,* Vol. I, pp. 26 f.

more than an other-worldly orientation. Many who undertake "religious activities," like going to church and singing hymns, or who say that certain events are according to "the will of God," do not show much interest in "a sphere above this world." Bultmann's definition meets only one aspect of the problem which concerns us.

Gerhard Ebeling, in an essay on Bonhoeffer's idea of religion, has given a more inclusive definition: the attempted "enlargement of reality by means of God."[2] Religion consists of appealing to God as a means of explaining, justifying, or otherwise "filling in the picture" of the world or human affairs. This summarizes the characteristics of religion, as Bonhoeffer saw them: thinking of two spheres of reality, the natural and the supernatural; interest in the other-worldly; metaphysical thinking; an idea of transcendence which surpasses human possibilities.[3] The religionless posture, on the other hand, is that of "coming to terms with reality apart from God," or without use of the God-hypothesis.[4]

Contemporary theologians from Barth to Ogden are agreed that Christianity does not conform to this definition of religion. Religion, they would say, is man's use of God to solve some human problem, whereas the Gospel proclaims God's unexpected use of man for his own purposes; this distinction lies behind Bonhoeffer's search for a "nonreligious" interpretation of biblical concepts. The fact remains, however, that all of these theologians continue to speak of God, even though, as Ebeling put it, "a considerable proportion of our contemporaries haven't the least idea of what we are even talking about when we speak of God."[5] Ebeling himself proposes what he calls a "worldly" way to speak of God, a way which must be concrete, clear, and effective, but the same "considerable proportion of our contemporaries" would undoubtedly judge this way to be talk about God nevertheless. Ebeling sees the problem, but he has not solved it.

The solution proposed by existentialist theologians consists of eliminating all "objectification" of God in thought and word,[6] but since Bultmann also objects to using the word "God" simply as a symbol of human experience, the word "God" appears to refer to nothing at all.

---

2. G. Ebeling, *Wort und Glaube* (Tübingen: Mohr, 1960), p. 145.

3. Bonhoeffer, *Ethics,* trans. N. H. Smith (London: SCM Press, 1955), p. 62; *WE,* pp. 180, 182, 184, 241 f., 259 f.

4. Ebeling, *op. cit.,* p. 159.

5. *Ibid.,* p. 363.

6. Cf., for example, E. Fuchs, "Glaube und Geschichte im Blick auf die Frage nach dem historischen Jesus," *Zeitschrift für Theologie und Kirche,* 54.2, 1957; also the discussion in Chapter III, *supra.*

The "nonobjective" use of the word "God" allows of no verification and is therefore meaningless. The moment we begin to use the word in a qualified sense, as in Flew's parable,[7] we begin to kill our assertions by the "death of a thousand qualifications," and we end by making no assertion at all.[8] We do not understand, therefore, by what logic Bultmann and Ebeling continue to use the word "God" as though it had a quite specific reference. The *we* must be emphasized and explained. Why do we not understand their use of the word "God" as though it had a quite specific reference? Such a use does appear to conflict with their confessed existentialist concerns and is therefore unclear, but our chief difficulty lies elsewhere. We set out upon this study with certain acknowledged commitments to what we called "secular thought," and we said that secularism, as we were using the term, is grounded in empirical attitudes in some way. Our objection to a certain use of the word "God" says as much about our own empirical attitudes as it does about Bultmann and Ebeling. The nature and extent of these empirical attitudes will become clearer as the study develops. It can only be suggested, not proved, that these attitudes are more common among contemporary "believers" than Bultmann or Ebeling appear to recognize, the force of this suggestion being measured by the degree to which a method consistent with such attitudes is found to be helpful for the reader.

The contemporary theological fashion of setting the Christian Gospel over against "religion" does not clarify our problem.[9] According to this view of the matter, the Gospel proclaims God's act of grace reaching down to rescue man, whereas religion has to do with man reaching up to find or define God. The "religionless" man, however, who can come to terms with life quite apart from this literally nonsensical entity called "God," will not be impressed by the difference between the Gospel and "religion." There is a difference between them, but both the Gospel and "religion" have so much more in common than either has with the scepticism of a man like Flew that the distinction loses its interest. The empiricist in us finds the heart of the difficulty not in what is said about God, but in the very talking about God

---

7. The parable by Flew, to which Van Buren refers here, is a variant of John Wisdom's story about an invisible gardener in "Gods" (see pp. 221–22 in this volume). Flew's version of the story is to be found in A. Flew and A. MacIntyre, eds., *New Essays in Philosophical Theology*, pp. 96 f.—Eds.

8. Cf. T. R. Miles, *Religion and the Scientific Outlook*, pp. 147 ff., on the meaninglessness of "qualified literal theism," a faith expressed by Flew's believing explorer.

9. Bonhoeffer, who approved of this fashion, gave Barth credit for being one of its main champions. *WE*, p. 219.

at all. We do not know "what" God is, and we cannot understand how the word "God" is being used. It seems to function as a name, yet theologians tell us that we cannot use it as we do other names, to refer to something quite specific. If it is meant to refer to an "existential encounter," a point of view, or the speaker's self-understanding, surely a more appropriate expression could be found. The problem is not solved, moreover, by substituting other words for the word *God:* one could supply the letter X (Flew used the word *gardener* in his parable) and the problem would remain, for the difficulty has to do with how X functions. The problem of the Gospel in a secular age is a problem of the logic of its apparently meaningless language, and linguistic analysts will give us help in clarifying it. We dare to call *our* problem *the* problem not because we have access to what everyone or anyone else means by "secular age" or "Gospel," but because we dare to hope that what we have found helpful for our own understanding may prove helpful for others, who may then identify the problem to some extent as we have identified it.

II. Linguistic Analyses of Religious Assertions

Flew's parable, with which we began our study, has been answered by R. M. Hare,[10] who begins by granting that Flew is "completely victorious" on the grounds which he has marked out. Hare grants that if religious or theological assertions are taken as statements about "how things are" (this is indeed the form they seem to have: *e.g.* "God loves all men"; "Jesus Christ is Lord"; "the wages of sin is death"), they must be judged as meaningless. The logic of Flew's parable is perfectly sound. Having made this concession, Hare has cleared the way for his reply. He begins by telling another parable about a student who has a peculiar attitude about dons: he is convinced that they all want to kill him. However many apparently friendly dons he meets, however friends try to persuade him by recalling his own experience or theirs, his attitude does not change.

Hare has invented the word *blik* for a fundamental attitude. The student in his parable has an insane "blik" about dons; we have a sane one, we would say, for Hare points out that we are never without a "blik," or we could not say that the student is insane, that he is wrong and we are right. A "blik" is not achieved by empirical inquiry. The basic presuppositions we have about the world are not verifiable, and

---

10. Flew, A. and MacIntyre, A., eds: *New Essays in Philosophical Theology,* pp. 99–105.

yet everything we do depends on them, as Hume taught us. Such a presupposition or set of presuppositions (and all men have them) are not to be regarded as *explanations*. That is Flew's mistake; he took his Believer's "blik" to be an explanation of the clearing in the jungle, which it clearly is not. Hare points out that "bliks" are serious matters for those who hold them, whether we judge any particular "blik" to be right or wrong, and everyone has a "blik." Consequently, the detachment of Flew's two explorers is unreal.

Flew's response to Hare's suggestion focuses nicely on our problem:[11]

> Any attempt to analyse Christian religious utterances as expressions or affirmations of a *blik* rather than as (at least would-be) assertions about the cosmos is fundamentally misguided. *First,* because thus interpreted they would be entirely unorthodox. If Hare's religion really is a *blik,* involving no cosmological assertions about the nature and activities of a supposed personal creator, then surely he is not a Christian at all? *Second,* because thus interpreted, they would scarcely do the job they do. If they were not even intended as assertions then many religious activities would become fraudulent, or merely silly. If "You ought *because* it is God's will" asserts no more than "You ought," then the person who prefers the former phraseology is not really giving a reason, but a fraudulent substitute for one, a dialectical dud cheque.

The issue between these two philosophers does not concern the logic or function of language. Neither of them, moreover, has questioned the empirical picture of the world of the twentieth century. Both grant that a simple literal theism, whose assertions could be put to an empirical test like that of Elijah before Mt. Carmel, is untenable. In other words, they agree in denying an "objectified" God. They also agree, however, that if a simple literal theism is untenable, a qualified literal ("nonobjectified") theism is meaningless. It is dead by the death of a thousand qualifications. If God is really "wholly other," we cannot speak of him at all. If statements about God are "to be interpreted exhaustively and without remainder" as statements about man, they cannot be meaningful statements about God. Where these philosophers disagree is on the nature of Christianity. One calls the statements of faith a collection of cosmological assertions; the other sees them as expressions of a "blik," an orientation, a commitment to see the world in a certain way, and a way of life following inevitably upon

---

11. *Ibid.,* pp. 107–08.

this orientation. What Hare is suggesting is that a man's faith and his theology have a meaning, even though the theistic rug has been pulled out from under him.

Not all analysts of the language of faith have gone this far, but Ian T. Ramsey, in arguing for the meaningfulness of language about God, offers support for and further elaboration of Hare's concept of a "blik." He argues that the language of faith combines the language of discernment, of an admittedly special sort, with the language of commitment, of a sort which covers the totality of life and the world.[12] Statements of faith direct our attention to certain kinds of stiuations: situations of disclosure, when "the light dawns," and the situation becomes alive and new. The emphasis is not only on the disclosure or discernment, but also on the resulting commitment, whereby what we now "see" becomes important and determines our subsequent seeing. In such situations, the believer makes use of odd words like "God."

The function of such words is clarified with the help of Ramsey's idea of models and qualifiers. The model of "father," for example, points in a certain direction, inviting us to follow this direction. But it is qualified by such words as "eternal" or "omnipotent," to indicate that the word is only a model, that we should push on and on and on . . . until the light dawns, and the situation, and, with it, all things, takes on "depth," or rather, until we see that the "depth" is there to be discerned. Ramsey grants that all this sounds very close to a psychological explanation of religious language, but he argues that it is false to say that such an interpretation of human experience is "purely subjective," since there is in fact no such thing as a purely subjective experience. Every experience is an experience of something.

The language of faith is nothing if not odd, Ramsey says, and he stresses its peculiarity in order to counter two "popular misconceptions: that those with an intense affection for ordinary language must necessarily deny metaphysics," and "that those who defend metaphysics must necessarily trade in occult realms and shadowy worlds."[13] One example of the odd character of the language of faith is the name of God, which the Hebrews avoided whenever possible. The significance of this avoidance of God's name lies in the linguistic fact that discovering a name is typical of situations of disclosure or discernment. When we *assign* a name to something, no disclosure is involved; we are simply in the realm of external information. When someone tells us his name, however, or when we learn a name, the situation is

---

12. *Religious Language,* pp. 18 ff.
13. I. T. Ramsey, *Freedom and Immortality* (London: SCM Press, 1960), p. 152.

a religious one, involving mystery and eliciting awe. The use of the revealed name recalls the mystery of self-disclosure.[14] The text of the revelation of the divine name in chapter 3 of Exodus is, moreover, an example of the final form of the language of loyalty. The last answer to why I have acted as I have, after all the partial explanations, is the statement, "I'm I." Behind any other things I might say, like "because I decided to do it," or "because he asked me to do it," lies this ultimate causal explanation. The series of "whys" of any decision, any case of loyalty or commitment, must finally come to rest at the "logical stop-card": "I'm I."[15] The word "God" also, Ramsey says, functions as the tautology "I'm I," and it is just this statement, "I am who I am," which stands in place of the revealed name in chapter 3 of Exodus. This tautology marks the limit which religious language approaches and to which it tries to point. The limit is never part of the series of variables which approach that limit, yet there is a relationship between the variables and the limit.[16]

Another example of the oddness of biblical language is the story of the resurrection of Jesus. The question "Did the resurrection occur?" is misleadingly simple, for if "resurrection" referred only to such things as an empty tomb and a resuscitated body, then one could acknowledge the resurrection and yet not be a believer. What the Christian believes about the resurrection of Jesus has something to do with these observable factors, but it is not identical with them. In fact, the question "Did the resurrection occur?" is logically much more like

---

14. *Religious Language*, pp. 108 ff.

15. *Ibid.,* pp. 63 ff.

16. At several places, Ramsey touches on a point which has been of concern to William Poteat: the possibility of understanding the function of theological language in the light of the similarly strange use of the word "I." (William Poteat, " 'I Will Die': An Analysis," *Philosophical Quarterly,* Vol. IX, No. 34 [1959], pp. 3–15.) Poteat has urged reflection upon the way in which "I" functions when we say, "I was born," or "I will die," where it operates in a way quite different from that of "he" when we say, "He was born," or "He will die." "He" functions in a straightforwardly empirical manner. We can say, "He will die," and also, after the fact, "He died." But we cannot use the first person singular of the verb "to die" in the past, unless we have first changed radically the manner of using the word "die." This indicates something odd about the logic of the verbs "to die" and "to be born," but more important, it indicates the odd logic of the first person singular pronoun. Of course, I can say many things about myself which are empirical and can also be said of me by someone else. But there are also other things which only I can say about myself and which cannot be translated "exhaustively and without remainder" into what others may say about me. This line of reflection is related to the distinction which existentialists make between the words "existential" and "existentialist." The first has to do with the "I"; the second can be talked about equally well in the third person.

the question asked of a situation in which a man has jumped from a bridge to rescue a drowning child: "Was that a case of duty?" The empirical evidence is not irrelevant, but the evidence will never settle either question. The word "resurrection" (like the words "duty," "love," and "God") directs us to the sort of situation in which a discernment fundamental to our whole conception of life and a response of commitment may take place. Such situations exceed empirical description, however relevant description may be to our discernment.

A further illustration of Ramsey's analysis of the language of faith may be seen in his treatment of the language of classical Christology:

> For the Early Christians, Jesus Christ was the occasion of and the object of "disclosure" situations for which the word "God" would have been appropriate currency. Further, much could be said about Jesus Christ which was, on the face of it, straightforwardly empirical, viz. that he was tired, that he wept, and so on. So we have what are *prima facie,* two logically different languages competing as descriptions of the object of "disclosure" or "revelation." There then arises the problem of how these two languages can somehow be integrated, for in the Christian disclosure *only one* "object" is disclosed.
>
> Hence arises the concept of "hypostatic" unity, which we may interpret both from a linguistic and a "factual" point of view.
>
> (i) To know what hypostatic unity is *in fact,* there must be evoked a Christian disclosure situation with Jesus Christ as the occasion and object of it.[17]

Preaching and the celebration of the Lord's Supper are obviously intended to evoke such a situation. The object and occasion of disclosure is the man Jesus, and the disclosure comes (if it does come) when "the light dawns" and we find ourselves involved in what existentialists would call an "encounter." All sorts of models may help us toward this situation, but none can either produce or describe it. Ramsey's analysis continues:

> (ii) As far as *language* goes, . . . the doctrine of *communicatio idiomatum* (the participation of either "nature" of Christ in the properties or attributes of the other) and the word "hypostasis" may

---

17. *Religious Language,* pp. 166 f.

both be seen as an ancient attempt to deal with what nowadays would be called the problem of complementary languages and their unity, a problem which is raised especially by recent developments in scientific method.

Let me emphasize that hypostasis would only be successful in unifying two languages if it is odd enough never to be given except by reference to a Christian disclosure situation. If it is to be the logical bond that Christian doctrine wishes it to be, it cannot be modelled. If it is to do this work it is quite impossible (*logically* impossible) to produce a model for it.[18]

We have quoted Ramsey at length because this passage is one of the rare examples of the beginning of an analysis of the language of Christology. Moreover, Ramsey has made in effect a further development of Hare's concept of "blik." A "blik" involves a perspective entailing a commitment, and Ramsey has clarified this with his analysis of the language of discernment and commitment. When this analysis is applied to the language of Christology, it discloses two sorts of languages: one is the language of a "blik"; the other is that of straightforward empirical observation. Both sorts of language are used about the same person, Jesus of Nazareth. But the language of Christology is appropriate only to one who himself has discerned what Christians discern, for whom Jesus has become the occasion for a new discernment which has led to a commitment involving his whole perspective. We can summarize by saying that the language of Christology is language about Jesus of Nazareth on the part of those for whom he has been the occasion and remains the definition of their "blik."

Another analysis of the language of faith, similar to those of Hare and Ramsey, has been made by T. R. Miles. Accepting, as Hare has done, the argument of Flew, Miles recommends what he calls "the way of silence qualified by parables." In place of the language of "simple literal theism" (God walking in the garden of Eden, coming down to and scattering the builders of the tower of Babel, smelling Noah's sacrifice), which few men would use today, and the language of "qualified literal theism" (the language of the Believer in Flew's parable), which proves to have no "cash value," Miles urges the course of silence, in which no claims or assertions are made. The Believer may qualify his silence, however, by what Miles calls the theistic parable.[19]

Any parable has three characteristics: the question of the literal truth

18. *Ibid.*, pp. 168 f.
19. Miles, *op. cit.*, pp. 161 ff.

of the parable is unimportant, the language is straightforwardly empirical, and, most important, the parable has a message. It invites us to view in a certain way the situation in connection with which the parable is told. Empirical considerations may be relevant for deciding on the usefulness of a particular parable, however. If, for example, it could be proved historically that Jesus "was fallible on matters of importance, it would be all the more difficult to accept any parable which says that he is the incarnate son of God."[20] Ultimately, however, the choice of parables is a matter of "personal conviction rather than rational argument."[21] The believer is the man who has chosen to qualify his silence with the theistic parable, like the one expressed in the doctrine of the creation of the world by a loving Father. The question of whether the parable is "objectively true" can only be met by silence; but the whole outlook of the man who chooses the theistic parable is changed.

One of the most radical contributions to the analysis of the language of faith has been made by R. B. Braithwaite. We shall summarize his lectures[22] because his argument is important for our study. Braithwaite begins by applying the verification principle of modern philosophy in its sharpest form to the language of the Christian faith. This principle implies

> that the primary question becomes, not whether a religious statement such as that a personal God created the world is true or false, but how it could be known to be true or false. Unless this latter question can be answered, the religious statement has no ascertainable meaning and there is nothing expressed by it to be either true or false. Moreover a religious statement cannot be believed without being understood, and it can only be understood by an understanding of the circumstances which would verify or falsify it. Meaning is not logically prior to the possibility of verification: we do not first learn the meaning of a statement, and afterwards consider what would make us call it true or false; the two understandings are one and indivisible.[23]

Now "a hypothesis which is consistent with every possible empirical fact is not an empirical one." Unless an answer can be given as to how

---

20. *Ibid.,* p. 172.

21. *Ibid.,* p. 171.

22. *An Empiricist's View of Religious Belief* (Cambridge: Cambridge University Press, 1955).

23. Braithwaite, *op. cit.,* pp. 2, 3.

the world or the course of history would have been different without God, or unless it were admitted that if either had been different we could have concluded that there is no God, religious or theological propositions cannot be empirical.[24] In short, if Elijah's empirical test is no longer to be allowed, then neither are assertions that Elijah's God has acted empirically in this world!

Braithwaite then states his thesis: religious assertions are in fact *used as* moral assertions.[25] Moral assertions share with religious ones the characteristic of being neither logically necessary nor empirical; yet they have a use: that of guiding conduct. With the significant modification which has been made in the early verification principle (so that philosophers would now say that "the meaning of a statement is given by the way in which it is used"),[26] it is now realized that "the primary use of a moral assertion [is] that of expressing the intention of the asserter to act in a particular sort of way specified in the assertion."[27]

Braithwaite then returns to his thesis that religious assertions are "primarily declarations of adherence to a policy of action, declarations of commitment to a way of life," and continues his argument:

> That the way of life led by the believer is highly relevant to the sincerity of his religious convictions has been insisted upon . . . by Christianity. . . . The view which I put forward for your consideration is that the intention of a Christian to follow a Christian way of life is not only the criterion for the sincerity of his belief in the assertions of Christianity; it is the criterion for the meaningfulness of his assertions. Just as the meaning of a moral assertion is given by its use in expressing the asserter's intention to act, so far as in him lies, in accordance with the moral principle involved, so the meaning of a religious assertion is given by its use in expressing the asserter's intention to follow a specified policy of behaviour. To say that it is belief in the dogmas of religion which is the cause of the believer's intending to behave as he does is to put the cart before the horse: it is the intention to behave which constitutes what is known as religious conviction.[28]

Braithwaite is aware of two objections which might be raised here:

---

24. *Ibid.,* pp. 6, 7.
25. *Ibid.,* p. 11.
26. *Ibid.,* p. 10. Braithwaite refers to Wittgenstein, *op. cit.,* §§ 340, 352, 559 f.
27. *Ibid.,* p. 12.
28. *Ibid.,* pp. 15 f.

not all theological assertions imply action; and, there is a difference between religion and morality. He meets these objections, first, by admitting that religious assertions should be taken as a group and in context. He insists, however, that "unless a Christian's assertion that God is love (*agape*)—which I take to epitomize the assertions of the Christian religion—be taken to declare his intention to follow an agapeistic way of life, he could be asked what is the connection between the assertion and the intention, between Christian belief and Christian practice."[29] (This would presumably be Braithwaite's exegesis of I John 4:20: "If any one says, 'I love God,' and hates his brother, he is a liar.") Second, he also grants that being filled with *agape* is more than acting agapeistically: "it also includes an agapeistic frame of mind."[30] But more important, for Braithwaite, is the following distinction: "A religious assertion will . . . have a propositional element which is lacking in a purely moral assertion, in that it will refer to a story as well as to an intention." Consequently, "to assert the whole set of assertions of the Christian religion is both to tell the Christian doctrinal story and to confess allegiance to the Christian way of life."[31] He notes that what he calls "story" has also been called by other names: parable, fairy tale, allegory, fable, tale, and myth. He prefers the word "story" because it is neutral, "implying neither that the story is believed nor that it is disbelieved."[32] The Christian story includes straight history and also material clearly not historical. But Braithwaite insists that belief in the empirical truth of the stories "is not the proper criterion for deciding whether or not an assertion is a Christian one. A man is not, I think, a professing Christian unless he both proposes to live according to Christian moral principles and associates his intention with thinking of Christian stories; but he need not believe that the empirical propositions presented by the stories correspond to empirical fact."[33]

What is the function of these stories and how are they related to this

---

29. *Ibid.,* p. 18.

30. *Ibid.,* p. 21.

31. *Ibid.,* p. 24: "Entertainment in thought (of a part or the whole of the Christian story) forms the context in which Christian resolutions are made, which serves to distinguish Christian assertions from those made by adherents of another religion or of no religion." We would urge the reader, who may feel that this is insufficient and that there must be something distinctively "Christian" about the actions or words themselves of believers, to reflect on the motives of such feelings.

32. *Ibid.,* p. 26.

33. *Ibid.,* pp. 26 f. The word "principles" in this context means "assertions" or "convictions."

intention to act? Braithwaite answers that the stories have a psychological and causal relationship to the intention: to say that an action is "doing the will of God" helps us to carry it through, and Braithwaite feels that theologians need to keep in mind the psychological fact that men's behaviour is determined not only by intellectual considerations, but also by phantasies, imaginations, and hopes.[34] He concludes his essay by remarking that in his analysis of theological language, he has not come across an entity called belief. "Religious belief," he concludes, is not "a species of ordinary belief, of belief in propositions. A moral belief is an intention to behave in a certain way: a religious belief is an intention to behave in a certain way (a moral belief) together with the entertainment of certain stories associated with the intention in the mind of the believer."[35]

If there is a weak link in this chain of reasoning, it is Braithwaite's understanding of the function of the Christian "story" and its relationship to the intention to lead the Christian "way of life." While his psychological observation is in order, his solution does not do justice to the indispensable role of the "story" in the kerygma. We shall return to a further analysis of this role in our reconstruction. The position of Braithwaite is, however, sufficiently close to the others we have examined to allow us to speak of a rough consensus among contemporary analysts of the language of faith, in spite of the variety of thought within that consensus.

Not all analytic philosophers, of course, have approached the language of faith in the way we have presented. A number of philosophers have argued that faith is a kind of knowledge and that faith-statements are to be understood cognitively, somewhat as Flew understands them. They would take issue with Hare, Braithwaite, and Miles, among others, insisting that faith is logically "belief that . . ." before it is "belief in. . . ." Christianity, they argue, is not essentially a conviction, commitment, or attitude, but entry into and living in a relationship with a transcendent being, and it stands or falls with the meaningfulness of its assertions concerning that transcendent being. Passing over the difficulties arising from placing the word "relationship" alongside of the expression "transcendent being," we notice a common line of argument among several philosophers holding this position.[36] Funda-

---

34. *Ibid.,* pp. 27, 28, 31.

35. *Ibid.,* pp. 32 f.

36. Representative of this position are I. M. Crombie, "The Possibility of Theological Statements," *Faith and Logic,* pp. 31 ff., and John Hick, *Faith and Knowledge* (Ithaca, N.Y.: Cornell University Press, 1957); "Theology and Verification," *Theology Today,* Vol. XVII, No. 1 (1960), pp. 12 ff.

mental to their case is the concept of undifferentiated or natural theism. Arguing from a sense of contingency, or from some other variation of the argument from design, they believe that most men, or a number great enough to lead us to take note of their ideas, have at least some vague concept of that which is *not* contingent and to which the designation "divine" would seem to them to be appropriate. On the basis of this general concept of the divine, certain events are interpreted by religious men as manifesting in some way and to some degree the character, will, or activity of this transcendent being. In some forms of this argument, a strong appeal is made to Jesus as the authority for looking to certain particular events and interpreting them as revelations of the divine. In the last resort, those who take this approach to the language of faith grant that verification must apply to this language, but they argue that this can only be done in the *eschaton,* in the final day of the Kingdom. In the *eschaton,* we shall see clearly whether or not faith as knowledge is correct. If that is no proof for the present, it is at least a justification for saying that faith-statements are meaningful, even though we cannot yet be in the position to carry through this verification. Logically, however, the statements of faith are in principle verifiable, and therefore meaningful, as cognitive assertions.

The choice of a noncognitive, "blik" conception of faith, rather than of a cognitive conception, will be fundamental to our study. We make this choice for both logical and theological reasons. The cognitive approach requires speaking of that which it admits is ineffable. It involves speaking of God by analogy, yet it is granted by its proponents that they cannot say to what extent the analogies are apt and proper. More difficult, however, is the problem of an appeal to eschatological verification. If "in heaven" there is neither marriage nor giving in marriage, then it is at least questionable if there is what philosophers call "verification" in the *eschaton.* On what basis could the possibility of eschatological verification be affirmed or denied? The language in which this question must be settled is, for better or worse, the language of men, not the "language of angels." To speak of verification as philosophers do presupposes certain empirical attitudes, and no one knows the empirical attitudes which would be either possible in or appropriate to the *eschaton.*

We reject the cognitive approach to theological language, however, not primarily because it is logically puzzling, but because of certain theological commitments out of which this study has arisen. That approach builds its case on a natural sense of the divine, on natural religion and a natural revelation. The history of theology, seen from the perspective of modern kerygmatic theology, suggests that this is a road leading into the wilderness. Within the Protestant tradition, that road has been clearly charted and firmly marked with a "dead-end" sign by the work of Karl Barth, and we see no reason to ignore the warning. Christian faith has troubles enough in the twentieth century without retracing the misleading path opened up for Protestantism by the rationalist orthodoxy of the seventeenth century, followed to its unproductive end in the nineteenth century.

The cognitive approach to faith-statements presented by some linguistic analysts leads into the old inner contradiction of earlier forms of natural theology. It begins by speaking of a divine being of whom it *cannot* be said that this is the God of grace, the God who finds man wandering into idolatry with every conception he forms of the divine, the God who comes and makes himself known to man, not through, but in spite of, man's natural conceptions of the divine. Either the "God" of which Christians have tried to speak is the God of grace and *self*-revelation, or he is the neutral "it" of natural theology. The "divine being" of the cognitive approach is not easily assimilable to Pascal's " *'Dieu d'Abraham, Dieu d'Isaac, Dieu de Jacob,' non des philosophes et des savants."*

To follow the cognitive approach to religious language would contradict our point of departure. It tends to mark off a certain area of experience as "religious," and it argues for a religious way of knowing, in contrast to other (secular?) ways of knowing. This approach leads Christians into the trap of the reductionist tendency of nineteenth-century theology, where they are tempted to fight a defensive action against all other knowledge in order to defend some small area of their own which they may call the proper sphere of theology, concerning which they may cry—but surely cry in vain—that nonreligious knowledge should not try to tread on this holy ground. On the basis of these logical and theological objections, we judge the cognitive approach to theological language to be inadequate to the character of secular thought and to the heart of the Gospel.

We cannot argue, of course, for some objective, normative definition of verification or of the Gospel. When we call this approach inadequate, we are exposing our own categorial commitments which we see reflected in some modern kerygmatic theology, some modern analytic philosophy, and indicated with the word "secular." We can only acknowledge that our commitments are such as to lead us to reject a search for a religious preserve to be investigated by a special religious way of knowing, and we are committed to a Gospel which begins, not with an argument for undifferentiated theism, but with the impact of whatever it was that happened on Easter in the context of a particular history. With such commitments, we have no choice but to return to the consensus of such analysts as Hare and Braithwaite about the character of the language of faith and to assess its possibilities as a tool for determining what we have called the secular meaning of the Gospel.

The first point of consensus is that "simple literal theism" is wrong and that "qualified literal theism" is meaningless. The second agreement lies in the implicit or explicit conviction that the language of faith does have a meaning, and that this meaning can be explored and clarified by linguistic analysis. The third consensus is a concern to take Christianity seriously as a way of life, even though a straightforward use of the word "God" must be abandoned.

Simple literal theism is wrong and qualified literal theism is meaningless. The first of these assertions is another way of making Bultmann's point that myth is no longer tenable; the idea of the empirical intervention of a supernatural "God" in the world of men has been ruled out by the influence of modern science on our thinking. In making such statements, we reveal our own commitments to modern science, and we would only add that modern thought tends to grant the validity of the findings of the natural sciences. For those holding these commitments, thunderbolts can no longer be explained as weapons of the wrath of an invisible God, and the phrase "God did this," therefore, cannot logically mean what it says.[37] If we begin to qualify this phrase, however, we find one qualification calling for another until nothing is left of the original assertion. Linguistic analysis challenges the qualified theism of Bultmann and Ogden as much as that of more conservative theologians. Whether objectifying or nonobjectifying, language about a "God who acts" must be interpreted in some other way.

The language of faith has a meaning, nonetheless; it has a function which may be clarified by linguistic analysis. The language of Christian faith is the language of a believer, one who has been "caught" by the Gospel. In so far as his "blik" is functioning, his language is the language of faith, whether he is speaking about some generally recognized religious subject, such as "God," or of some so-called secular subject, like politics or his job. The function of his words may be to enlighten his listener concerning his "blik." In other circumstances

---

37. For a similar criticism of such assertions of biblical theology as "God acts" and "God speaks," cf. Langdon B. Gilkey, "Cosmology, Ontology, and the Travail of Biblical Language," *The Journal of Religion,* Vol. XLI, No. 3 (1961), pp. 194 ff.

they may take the form of an invitation to share that "blik." Or they may simply be a notification that he must take a particular course of action, for the unexpressed reason that he sees things in a certain way. In each case, the fact that a believer is speaking and the circumstances in which he is speaking may not be ignored. The actual function of the words is the key to understanding the language of faith.

Finally, the language of faith has meaning when it is taken to refer to the Christian way of life; it is not a set of cosmological assertions. The Christian "way of life," an expression recalling the New Testament designation of life in Christ as "the Way" (Acts 9:2), is central to the linguistic interpretation we have been considering. It contains elements of wonder, awe, and worship, but it is bound up with a basic conviction concerning the world and man's place in it which bears directly on decisions and actions. There is a parallel to the existentialists' emphasis on decision, but room is left for attitudes and ways of seeing things for which we would not ordinarily use the word "decision." There is a note of British calm and logical reflection in this conception of what goes to make up the Christian "way of life" or "authentic existence." Yet for these thinkers also, a "blik," the discernment and commitment of faith, is by definition something which is "lived."

This attempt to define a consensus does justice to no single position of the language analysts, yet our summary indicates the trend of their interpretations of Christianity. It remains to evaluate the method and results of these philosophers for a reconstruction of the kerygma and Christology.

22.   The Absurd

Most people feel on occasion that life is absurd, and some feel it vividly and continually. Yet the reasons usually offered in defense of this conviction are patently inadequate: they *could* not really explain why life is absurd. Why then do they provide a natural expression for the sense that it is?

I

Consider some examples. It is often remarked that nothing we do now will matter in a million years. But if that is true, then by the same token, nothing that will be the case in a million years matters now. In particular, it does not matter now that in a million years nothing we do now will matter. Moreover, even if what we did now *were* going to matter in a million years, how could that keep our present concerns from being absurd? If their mattering now is not enough to accomplish that, how would it help if they mattered a million years from now?

Whether what we do now will matter in a million years could make the crucial difference only if its mattering in a million years depended

---

This selection first appeared in *The Journal of Philosophy* vol. LXVIII, no. 20 (October 21, 1971). Used with the permission of the Journal and the author. Compare with selection 17 by Albert Camus.

on its mattering, period. But then to deny that whatever happens now will matter in a million years is to beg the question against its mattering, period; for in that sense one cannot know that it will not matter in a million years whether (for example) someone now is happy or miserable, without knowing that it does not matter, period.

What we say to convey the absurdity of our lives often has to do with space or time: we are tiny specks in the infinite vastness of the universe; our lives are mere instants even on a geological time scale, let alone a cosmic one; we will all be dead any minute. But of course none of these evident facts can be what *makes* life absurd, if it is absurd. For suppose we lived forever, would not a life that is absurd if it lasts seventy years be infinitely absurd of it lasted through eternity? And if our lives are absurd given our present size, why would they be any less absurd if we filled the universe (either because we were larger or because the universe was smaller)? Reflection on our minuteness and brevity appears to be intimately connected with the sense that life is meaningless; but it is not clear what the connection is.

Another inadequate argument is that because we are going to die, all chains of justification must leave off in mid-air: one studies and works to earn money to pay for clothing, housing, entertainment, food, to sustain oneself from year to year, perhaps to support a family and pursue a career—but to what final end? All of it is an elaborate journey leading nowhere. (One will also have some effect on other people's lives, but that simply reproduces the problem, for they will die too.)

There are several replies to this argument. First, life does not consist of a sequence of activities each of which has as its purpose some later member of the sequence. Chains of justification come repeatedly to an end within life, and whether the process as a whole can be justified has no bearing on the finality of these end-points. No further justification is needed to make it reasonable to take aspirin for a headache, attend an exhibit of the work of a painter one admires or stop a child from putting his hand on a hot stove. No larger context or further purpose is needed to present these facts from being pointless.

Even if someone wished to supply a further justification for pursuing all the things in life that are commonly regarded as self-justifying, that justification would have to end somewhere too. If *nothing* can justify unless it is justified in terms of something outside itself, which is also justified, then an infinite regress results, and no chain of justification can be complete. Moreover, if a finite chain of reasons cannot justify anything, what could be accomplished by an infinite chain, each link of which must be justified by something outside itself?

Since justifications must come to an end somewhere, nothing is gained by denying that they end where they appear to, within life—or by trying to subsume the multiple, often trivial ordinary justifications of action under a single, controlling life scheme. We can be satisfied more easily than that. In fact, through its misrepresentation of the process of justification, the argument makes a vacuous demand. It insists that the reasons available within life are incomplete but suggests thereby that all reasons that come to an end are incomplete. This makes it impossible to supply any reasons at all.

The standard arguments for absurdity appear therefore to fail as arguments. Yet I believe they attempt to express something that is difficult to state, but fundamentally correct.

II

In ordinary life a situation is absurd when it includes a conspicuous discrepancy between pretension or aspiration and reality: someone gives a complicated speech in support of a motion that has already been passed; a notorious criminal is made president of a major philanthropic foundation; you declare your love over the telephone to a recorded announcement; as you are being knighted, your pants fall down.

When a person finds himself in an absurd situation, he will usually attempt to change it, by modifying his aspirations, or by trying to bring reality into better accord with them, or by removing himself from the situation entirely. We are not always willing or able to extricate ourselves from a position whose absurdity has become clear to us. Nevertheless, it is usually possible to imagine some change that would remove the absurdity—whether or not we can or will implement it. The sense that life as a whole is absurd arises when we perceive, perhaps dimly, an inflated pretension or aspiration which is inseparable from the continuation of human life and which makes its absurdity inescapable, short of escape from life itself.

Many people's lives are absurd, temporarily or permanently, for conventional reasons having to do with their particular ambitions, circumstances, and personal relations. If there is a philosophical sense of absurdity, however, it must arise from the perception of something universal—some respect in which pretension and reality inevitably clash for us all. This condition is supplied, I shall argue, by the collision between the seriousness with which we take our lives and the perpetual possibility of regarding everything about which we are serious as arbitrary, or open to doubt.

We cannot live human lives without energy and attention, nor with-

The Absurd

out making choices which show that we take some things more seriously than others. Yet we have always available a point of view outside the particular form of our lives, from which the seriousness appears gratuitous. These two inescapable viewpoints collide in us, and that is what makes life absurd. It is absurd because we ignore the doubts that we know cannot be settled, continuing to live with nearly undiminished seriousness in spite of them.

This analysis requires defense in two respects: first as regards the unavoidability of seriousness; second as regards the inescapability of doubt.

We take ourselves seriously whether we lead serious lives or not and whether we are concerned primarily with fame, pleasure, virtue, luxury, triumph, beauty, justice, knowledge, salvation, or mere survival. If we take other people seriously and devote ourselves to them, that only multiplies the problem. Human life is full of effort, plans, calculation, success and failure: we *pursue* our lives, with varying degrees of sloth and energy.

It would be different if we could not step back and reflect on the process, but were merely led from impulse to impulse without self-consciousness. But human beings do not act solely on impulse. They are prudent, they reflect, they weight consequences, they ask whether what they are doing is worthwhile. Not only are their lives full of particular choices that hang together in larger activities with temporal structure: they also decide in the broadest terms what to pursue and what to avoid, what the priorities among their various aims should be, and what kind of people they want to be or become. Some men are faced with such choices by the large decisions they make from time to time; some merely by reflection on the course their lives are taking as the product of countless small decisions. They decide whom to marry, what profession to follow, whether to join the Country Club, or the Resistance; or they may just wonder why they go on being salesmen or academics or taxi drivers, and then stop thinking about it after a certain period of inconclusive reflection.

Although they may be motivated from act to act by those immediate needs with which life presents them, they allow the process to continue by adhering to the general system of habits and the form of life in which such motives have their place—or perhaps only by clinging to life itself. They spend enormous quantities of energy, risk, and calculation on the details. Think of how an ordinary individual sweats over his appearance, his health, his sex life, his emotional honesty, his social utility, his self-knowledge, the quality of his ties with family, colleagues, and friends, how well he does his job, whether he understands the world and what is going on in it. Leading a human life is a full-time occupation, to which everyone devotes decades of intense concern.

This fact is so obvious that it is hard to find it extraordinary and important. Each of us lives his own life—lives with himself twenty-four hours a day. What else is he supposed to do—live someone else's life? Yet humans have the special capacity to step back and survey themselves, and the lives to which they are committed, with that detached amazement which comes from watching an ant struggle up a heap of sand. Without developing the illusion that they are able to escape from their highly specific and idiosyncratic position, they can view it *sub specie aeternitatis*—and the view is at once sobering and comical.

The crucial backward step is not taken by asking for still another justification in the chain, and failing to get it. The objections to that line of attack have already been stated; justifications come to an end. But this is precisely what provides universal doubt with its object. We step back to find that the whole system of justification and criticism, which controls our choices and supports our claims to rationality, rests on responses and habits that we never question, that we should not know how to defend without circularity, and to which we shall continue to adhere even after they are called into question.

The things we do or want without reasons, and without requiring reasons—the things that define what is a reason for us and what is not —are the starting points of our skepticism. We see ourselves from outside, and all the contingency and specificity of our aims and pursuits become clear. Yet when we take this view and recognize what we do as arbitrary, it does not disengage us from life, and there lies our absurdity: not in the fact that such an external view can be taken of us, but in the fact that we ourselves take it, without ceasing to be the persons whose ultimate concerns are so coolly regarded.

III

One may try to escape the position by seeking broader ultimate concerns, from which it is impossible to step back—the idea being that absurdity results because what we take seriously is something small and insignificant and individual. Those seeking to supply their lives with meaning usually envision a role or function in something larger than themselves. They therefore seek fulfillment in service to society, the state, the revolution, the progress of history, the advance of science or religion and the glory of God.

But a role in some larger enterprise cannot confer significance unless that enterprise is itself significant. And its significance must come back to what we can understand, or it will not even appear to give us what we are seeking. If we learned that we were being raised to provide food for other creatures fond of human flesh, who planned to turn us into cutlets before we got too stringy—even if we learned that the human race had been developed by animal breeders precisely for this purpose—that would still not give our lives meaning, for two reasons. First, we would still be in the dark as to the significance of the lives of those other beings; second, although we might acknowledge that this culinary role would make our lives meaningful to them, it is not clear how it would make them meaningful to us.

Admittedly, the usual form of service to a higher being is different from this. One is supposed to behold and partake of the glory of God, for example, in a way in which chickens do not share in the glory of coq au vin. The same is true of service to a state, a movement, or a revolution. People can come to feel, when they are part of something bigger, that it is part of them too. They worry less about what is peculiar to themselves, but identify enough with the larger enterprise to find their role in it fulfilling.

However, any such larger purpose can be put in doubt in the same way that the aims of an individual life can be, and for the same reasons. It is as legitimate to find ultimate justification there as to find it earlier, among the details of individual life. But this does not alter the fact that justifications come to an end when we are content to have them end —when we do not find it necessary to look any further. If we can step back from the purposes of individual life and doubt their point, we can step back also from the progress of human history, or of science or the success of a society, or the kingdom, power, and glory of God,[1] and put all these things into question in the same way. What seems to us to confer meaning, justification, significance, does so in virtue of the fact that we need no more reasons after a certain point.

What makes doubt inescapable with regard to the limited aims of individual life also makes it inescapable with regard to any larger purpose that encourages the sense that life is meaningful. Once the fundamental doubt has begun, it cannot be laid to rest.

Camus maintains in *The Myth of Sisyphus* that the absurd arises because the world fails to meet our demands for meaning. This suggests that the world might satisfy those demands if it were different. But now we can see that this is not the case. There does not appear to be any conceivable world (containing us) about which unsettlable doubts could not arise. Consequently the absurdity of our situation

---

1. Cf. Robert Nozick, "Teleology," *Mosaic,* XII, 1 (Spring 1971): 27/8.

derives not from a collision between our expectations and the world, but from a collision within ourselves.

IV

It may be objected that the standpoint from which these doubts are supposed to be felt does not exist—that if we take the recommended backward step we will land on thin air, without any basis for judgment about the natural responses we are supposed to be surveying. If we retain our usual standards of what is important, then questions about the significance of what we are doing with our lives will be answerable in the usual way. But if we do not, then those questions can mean nothing to us, since there is no longer any content to the idea of what matters, and hence no content to the idea that nothing does.

But this objection misconceives the nature of the backward step. It is not supposed to give us an understanding of what is *really* important, so that we see by contrast that our lives are insigificant. We never, in the course of these reflections, abandon the ordinary standards that guide our lives. We merely observe them in operation, and recognize that if they are called into question we can justify them only by reference to themselves, uselessly. We adhere to them because of the way we are put together; what seems to us important or serious or valuable would not seem so if we were differently constituted.

In ordinary life, to be sure, we do not judge a situation absurd unless we have in mind some standards of seriousness, significance, or harmony with which the absurd can be contrasted. This contrast is not implied by the philosophical judgment of absurdity, and that might be though to make the concept unsuitable for the expression of such judgments. This is not so, however, for the philosophical judgment depends on another contrast which makes it a natural extension from more ordinary cases. It departs from them only in contrasting the pretensions of life with a larger context in which *no* standards can be discovered, rather than with a context from which alternative, overriding standards may be applied.

V

In this respect, as in others, philosophical perception of the absurd resembles epistemological skepticism. In both cases the final, philosophical doubt is not contrasted with any unchallenged certainties, though it is arrived at by extrapolation from examples of doubt within the system of evidence or justification, where a contrast with other

certainties *is* implied. In both cases our limitedness joins with a capacity to transcend those limitations in thought (thus seeing them as
limitations, and as inescapable).

Skepticism begins when we include ourselves in the world about
which we claim knowledge. We notice that certain types of evidence
convince us, that we are content to allow justifications of belief to come
to an end at certain points, that we feel we know many things even
without knowing or having grounds for believing the denial of others
which, if true, would make what we claim to know false.

For example, I know that I am looking at a piece of paper, although
I have no adequate grounds to claim I know that I am not dreaming;
and if I am dreaming then I am not looking at a piece of paper. Here
an ordinary conception of how appearance may diverge from reality is
employed to show that we take our world largely for granted; the
certainty that we are not dreaming cannot be justified except circularly,
in terms of those very appearances which are being put in doubt. It is
somewhat far-fetched to suggest I may be dreaming; but the possibility
is only illustrative. It reveals that our claims to knowledge depend on
our not feeling it necessary to exclude certain incompatible alterna-
tives, and the dreaming possibility or the total-hallucination possibility
are just representatives for limitless possibilities most of which we
cannot even conceive.[2]

Once we have taken the backward step to an abstract view of our
whole system of beliefs, evidence, and justification, and seen that it
works only, despite its pretensions, by taking the world largely for
granted, we are *not* in a position to contrast all these appearances with
an alternative reality. We cannot shed our ordinary responses, and if
we could it would leave us with no means of conceiving a reality of any
kind.

It is the same in the practical domain. We do not step outside our
lives to a new vantage point from which we see what is really, objectively significant. We continue to take life largely for granted while
seeing that all our decisions and certainties are possible only because
there is a great deal we do not bother to rule out.

Both epistemological skepticism and a sense of the absurd can be
reached via initial doubts posed within systems of evidence and justification that we accept, and can be stated without violence to our ordinary concepts. We can ask not only why we should believe there is a

---

2. I am aware that skepticism about the external world is widely thought to have been
refuted, but I have remained convinced of its irrefutability since being exposed at
Berkeley to Thompson Clarke's largely unpublished ideas on the subject.

floor under us, but also why we should believe the evidence of our senses at all—and at some point the framable questions will have outlasted the answers. Similarly, we can ask not only why we should take aspirin, but why we should take trouble over our own comfort at all. The fact that we shall take the aspirin without waiting for an answer to this last question does not show that it is an unreal question. We shall also continue to believe there is a floor under us without waiting for an answer to the other question. In both cases it is this unsupported natural confidence that generates skeptical doubts; so it cannot be used to settle them.

Philosophical skepticism does not cause us to abandon our ordinary beliefs, but it lends them a peculiar flavor. After acknowledging that their truth is incompatible with possibilities that we have no grounds for believing do not obtain—apart from grounds in those very beliefs which we have called into question—we return to our familiar convictions with a certain irony and resignation. Unable to abandon the natural responses on which they depend, we take them back, like a spouse who has run off with someone else and then decided to return; but we regard them differently (not that the new attitude is necessarily inferior to the old, in either case).

The same situation obtains after we have put in question the seriousness with which we take our lives and human life in general and have looked at ourselves without presuppositions. We then return to our lives, as we must, but our seriousness is laced with irony. Not that irony enables us to escape the absurd. It is useless to mutter: "Life is meaningless; life is meaningless . . ." as an accompaniment to everything we do. In continuing to live and work and strive, we take ourselves seriously in action no matter what we say.

What sustains us, in belief as in action, is not reason or justification, but something more basic than these—for we go on in the same way even after we are convinced that the reasons have given out.[3] If we tried to rely entirely on reason, and pressed it hard, our lives and beliefs would collapse—a form of madness that may actually occur if the inertial force of taking the world and life for granted is somehow lost. If we lose our grip on that, reason will not give it back to us.

---

3. As Hume says in a famous passage of the *Treatise:* "Most fortunately it happens, that since reason is incapable of dispelling these clouds, nature herself suffices to that purpose and cures me of this philosophical melancholy and delirium, either by relaxing this bent of mind, or by some avocation, and lively impression of my senses, which obliterate all these chimeras: I dine, I play a game of backgammon, I converse, and am merry with my friends; and when after three or four hours' amusement, I would return to these speculations, they appear so cold, and strain'd, and ridiculous, that I cannot find in my heart to enter into them farther" (Book 1. Part 4, Section 7; Selby-Bigge, p. 269).

VI

In viewing ourselves from a perspective broader than we can occupy in the flesh, we become spectators of our own lives. We cannot do very much as pure spectators of our own lives, so we continue to lead them, and devote ourselves to what we are able at the same time to view as no more than a curiosity, like the ritual of an alien religion.

This explains why the sense of absurdity finds its natural expression in those bad arguments with which the discussion began. Reference to our small size and short lifespan and to the fact that all mankind will eventually vanish without a trace are metaphors for the backward step which permits us to regard ourselves from without and to find the particular form of our lives curious and slightly surprising. By feigning a nebula's-eye view, we illustrate the capacity to see ourselves without presuppositions, as arbitrary, idiosyncratic, ·highly specific occupants of the world, one of countless possible forms of life.

Before turning to the question whether the absurdity of our lives is something to be regretted and if possible escaped, let me consider what would have to be given up in order to avoid it.

Why is the life of a mouse not absurd? The orbit of the moon is not absurd either, but that involves no strivings or aims at all. A mouse, however, has to work to stay alive. Yet he is not absurd, because he lacks the capacities for self-consciousness and self-transcendence that would enable him to see that he is only a mouse. If that did happen, his life would become absurd, since self-awareness would not make him cease to be a mouse and would not enable him to rise above his mousely strivings. Bringing his new-found self-consciousness with him, he would have to return to his meagre yet frantic life full of doubts that he was unable to answer, but also full of purposes that he was unable to abandon.

Given that the transcendental step is natural to us humans, can we avoid absurdity by refusing to take that step and remaining entirely within out sublunar lives? Well, we cannot refuse consciously, for to do that we would have to be aware of the viewpoint we were refusing to adopt. The only way to avoid the relevant self-consciousness would be either never to attain it or to forget it—neither of which can be achieved by the will.

On the other hand, it is possible to expend effort on an attempt to destroy the other component of the absurd—abandoning one's earthly, individual, human life in order to identify as completely as possible with that universal viewpoint from which human life seems arbitrary and trivial. (This appears to be the ideal of certain Oriental religions.) If one succeeds, then one will not have to drag the superior awareness through a strenuous mundane life, and absurdity will be diminished.

However, insofar as this self-etiolation is the result of effort, will-power, asceticism, and so forth, it requires that one take oneself seriously as an individual—that one be willing to take considerable trouble to avoid being creaturely and absurd. Thus one may undermine the aim of unworldliness by pursuing it too vigorously. Still, if someone simply allowed his individual, animal nature to drift and respond to impulse, without making the pursuit of its needs a central conscious aim, then he might, at considerable dissociative cost, achieve a life that was less absurd than most. It would not be a meaningful life either, of course; but it would not involve the engagement of a transcendent awareness in the assiduous pursuit of mundane goals. And that is the main condition of absurdity—the dragooning of an unconvinced transcendent consciousness into the service of an immanent, limited enterprise like a human life.

The final escape is suicide; but before adopting any hasty solutions, it would be wise to consider carefully whether the absurdity of our existence truly presents us with a *problem,* to which some solution must be found—a way of dealing with prima facie disaster. That is certainly the attitude with which Camus approaches the issue, and it gains support from the fact that we are all eager to escape from absurd situations on a smaller scale.

Camus—not on uniformly good grounds—rejects suicide and the other solutions he regards as escapist. What he recommends is defiance or scorn. We can salvage our dignity, he appears to believe, by shaking a fist at the world which is deaf to our pleas, and continuing to live in spite of it. This will not make our lives un-absurd, but it will lend them a certain nobility.[4]

This seems to me romantic and slightly self-pitying. Our absurdity warrants neither that much distress nor that much defiance. At the risk of falling into romanticism by a different route, I would argue that absurdity is one of the most human things about us: a manifestation of our most advanced and interesting characteristics. Like skepticism in epistemology, it is possible only because we possess a certain kind of insight—the capacity to transcend ourselves in thought.

If a sense of the absurd is a way of perceiving our true situation (even

---

4. "Sisyphus, proletarian of the Gods, powerless and rebellious, knows the whole extent of his wretched condition; it is what he thinks of during his descent. The lucidity that was to constitute his torture at the same time crowns his victory. There is no fate that cannot be surmounted by scorn" *(The Myth of Sisyphus,* Vintage edition, p. 90).

though the situation is not absurd until the perception arises), then what reason can we have to resent or escape it? Like the capacity for epistemological skepticism, it results from the ability to understand our human limitations. It need not be a matter for agony unless we make it so. Nor need it evoke a defiant contempt of fate that allows us to feel brave or proud. Such dramatics, even if carried on in private, betray a failure to appreciate the cosmic unimportance of the situation. If *sub specie aeternitatis* there is no reason to believe that anything matters, then that doesn't matter either, and we can approach our absurd lives with irony instead of heroism or despair.

Biographical Sketches

ALFRED JULES AYER (1910–) (Selection 13) is one of the best-known of contemporary analytic philosophers. He was educated at Oxford and, after many years as Grote Professor at University College, London, he returned to Oxford in 1959 as Wykeham Professor of Logic. Among his writings are *The Foundations of Empirical Knowledge; Language, Truth and Logic; The Problem of Knowledge;* and most recently, *Russell and Moore: The Analytic Tradition.*

NORMAN O. BROWN (1913–) (Selection 19) was born in El Oro, Mexico. He graduated from Oxford and the University of Wisconsin. He was a Professor of Classics at Wesleyan University and has taught at the University of Rochester and the University of California at Santa Cruz. In addition to *Life Against Death* he also has published another work in philosophy of religion entitled *Love's Body.*

RUDOLF BULTMANN (1884–) (Selection 15) is a famous contemporary theologian, who has explored the consequences for theology of existentialism. From 1921–51 he was on the faculty of the University of Marburg. His writings include *Glauben Und Verstehen* (four volumes); *Primitive Christianity; Jesus Christ and Mythology;* and *Kerygma and Myth.*

ALBERT CAMUS (1913–1960) (Selection 17) was born in Mondovi, Algeria. After receiving a degree in philosophy from the University of

Algiers, he worked as a journalist, ran a theatrical company, and was active in the French Resistance during the Second World War. He received the Nobel Prize for Literature in 1957. Among his major writings are *The Stranger; The Myth of Sisyphus; The Rebel; The Plague;* and *The Fall.*

FYODOR DOSTOYEVSKY (1821–1881) (Selection 6) was one of the most famous of Russian novelists. He was arrested by the government for conspiracy and exiled to Siberia for six years (1849–54). He was plagued by financial difficulties most of his life, despite his growing fame as a major novelist. Among his most important writings are *The House of the Dead; Letters From Underground; Crime and Punishment; The Idiot; The Possessed;* and *The Brothers Karamozov.*

FRIEDRICH ENGELS (1820–1895) (Selection 5) was the founder, along with Karl Marx, of Dialectical Materialism, the theoretical foundation of Communism. A successful business man in England, he began collaborating with Marx in 1844 and aided and befriended him for the rest of his life. In addition to editing the second and third volumes of Marx's *Capital,* he also wrote *The Condition of the Working Class in England in 1844; The Origin of the Family, Private Property and the State;* and *Anti-Duhring.*

LUDWIG FEUERBACH (1804–1872) (Selection 2) was a very influential German philosopher. Originally a student of Hegel, he subsequently abandoned Hegelian idealism for a naturalistic materialism, which he employed in an attack on and reinterpretation of orthodox religion. Marx was influenced greatly by him. He was the author of *The Essence of Christianity* and *The Essence of Religion.*

SIGMUND FREUD (1856–1939) (Selection 12) was the most famous and influential psychologist of modern times. He was the founder of psychoanalysis. He lived most of his long, highly productive life in Vienna. He was forced to flee from Austria in 1938 to escape the Nazis. His major works include *The Interpretation of Dreams; A General Introduction to Psychoanalysis; Totem and Taboo; Moses and Monotheism; The Future of an Illusion;* and *Civilization and Its Discontents.*

DAVID HUME (1711–1776) (Selection 1) was one of the great figures of Western philosophy. He is best known for his skeptical philosophy, which is still very influential today. Born in Scotland, he never held an academic post but became famous throughout Europe for his writings in history and philosophy. Among his most famous works are *A Treatise of Human Nature; An Enquiry Concerning Human Under-*

standing; History of England; and *Dialogues Concerning Natural Religion.*

WILLIAM JAMES (1842–1910) (Selections 10 and 11) was America's most famous philosopher and psychologist. He was the brother of the novelist Henry James. Born in New York City, he was educated at Harvard University, where he returned to teach in 1872. He is one of the founders of the philosophical movement known as pragmatism. He was the author of *The Principles of Psychology; The Meaning of Truth; Essays in Radical Empiricism;* and *The Varieties of Religious Experience.*

SOREN KIERKEGAARD (1813–1855) (Selection 3) was a famous Danish philosopher and theologian. He was born in Copenhagen and, except for a few years studying in Berlin, lived there all his life. His highly unique approach to philosophy resulted in influential books dealing with morality and aesthetics as well as religion. Among his most famous writings are *Either/Or; Fear and Trembling; Stages on Life's Way; Concluding Unscientific Postscript; Sickness Unto Death;* and *The Attack Upon Christendom.*

KARL MARX (1818–1883) (Selection 4) was the most influential of political philosophers of modern times. Born in Trier, Prussia, he received his education at the University of Berlin. Because of political activity, he was expelled from Prussia in 1849 and lived in London until his death. Contemporary Communism claims him as the originator of its theory. His *magnum opus* is the three-volumed masterpiece, *Capital.* He also authored (with Engels) *The Communist Manifesto* and numerous other important books and essays.

THOMAS NAGEL (1937–) (Selection 22) is presently a Professor of Philosophy at Princeton University. Born in Belgrade, Yugoslavia, he graduated from Oxford and Harvard University. He has taught at Princeton since 1966. In addition to many technical articles, he is the author of *The Possibility of Altruism.*

FRIEDRICH NIETZSCHE (1844–1900) (Selections 7 and 8) was possibly the most original and influential of nineteenth-century German philosophers. For ten years he was a Professor of Philology at Basel, Switzerland. Despite chronic poor health, he wrote significant books concerning music, Greek antiquity, philology, and religion. He suffered a mental breakdown in 1889 from which he never recovered. Some of his most famous works are *The Birth of Tragedy; Beyond Good and Evil; Human, All-Too-Human; On the Genealogy of Morals; Ecce Homo;* and *Thus Spake Zarathustra.*

JOHN ROBINSON (1915–) (Selection 20) was for many years Bishop of Woolwich and is presently Assistant Bishop of Southwark in the Church of England. He received his education at Cambridge University and is currently a Fellow and Dean of the Chapel at Trinity. He has lectured frequently in the United States. Among his writings are *Honest to God; Christian Morals Today; But That I Can't Believe;* and *Christian Freedom in a Permissive Society.*

JEAN-PAUL SARTRE (1905–) (Selection 16) is the most famous of contemporary French philosophers. In addition to his philosophical works, he is also world famous as a novelist and playwright. During the Second World War he was captured by the Germans but later fought in the French Resistance. His best known philosophical work is *Being and Nothingness.* Among his other writings are *Nausea; No Exit; The Wall;* and *Critique of Dialectical Reason.*

PAUL TILLICH (1886–1965) (Selection 18) was one of the two or three most famous of twentieth-century theologians. He taught for many years at the Union Theological Seminary (1933–55) and at Harvard University until 1962. He is the author of *Systematic Theology* (three volumes); *The Shaking of the Foundations; Dynamics of Faith;* and *The Courage To Be.*

COUNT LEO TOLSTOY (1828–1910) (Selection 9) is generally recognized as the greatest of Russian novelists. He is also famous for his many writings concerning social and moral problems and his attempt to formulate a new Christianity. Among his most important works are *War and Peace; Anna Karenina; Resurrection;* and *A Confession.*

PAUL M. VAN BUREN (1924–) (Selection 21) is presently a Professor of Religion at Temple University. He was educated at Harvard University, Episcopal Theological School, and the University of Basel. He has been teaching at Temple since 1964. Among his writings are *Christ in Our Place; The Secular Meaning of the Gospel;* and *Theological Explorations.*

JOHN WISDOM (1904–) (Selection 14) has played an important role in analytic philosophy for many decades. He acknowledges that his approach to philosophical and religious questions, original as it is, was much influenced by his contact with Ludwig Wittgenstein. He taught for many years at Cambridge University. Since 1968 he has been a Professor of Philosophy at the University of Oregon. His major writings are *Other Minds; Philosophy and Psychoanalysis;* and *Paradox and Discovery.*

Selected Bibliography

The following bibliography is intended to aid those who wish to explore further the topics discussed in this book and related subjects. It is not an exhaustive listing, but it should help the interested reader to locate many of the more important classic and contemporary works in the philosophy of religion. The entries have been grouped topically. In many instances, however, a book may cover a greater area than the editorial category indicates.

I. General

A. ANTHOLOGIES

Abernethy, George L., and Langford, Thomas A., eds. *Philosophy of Religion: A Book of Readings.* 2d ed. New York: Macmillan, 1968.

Alston, William P. *Religious Belief and Philosophical Thought: Readings in the Philosophy of Religion.* New York: Harcourt, Brace & World, 1963.

Arnett, Willard E., ed. *A Modern Reader in the Philosophy of Religion.* New York: Appleton-Century-Crofts, 1966.

Feaver, J. Clayton, and Horosz, William, eds. *Religion in Philosophical and Cultural Perspective.* Princeton, N.J.: Van Nostrand, 1967.

Hartshorne, Charles, and Reese, William L., eds. *Philosophers Speak of God.* Chicago: University of Chicago Press, 1953.

Hartsock, Donald E. *Contemporary Religious Issues.* Belmont, Calif.: Wadsworth, 1968.

Hick, John, ed. *Classical and Contemporary Readings in the Philosophy of Religion.* Englewood Cliffs, N.J.: Prentice-Hall, 1964.

————. *The Existence of God.* New York: Macmillan, 1964.

Kaufmann, Walter, ed. *Religion from Tolstoy to Camus.* New York: Harper & Row, 1961.

Mavrodes, George I., and Hackett, Stuart C., eds. *Problems and Perspectives in the Philosophy of Religion.* Boston: Allyn & Bacon, 1967.

Mitchell, Basil, ed. *The Philosophy of Religion.* London: Oxford University Press, 1971.

Needleman, Jacob; Bierman, A. K.; and Gould, James A. *Religion For a New Generation.* New York: Macmillan, 1973.

Reardon, B. M. G., ed. *Religious Thought in the Nineteenth Century.* Cambridge: Cambridge University Press, 1966.

Weinberg, Julius, and Yandell, Keith E., eds. *Philosophy of Religion.* New York: Holt, Rinehart, & Winston, 1972.

Yandell, Keith, ed. *God, Man, and Religion.* New York: McGraw-Hill, 1973.

B. TEXTS

Bertocci, Peter Anthony. *Introduction to the Philosophy of Religion.* New York: Prentice-Hall, 1951.

Bouquet, A. C. *Comparative Religion: A Short Outline.* Baltimore: Penguin, 1958.

Burtt, Edwin A. *Types of Religious Philosophy.* rev. ed. New York: Harper & Bros., 1951.

Caird, Edward. *The Evolution of Religion.* 2d ed. 2 vols. New York: Macmillan, 1894.

Ducasse, C. J. *A Philosophical Scrutiny of Religion.* New York: Ronald Press, 1953.

Eliade, Mircea. *Patterns in Comparative Religion.* New York: Sheed & Ward, 1958.

Garnett, Arthur Campbell. *A Realistic Philosophy of Religion.* Chicago: Willett, Clark, & Co., 1942.

Hick, John. *Philosophy of Religion.* Englewood Cliffs, N.J.: Prentice-Hall, 1963.

MacGregor, Geddes. *Philosophical Issues in Religious Thought.* Boston: Houghton Mifflin, 1973.

Paton, H. J. *The Modern Predicament.* London: Allen & Unwin, 1955.

Radhakrishnan, S. *Eastern Religions and Western Thought.* 2d ed. London: Oxford University Press, 1940.

Smart, Ninian. *Philosophers and Religious Truth.* London: SCM Press, 1969.

————. *The Philosophy of Religion.* New York: Random House, 1970.

————. *Reasons and Faiths.* London: Routledge & Kegan Paul, 1958.

————. *World Religions: A Dialogue.* Baltimore: Penguin, 1960.

Stace, Walter. *Religion and the Modern Mind.* Philadelphia: Lippincott, 1952.

Yandell, Keith. *Basic Issues in the Philosophy of Religion.* Boston: Allyn & Bacon, 1971.

C. HISTORIES

Dillenberger, John, and Welch, Claude. *Protestant Christianity Interpreted Through Its Development.* New York: Scribner's, 1954.

Eusebius. *The History of the Church from Christ to Constantine.* Translated by G. A. Williamson. New York: New York University Press, 1966.

Gilson, Etienne. *History of Christian Philosophy in the Middle Ages.* London: Sheed & Ward, 1955.

Heine, Heinrich. *Religion and Philosophy in Germany.* Translated by John Snodgrass. Boston: Beacon Press, 1959.

Husik, Isaac. *A History of Mediaeval Jewish Philosophy.* New York: Macmillan, 1916.

Hutchison, John A. *Paths of Faith.* New York: McGraw-Hill, 1969.

Latourette, Kenneth Scott. *A History of Christianity.* New York: Harper & Bros., 1953.

Lea, Henry Charles. *The Inquisition of the Middle Ages.* Abridged by Margaret Nicholson. New York: Macmillan, 1961.

McNeill, John T. *The History and Character of Calvinism.* New York: Oxford University Press, 1967.

Moore, George Foote. *History of Religions.* 2 vols. Edinburgh: T. & T. Clark, 1914.

Murray, Gilbert. *Five Stages of Greek Religion.* Garden City, N.Y.: Doubleday, 1955.

Noss, John B. *Man's Religions.* 4th ed. London: Macmillan & Collier-Macmillan Ltd., 1969.

Robertson, J. M. *A Short History of Free Thought, Ancient and Modern.* New York: Russell & Russell, 1957.

Sachar, Abraham Leon. *A History of the Jews.* 5th ed., rev. & enlarged. New York: Knopf, 1965.

Williamson, G. A., ed. *Foxe's Book of Martyrs.* Abridged. Boston: Little, Brown, 1965.

D. REFERENCE WORKS

Attwater, Donald, ed. *A Catholic Dictionary.* 3d ed. New York: Macmillan, 1961.

Baldwin, James M. *Dictionary of Philosophy and Psychology.* 4 vols. Gloucester, Mass.: Peter Smith, 1901.

Edwards, Paul, ed.-in-chief. *Encyclopedia of Philosophy.* 8 vols. New York: Macmillan, 1967.

Encyclopedia Britannica. 11th ed. Cambridge: Cambridge University Press, 1910.

Ferm, Virgilius. *Encyclopedia of Morals.* Westport, Conn.: Greenwood Press, 1956.

Macquarrie, John, ed. *Dictionary of Christian Ethics.* Philadelphia: Westminster Press, 1967.

Mead, Frank S., ed. *Handbook of Denominations in the United States.* 4th ed. New York: Abingdon Press, 1965.

New Catholic Encyclopedia. New York: McGraw-Hill, 1967.

Rosten, Leo, ed. *Religions in America.* New York: Simon & Schuster, 1963.

Roth, Cecil, ed.-in-chief. *The Standard Jewish Encyclopedia.* rev. ed. Garden City, New York: Doubleday, 1966.

E. CLASSIC WORKS OF THEOLOGY AND RELIGION

1. *Theology*

Anselm. *Proslogion, Monologion.*

Aquinas, St. Thomas. *Summa Theologica.*

Aristotle. *Metaphysics.* Bk. XII, 1071b ff.

Augustine. *Confessions, City of God.*

Butler, Bishop Joseph. *The Analogy of Religion.*

Calvin, John. *Institutes of the Christian Religion.*

Descartes, René. *Meditations* III and V.

Edwards, Jonathan. *Freedom of the Will; Narrative of Surprising Conversions; Treatise of Religious Affections.*

Emerson, Ralph Waldo. "The Transcendentalist." In *Works of Ralph Waldo Emerson.* New York: Houghton Mifflin, 1883, vol. I.

Erasmus. *Enchiridion Militus Christi (Handbook of the Militant Christian).*

Hegel, Georg Friedrich. *Early Theological Writings.* Translated by T. M. Knox. Chicago: University of Chicago Press, 1948.

Hume, David. *Dialogues Concerning Natural Religion; Natural History of Religion.*

Kant, Immanuel. *Religion within the Limits of Reason Alone; Critique of Practical Reason,* Pt. I, Bk. II. *Lectures on Ethics.* Translated by Louis Infield. New York: Harper & Row, 1963, pp. 78–116.

Leibniz, Baron Gottfried Wilhelm von. *Theodicy.*

Luther, Martin. *Three Treatises.* Philadelphia: Muhlenberg Press, 1943.

Maimonides, Moses. *Guide for the Perplexed.*

Mill, John Stuart. *Three Essays on Religion.*

Paine, Thomas. *The Age of Reason: Being an Investigation of True and Fabulous Theology.*

Paley, William. *Natural Theology, or Evidences of the Existence and Attributes of the Deity Collected from the Appearances of Nature.*

Philo, Saadya Gaon, and Halevi, Jehuda. *Three Jewish Philosophers.* Edited by Hans Lewy. New York: Harper & Row, 1965.

Plato. *The Phaedo.*

Spencer, Herbert. *Synthetic Philosophy.*

Spinoza, Baruch. *Ethics.*

Voltaire. *Candide.*

2. *Religion*

Ballou, Robert O., ed. *The Portable World Bible.* New York: Viking, 1944.

Bouquet, A. C., ed. *Sacred Books of the World: A Companion Source-Book to "Comparative Religion."* Baltimore: Penguin, 1954.

Browne, Lewis, ed. *The Wisdom of Israel.* New York: Random House, 1945.

Fosdick, Harry Emerson, ed. *Great Voices of the Reformation.* New York: Random House, 1952.

Jeffrey, Arthur, ed. *Islam: Muhammed and His Religion.* Indianapolis: Bobbs-Merrill, 1958.

Pegis, Anton C., ed. *The Wisdom of Catholicism.* New York: Random House, 1949.

Stryk, Lucien, ed. *World of the Buddha: A Reader.* New York: Doubleday, 1968.

Watts, Alan W. *The Way of Zen.* New York: New American Library, 1957.

Yutang, Lin, ed. *The Wisdom of China and India.* New York: Random House, 1942.

II. God Is Dead

Altizer, Thomas J. J. *The Gospel of Christian Atheism.* Philadelphia: Westminster, 1966.

Altizer, Thomas J. J., ed. *Toward a New Christianity.* New York: Harcourt, Brace & World, 1967.

Altizer, Thomas J. J., and Hamilton, William. *Radical Theology and the Death of God.* Indianapolis: Bobbs-Merrill, 1966.

Bent, Charles N., S. J. *The Death of God Movement.* New York: Paulist Press, 1967.

Bonnhoeffer, Dietrich. *Letters and Papers from Prison.* Translated by Reginald H. Fuller. Edited by Eberhard Bethge. New York: Macmillan, 1962.

Callahan, Daniel, ed. *The Secular City Debate.* New York: Macmillan, 1966.

Casserly, J. Langmead. *The Death of Man: A Reinterpretation of Christian Atheism.* New York: Morehouse-Barlow, 1967.

Cooper, John C. *The Roots of Radical Theology.* Philadelphia: Westminster Press, 1967.

Cox, Harvey. *The Secular City.* rev. ed. New York: Macmillan, 1966.

Edwards, David L., ed. *The Honest to God Debate.* Philadelphia: Westminster Press, 1963.

Graham, Billy et al. *Is God Dead?* Grand Rapids, Mich.: Zondervan, 1966.

Hamilton, William. *The New Essence of Christianity.* New York: Association Press, 1961.

Ice, Jackson, ed. *The Death of God Debate.* Philadelphia: Westminster, 1966.

Nietzsche, Friedrich. *Joyful Wisdom.* Translated by Thomas Commans. New York: Frederick Ungar, 1960.

————. *Thus Spake Zarathustra.* In *The Portable Nietzsche,* translated by Walter Kaufmann. New York: Viking, 1954.

Pike, James A. *A Time for Christian Candor.* New York: Harper & Row, 1964.

Robinson, John. *But That I Can't Believe.* New York: New American Library, 1967.

Rubenstein, Richard L. *After Auschwitz: Essays in Contemporary Jewish Theology.* Indianapolis: Bobbs-Merrill, 1966.

Vahanian, Gabriel. *The Death of God.* New York: Braziller, 1961.

Vahanian, Gabriel, ed. *The Death of God Debate.* New York: McGraw-Hill, 1967.

III. Marxism and Alienation

Fromm, Erich. *Beyond the Chains of Illusion.* New York: Pocket Books, 1962.

————. *Marx's Concept of Man.* New York: Frederick Ungar, 1961.

————. *The Sane Society.* New York: Fawcett Premier Books, 1955.

Hooke, Sidney. *From Hegel to Marx: Studies in the Intellectual Development of Karl Marx.* New York: Michigan, 1950.

Kamenka, Eugene. *Marxism and Ethics.* London: Macmillan, 1969.

Marcuse, Herbert. *One-Dimensional Man.* Boston: Beacon, 1964.

_____. *Eros and Civilization.* Boston: Beacon, 1955.

Schacht, Richard. *Alienation.* Garden City, New York: Doubleday, 1970.

Sommerville, John. *The Philosophy of Marxism.* New York: Random House, 1967.

Stalin, Joseph. *Dialectical and Historical Materialism.* New York: International Publishers, 1940.

Tucker, Robert C. *The Marxian Revolutionary Idea.* New York: Norton, 1969.

_____. *Philosophy and Myth in Karl Marx.* rev. ed. New York: Cambridge, 1972.

Wolfe, Bertrand D. *Marxism: One Hundred Years in the Life of a Doctrine.* New York: Dial Press, 1964.

Wolff, Robert Paul; Moore, Barrington; and Marcuse, Herbert. *A Critique of Pure Tolerance.* Boston: Beacon, 1965.

Zeitlin, Irving M. *Marxism: A Re-Examination.* Princeton, N.J.: Van Nostrand, 1967.

IV. Miracles, Science, and Myth

Bultmann, Rudolf. *Jesus Christ and Mythology.* New York: Scribner's, 1958.

Dillenberger, John. *Protestant Thought and Natural Science.* New York: Doubleday, 1960.

Farmer, H. H. *The World and God.* London: James Nisbet & Co., Ltd., 1935, chs. 7–10.

Flew, Antony. *Hume's Philosophy of Belief.* London: Routledge & Kegan Paul, 1961, ch. 8.

Hepburn, Ronald. *Christianity and Paradox.* London: Watts, 1958.

Hitchcock, Edward. *The Religion of Geology and Its Connected Sciences.* Boston: Phillips, Sampson and Co., 1854.

Huxley, Julian. *Religion Without Revelation.* New York: Harper & Row, 1957.

Jaspers, Karl, and Bultmann, Rudolf. *Myth and Christianity: An Inquiry into the Possibility of Religion Without Myth.* New York: Noonday Press, 1958.

Kennedy, Gail, ed. *Evolution and Religion.* Boston: D. C. Heath, 1957.

Kuhn, Thomas S. *The Structure of Scientific Revolutions.* Chicago: University of Chicago Press, 1962.

Lewis, C. S. *Miracles: A Preliminary Study.* New York: Macmillan, 1947.

Lunn, Arnold. "Miracles—The Scientific Approach." *Hibbert Journal,* 1950.

Macquarrie, John. *The Scope of Demythologizing: Bultmann and His Critics.* London: SCM Press, 1960.

Malinowski, Bronislaw. *Magic, Science and Religion and Other Essays.* Garden City, N.Y.: Doubleday, 1954.

Ramsey, Ian T. *Miracles: An Exercise in Logical Mapwork.* Oxford: Clarendon Press, 1952.

Russell, Bertrand. *Religion and Science.* London: Oxford University Press, 1935.

Taylor, A. E. "David Hume and the Miraculous." *Philosophical Studies.* London: Macmillan, 1934, ch. 9.

Tennant, F. R. *Miracle and Its Philosophical Presuppositions.* Cambridge: Cambridge University Press, 1925.

Whitehead, Alfred North. *Science and the Modern World.* New York: New American Library, 1948.

V. Psychology, Psychoanalysis, and Psychical Research

Bakan, David. *Sigmund Freud and the Jewish Mystical Tradition.* New York: Schocken Books, 1958.

Broad, C. D. *Lectures in Psychical Research.* London: Routledge & Kegan Paul, 1962.

————. *Religion, Philosophy, and Psychical Research.* London: Routledge & Kegan Paul, 1953.

Brown, Norman O. *Love's Body.* New York: Vintage, 1966.

Erickson, Erik H. *Young Man Luther.* New York: Norton, 1962.

Ferenczi, Sandor. *Thalassa: A Theory of Genitality.* New York: The Psychoanalytic Quarterly, 1938.

Frazer, Sir James George. *The Golden Bough.* Abridged ed. New York: Macmillan, 1963.

Freud, Sigmund. *Civilization and Its Discontents.* Edited and translated by James Strachey. New York: Norton, 1961.

_____. *The Ego and the Id.* Translated by Joan Riviere. Revised and edited by James Strachey. New York: Norton, 1960.

_____. *Group Psychology and the Analysis of the Ego.* Translated by James Strachey. New York: Bantam, 1960.

_____. *Moses and Monotheism.* Translated by Katherine Jones. New York: Random House, 1939.

_____. *Studies in Parapsychology.* New York: Collier, 1963.

_____. *Totem and Taboo.* Translated by James Strachey. New York: Norton, 1950.

Freud, Sigmund, and Pfister, Oskar. *Psychoanalysis and Faith: The Letters of Sigmund Freud and Oskar Pfister.* Edited by Heinrich Meng & Ernst L. Freud. Translated by Eric Mosbacher. New York: Basic Books, 1963.

Fromm, Erich. *Psychoanalysis and Religion.* New Haven, Conn.: Yale University Press, 1950.

Fromm, Erich; Suzuki, D. T.; and Martino, R. *Zen Buddhism and Psychoanalysis.* New York: Harper, 1960.

Havens, Joseph, ed. *Psychology and Religion: A Contemporary Dialogue.* Princeton, N.J.: Van Nostrand, 1968.

James, William. *The Will to Believe and Other Essays in Popular Philosophy.* New York: Longmans Green, 1897.

Jung, Carl G. *Psychology and Religion.* New Haven, Conn.: Yale University Press, 1938.

Marcuse, Herbert. *Eros and Civilization.* Boston: Beacon Press, 1955.

Murphy, Gardner. *The Challenge of Psychical Research.* New York: Harper & Bros., 1961.

Podmore, Frank. *Mediums of the Nineteenth Century.* 2 vols. New Hyde Park, N.Y.: University Books, 1963.

Pratt, J. Gaither. *Parapsychology: An Insider's View of ESP.* New York: Dutton, 1966.

Rank, Otto. *The Myth of the Birth of the Hero and Other Writings.* Edited by Philip Freund. New York: Vintage, 1964.

Rubinstein, Richard. *The Religious Imagination: A Study in Psychoanalysis and Jewish Theology.* Indianapolis: Bobbs-Merrill, 1968.

Scriven, Michael. "The Frontiers of Psychology: Psychoanalysis and Parapsychology." In *Frontiers of Science and Philosophy,* edited by Robert Colodny. London: Allen & Unwin, 1964.

Smythies, J. R., ed. *Science and ESP.* London: Routledge & Kegan Paul, 1967.

Spinks, G. Stephens. *Psychology and Religion: An Introduction to Contemporary Views.* Boston: Beacon Press, 1963.

Thouless, Robert H. *The Psychology of Religion.* Cambridge: Cambridge University Press, 1961.

Zilboorg, Gregory. *Psychoanalysis and Religion.* New York: Farrar, Straus & Cudahy, 1962.

VI. The Meaning of Religious Language

Barrett, Cyril. *Wittgenstein: Lectures and Conversations on Aesthetics, Psychology and Religious Beliefs.* Oxford: Basil Blackwell, 1966.

Blackstone, William T. *The Problem of Religious Knowledge: The Impact of Philosophical Analysis on the Question of Religious Knowledge.* Englewood Cliffs, N.J.: Prentice-Hall, 1963.

Bochenski, Joseph M. *The Logic of Religion.* New York: New York University Press, 1957.

Braithewaite, R. B. *An Empiricist's View of the Nature of Religious Belief.* Cambridge: Cambridge University Press, 1955.

Ferre, Frederick. *Language, Logic and God.* New York: Harper & Row, 1961.

Flew, Antony, and MacIntyre, Alasdair. *New Essays in Philosophical Theology.* New York: Macmillan, 1964.

Hick, John. *Faith and Knowledge.* Ithaca, N.Y.: Cornell University Press, 1957, ch. 8.

Hick, John, ed. *The Existence of God.* New York: Macmillan, 1964, Pt. III.

High, Dallas M. *Language, Persons and Belief: Studies in Wittgenstein's "Philosophical Investigations" and Religious Uses of Language.* New York: Oxford University Press, 1962.

High, Dallas M., ed. *New Essays on Religious Language.* New York: Oxford University Press, 1969.

MacIntyre, Alasdair, ed. *Metaphysical Beliefs.* London: SCM Press, 1957.

Mascall, Eric L. *Words and Images: A Study in Theological Discourse.* London: Longmans Green, 1957.

Mitchell, Basil, ed. *Faith and Logic.* Boston: Beacon Press, 1957.

Ramsey, Ian T., ed. *Prospect for Metaphysics.* London: Allen & Unwin, 1961.

_____. *Religious Language.* New York: Macmillan, 1957.

Santoni, Ronald E., ed. *Religious Language and the Problem of Religious Knowledge.* Bloomington: Indiana University Press, 1968.

Talk of God: Royal Institute of Philosophy Lectures, vol. 2, 1967–68. New York: Macmillan, 1969.

VII. Morality and Religion

Aiken, Henry David. "God and Evil: A Study of Some Relations Between Faith and Morals." In *Reason and Conduct: New Bearings in Moral Philosophy,* by Henry David Aiken. New York: Knopf, 1962.

Bergson, Henri. *The Two Sources of Morality and Religion.* New York: Henry Holt, 1935.

Dewey, John. *A Common Faith.* New Haven, Conn.: Yale University Press, 1934.

Dostoyevsky, Fyoder. *Notes from Underground.* Baltimore: Penguin, 1972.

Fletcher, Joseph. *Situation Ethics: The New Morality.* Philadelphia: Westminster Press, 1966.

_____. *Moral Responsibility: Situation Ethics at Work.* Philadelphia: Westminster Press, 1967.

Hick, John. *Evil and the God of Love.* New York: Harper & Row, 1966.

Gandhi, Mohandas K. *Non-Violent Resistance (Satyagraha).* New York: Schocken Books, 1961.

Garnett, Arthur Campbell. *Religion and the Moral Life.* New York: Ronald Press, 1955.

King, Martin Luther. *Where Do We Go From Here: Chaos or Community.* New York: Harper & Row, 1967.

MacLagan, W. G. *The Theological Frontiers of Ethics.* London: Allen & Unwin, 1961.

Niebuhr, Reinhold. *Moral Man and Immoral Society: A Study in Ethics & Politics.* New York: Scribner's, 1932.

Nietzsche, Friedrich. *Beyond Good and Evil.* In *Basic Writings of Nietzsche,* translated and edited by Walter Kaufmann. New York: Modern Library, 1968.

Paton, H. J. *The Modern Predicament.* London: Allen & Unwin, 1955, chs. 21–23.

Pike, Nelson, ed. *God and Evil.* Englewood Cliffs, N.J.: Prentice-Hall, 1964.

Ramsey, Ian T., ed. *Christian Ethics and Contemporary Philosophy.* New York: Macmillan, 1966.

Russell, Bertrand. *Why I Am Not a Christian and Other Essays on Religion and Related Subjects.* London: Allen & Unwin, 1957.

Shaw, George Bernard. *The Adventures of the Black Girl in Her Search for God.* New York: Capricorn Books, 1959.

Tolstoy, Leo. *Tolstoy's Writings on Civil Disobedience and Non-violence.* New York: Bergman Publishers, 1967.

Weber, Max. *The Protestant Ethic and the Spirit of Capitalism.* Translated by Talcott Parsons. New York: Scribner's, 1958.

VIII. Death

Agee, James. *A Death in the Family.* New York: McDowell, Obolensky, 1957.

Broad, C. D. *Mind and Its Place in Nature.* London: Routledge & Kegan Paul, 1925, chs. 11–14.

Charon, Jaques. *Death and Modern Man.* New York: Collier Books, 1964.

————. *Death and Western Thought.* New York: Collier, 1963.

Ducasse, C. J. *Nature, Mind, and Death.* La Salle, Ill.: Open Court, 1951, Pt. IV.

————. *A Critical Examination of the Belief in Life After Death.* Springfield, Ill.: Charles C. Thomas, 1961.

Epicurus. *Epicurus, to Menoceus; Principle Doctrines.* Both translated by C. Bailey. In *The Stoic and Epicurean Philosophers,* edited by Whitney J. Oates. New York: Random House, 1940.

Feifel, Herman, ed. *The Meaning of Death.* New York: McGraw-Hill, 1959.

Fletcher, Joseph. "The Patient's Right to Die." *Harper's Magazine,* October 1960.

Freud, Sigmund. *Reflections on War and Death.* New York: Moffat, Yard and Co., 1918.

Gurney, Edmund; Myers, Frederic W. H.; and Podmore, Frank. *Phantasms of the Living.* In *Phantasms of the Living,* edited by Eleanor Sidgwick. New Hyde Park, N.Y.: University Books, 1962.

Hendin, David. *Death as a Fact of Life.* New York: Norton, 1973.

Hinton, John. *Dying.* Baltimore, Md.: Penguin Books, 1967.

Hume, David. "On the Immortality of the Soul." In *Essays: Moral, Political and Literary.* London: Oxford University Press, 1963.

James, William. *Human Immortality.* In *The Will to Believe and Human Immortality.* N.Y.: Dover, 1956.

Kubler-Ross, Elizabeth. *On Death and Dying.* New York: Macmillan, 1969.

Mitford, Jessica. *The American Way of Death.* New York: Simon & Schuster, 1963.

Myers, F. W. H. *Human Personality and Its Survival of Bodily Death.* Edited by Susy Smith. New Hyde Park, N.Y.: University Books, 1961.

Ryle, Gilbert. *The Concept of Mind.* London: Hutchinson, 1949.

St. John-Stevas, Norman. *Life, Death and the Law.* New York: World, 1961.

Taylor, Gordon Rattray. *The Biological Time Bomb.* New York: World, 1968, ch. 4.

Thurston, Herbert, S. J. *Ghosts and Poltergeists.* Chicago: Henry Regnery, 1954.

Tolstoy, Leo. "The Death of Ivan Ilyitch." In *Religion From Tolstoy to Camus,* edited by Walter Kaufmann. New York: Harper & Row, 1961.

Toynbee, Arnold et al. *Man's Concern with Death.* New York: McGraw-Hill, 1968.

Waugh, Evelyn. *The Loved One.* Boston: Little, Brown, 1948.

Williams, Glanville. *The Sanctity of Life and the Criminal Law.* New York: Knopf, 1966.

Wyschogrod, Edith. *The Phenomenon of Death.* New York: Harper & Row, 1973.